D0331867

UNDERSTANDING HUMAN RESOURCE DEVELOPMENT

This book contains original chapters by some of the leading researchers and writers in the field of human resource development. It acts as a definitive source of information on the design and conduct of research in HRD and simultaneously identifies key issues and debates concerning methodological principles, and the possibilities and limitations of particular methods and techniques. Each chapter in the book includes the following features:

- statement of aims
- description of theoretical and empirical context
- identification and examination of methodological issues
- description and assessment of research design
- critical analysis and evaluation
- key learning points.

Understanding Human Resource Development is essential reading for all students, teachers and practitioners involved in HRD.

Jim McGoldrick is Professor of Human Resource Management at the University of Abertay, Dundee, where he is also Vice-Principal. **Jim Stewart** is Professor of Human Resource Development at Nottingham Business School. **Sandra Watson** is Head of Human Resource Management at Napier University Business School.

ROUTLEDGE STUDIES IN HUMAN RESOURCE DEVELOPMENT
Edited by Monica Lee
Lancaster University, UK

This series presents a range of books which explore and debate the changing face of human resource development, offering discussion and delineation of HRD theory and, thus, the development of practice.

This series is aimed at human resource and organization theoreticians, and is also of direct relevance to sociologists, psychologists and philosophers, as well as those working in the areas of culture and globalization. HR practitioners and those interested in the practical aspects of HR theory will also find this series to be an important catalyst in understanding and enhancing their practice.

ACTION RESEARCH IN ORGANISATIONS
Jean McNiff, accompanied by Jack Whitehead

UNDERSTANDING HUMAN RESOURCE DEVELOPMENT
A research-based approach
Edited by Jim McGoldrick, Jim Stewart and Sandra Watson

UNDERSTANDING HUMAN RESOURCE DEVELOPMENT

A research-based approach

Edited by Jim McGoldrick, Jim Stewart and Sandra Watson

London and New York

First published 2002 by Routledge
11 New Fetter Lane, London EC4P 4EE

Simultaneously published in the USA and Canada
by Routledge
29 West 35th Street, New York, NY 10001

Routledge is an imprint of the Taylor & Francis Group

© 2002 Editorial matter and selection by Jim McGoldrick,
Jim Stewart and Sandra Watson; individual chapters
the contributors

Typeset in 10/12pt Baskerville by Graphicraft Limited, Hong Kong
Printed and bound in Great Britain by St Edmundsbury Press, Bury
St Edmunds, Suffolk

All rights reserved. No part of this book may be reprinted or
reproduced or utilised in any form or by any electronic,
mechanical, or other means, now known or hereafter
invented, including photocopying and recording, or in any
information storage or retrieval system, without permission in
writing from the publishers.

British Library Cataloguing in Publication Data
A catalogue record for this book is available
from the British Library

Library of Congress Cataloging in Publication Data
Understanding human resource development: a research-based
approach / edited by Jim McGoldrick, Jim Stewart, and Sandra
Watson.
 p. cm. — (Routledge studies in human resource development)
Includes bibliographical references and index.
1. Personnel management—Research. I. McGoldrick, Jim, 1952–
II. Stewart, Jim, 1950– III. Watson, Sandra. IV. Series.

HF5549.15 .U52 2001
658.3—dc21   2001019638

ISBN 0–415–22609–0 (hbk)
ISBN 0–415–22610–4 (pbk)

CONTENTS

CONTENTS

ILLUSTRATIONS

Figures

Tables

CONTRIBUTORS

Joint editors

Jim McGoldrick   Professor of Human Resource Management and Vice-Principal of the University of Abertay, Dundee; President of the University Forum for HRD and former Vice-President (Training and Development) of the Chartered Institute of Personnel and Development. Member of the Management Board of *Human Resource Development International.*

Jim Stewart   Professor of Human Resource Development, Nottingham Business School, Nottingham Trent University; Chair of the University Forum for HRD.

Sandra Watson   Head of Human Resource Management, Napier Business School, Napier University, Edinburgh.

Contributors

Alison Alker   Lecturer in Employee Development, Lancashire Business School, the University of Central Lancashire.

Rona S. Beattie   Senior Lecturer in Human Resource Management and Development, Caledonian Business School, Glasgow Caledonian University. Leader of the Voluntary Sector Research Centre.

Goronwy Davies   Principal Lecturer in Training and Development, Wolverhampton Business School, Wolverhampton University.

Catherine Edwards   Lecturer in Continuing Education, the University of Warwick.

Jeff Gold   Principal Lecturer in Human Resource Development, Leeds Business School, Leeds Metropolitan University.

John Hamblett   Senior Lecturer in the School of Economics and Human Resource Management, Leeds Business School, Leeds Metropolitan University.

Bob Hamlin   Principal Lecturer in Human Resource Development and Human Resource Programmes Manager, Wolverhampton Business School, the University of Wolverhampton. Honorary Treasurer of the University Forum for Human Resource Development. Awarded the Distinguished Badge of Merit of the Chartered Institute of Personnel and Development.

Rosemary Hill, PhD MSc HRD (distn.) FCIPD MIQA Principal, *RHR Consultants.*

Rick Holden   Principal Lecturer in the School of Economics and Human Resource Management, Leeds Business School, Leeds Metropolitan University.

K. Peter Kuchinke   Assistant Professor in the Department of Human Resource Education, College of Education, the University of Illinois at Urbana-Champaign, Illinois, USA. Member of the Executive Board of the Academy of Human Resource Development.

Monica Lee   Editor in Chief, *Human Resource Development International,* the Management School, the University of Lancaster. Member of the Editorial Board of *Human Resource Development Quarterly.*

Marilyn McDougall   Professor of Human Resource Development, Caledonian Business School, Glasgow Caledonian University.

Christina MacNeil   Senior Lecturer in Human Resource Development, Oxford Brookes University.

Graeme Martin   Director of Research, Dundee Business School, the University of Abertay, Dundee; Associate Professor of Human Resource Management, the University of Colorado, Denver, Colorado, USA.

Judy Pate   Lecturer in Human Resource Management, Dundee Business School, the University of Abertay, Dundee.

Monder Ram   Professor of Small Business Development, Department of Corporate Strategy, University of Central England Business School, Birmingham. Co-Director of the Small Business Research Group at De Montfort University.

Clare Rigg   Senior Lecturer in Human Resource Development, University of Central England Business School, Birmingham.

Mike Rix   Managing Director, *Meridian Consultants,* Doncaster.

Sally Sambrook   Lecturer in Human Resource Development, the University of Wales, Bangor.

Sue Shaw   Head of Department of Human Resource Management, Manchester Metropolitan University.

Darren C. Short President of *Perspectives*, a Human Resource Development Consulting Firm and an Internal Consultant for an UK Government Agency, London. Member of the Research Committee of the American Society for Training and Development.

Denise Thursfield Senior Lecturer in the School of Economics and Human Resource Management, Leeds Business School, Leeds Metropolitan University.

Kiran Trehan Head of the Division of Management, the University of Central England Business School in Birmingham.

Stuart Watson Senior Lecturer in Human Resource Management, Leeds Business School, Leeds Metropolitan University.

Penny West Senior Lecturer in Management, Centre for Business and Management Studies, Edge Hill College, Lancashire.

Tony Wilson Training and Development Consultant.

Jonathan Winterton Director of Research and Professor of Human Resource Development, Groupe ESC, Toulouse, France and Associate Professor of Human Resource Development, Napier Business School, Napier University, Edinburgh.

Ruth Winterton Lecturer in the Department of Psychology and Sociology and Master's Programme Director of Social Research, Napier University, Edinburgh.

Jean Woodall Professor of Human Resource Development and Director of Management Programmes, the Kingston Business School, Kingston University; Associate Editor of *Human Resource Development International*.

PREFACE

Aims and purpose

As the title of the book indicates, the overarching purpose of the book is to advance knowledge and understanding of human resource development (HRD). In particular it is our aim to do so by drawing upon the emerging body of research in HRD, primarily UK-based, which will provide the underpinning for the conceptual, theoretical and practical advance of HRD.

This book is neither a 'how to' manual of conducting research, nor is it *not* a 'how to' manual. This rather ambiguous, not to say contradictory, description is the first guiding principle that informed the conception and construction of this book. Our aim has been to produce a work which is of practical value to those who are inexperienced in the conduct of research. The major means of achieving that aim is to include only chapters that are derived from recent or ongoing research projects, and to have contributors both describe and justify their decisions related to research design and choice of methods. In that sense, we have produced a 'how to' manual since there is much content which will be new knowledge for the inexperienced researcher.

We have though pursued a second aim. Conducting research is a complex process. It requires hard thought to engage with sometimes quite difficult ontological and epistemological issues that inform the conceptual clarity needed to produce coherent designs. Applying those designs rarely, if ever, works out as planned or expected and decision making is consequently a continuous and iterative process. Our second aim therefore has been to 'problematize' the research process in two senses. First, to simply acknowledge and describe the practical problems that research projects encounter in implementation of 'elegant' designs. Second, and more importantly, to directly address the often unstated assumptions and philosophical positions which inform the design and conduct of research. So, in the sense of 'problematizing' the research process, we go beyond a simple 'how to' manual and provide content of interest and value to experienced as well as inexperienced researchers.

A second guiding principle has directed our work. The book originated as a collaborative project to be undertaken by the University Forum for Human Resource Development (UFHRD). Almost all of our contributors and we are members of the UFHRD. Forum members identified a shared dissatisfaction with existing research-oriented texts, for one or both of two reasons. First, books on 'how to do research' tend to be too broad in their focus on business and management and too narrow in the perspectives adopted, reflecting perhaps the views of single or double authors. They also tend to discuss important concepts in abstract and generalized ways, rather than examining their concrete application in specific projects. Second, those with a more specific focus on HR research do little to advance knowledge of the subject overall. This reflects a common enough distinction between 'content' and 'process', applied in this case to a distinction being drawn between understanding how to do research and understanding HRD itself.

We find this distinction unhelpful and so have sought to achieve two related aims derived from the guiding principle of advancing knowledge and understanding of HRD. These aims are to provide discussions of research findings as well as the research process, and to provide a wide coverage of established and emerging issues within HRD. Achieving these aims has been sought by the selection of contributions and chapters, and by the content of each chapter.

Parallel tracks

The development of the concept of this book has not taken place in a vacuum. In the last ten years the study of HRD as an academic field has seen tremendous growth in the UK and latterly in mainland Europe. In the UK the early momentum came from the promotion of Master's programmes in training and development by the former Institute of Training and Development (which merged in 1994 with the former Institute of Personnel Management to create the Chartered Institute of Personnel and Development). That initiative was also the precursor to the formation of the UFHRD, which in turn, as noted above, provided the sponsorship for this book. In order to support programmes at Master's level a concomitant development in the literature of HRD occurred. There are two distinct strands to the literature of HRD worth noting at this point.

First, there are what we might call key texts explicitly self-labelled as 'HRD texts' which are differentiated from related fields such as organization studies, human resource management, organizational development and the like. We do not intend to undertake a comprehensive review of all the literature but rather to illustrate the parallel processes by which HRD has advanced in the UK. Perhaps the pioneering text in HRD was published in 1993 by Megginson, Joy-Matthews and Banfield followed three years later by an edited volume put together by Stewart and McGoldrick

(1996). Both these texts helped 'shape' the field of HRD in the mid-1990s and established that there was an emerging 'market' for HRD texts. This has been reinforced recently by the publication in 1999 of two additional texts. John Wilson's volume is an edited collection focusing on individual and organizational learning and John Walton's award-winning epic stakes a powerful claim for the strategic significance of HRD. Our point here is not one of partially disguised self-publicism, but rather to argue that there is a clear and definite 'space' for this volume – both in academic and market terms. A more detailed analysis of the literature of HRD is contained in this volume (see Chapter 18 by Sally Sambrook).

The second strand of HRD literature is the emergence during the mid to late 1990s of research-based journal articles. Central to this was the launch of three internationally focused and fully refereed academic journals. Two of these are UK-based journals, the *International Journal of Training and Development (IJTD)* and *Human Resource Development International (HRDI)*. In their launch editions each editor took the opportunity to set their agenda for HRD. Paul Lewis (1997), editor of the *IJTD*, set out a vision of a systems-oriented perspective on research whilst Monica Lee (1998) the editor of *HRDI* offers a vision of a journal aimed at giving expression to the 'undefinable' nature of HRD. A point worth noting in passing is that HRDI was one of the first tangible outcomes of the formation of the UFHRD. The third journal, the *Journal of European Industrial Training (JEIT)* is based in Ireland and has been established for nearly two decades. It brands itself as 'a journal for HRD specialists' and is perhaps best known for the highly influential article setting out a strategic agenda for HRD by Thomas Garavan in 1991. The opportunity for the advance of HRD research created by these journals is of fundamental importance and is central to our argument for a research-based approach to HRD.

Perhaps the main advance of HRD as a field of academic study has taken place in the USA pioneered initially by the American Society for Training and Development (ASTD), and taken further forward by its academic offshoot, the Academy of Human Resource Development (AHRD). In the USA there has been a long-established tradition of study and qualification in training and development and instructional design which also means that there is a depth of research and scholarship in American universities. The AHRD sponsors the leading journal in the field *Human Resource Development Quarterly (HRDQ)* which has been added to in the last year by a new journal, *Advances in Human Resource Development*. Additionally, the Academy organizes an annual conference, which has recently begun to attract significant interest from UK and European scholars and researchers. Of particular interest is the common concern of academics from all areas of HRD and from different countries in the conceptual and theoretical development of HRD – a concern which is a major issue in this volume, which we discuss in detail in Chapter 1.

The HRM/HRD nexus

In the UK the biggest single factor in the advance of HRD was the rapid development and establishment of human resource management (HRM) as a field of study. To be sure such a statement is not without controversy, but the explosion in the literature of HRM in terms of texts and academic journals of international standing is truly remarkable. Whilst many critics of HRM doubted its durability (Storey 1989 and 1995) it is now a major field of academic research and writing. There are numerous UK-oriented texts that provide a comprehensive overview of the state of development of the literature of HRM (Beardwell and Holden 1994; Bratton and Gold 1999). McGoldrick and Stewart (1996) were perhaps the first writers in the area of HRD to acknowledge the parallel pathways of HRM and HRD and in particular their resonance with the language of corporate strategy rather than with personnel management and training and development. The further development of research and writing in HRM has led to the emergence of a more critical perspective now evident in the literature (Legge 1995; Keenoy 1999). The need for critical theory for HRD is one of the key concerns of this book and is explored in depth in our opening chapter.

Readership of this book

The discussion of the broad aims of the book and the discussion of the parallel developments in the field of HRD suggest the type of readership categories we have had in mind in producing the book. In no particular order of priority or importance, these are as follows.

- *Postgraduate students of HRD*
  There are a number of constituencies within this broad heading. The most obvious are those studying for postgraduate degrees and diplomas in HRD and HRM. A perhaps equally obvious readership will be research students, whether embarked on a PhD, MPhil or Doctorate in Business Administration. Despite its specific subject focus, we believe the book to be of value to those studying more generalist management programmes such as the UK Diploma in Management Studies (DMS) and MBA, perhaps particularly where there is a strong HR element in the content and related possibilities for HR-focused dissertations.
- *Undergraduate students of HRD*
  The broad area of HR is now well established in undergraduate degrees, as is the conduct of research leading to a research-based final year dissertation. Specific modules on HRD and employee development are also becoming increasingly common. We have therefore had in mind an increasing undergraduate readership.

- *Academics and researchers*
  The book provides a rigorous examination of both the research process and of the most recent thinking and writing on HRD. Thus, we believe it will be of interest and value to academics teaching and researching in HR practice.

It is our view that the selection of contributions in the book will appeal to all of the readership categories noted above. The variety of topics, theoretical and methodological approaches covered will be of interest to both specialist readers and those with a general interest in HRD.

Structure and organization of the book

The overall structure of the book reflects, primarily, our first guiding principle of advancing knowledge and understanding of HRD. The first sequence of chapters identify and examine the assumptions and philosophical issues which arise, and need to be 'sorted out', when thinking about doing research. The second sequence focuses on chapters which draw out issues to do with research design. The chapters collectively address design questions which arise at each stage of the research process, and some issues, such as ethical considerations, which are part of decision making at all stages of the process. The final sequence of chapters of the book is concerned with accounts which examine more specific questions to do with methods and techniques. Thus, the overall structure reflects a process of research which, analytically, consists of producing a reasoned response to philosophical questions, which then informs a research design, which then informs selection and application of methods and techniques.

This overall structure is carried into each chapter. Individual chapters provide, to some extent, an account of each of the three stages. They also follow a common format which applies our second guiding principle, represented by the following features and sections:

- statement of aims and contribution
- description and evaluation of theoretical context
- description of empirical context
- critical examination of research design
- evaluative analysis of main outcomes
- conclusions
- summary of key learning points.

This commonality of structure allows the varying accounts given in the individual chapters to be compared and contrasted. It also supports the use of the book as a resource for stimulating debate and reflection on both the conduct of research and current knowledge of HRD. As editors, we have attempted to provide a synthesis of the main content of the book in our introductory and concluding chapters. However, these represent our arguments and we do not claim that they are definitive. We encourage readers to produce their own in order to critique ours. It is our firm conviction that this will genuinely advance your understanding of research and of HRD.

Acknowledgements

The editors wish to acknowledge the following people without whose contribution the production of this volume would have been impossible. Jessie Mathieson of the University of Abertay provided enormous help in communications with all the contributors but more importantly managed much of the scheduling of editorial meetings, no mean feat considering that principally involved controlling Jim McGoldrick's chaotic diary. Additionally, a debt is owed to Fiona MacDonald for helping Jim McGoldrick (again) master some of the basics of page formatting and layout of the draft manuscript. Sincere thanks are due also to colleagues in the University Forum for HRD for their initial support for the concept of the book and, indeed, for many of their contributions to the book. Thanks should also be acknowledged to Michelle Gallagher at Routledge who was thrust into her managing editorial role on the departure of Stuart Hay who had provided initial encouragement for the project.

We would also like to record our personal thanks to our partners who have had to put up with a lot in the last eighteen months.

References

Beardwell, I. and Holden, L. (eds) (1994) *Human Resource Management: a Contemporary Perspective*, London: Pitman.

Blyton, P. and Turnbull, P. (eds) (1992) *Reassessing Human Resource Management*, London: Sage.

Bratton, J. and Gold, J. (eds) (1999) *Human Resource Management: Theory and Practice*, Basingstoke: Macmillan Business.

Keenoy, T. (1999) 'HRM as hologram: a polemic', *Journal of Management Studies*, 36(1): 1–23.

Garavan, T.N. (1991) 'Strategic human resource development', *Journal of European Industrial Training*, 15(1): 17–30.

Lee, M. (1998) 'HRDI: a journal to define', *Human Resource Development International*, 1(1): 1–6.

Legge, K. (1995) *Human Resource Management: Rhetoric and Realities*, Basingstoke: Macmillan.

Lewis, P. (1997) 'A framework for research into training and development', *International Journal of Training and Development*, 1(1): 2–8.

McGoldrick, J. and Stewart, J. (1996) 'The HRM/HRD nexus', in J. Stewart and J. McGoldrick (eds) (1996) *Human Resource Development: Perspectives, Strategies and Practice*, London: Pitman.

Megginson, D., Joy-Mathews, J. and Banfield, P. (1993) *Human Resource Development*, London: Kogan Page.

Storey, J. (ed.) (1989) *New Perspectives on Human Resource Management*, London: Routledge.

Storey, J. (1992) *Developments in the Management of Human Resources*, Oxford: Blackwell.

—— (1995) 'Human resource management: still marching on, or marching out', in J. Storey *Human Resource Management: a Critical Text*, London: Routledge.

Walton, J. (1999) *Strategic Human Resource Development*, London: Financial Times/ Prentice Hall.

Wilson, J. (ed.) (1999) *Human Resource Development*, London: Kogan Page.

ACKNOWLEDGEMENTS

The authors and publishers would like to thank the following for granting permission to reproduce material in this work:

Blackwell Publishers for Box 6.1, adapted from:
Journal of Management Studies, May 1976, Stanworth, M.J.K. and Curran, J., 'Growth and the Small Firm – An Alternative View', p. 96. Originally published as: Bolton Committee, *Small Firms – Report of the Committee of Inquiry on Small Firms*, Cmnd. 4811, London: HMSO, November 1971

Elsevier Science for the following:
Figure 3.1, adapted from:
European Management Journal, vol. 13, no. 3, Hiltrop, J.M., 'The Changing Psychological Contract', pp. 286–94, 1995
Figure 3.2, adapted from:
Organizational Dynamics, vol. 26, no. 3, Hall, D.T. and Moss, J.E., 'The Protean Career Contract', pp. 22–37, 1998

John Wiley & Sons Limited for Figure 3.3, adapted from:
Journal of Organizational Behaviour 19 (SPI), Guest, D.E., 'Is the psychological contract worth taking seriously', pp. 649–64, 1998

Pearson Education Ltd for permission to reproduce three figures from:
Organizational Change and Development: a Reflective Guide for Managers, Hamlin, B., Keep, J. and Ash, K., 2001 (Figs 5.2, 5.3 and 5.4)

Sage Publications Ltd for the following:
Table 17.1, adapted from:
Table 1: 'Fifteen Characteristics of Action Research' Eden, C. and Huxham, C., 'Action Research for the Study of Organizations', in Clegg, S. *et al.* (eds) *Handbook of Organization Studies*, 1999, p. 285
Figure 17.3, adapted from 'Stages in Co-operative Inquiry', in Reason, P., *Human Inquiry in Action*, 1998

Every effort has been made to contact copyright holders for their permission to reprint material in this book. The publishers would be grateful to hear from any copyright holder who is not here acknowledged and will undertake to rectify any errors or omissions in future editions of this book.

1

RESEARCHING HRD

Philosophy, process and practice

Jim McGoldrick, Jim Stewart and Sandra Watson

Aims and contribution

This chapter has three aims. The first is to provide the foundation for locating the research presented throughout the text within the theoretical context of HRD. The second is to examine underpinning research perspectives and paradigms represented in the book. Third, to provide an overview of the key issues raised in the contributed chapters to enable readers to apply these theoretical arguments in their reading of the individual chapters. In order to achieve these aims we provide an overview of many of the conceptual and theoretical concerns surrounding the meaning and understanding of HRD. These issues and concerns are affiliated to both the ontological and epistemological perspectives of HRD, which in turn influence our vision of researching and understanding HRD. The commentary is derived from a meta-analysis of recent European and American literature. This is supplemented with selected examples of the theoretical, empirical and methodological contexts of the research projects reported in the contributed chapters of this volume. Finally, a critical analysis of paradigms, theories and concepts associated with understanding the meaning of HRD is provided.

Achieving these aims will contribute to the ongoing debate surrounding the theoretical foundations of HRD (Walton 1999; Lynham 2000) and the purpose and value of HRD professional practice (Holton 2000). The chapter presents an analysis of the key tenets of the various positions in these debates. In doing so, the authors provide a rare comparison of American and European conceptions of HRD. This informs the overview, also provided through this chapter, of the diverse range of research philosophies, processes and practices currently being applied in the UK. The chapter also draws on the work of Keenoy (1999), a sharp critic of the literature of human resource management and tries to take his insights and critique into a better conceptual understanding of HRD.

Theoretical context

Recent attempts to define the concept of human resource development (HRD) by academics, researchers and practitioners are proving frustrating, elusive and confusing. This suggests that HRD has not established a distinctive conceptual or theoretical identity (Garavan, Gunnigle and Morley 2000; Hatcher 2000). The process of defining HRD is frustrated by the apparent lack of boundaries and parameters, elusiveness is created through the lack of depth of empirical evidence of some conceptual aspects of HRD e.g. strategic HRD, learning organization and knowledge management (Keenoy, op. cit.). Confusion also arises over the 'philosophy', 'purpose', 'location' and 'language' of HRD. This is further complicated by the epistemological and ontological perspectives of individual stakeholders and commentators in the HRD arena (Swanson *et al.* 2000). All research, to varying degrees, is tied to a particular theoretical framework and to a general body of knowledge. These, in turn, are themselves the product of a complex interplay of philosophical arguments thus, the 'complication' noted by Swanson (op. cit.) is perfectly natural but renders the task of analysing the 'meaning' of HRD more difficult. Inevitably this draws us into the realm of philosophy.

In reviewing the literature surrounding the meaning and understanding of HRD, a number of dimensions can be seen to be influencing an almost chameleon-like characteristic to emerge. The following discussion is organized around what are seen to be the most significant of these dimensions.

Philosophical and conceptual dimensions

As Swanson *et al.* (op. cit.: 1126) argue, 'philosophy is a systematic examination of the assumptions that underlie action'. Therefore, in order to understand action, in this case HRD activities, it is necessary to engage with philosophies of HRD to make explicit the rationales underpinning competing perspectives. They put forward three interactive elements of the philosophical framework of HRD. These are as follows: first, *ontology* (how we see our world); second, *epistemology* (how we think about our world); and, third, *axiology* (the values that determine how we should and actually act in research and practice). The dynamic relationship of these three elements will influence an individual's understanding and expression of HRD. Therefore it is useful and appropriate to address philosophical issues in attempting to understand HRD as this supports the view expressed by Swanson *et al.* (op. cit.: 1126): 'interpretation of texts and the criticism of common wisdoms that are often taken for granted'.

The philosopher Thomas Kuhn first introduced the idea of scientific paradigms in his path-breaking book *The Structure of Scientific Revolutions* in 1962. This book has proven to be seminal in the development of theory and research in the social sciences and is likely to have an equally profound and enduring influence on the conceptual and theoretical development in HRD. The concept of paradigms, introduced by Kuhn (1962), is often used to describe philosophical frameworks informing and guiding scientific research. McAndrew (2000) usefully applies this notion in analysing significant influences on HRD theory and practice. She particularly highlights the Newtonian and quantum paradigms, as well as a number from biology and chemistry to illustrate these influences. For example Newtonian physics is shown to be related to mechanistic conceptions of humans and organizations, while more recent ideas such as *autopoiesis* are argued to both question established paradigms and to support the development of alternatives. Earlier work in social theory adopted similar approaches to explain varying accounts of and prescriptions for organizing and managing.

One of the best known of these is the paradigmatic framework developed by Burrell and Morgan (1979). They forward four broad paradigms, which affect the development of social theory. These are the *functionalist paradigm*, which assumes an objective, social reality, and which can be empirically analysed and understood through application of scientific methods. Social systems are seen as inherently concerned with stability and continuity to serve regulatory purposes. The *interpretive paradigm* assumes that individuals and their interactions create social reality, subjectively. Multiple social realities are created, maintained and changed and there is no single, objective entity to be analysed and understood. However, in common with the functional perspective, the interpretive paradigm assumes an underlying pattern and order in the social world, i.e. regulatory focus, rather than a change orientation. Much of Burrell and Morgan's (op. cit.) insight still informs contemporary debates in organizational analysis.

Variants of these arguments are evident in the emergence of new perspectives on HRD framed as *post-positivist* (Trochim 1999) and *critical realist* (Sayer 2000) positions. The former of these develops elements of the Burrell and Morgan functionalist and interpretive paradigms whilst the critical realist perspective takes forward a concern with meaning and interpretation that echoes the radical humanist and radical structuralist paradigms. However, these have not crystallized into a simple bipolarization. Rather the whole area is characterized by what Martin (2000: 13) refers to as paradigm incommensurability, which in turn reflects an impact on methodological development to which we will return later.

The *radical humanist paradigm* assumes that reality is socially and subjectively created and therefore not capable of objective analysis seeing social institutions as negative in the sense of constraining and controlling human thought, action and potential. These negative aspects tend to alienate rather than focus on positive outcomes. The concern is with radical change rather than regulation. The *radical structuralist paradigm* assumes that social systems have independent, concrete and objective existence and are capable of scientific analysis. This perspective also encompasses

3

social systems as oppressive and alienating and assumes an inherent drive for radical change in society. A more detailed analysis of the complex strands of these arguments is contained in the contribution to this volume by Hamblett, Holden and Thursfield (Chapter 4).

To date, there appears to be little sustained and detailed attention given to philosophical influences on HRD, but as Kuchinke (2000: 32) argues 'paradigm debates can deepen theory and provide the foundation for new research'. This view is supported by Swanson *et al.* (op. cit.), amongst others who identify implications of philosophy for research, theory building, practice and the evolution of HRD. The role of the varying paradigms discussed here, representing as they do different philosophical frameworks, in shaping HRD theory and practice is well illustrated by the work of Lynham (2000). It is evident that a significant outcome of adopting different paradigms will be varying emphasis on the possible alternative purposes of HRD.

The chapters in this volume display a broad range of epistemological perspectives embracing the whole range of paradigms discussed earlier in relation to Burrell and Morgan (1979). Some contributions to the text can be readily seen to derive from, or have been influenced by distinct and different knowledge paradigms. For example, Short and Kuchinke's contribution (Chapter 10) focuses on a quantitative analysis and can be seen to approximate to the positivist or post-positivist paradigm. Similarly, Winterton and Winterton (Chapter 7) and Hamlin (Chapter 5), with their strong emphasis on evidential clarity, may also be seen to resonate with post-positivism. The large majority of contributed chapters cluster around various aspects of an interpretive paradigm with a very strong emphasis on process as much as content in their research. These include up-front adherents to qualitative research and particularly 'action research', for example, Rigg, Trehan and Ram (Chapter 17). The interpretive approach with a clear emphasis on subjectivity includes Wilson and Davies (Chapter 14), Beattie (Chapter 15), Gold *et al.* (Chapter 8) and Sambrook (Chapters 11 and 18). McGoldrick, Martin and Pate (Chapter 3) more consciously associate their approach closer to a critical realist epistemology whilst the radical humanist paradigm is echoed to varying degrees by Lee (Chapter 2) and Edwards (Chapter 13). The closest to a radical structuralist epistemology is displayed by Hamblett, Holden and Thursfield (Chapter 4).

This variety of perspectives demonstrates vividly that there is no dominant paradigm of HRD research. It also illustrates what may be meant by 'paradigm incommensurablity' in organizational research. However, such a position is healthy. There is no single *lens* for viewing HRD research and there are many *voices* expressing individual opinions. It may be that, as HRD academics become more sophisticated in theorizing, then greater clarity and paradigm commensurablity will occur. It may also be the case that the increasingly influential discourse of postmodernism, which is strongly established in the field of organization studies (Alvesson and Deetz

1999; Burrell 1999) and is now evident in the literature of strategic change, will come to have an impact on HRD researchers (Ford and Ford 1995). A further, but more mundane, point is that the paradigmatic pluralism evident within this text also results in a very broad ranging discussion of research methods being conducted throughout all of the chapters below.

Purpose of HRD

Lying behind the main philosophical debates concerning the nature of HRD, there is a concurrent set of debates concerning the purpose of HRD. According to Holton (2000) the debates on purpose centre on the 'learning' versus 'performance' perspectives. Should HRD practice focus on the well being of the individual or should interests of the shareholders predominate? This section presents a rudimentary map of what the various claims of the purpose of HRD might be. Hatcher (2000) proposes that HRD research should focus on the economic benefits, systems theory, social benefits and ethics of HRD and thus indirectly attempts a reconciliation of these two perspectives. Kuchinke (op. cit.) presents a classification of schools of thought according to the central focus of the developmental activity: *person-centred, production-centred* and *principled problem solving*, each deriving from different philosophical traditions. Gourlay (2000: 99) in attempting to clarify the nature of HRD states that 'it focuses on theory and practice relating to training, development and learning within organisations, both for individuals and in the context of business strategy and organisational competence formation'.

Whilst the authors contributing to this volume were not specifically concerned to explore 'the purpose of HRD' as such, there are nonetheless echoes of the more conceptual debates evident in some of the chapters. Kuchinke's (op. cit.) classification of *person-centred, production-centred* and *principled problem-solving* perspectives can be seen in the contribution of Lee with respect to the 'person-centred' category. Whereas the contributions of Hill (Chapter 6) and West (Chapter 9) can be seen to have elements of the 'production-centred' category, the contributions of Sambrook (Chapter 18) and Gold, Watson and Rix (Chapter 8) resonate with the 'principled problem solving' category.

Garavan, Gunnigle and Morley (2000) articulate three perspectives of HRD as being concerned with *capabilities, psychological contracts* and *learning organization/organizational learning*. Each of these is associated with different root disciplines. They also imply different purposes in their prescriptions for HRD practice. The issues identified by Garavan *et al.* are addressed to varying degrees by many of the chapters in this volume. The contribution by McGoldrick, Martin and Pate (Chapter 3) whose research focus is on lifelong learning and the psychological contract is perhaps the closest match.

There is also variability in relation to the purpose of HRD arising from the root disciplines seen to be underpinning HRD. These include 'adult education, instructional design and performance technology, psychology, business and economics, sociology, cultural anthropology, organization theory and communications, philosophy, axiology (the study of values), and human relations theories' (Willis 1997; cited by Walton 1999). There is also a running subterranean debate within the field of HRD on the 'discipline' status of some of these root disciplines. As well as variability of purpose, conceptual propositions derived from and built on these root disciplines also influence individual perspectives of HRD. For example, in the typology devised by Garavan, Gunnigle and Morley (2000) the *capabilities* perspective is primarily associated with human capital theory and the application of economics in the resource based view of the firm. In a similar vein, Weinberger (1998) identifies *systems theory* as being distinct from *learning theory* in relation to their influence on HRD, leading to different formulations on the nature and purpose of HRD practice.

What is apparent from the above commentary is that there is no consensus over the conceptual-theoretical identity of HRD and related purpose. The purpose is contingent upon both philosophical and theoretical perspectives. Arguments on the theoretical foundations of HRD also constitute the core of debates on its scope and boundaries.

Boundaries and parameters of HRD

As has been amply demonstrated earlier in this discussion, the multi-disciplinary nature of what is contended to be HRD makes attempts to precisely define HRD difficult. There is some evidence in the literature of ideological or descriptive-normative models for aspects of HRD. For example Walton (1999) has identified 'Strategic HRD' as a distinctive and almost freestanding dimension of HRD. Similarly, the much discussed idea of the 'learning organisation' (Senge 1997), is a good example of the ways in which the normative prescriptive models are used as the basis for examining current practice (Dibella and Nevis 1998). HRD is often presented as different to training and development with the focus being on learning and development for the organization as well as the individual. There is often a futuristic focus, with prescribed contingent outcomes. Although there are often attempts to address both the practice and the conceptual aspects of HRD, the drive to express HRD in relation to models, frameworks and typologies could result in a distancing between rhetoric and reality, similar to that found in HRM debates. As Hatcher argues, 'Without a focus on the theoretical foundations of research and practice, HRD is destined to remain atheoretical in nature and poor practice will continue to undermine its credibility' (2000: 45).

Historically, the development of HRD can be traced from training and instructional design, to training and development, to employee development (Jacobs 2000). Traditionally, the field of HRD was defined by practice, not from a theoretical frame or set of research (Lyhnam op. cit.). Pat McLagan (1983) postulates the boundaries of HRD as *individual development, organization development* and *career development*. O'Brien and Thompson (1999) apply a similar framework in the Irish and European context. More recently, the emergence of HRD related journals have presented an opportunity to define the field on the basis of theory and practice (Jacobs op. cit.). There is also a blurring of the boundaries in relation to the affiliation of researchers. Many early American researchers emanated from either an instructional design or an adult educational base. Recently Jacobs (op. cit.) has reported that there are an increased number of manuscripts coming from business schools. This trend is a reversal of the European and UK situation. In the UK, HRD is very much the child of the explosion of HRM literature in the 1980s and 1990s (McGoldrick and Stewart 1996). In the introduction to this volume we discuss the emergence of the HRD literature in the form of HRD texts, journals and academic symposia.

In addition, the scope of HRD research can be seen to be expanding, with recent focus on areas that were not traditionally considered to be within the domain of HRD. These include organizational leadership, organizational values, workforce development issues at the societal level and labour economics (Donovan and Marsick 2000). Multidisciplinary foundations and an expanding scope both have the effect of expanding the discursive resources and therefore language available to and used by HRD academics and practitioners.

The chapters themselves also display a wide range of concepts and content issues aimed at expanding the border areas around HRD. These range from Hamblett, Holden and Thursfield's interest in the social benefits of employee-led development programmes, to the economic focus taken by Winterton and Winterton, who examine the impact of management development on business performance. Issues related to the ethics of mentoring provide the focus of Beattie and McDougall's contribution (Chapter 12). Other concepts covered in the text include lifelong learning (McGoldrick, Martin and Pate), learning networks (Edwards) and leadership by Short and Kuchinke (Chapter 10). All of these, it could be argued, are neither novel nor original issues in themselves. The point is that they are addressed and analysed in new and interesting ways and from differing epistemological perspectives.

This last point is worth a little more elaboration, particularly with respect to Hatcher's remark, noted above, concerning the poverty of HRD practice being a function of the poverty of HRD theory. Rather than seeking to stake a claim to particular territory, HRD should be looking to enhance its capability to theorize on the basis of a solid research base. As was noted earlier, there is no single lens through which HRD is viewed, nor should there be. The debates which are now emerging from the Academy of HRD in the US and the University Forum for HRD in Europe and the UK, indicate a growing vitality for the development of good HRD theory. In taking these discussions and debates forward it is essential to pay close attention to issues of language and meaning.

Language of HRD: 'jargon-ridden' or 'meaning-hidden'?

There is a clear and continuing paradox concerning the language used in the discourse of HRD. Walton (1999) neatly sums it up as follows: 'this constant concern with meaning and learning and their subtleties/shades/tones/cadences by those responsible for HRD can paradoxically be (yet another) reason why the HRD language appears so jargon-ridden and meaning-hidden'. He continues: 'Words are being asked to express the ambiguities faced by those trying to translate the subtleties of meaning into learning frameworks and language that hopefully capture all the nuances of actual experience and associated reflection, conceptualisation and experimentation' (1999: 54). Social processes through which this has been attempted involve the construction of linguistic categories and an alteration in the received meaning of existing expressions. New terms in HRD include *lifelong learning* and *psychological contracts*, whilst terms with scope for new meaning include *competence* and *competences, integration, teamwork, communication* and *commitment.* Although all of these are useful to describe practices, conceptually there is a danger that these denote rhetorical, often managerial, aspirations and desired states of being. A lack of effective linguistic categories to clarify what is happening within HRD could result in a combination of illusion and allusion, as there are no definitive words to signify its identity.

Many of Walton's concerns resonate with Legge's (1995) sharp critique of rhetoric and reality of HRM. However, this point is challenged by Sambrook (2000) who provides an analysis which draws no distinction between *rhetoric and reality* or *words and action.* In her view rhetoric *is* reality and words *constitute* action. From this approach, she is able to formulate a typology of 'ideal types' which is capable of accommodating discourse from both academic disciplines and professional practice. Such typologies, as well as those suggested by Garavan, Gunnigle and Morley (op. cit.) and Lynham (op. cit.) may well be useful in capturing and making sense of current variety of discourses within the HRD domain. However, a proliferation of linguistic terms with variable meanings has obvious consequences for investigating empirical realities.

The contributions to this volume reflect many of the points made above. Language is definitely seen to be a prominent theme emerging in the body of HRD research in the UK. This is seen to be particularly important with respect to research involving models and concepts of HRD with a focus on words, phrases, discursive resources used to create, describe and achieve HRD. This is particularly demonstrated by the contribution from Sambrook (Chapter 18). She is interested in exploring the use of language in researching models and concepts of HRD from academic and practitioner perspectives. For Sambrook, the importance of language is paramount. She argues strongly and persuasively that HRD *has been talked into being* and is talked about, by HRD specialists – whether academics or practitioners. In Chapter 11 she uses the technique of story-telling to create new meaning and understanding of the emergence of HRD in the health service. Gold *et al.* (Chapter 8) utilize narrative analysis and linguistics of story-telling to understand the process and results of the social construction of learning.

Empirical elusiveness

Empirical elusiveness (Keenoy op. cit.) derives from an inability to show that HRD has a substantive presence in organizations. In some respects the issues surrounding the empirical absence or presence of HRD are analogous with those discussed earlier with respect to the conceptual parameters and boundaries. The American Society for Training and Development Research committee identified two major empirical gaps in relation to evidence as being between practitioners and researchers, and between practitioners and senior executives (Dilworth and Redding 1999). Several European commentators, including Harrison (1998), have found little empirical evidence of 'Strategic HRD' in organizations. Others including Sambrook (1998) identify divergence in the stories told by HRD practitioners and non-HRD managers and employees. These studies suggest a need for closer collaboration between researchers and practitioners in order to build more accurate empirical evidence. Such a need has been expressed by both European (Hamlin, Reidy and Stewart 1998) and American (Lynham 2000) academics.

This empirical elusiveness is portrayed by a number of our authors. For example Hamlin (Chapter 5) identifies a *HRD research-practice gap*, Hill (Chapter 6) and Rigg, Trehan and Ram (Chapter 17) decry the paucity of understanding of the HRD needs of SMEs and entrepreneurs, whilst Gold *et al.* (Chapter 8) emphasize the need to explore the learning below 'the tip of the iceberg'. The empirical elusiveness, discussed above, can be further compounded by the emergence of new organizational forms. However, the underlying concern is less to do with whether or not something labelled 'HRD' is present or absent. Rather it is to do with the development of a serious body of research and academic writings and the identification of issues which are worth researching.

Locations of HRD

Locations of HRD can be understood in two senses. First, as a description of a physical or sectoral location and second, and more importantly, as a feature of the process of organizational design. Reconfiguration of contemporary organizations, the emergence of the small business sector and continued growth in non-standard forms of employment are extending the perimeters of HRD activity. Internal creation of independent business units and growth of outsourcing, subcontracting and downsizing are all impacting on the structures and boundaries of organizations. Similarly, the notion of 'employee' appears increasingly under threat; employment security is no longer salient, with apparent continuing growth in temporary, part-time, subcontract and agency work.

As a consequence HRD can no longer be seen to operate within the traditional boundaries of an organization, but spread its influence to the development of those outside, on whom it depends (Walton 1996, 1999). In addition the small and medium-sized enterprises (SME) sector is likely to provide a growing location for HRD practice, which may imply an expansion of the meaning of HRD (Hill and Stewart 2000).

Two of the chapters in this volume, McGoldrick, Martin and Pate (Chapter 3) and Davies and Wilson (Chapter 14) focus on the area of career development and change. Each of them addresses in their own ways the current debates surrounding organizational reconfiguration and careers. The debates focus on the degree to which the traditional concept of 'career' is now replaced by 'portfolio' of transferable skills and competences. Occupational limits are also becoming 'boundaryless' (Arthur and Rousseau 1996) and new ideas and understandings of careers place much more weight on the active agency of individuals (Watson and Harris 1999). In addressing these concerns, the AHRD conference in North Carolina, endeavoured to reconcile the different perspectives, conceptual frameworks and locations of HRD and put forward the following summation: 'The purpose of HRD is to enhance human learning, human potential and high performance in work related systems' (Holton 2000, oral summation).

As well as presenting a range of contexts for locating HRD, the contributions also vary in relation to sectors, including manufacturing, West (Chapter 9) locates her research within the automative car industry, Short and Kuchinke (Chapter 10) use research based within a telecommunications organization to illustrate core principles and conventions in quantitative research. Hill (Chapter 6) and Winterton and Winterton (Chapter 7) utilize a range of sectors for their research and public-sector examples can be found in the work of Sambrook (Chapters 11 and 18) and Hamlin (Chapter 5). The research examples presented in this text are derived from a diverse range of organizations in terms of ownership and size, including SMEs, Hill (Chapter 6) 'voluntary sector' (Beattie, Chapter 15) and National Health Service by Sambrook (Chapters 11 and 18).

What is apparent from the discussion in the previous sections of this chapter is that there is no consensus over the conceptual-theoretical identity of HRD. It can be seen to constitute multiple, shifting, competing and contingent identities, dependent on philosophical perspectives and influenced by the range of methodological dimensions derived from the literature and from the continuing analysis of ongoing research work. This volume perhaps epitomizes the conceptual incongruence, with chapters from researchers who utilize a broad range of perspectives, concepts and theories. They also represent a focus on both theory and practice.

Methodological issues

The consideration given to the philosophical and theoretical aspects of HRD also raise some interesting issues with respect to methodological development for HRD research. It is clear that there is no 'one best way' but there is an interesting exercise to be done at sometime which might scrutinize published HRD research and tease out the methodological issues. Whilst the chapters included in this volume were selected in order to demonstrate, to some extent, the diversity of HRD research in the UK they were never intended to be seen as *representative* of the state of development of research. However, the chapters are nonetheless *indicative* of the kinds of issues of interest to UK academics.

Of the eighteen substantive chapters all but two engage in some reflection on choices and methods in the research work underpinning the specific contributions. Overwhelmingly the chapters indicate a preference for qualitative over quantitative research. Only two chapters are explicitly quantitative. Notwithstanding the variations in epistemological influence the data sources were predominantly 'subjective'. There is a clear focus in some on process epistemology in that the design of the research and the doing of the research were inextricably bound up with each other. Action research featured strongly in this regard but was not the only way in which process dimensions were addressed. The contributions display an array of specific methods of data gathering and analysis and all address in their own ways issue of reliability and validity.

There is also an overwhelming use of case studies as the empirical vehicle for the research. Taken together, the combination of case studies with qualitative data gathering methods indicates a strong preference for depth and richness of data and for texture and nuance rather than numerical patterns and statistical validity. The latter point is perhaps an area of weakness. Even a quick glance at North American HRD journals and conference proceedings conveys a flavour of an epistemological and methodological ocean separating HRD academics in Europe from their colleagues in the USA. Papers from the Academy of HRD in the USA are redolent with measurement and modelling and with statistical testing and rigour. This is not to the exclusion of other types of paper but paradigmatic diversity is less evident. These comments are not intended to offer a judgement as to whether or not quantitative research is more robust or more reliable than qualitative but rather offer the optimistic conclusion that there is much that can be learned through HRD academics sharing ideas and research.

11

Critical analysis

In our preface to this volume we offered an overview of how we have seen the evolution of HRD in the UK. Our argument is that conceptually HRD is still in the intellectual shadows of HRM (McGoldrick and Stewart 1996). It is instructive, however, to see all the lessons HRD academics can learn from the theoretical development of HRM. Since its emergence in the late 1980s there have been two distinct strands to the literature advancing HRM. The first of these has been the solid development of texts and journal publications. The second has been a highly critical, even polemical literature, questioning the academic and root discipline claims of HRM. The strongly critical literature is exemplified by Keenoy and Anthony's (1992) portrayal of HRM as 'metaphor' and Legge's (1995) critique of the rhetoric of HRM.

One of the critics is Tom Keenoy (1999) who has written a sharp and deeply polemical review of the rise of HRM – which he dubs 'HRMism'. The article is both challenging and stimulating and poses questions as relevant to the emerging debates about HRD as to the discussion of HRM. His argument is that HRM concepts, practices and theory are 'a source of controversy, confusion and misapprehension'. Indeed, he goes further than this and argues that 'at the centre of this unfolding obfuscation lies an infuriating but curious paradox: despite mounting evidence of conceptual fragmentation, empirical incoherence and theoretical vacuity, HRMism has gone from strength to strength' (op. cit.: 1). These charges of conceptual fragmentation, empirical incoherence and theoretical vacuity may equally be applied to HRD. However, emerging from his polemical discourse there is a potentially useful metaphor for HRD.

A holographic paradigm?

The key argument that we wish to advance here, in contra-distinction to the way that Keenoy's argument is developed, is that utilizing the metaphor of a hologram enables the reconciliation of intrinsic confusions and contradictions of conceptual-theoretical and empirical identities of HRD to be understood.

'Holograms are projected images, which, as we shift our visual field in relation to them, appear to have contours, depth and in some cases movement' (Keenoy op. cit.: 9). The hologram is composed of two distinct, discrete processes of technology and social, which are entwined. Both must occur simultaneously for the hologram to exist. Human social action and perception are an integral part of the process required to construct the image and illusions. Holograms can be described as 'techno-social' artefacts with a complex ontology (Keenoy op. cit.: 10). Each is real, but each exists in a different domain. We only see what we are looking for. In order to see the other side, the shaded, deeper side and fracture of its identity, we need to change our perspective. The hologram provides a metaphor, which depicts 'social reality' as multi-dimensional, multi-causal, mutually dependent and constantly changing. The holographic reality is only accessible through a reflexive epistemology, which explicitly acknowledges the role of human beings in creating 'social reality'.

The following quotation from Keenoy is modified and substitutes HRD for HRM: 'The more [HRD] is undermined by conventional academic analysis, the stronger it seems to have become. Viewed from a holographic perspective this paradox is a consequence of employing a limiting two-dimensional epistemology. . . . Trying to fragment the phenomena and then mapping each fragment against a predetermined definition could be responsible for failure to "see" [HRD] for what it is' (op. cit.: 10–11). Seeking the reflections of abstracted concepts of [HRD] in 'empirical reality and when reality fails the test we conclude that [HRD] does not exist is fraught with contradictions'.

For Keenoy, all of those implicated in [HRD] may all hold different 'conceptual-projections' of HRD, which are likely to contradict their actual experience of HRD. From this HRD can be seen as a series of mutually expressive phenomena, which are transient (op. cit.: 17). Therefore it is impossible to conclude that HRD does not exist and impossible to conclude that it does exist. HRD exists in so far as it is the process of coming into being. Although we may not be used to conceptualizing HRD as social phenomena in this way, such a conception is already present in the learning organization discourse, which is postulated as a continuous and never-ending process.

The holographic metaphor of HRD has some attraction for some of the reasons that Keenoy is sceptical. Whilst most of this chapter has argued that HRD has no singular identity, if it is understood as a hologram it *could* be defined as singular. HRD's singularity would be defined through the properties of the hologram which could be described as 'the fluid, multi-faceted, integrated social artefacts', which are the 'continuing-outcome' of contextualized learning. HRD then serves as the 'collective noun' for the various concepts, theories and methods devised to manage and control learning. This definition embodies our earlier argument concerning the complex interplay of competing ontological, epistemological and methodological assumptions, which assist in understanding the reality of HRD.

The benefits of the holographic metaphor are the following.

- It acknowledges anomaly, uncertainty, ambiguity, multiple identities and transience. It is sensitive to the problem of linguistic expression.
- It permits the encompassment and softening of contradictions and paradoxes of different perspectives of HRD.
- It emphasizes the analytical significance of the mutually involved processes of social and discursive construction, i.e. the role of social actors in reconstructing reality, whilst being components of reality.

13

- It provides interesting methodological questions concerning empirical research. This does not necessarily mean the abandonment of conventional modernist methodology, but emphasizes the need for greater interpretative sensitivity. It requires analytical space to accommodate paradox, ambiguity instability as normal predictable outcomes within the praxis relationship.
- The holographic metaphor seems to offer an alternative to the dualistic limitations of the modernism perspective and avoids the 'limitless relativism' found in some varieties of social constructionism.

The use of metaphors in HRD is not a new phenomenon by any means. Short (2000) provides an excellent review of the use of metaphors in a recent paper. However, the attractions of the holographic metaphor are that it allows for a whole new *perspective* radically different to those currently associated with the debates on HRD. It provides a perspective which is grounded in the belief that social reality has to be understood as a 'fluid, unfolding *process* of social accomplishment' and, in addition, 'draws attention to the experiential nature of observation and the *observational nature of experience*. "Reality" is a fuzzy shimmer between these two movements' (Keenoy op. cit.: 18).

The implications for theorizing and methodological development afforded by consideration of the holographic perspective may not yet amount to a new paradigm. However, it does offer a counter to the initial charges that may be laid at the door of HRD theory of conceptual fragmentation and theoretical vacuity. The methodological implications for research design are immense and challenging. But that is a matter for another paper, another time.

Conclusions and key learning points

At the start of this chapter we indicated three aims. First, to locate the research presented throughout the text within the theoretical context of HRD. Second, to examine underpinning research perspectives and paradigms. Third, to provide an overview of the key issues raised in the contributed chapters.

In our view these have been achieved. We offered a detailed analysis of the theoretical context of HRD research by focusing initially on the *philosophical and conceptual dimensions*. We argued that HRD has no dominant paradigm, at least in the UK. There is no single *lens* for viewing HRD and indeed there are many *voices* articulating particular perspectives. In relation to our questions on *the purpose of HRD* we found that there is no consensus over the conceptual-theoretical identity of HRD and related purpose. The purpose is contingent upon both philosophical and theoretical perspectives. Arguments on the theoretical foundations of HRD also constitute the core of debates on its scope and boundaries.

We also discussed at length the issues of the *boundaries and parameters of HRD* where we argued that rather than seeking to stake a claim to particular territory, HRD should be looking to enhance its capability to theorize on the basis of a solid research base.

We also addressed the language of HRD as central to advancing theory and research. Such is the significance of the language of HRD that we concluded that the distinction between rhetoric and reality in HRD is a false one. This is a particular theme in a number of chapters. Finally, in the theoretical overview we examined the empirical elusiveness and locations of HRD and argued that both of these were intimately bound up with the changing forms and designs of organizations and the need therefore for research in HRD to address these changes.

Throughout the first part of the chapter we drew 'evidence' from the individual contributions. This was particularly helpful with respect to our discussion of methodological issues.

The concluding section of the chapter focused on the holographic metaphor as a novel perspective on HRD. Our thinking in this regard is at an early stage but we felt it provided the basis of a paradigm through which HRD can be expressed as a transient phenomenon more difficult to explain than understand. It is also seen as useful in developing new explanatory models of what HRD 'is', 'might be', or 'can be'.

Although there is no agreement on what HRD means, it can be researched, practised and taught. *Researching HRD* is intended to portray the diversity, contradictions and ambiguities of HRD as a medium to develop understanding of the complexities of HRD, conceptually and in practice.

References

Alvesson, M. and Deetz, S. (1999) 'Critical theory and postmodernism: approaches to organisational studies', in S. Clegg (ed.) *Studying Organisation Theory and Method*, London: Sage.

Arthur, M.B. and Rousseau, D.M. (eds) (1996) *The Boundaryless Career: A New Employment Principle for a New Organisational Era*, New York: Oxford University Press.

Burrell, G. (1999) 'Normal Science, paradigms, metaphors, discourses and genealogies of analysis', in S. Clegg (ed.) *Studying Organisation Theory and Method*, London: Sage.

Burrell, G. and Morgan, G. (1979) *Sociological Paradigms and Organisational Analysis*, London: Heinemann.

Clegg, S. (ed.) (1999) *Studying Organisation Theory and Method*, London: Sage.

Dibella, A.J. and Nevis, E.C. (1998) *How Organisations Learn – an integrated strategy for building learning capability*, San Francisco: Jossey-Bass.

Dilworth, J. and Redding, R.L. (1999) 'Bridging gaps: an update from the ASTD Research Committee', *Human Resource Development Quarterly*, 10(3): 199–202.

Donovan, L.L. and Marsick, V.J. (2000) 'Trends in the literature: a comparative analysis of 1998 HRD research', *Proceedings of the Academy of Human Resource Development*, North Carolina.

Ford, J.D. and Ford, L.W. (1995) 'The role of conversations in producing intentional organizational change', *Academy of Management Review*, 20(3): 541–70.

Garavan, T.N. (1991) 'Strategic human resource development', *Journal of European Industrial Training*, 15(1): 17–30.

Garavan, T.N., Gunnigle, P. and Morley, M. (2000) 'Contemporary HRD research: a triarchy of theoretical perspectives and their prescriptions for HRD', *Journal of European Industrial Training*, 24(1, 2, 3, 4): 65–93.

Gourlay, S. (2000) 'Knowledge management and HRD', *HRD Research and Practice across Europe Conference Proceedings*, Kingston University, 90–104.

Hamlin, B., Reidy, M. and Stewart, J. (1998) 'Bridging the research–practice gap through professional partnerships: a case study', *Human Resource Development International*, 1(3): 273–90.

Harrison, R. (1998) *Employee Development*, London: IPD.

Hatcher, T. (2000) 'A study of the influence of the theoretical foundations of human resource development on research and practice', *Proceedings of the Academy of Human Resource Development*, North Carolina.

Hill, R. and Stewart, J. (2000) 'Human resource development in small organisations', *Journal of European Industrial Training*, 24(1, 2, 3, 4): 105–17.

Holton, III, E.F. (2000) 'Clarifying and defining the performance paradigm of human resource development', *Proceedings of the Academy of Human Resource Development*, North Carolina.

Jacobs, R.L. (2000) 'Developing the boundaries of HRDQ and HRD', *Human Resource Development Quarterly*, 11(2).

Keenoy, T. (1999) 'HRM as hologram: a polemic', *Journal of Management Studies*, 36(1): 1–23.

Keenoy, T. and Anthony, P. (1992) 'HRM: Metaphor, meaning and morality', in Blyton, P. and Turnbull, P. (eds) *Reassessing Human Resource Management*, London: Sage.

Kuchinke, P.K. (2000) 'Development towards what end? An analysis of the notion of development for the field of human resource development', *Proceedings of the Academy of Human Resource Development*, North Carolina.

Kuhn, T.S. (1962) *The Structure of Scientific Revolutions*, Chicago: University of Chicago Press.

Legge, K. (1995) *Human Resource Management: Rhetoric and Reality*, London: Macmillan.

Lynham, S.A. (2000) 'Theory building in the human resource development profession', *Human Resource Development Quarterly*, 11(2).

McAndrew, A.E. (2000) 'Scientific paradigms and their implications for a vision of HRD, *Proceedings of the Academy of Human Resource Development*, North Carolina.

McGoldrick, J. and Stewart, J. (1996) 'The HRM/HRD nexus', in J. Stewart and J. McGoldrick (eds) (1996) *Human Resource Development: Perspectives, Strategies and Practice*, London: Pitman.

McLagan, P.A. (1983) 'Models for excellence: the conclusions and recommendations of the ASTD training and development competency study', Washington, DC: ASTD.

O'Brien, G. and Thompson, J.E. (1999) 'The development of Irish HRD professionals in comparison with European professionals' roles, outputs and competencies', *International Journal of Training and Development*, 3(4): 250–68.

Sambrook, S.A. (1998) 'Models and concepts of human resource development; academic and practitioner perspectives', Unpublished Ph.D. thesis, The Nottingham Trent University.

—— (2000) 'Talking of HRD', *Human Resource Development International*, 3(2): 159–78.

Sayer, A. (2000) *Realism and Social Science*, London: Sage.

Senge, P. (1997) *The Fifth Discipline*, London: Century Business.

Short, D. (2000) 'Analysing HRD through metaphor: why, how, and some likely findings', *Proceedings of the Academy of Human Resource Development*, North Carolina, 1(4–1): 78–85.

Stewart, J. and McGoldrick, J. (eds) (1996) *Human Resource Development: Perspectives, Strategies and Practice*, London: Pitman.

Storey, J. (1995) 'Human resource management: still marching on, or marching out?', in *Human Resource Management: A Critical Text*, London: Routledge.

Swanson, R.A., Lynham, S.A., Ruona, W.E. and Torraco, R.J. (2000) 'Theory building researching HRD – pushing the envelope!', *Proceedings of the Academy of Human Resource Development*, North Carolina.

Trochim, W.K. (1999) *Positivism and Post-positivism: Research Methods, Knowledge Base* (2nd edn), http://trochim.human.cornell.edn/Kb/positivism.htm.

Walton, J. (1996) 'The provision of learning support for non-employees', in J. Stewart and J. McGoldrick (eds) (1996) *Human Resource Development: Perspectives, Strategies and Practice*, London: Pitman.

—— (1999) *Strategic Human Resource Development*, London: Financial Times/Prentice Hall.

Watson, T.J. and Harris, P. (1999) *The Emergent Manager*, London: Sage.

Weinberger, L.A. (1998) 'Commonly held theories of human resource development', *Human Resource Development International*, 1(1).

Willis, V.J. (1997) 'HRD as evolutionary system: from pyramid building to space walking and beyond', *Proceedings of the Academy of Human Resource Development*, Atlanta.

2

DEFINING THE RESEARCH QUESTION

On seizing the moment as the research question emerges

Monica Lee

Aims and contribution

The 'correct' identification of one's 'research question' and the judgement as to whether or not one has effectively, comprehensively and skilfully answered that question are central to the way in which our work, as researchers, is measured. This applies to those in the higher echelons of the research community and the neophyte research student alike – though the grounds for the judgement might differ. The notion appears easy and many a research student has been slickly told 'do your literature review, find the hole in the literature, find your question and then answer it', irrespective of their area of study and personal style. This approach does not do the supervisor or the student any favours at all – the student is presented with an almost impossible task, and the supervisor is perpetuating an unworkable myth.

My aim in this chapter is to delve below the superficial gloss to explore the murky world of research questions . . . and I believe this is important for several reasons. First, I would be quite pleased if it helped just one or two research students realize that the task is difficult, but not impossible. Second, as a supervisor I know how easy it is to become formulaic in my approach and to forget the uniquely situated nature of each student's research, so I hope this chapter might serve to redress the balance a little so that each student's work crystallizes as an example of their own excellence, rather than a merely satisfactory compromise of styles and custom. Third, leading directly from the second, I also hope that this chapter might serve as a call to foster the unique and innovative and to stretch our research. The discipline of HRD is changing and growing, and our approaches to research, and associated methodologies and methods also need to develop in harmony with this. Finally, as HRD has learnt from other disciplines, so, I suggest, other disciplines can learn from HRD, and

I would like to see this chapter help percolate a more flexible approach to research and 'the research question' to other areas of study.

In this chapter I loosely describe the hunt for the research question as that of a wild animal, and, in view of my wider aims, talk about 'research' as a generic process rather than one specific to HRD. Throughout this chapter I have inserted questions about research (though not 'the research question') in order to counterpoint the search for the 'right' question (after Rowan 1981).

Theoretical context

My choice of title for this chapter is deliberately obscure. Other possibilities spring to mind: 'how to identify a research question', 'finding the best research question', or, 'the importance of the research question' are just a few. None of these, however, would have adequately indicated my stance towards the 'research question'. I appreciate how odd this might seem. After all, this is a book on research in HRD and this chapter, placed early in the book in this way, might be thought to establish the scene, to lay out the process of research, starting in a clear linear fashion with the research question. Emphasizing the notion, thereby, that the research question is the thing that drives and informs the research. In one way, it is and does, but in my opinion, it is a very odd beast, and it is often hard to catch, so this chapter is really about hunting a wild and elusive animal.

Let us take up the hunt for the research question, then. In what terrain is it found? In the hills or in the valleys? Well, sometimes people are given them – they are employed to do a particular piece of research and answer a particular question. Such people might well have to refine their question (which involves a further hunt) but they do not have the flexibility that is at one time both a great blessing as the researcher can follow their dream, and a great trial . . . how does one capture the uncapturable? So, where does the research question emerge?

Being (One's engagement in a particular field)
Efficiency questions
- Am I familiar with the field and its literature?
- Am I actually involved with the relevant data?
- Have I got appropriate qualifications for dealing with the relevant matters?
- Do I have dependable work habits?
- Am I intelligent enough and intellectually tough enough?

Self and other questions
- Am I aware of my own motives?
- Am I questioning my involvement with the field?

- What relationship with others do I set up by my way of being?
- Can I listen to others?

Political and power questions
- Am I aware of the social implications of my daily practice?
- Am I aware of the sources of the money which supports me?
- Am I aware of the social pressures which influence my actions?
- Am I sexist? Racist? Classist? Ageist?
- Do I see life in terms of domination and submission? Competition and acclaim? Struggle for recognition?
- Am I aware of the patriarchal patterns which surround me?

Dialectical questions
- Do I look for the contradictions underlining daily experience?
- Do I take responsibility for my own life?
- Do I perceive the world in terms of conflicts and their resolution?
- Do I see the paradox of rhythm and the rhythm of paradox?

Legitimacy questions
- Is a client involved? If so, is there honesty or deception or lack of communication between the client and me?
- Who provides the problem? Who defines what the problem is? Who owns the problem? Who legitimates the problem?
- Who is the client? And who is the real client?

Relevance questions
- Am I choosing a problem that is relevant to my life? My career? A client? Ordinary people? Questioning patriarchy? The advancement of science? A class of problems? My unconscious?
- What am I really trying to do?

Two research paradigms

I will suggest that 'the research question' is that one unique question whose answer encapsulates the research such that 'real' research (by which I mean the development of the understanding of the area and the search for meaning within that) *becomes* the search for the 'research question'. In talking about the research question, therefore, I will spend quite a bit of time talking about research because understanding the parameters of the research is fundamental to our search for the question.

There appear to be two main basic beliefs or paradigms about how research should be conducted. I am using the word 'paradigm' here as something that

> supplies a relatively complete set of investigative tools including theory, methods and standards for evaluation in a coherent *Weltanschauung*. This perspective then guides all of the scientist's

researches within the field. It also provides a convenient 'map' of the field in which one can discern the fundamental under-pinnings of any theoretical stance (Kuhn 1969; Ritzer 1980; Burrell and Morgan 1979).

(Gray 1996: 127)

I am not sure whether they really are different paradigms, and, as I suggest later in this chapter, there are certainly some areas of similarity between them. However, they do appear to operate via very different rules: in brief, one is said to start with theory and then to validate this empirically via carefully controlled inquiry, as was propounded as early as *Mill's Canon of Induction* in 1872, and is described in Reason (1981). I have illustrated this in Figure 2.1.

A: Often known as 'linear', 'traditional', 'positivist', 'quantitative' or 'scientific' approach

Figure 2.1 Paradigm A: scientific approach to research

The second is said to start in the empirical world, and then to generate theory, and is discussed in Flick (1998) and illustrated in Figure 2.2.

Both paradigms involve a 'research question', but the position and nature of the 'question' differs considerably. In Paradigm A, which I shall call the *scientific* approach (as it derives from the natural sciences and is a necessary part of study in this area) experiments are designed by which the truth of null hypotheses can be ascertained – and these are built from, or around, the research question. The research question, therefore, is assumed to be absolutely clearly stated and concisely worded before any experimentation occurs. I say 'experimentation' deliberately, as this approach is normally adopted in the realm of carefully designed and controlled experiments

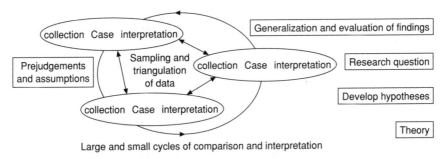

Large and small cycles of comparison and interpretation

Figure 2.2 Paradigm B: phenomenological approach to research

21

in which the 'human factor' is eliminated – or at least minimized as much as possible.

By its nature, research into HRD involves people, and therefore we could assume that there is no role for the scientific approach. This assumption is likely to be wrong, at least in parts. Although strict experimental method is often not used in HR research, the terminology and concepts behind it remain valid for the 'statistical' approach in which people just happen to be the objects that are being measured or sampled. This approach assumes that there is a 'normal' population and that the more data that are gathered the better the description, or the more valid the findings. Hypotheses are established at the beginning (though in this case it is positive hypotheses rather than null hypotheses) and they, and the clearly established and controlled sampling methods, are directly linked to an already established and clearly stated research question.

The shift from null hypothesis to positive hypothesis is much deeper than might appear on first glance. For example, we could hypothesize that all cats have tails. When we adopt a null hypothesis approach we are saying that the hypothesis we will examine is that some cats do not have tails . . . so, if we find any cats without tails then we know that the original hypothesis is wrong . . . not all cats do have tails. However, if we do not find any no-tailed cats, then we can only say that we do not know that somewhere, undetected by us, there might be cats without tails. This approach offers the absolute certainty that proving the null hypothesis disproves the original.

If we adopt a positive hypothesis, then we say that we have seen lots and lots of cats and they all have tails so all cats must have tails. So – we can not be absolutely certain that the hypothesis is really true. This is a confirmatory approach to life and is how most of us normally make assumptions about life, but it does lead to the sort of apparent paradox highlighted in *The HitchHiker's Guide to the Galaxy* when Adams describes the population of the universe as 'none', saying

> It is known that there are an infinite number of worlds, simply because there is an infinite amount of space for them to be in. However, not every one of them is inhabited. Therefore there must be a finite number of inhabited worlds. Any finite number divided by infinity is as near nothing as makes no odds, so the average population of all the planets in the Universe can be said to be zero. From this it follows that the population of the whole Universe is also zero, and that any people you may meet from time to time are merely the products of a deranged imagination.

The 'research questions' in this approach are normally about things that we wish to confirm, rather than disprove.

It might be that these sorts of confirmatory or disproving research question are the beast we are searching for. But in both the scientific and the statistical approach, as I present it here, the question seems to pop out of the hole, right in front of us, already formulated in a way that spawns hypotheses and such that the methods of data gathering emanate directly from the question. Such ease in identifying the question, however, is nothing but an illusion created by the way in which the research is reported, which I shall discuss in more detail towards the end of this chapter. Although the research is conducted differently within the different approaches, and although it is reported in very different ways, the processes of starting the research (getting to the roots of it and bringing forth the question that encapsulates this one, particular, research project) are very similar.

I shall call Paradigm B in Figure 2.2 the *phenomenological* approach to emphasize that it focuses on the subjective, unusual, and unexpected aspects of the world around us, as opposed to the normative aspects of the scientific approach. Within this broad description there are a very wide range of methodologies (critical incident, ethnography, action research, etc.), but they are similar with regard to the hunt for the research question. In *An Introduction to Qualitative Research*, Uwe Flick devotes several pages to the research question, and notes that 'almost no textbook dedicates a separate chapter to this topic. In most subject indexes one looks for it in vain' (1998: 53). I would recommend this book for background reading, but would question the view that

> Research questions are like a door to the research field under study. Whether empirical activities investigated produce answers or not depends on the formulation of such questions. Also dependant on this is the decision as to which methods are appropriate and who (i.e. which persons, groups or institutions) or what (i.e. what processes, activities, lifestyles) should be included in the study. The essential criteria for evaluating research questions include their soundness and clarity, but also whether they can be answered in the framework of given and limited resources (time, money etc.).
>
> (Ibid.)

My quibble with this is in the relationship described between the research question and all the factors that emanate from it and are dependent upon it. I agree that there are many factors involved, but does that single central question that characterizes one particular, unique, research project really come first and all other factors follow on? If the question is 'wrong' or 'faulty' is the project necessarily doomed? I have quite often come across nice coherent research projects or project proposals that are great in themselves, but have little to do with the 'research question' that they are said to address. To date, I have always succeeded in resolving this with the researcher by addressing the research question – re-working it to better encapsulate the research.

Two sorts of research question

It seems to me that in the phenomenological approach, as well as the scientific, there are two sorts of research question. One that gets written up neatly as if it were the precursor to the research, and the other that messily and slowly emerges from primary (empirical) and secondary (literature etc.) data as the real 'research' (the making sense of the area) is conducted. I will address these in reverse order, and talk about the coherently described research question towards the end of this chapter, and examine the nature of the emergent 'fuzzy beastie' in the next sections. From this perspective the research question beast emerges from an increasing understanding of the empirical evidence and is refined as the research progresses. In some sense, the 'research' *becomes* the search for the 'research question'.

In describing research as the search for meaning I am taking a minimalist view of research that does not really do justice to the world of research, to this book, or indeed, to this chapter. Research is more than just looking for meaning, it is also about managing and following through all the logistics of data gathering, it is about slogging away late at night analysing data, it is about writing and rewriting, and it is about exposing oneself, via one's research (that precious baby that has been nurtured for so long) to the scrutiny of colleagues and the wider community, and it is about trying not to be protective and remembering to say 'thank you' as they start to criticize the infant. It is also about enthusiasm, determination, self-development and career progression.

Thinking (refining the research problem)

Efficiency questions
- Can I marshal and collate information in such a way as to bring it to focus on a problem?
- Can I define and break down the problem into specific researchable questions?
- Can I use creative imagination to think of interesting and usable hypotheses?
- Can I discriminate between more and less central or crucial hypotheses to test?
- Can I use the library in an efficient way to gather existing data?
- Have I got the stamina to pursue what I want in the abstracts and reprints?

Self and other questions
- Do I believe that I can be value-free?
- Do I separate research from the rest of my life?
- Do I have something to gain or lose from the outcome of the research, in a direct, practical, personal way?
- Do I consult with others on a strict role basis?

- Do I focus on a specific question early, and spend the rest of the time defending that selection?
- If I disagree with others on a point, do I call for a vote?
- Do I consult authorities to gain new knowledge or insight, or to back-up what is being done already?

Political and power questions
- Do I check on the political commitment of sources of information?
- Am I aware of the social implications of certain lines of inquiry?
- Do I refuse to be politically isolated in my work?
- Do I take patriarchy for granted?
- Do I draw attention to patriarchal patterns when I discover them?

Dialectical questions
- Am I consistently adopting a reflexive approach – applying my concepts to myself?
- Am I looking for the reality beneath the appearances?
- Am I looking for the major contradiction underlying my problem, as opposed to the minor contradictions which might be easier to approach?

Legitimacy questions
- Is information being fed in from an interested party?
- Am I under pressure not to study certain problems?
- Is certain information being refused or not made available?
- Are certain lines of thought discouraged?

Relevance questions
- Am I looking for the data about how my problem can work out in practice?
- How has application taken place? How will it take place?

Empirical context

The search for meaning

Even so, I contend that the nub of the research, the central core, is about trying to make sense of the world. It follows from this that seeking the research question is largely about structuring this search for meaning. The core of the research is built upon a background of thinking and reading, of scouring the secondary data and of conducting 'thought experiments', all leading to knowledge of the area. In the scientific approach much of what I would call the 'true' research has already been done before the empirical work is undertaken, during the designing and planning the experiments, questionnaires, etc. In the phenomenological approach the development of this core part of the research is a more obvious and central part of the research project, such that under some models (e.g.

action research), the 'object' of the research becomes a participant who is given the power to influence (or is even given co-ownership of) the research question.

I am suggesting, therefore, that regardless of one's research paradigm the central core of research is about trying to make sense of the world, and that the process of finding the 'research question' is the process of structuring that search for meaning, such that it becomes a manageable and achievable task. But... what do I mean by a search for meaning? Meaning for whom? Is it just for me, the researcher, or is it a wider meaning?

For research to be 'recognized' by the academic community it needs to have meaning for that community, it needs to influence the community and to move the discipline area forward. It is possible that a brilliant bit of research is going to influence the field almost regardless of how it is presented. However, the attention paid to most research relies on how and where it is written, developed, contextualized or presented, how the 'meaning' in the research is developed for others. I shall come back to this point later, because I think there is another aspect of research here that is often ignored (sometimes to the serious detriment of the researcher and the research).

Meaning for one's self

I firmly believe that for most people the best research they do has a deep meaning for themselves, it says something to them about their life. I find that people are often attracted to a particular research area because of questions they are asking of themselves or of their lives. Perhaps they are trying to make sense of a circumstance that they find themselves in, perhaps they are trying to understand or rationalize a particular experience, perhaps trying to understand how their story fits within the range of human experience. Such personal involvement with a particular research area, if acknowledged and used, can be a tremendous help in the research process. It is the spark that keeps the researcher going through the late nights when the words have fled the lexicon – it is what keeps the research alive.

One of the problems with such personal involvement, however, is linked to the difficulty of firstly acknowledging, and then using it. I imagine that anyone who has ever supervised research students knows what it is like to be presented with a research proposal, which if it were to be done properly, would be equivalent to at least six PhDs, but which contains within it, somewhere, the one point – the single spark that encapsulates why that particular topic means something to that individual. The only thing to do is to sit down with the person and question, gradually pulling apart the web until the spark is revealed and the personal focus acknowledged. Obviously research can, and often is, conducted without this personal realization, but it tends to be a relatively unrewarding hard slog. I have been lucky to have always worked within systems of qualification in which students are allowed to change their topics or titles as their work and focus develops. Indeed, I would see this change as a sign that someone really is 'researching'.

The second difficulty faced is in making use of this spark. It is almost tautological to say that the more personal the research area the harder it is to stand back from it and objectively make decisions about what is to be researched, how it should be managed, and the interpretation of the findings. Yet if the research question is to be captured, then such clarity is necessary. Sometimes, therefore, however revealing investigation into a particular area might be for an individual, the individual might be so close to their work that they are unable to turn it into 'research'.

Therefore, the first stage in structuring the meaning, that of hunting the research question, is to start to establish how close one would like one's relationship to it to be. Too close and the question gets lost in the morass of the personal; too distant and the question disappears into the background of objectivity.

Project (planning the data gathering)

Efficiency questions
- Is a proper procedure in place so that all alternative possibilities are accounted for?
- Is a proper experimental design established to insure that alternative hypotheses are eliminated?
- Is the questioning procedure open when it needs to be open, and closed to where it needs to be closed?
- Are the questions phrased in the optimal manner?
- Are non-reactive methods used where possible?

Self and other questions
- Am I investing myself fully, and risking something personal?
- Am I setting up the project in a way that I really want?
- Are my resources fully engaged in the research plan?
- Am I relating to others solely in terms of roles and rules?
- Is the research plan fixed and rigid, or flexible and abandonable?

Political and power questions
- What are the political implications of the research design?
- Is the social context being taken into account?
- Does the set-up take patriarchy for granted?
- Does the research design reinforce patterns of domination in any way?

Dialectical questions
- Does the project negate what was there before?
- Does the project aim at a new state of affairs, which does not exist now, but which will exist then?

- Is the research planned to allow for the maximum of serendipity – lucky findings which were not anticipated?
- Is the impact of my own response accounted for in the research plan?

Legitimacy questions
- Is there pressure to have a particular type of project?
- Are limitations being imposed on who can be seen or involved?
- Are certain questions not being permitted?
- Is access restricted?

Relevance questions
- Could the results of this activity be relevant to the client? The underdog? My career? Social problems? Humanity?
- Will it make a difference to my life? Will it bring world peace?
- Will it matter a damn to anyone?

Methodological issues

Types of making sense

Part of this first stage of hunting the question, though perhaps moving more into the second stage, is helped by becoming aware of different ways of making sense. The precedents for this view are long and distinguished. It is rooted in the ideas of Carl Jung (1964, 1971) and has, more recently, been popularized by the Myers Briggs Type Indicator (MBTI). It is beyond the remit of this chapter to go into the MBTI-based literature in any depth, though see Briggs Myers (1987), Krebs Hirsh and Kummerow (1987) for more detail.

Jung suggested that whilst everyone seeks to make sense of the world around them, we do not all focus on the same things. He argued that there are two main operations involved as we perceive our world, those of gathering information and making decisions about what we have gathered. He suggested that these two processes are independent of each other, and that both are bi-polar, in that when gathering information people *prefer* to focus either on the 'here-and-now' information from their senses, or on the 'what if' information they 'intuit' from the possibilities and patterns they see developing. Similarly, when deciding about the information they have gathered, people *prefer* to make decisions based on objective thinking, by analysing and weighing the alternatives from a wide perspective, or to make decisions based on their feelings for each particular situation in an individualized manner.

I have placed particular emphasis on the word 'prefer' in my description of Jung's dimensions, as he was concerned to emphasize that any one person was able to adopt either way of gathering information (sensing or intuition) and deciding upon it (thinking or feeling), but they could only

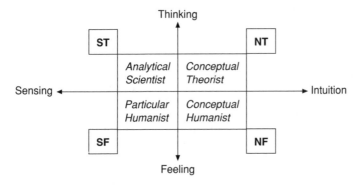

Figure 2.3 Four ways of seeing the world: the relationship between Jungian quartiles, Mitroff and Kilmann's four types of scientist and MBTI preferences
Source: Mitroff and Kilmann (1978)

adopt one approach at any one time, and thus built up and normally demonstrated a preference over time. Jung's theory, and the MBTI, are about preference, rather than about typecasting people or about classifying someone according to their 'personality'. This means that, if we accept Jung's dimensions, we can say that different people might have different preferred ways of researching, and that particular research projects might entail, or be better conducted, by one style of making sense, rather than another. The notions of *preference* and *style* carry with them the idea that people can choose to change their approach, and can adopt different approaches under different circumstances.

Other people have applied Jung's theory to research style, but, as can easily happen in a world that looks for certainties, a system based on preference easily gets translated into one of fixed typology. For example, Mitroff and Kilmann (1978) take these ideas and suggest that there are four psychological types which represent 'basic styles of thinking about and doing science'. These four basic styles fit well with Jungian quartiles and Myers Briggs, as can be seen in Figure 2.3.

Mitroff and Kilmann produced summary tables for each type, from which I shall extract just a little of the information in order to give a flavour of their work. As can be seen in Table 2.1, they have clearly and uniquely categorized the different types of scientist. By this I mean that their typology implies that a scientist can be in one group or another, and that if a scientist is in one particular group then the characteristics of that group describe those of that individual's personality.

In other words, Mitroff and Kilmann adopt a positivistic, or Paradigm A (above), approach to Jung's typology. In contrast, I would suggest that the same typology can be interpreted via Paradigm B, in which preference, flexibility and lack of clear delineation come into play. In doing this, we can keep the idea that different people prefer different ways of making sense of the world, which are associated with different preferences for how

Table 2.1 Summaries of types of scientist

	Analytical scientist	*Conceptual theorist*	*Conceptual humanist*	*Particular humanist*
Properties of the scientist	Disinterested, unbiased, impersonal, precise, expert, specialist, sceptical, exact, methodological	Disinterested, unbiased, impersonal, imaginative, speculative, generalist, holistic	Interested, free to admit and know his biases, highly personal, imaginative, speculative, generalist, holistic	Interested, 'all-too-human', biased, poetic, committed to the postulates of an action-oriented science
Preferred logic	Aristotelian, strict classical logic, non-dialectic and indeterminate	Dialectical logics, indeterminate logics	Dialectical behavioural logics	The 'logic' of the unique and singular
Preferred mode of inquiry	Controlled inquiry as embodied in the classical concept of the experiment	Conceptual inquiry; treatment of innovative concepts from multiple perspectives; invention of new schemas	Conceptual inquiry; treatment of innovative concepts; maximal co-operation between experimenter and subject	The case study; the in-depth detailed study of a particular individual

Source: Adapted from Mitroff and Kilmann (op. cit.), as given in Reason (1981)

research 'should' be structured and conducted. We can also appreciated that these preferences are linked to context and situation; they are *situated* preferences rather than exclusive *personality* differences.

I am certainly not denying that people do have different ways of working. Indeed, I'd fully support this notion. For example, in my experience it is much more important for a research student to find a supervisor whose way of working they respect and can relate to, than one who is an 'expert' in the field, though this does help a bit! I am, of course, adopting the Paradigm B approach here in assuming that research, and thus one's relationship with one's supervisor, is such a personal thing. I would argue that it is very important for researchers to think about their preferred style and preferred approach, and be able to justify them. Not only can the research become nothing more than hard and boring work if one tries to find meaning (researching) in a way that is alien to one's preference, but the end result can be less than convincing. It can be in these circumstances that the identified research question says one thing, and the real question (remaining hidden within the write-up of the research) says another.

Making sense (analysing, understanding and evaluating what has happened)
Efficiency questions?
- Do I have knowledge of relevant software systems?
- Can I recombine data in illuminating ways?
- Have I an adequate knowledge of content analysis?
- Are the most powerful statistical methods being used to maximize the information which can be extracted from the data?

Self and other questions
- Am I genuinely open to the experiences that I have gained in the encounter?
- Am I eager to get the results clear for my own sake, and for my own illumination?
- Can I get into the appropriate state of consciousness to let the data make new patterns?
- Are other people involved with the examination and processing of the results?
- Do colleagues involved in the data processing genuinely listen to one another?
- Are other people encouraged to make alternative sense of what has occurred?

Political and power questions
- What political interests are taken for granted in the categories being used?
- Are any invidious analyses being made?
- Am I being separated from other people by interested parties?
- What political assumptions are hidden in the statistics?
- Does the analysis make sexist, racist, classist, or ageist assumptions?
- Does the process involve contemplation as well as analysis?
- Is there emotional support for me during the process? How about support for other people?

Dialectical questions
- Is there an assumption that just one answer is being sought?
- Does the analysis bring out contradictions in a conscious way?
- Are the possibilities of dialogue between other people and myself being fully exploited?
- Is the risk being taken of destroying all that emerged from the encounter?

Legitimacy questions
- Is there pressure to analyse in a certain way?
- Is it compulsory to use certain machinery or certain methods?
- Are certain analyses discouraged?

Relevance questions
- Am I analysing for relevance, or for show?
- Is my analysis relevant to the people who took part?

The research

Politics: a boggy terrain

I emphasize the situated nature of the hunt, because, just as if we were seeking a strange beast across different environments and had to alter our behaviour according to our environs, so the way in which we conduct our search for meaning, and thus the meaning we find, is not, in my opinion at least, absolute, pure and objective. Research, and the search for meaning, is a political activity – and very few people have claimed that politics is pure!

By this I mean that we each carry with us our own political bent, as do the people, literature and events we refer to. We are political and our research will reflect that. In addition, as researchers, we are inevitably engaged in politics – it is only the very lucky few who can conduct research exactly as they wish, with no constraints or compromises. For most of us there are a whole web of factors that influence how we might conduct our research. Some of these might be obvious. The heavy-handed research sponsor who insists upon the right to influence all research done in their name is an obvious candidate. Another candidate might be research that is influenced by the accessed organization – who, for example, might decide (sometimes at a very late stage) that they do not want data published that they see as sensitive. Both of these have a direct impact on the research and the identification of the research question. For example, if the researcher needs to be able to publish their research in order to obtain a job in academe, then whilst having it kept under wraps for five years (as is possible for PhD theses containing sensitive material) might earn the person a PhD, it won't enhance their career a great deal. In the same way, in order to enhance their careers academics find themselves designing their research in order to get it published in particular outlets or at particular times.

A similar situation can occur if someone is hoping to enhance their career within their organization. Do they stick with their analysis and publish research that is damming to their organization and is likely to get them sacked? More subtly, do they adopt their much preferred qualitative approach to their research, when it is clear that their organization only values quantitative findings?

As well as being affected by politics, research is also a political tool. A research design that involves close work with senior staff might well help the researcher up the career ladder. A research topic that anticipates and 'solves' an area of organizational concern might well lead to a job and team being created for the researcher. A smoothly written dissertation that captures the imagination of the public might (when re-written) prove the first step on the road to 'guru' hood, and so on.

Alongside the larger political issues of reputation, intent and access, there are smaller (but no less troublesome) ones of resources and logistics.

For example, I did my PhD just as I was starting a family; so much of my empirical work was conducted carrying youngsters around with me. Thus my choice of organization to visit was a compromise between the needs of my inquiry and the (sometimes urgently stated) needs of my offspring! Similarly, however much the researcher might think a longitudinal study is needed to address a particular point – if the time-frame for the research is short then the emerging research question must reflect what is possible – not that which is desirable.

So where are we in our hunt for the research question?

Encounter (the empirical/primary data gathering part)

Efficiency questions
- Is the experimental control being kept in the way intended?
- Is the questioning procedure being carried out in a uniform manner?
- Is the correct sample being contacted?
- Am I retaining my objectivity?

Self and other questions
- Am I open to my own feelings and body reactions?
- Am I prepared to express feelings in a genuine way?
- Am I prepared to stay with the experience wherever it leads? Can I improvise?
- Has a trusting relationship been built?
- Am I open to other people?
- Are the other people determining the situation, as much as I am?
- Are roles being broken down?

Political and power questions
- Is the social context being taken into account?
- Is the encounter such as to raise the other people's power of self-determination?
- Are the 'back-home' situations of the other people being taken into account?
- Are patterns of control being eroded?
- Is there an assumption that everyone is heterosexual?

Dialectical questions
- Is conflict being encouraged and worked through?
- Am I fully engaged and committed to the process?
- Is there an appreciation of the way in which quantity can transform into quality?

Legitimacy questions
- Are there any restrictions placed on the actual interviews, observations, or experiments?
- Is the research stopped before completion?
- Are people suddenly changing the way they interact?

Relevance questions
- Is this work turning out in the practice to be relevant to the subject/respondents/co-researchers? How does it actually affect them?
- Am I doing any good? Any harm?

The research

Review of the hunt

Research seems to be inextricably linked with questioning: 'how does this work?'; 'why did that occur?'; 'what would happen if I did this?'; and so on. However, we talk of 'the research question' as fundamentally different from the many questions that can spark ideas, inspire investigation, and be associated with research in general.

I have suggested that 'the research question' is that one unique question whose answer encapsulates the research such that 'real' research (by which I mean the development of the understanding of the area and the search for meaning within that) *becomes* the search for the 'research question'. In talking about the research question, therefore, I have spent quite a bit of time talking about research because understanding the parameters of the research is fundamental to our search for the question.

I have likened the research question to a rare and elusive animal – one that we know exists and is nearby but does not thrust itself into the limelight. Instead, it hides in the shadows and when it does emerge we need to be ready and prepared – film in camera and alert to capture the moment. This moment needs to be seized with both hands as it can slide past, and instead of a sudden burst of clarity that pulls everything together and provides a focus for sense making we are left with the feeling that we have missed something. A realization that we are nearly there, but are faced with the inertia of preformed plans that surround and slowly strangle the life out of our insight.

I have likened it to an animal in order to emphasize the way in which it does seem to have a life of its own, and the sense of clarity and achievement that is gained on realizing that this particular question (whatever it is) is *the* one. In my experience it is very rare to arrive at that final question quickly. Normally many questions are considered and modified throughout the sense-making process, and throughout this chapter I include lots of questions (modified from Rowan op. cit.) that a researcher can ask of themselves and of their research project. Thus, quite often, as I find in my own research, the 'research question' only emerges in its final and succinct form as the whole of the research is being written up – the act of writing is often the final bait that entices the fuzzy beastie from its bolt-hole.

Interestingly, it is also this act of writing that creates the major illusion that the question was clearly established at the 'beginning' of the research, and that all the 'research' was conducted as an inevitable response to that question. Indeed, most research that is written up and published or submitted as part of Master's degree dissertations or doctoral theses tell the story as if this is exactly how the research was conducted; nice and clearly linear and logical. To some extent, what the research question does is provide a sense of inevitability about the way in which it must be answered. It is stated in such a way that there can only be one way of addressing it, it provides the feeling of legitimacy and appropriateness to the answer.

I assert that most people, however, who have ever done any research know that this is not what really happens, or at least, it is not what happens chronologically. Instead it is the acceptable face of research – the sanitized version in which all the parts, the thinking, the reading, the activity and the pain, are rearranged to make sense to the reader. Thus the research continues to live and develop within the process of writing and rewriting.

The writing up of the research is more than just dissemination of one's ideas and findings. It is what characterizes research over and above 'searching for meaning' for oneself. It is about influencing one's peer group and contributing to the debate. It has a purpose and a value that is directly linked to the quality of the research and the research question.

Communication (formally communicating the research to others)

Efficiency questions
- Are the results written up in a proper scientific form?
- Would the appropriate professional journal, such as *Human Resource Development International*, publish them?
- Are the results analysed in an objective way, which any outside observer could check?

Self and other questions
- Can I make the results part of my own process of living?
- Can I risk myself to say that I am disappointed, upset, frustrated?
- Can I own up to the fact that it is *my* truth I am sharing, not necessarily *the* truth?
- Can other people make the results part of their process of living?
- Are other people involved in the communication of the results?
- Have other people contributed all that they really want to the final outcome?

Political and power questions
- Is the social effect of the information taken into account when passing it on?
- If any information can be extracted, is it passed on to those who could make the best use of it?
- If information is passed on, is it done in such a way as not to put down those who receive it?
- Is the information elaborated into curlicues of abstraction?

35

Dialectical questions
- Do I appreciate communication is a two-way process?
- Do I try to establish a real relationship or with people before attempting to communicate with them – and while communicating with them?
- Do I assume that communication has to be done with words?
- Do I appreciate the importance of readiness in communication?
- Do I appreciate the importance of resistance in communication, and how it can be used to establish a relationship?

Legitimacy questions
- Is pressure being applied to publish only in a certain way? To omit relevant material?
- To destroy some or all of the report? Is there censorship or falsification of the final report?

Relevance questions
- Will publication help others? My career? The political struggle?
- Will publication change the world?
- Will my work take social science forward?
- How will this research be seen by those whose opinions I respect most?
- Will all this help my self-belief?

Critical analysis

Retelling of the hunt and world domination![1]

One of my teenage sons recently returned home from a three-day expedition with a couple of other lads, trekking with tents in the Lake District. He returned wet through, very cold and covered in vomit, having been sitting next to one of his friends at a bad moment on the return journey. Despite this, he seemed quite happy, perhaps aided by writing the following piece on the back of his map case.

> This map guides me
> Mentally and Physically
> If I am guided physically I know
> where I am; Others don't:
> This gives me knowledge over others;
> Knowledge is Power: therefore
> I have power over others:
> If I am guided mentally I
> Can exploit this power;
> Others will do my bidding;
> We will rule the world;
> Me and the map.
>
> (Michael Lee 1999)

Michael was writing about the sort of map that represents physical features of the landscape by societally agreed symbols – one which anybody, if they knew the coding, could read. He talks of the power associated with being able to correctly interpret the signals, and possessing the map in the first place. The power comes from capturing what is there, what exists, and in making it his own. The structure of the geography and of the map provide structure for the symbols used, hone the mental rigour required to work with the symbols, and so guide the development of understanding. So what has this to do with finding the research question?

The structure of the search for meaning is signalled by, and derives from, the research question, whilst at the same time the need to identify the question forces clarity into the account. The 'quality' ones stand out in those accounts in which the question has been seized – regardless of the approach, area, or intent, they are the ones that are well structured and rigorous. By this I mean that they allow me, the reader, to know where their argument is going, and why. Each paragraph addresses a separate or discrete point, and each leads, one from to the other, to what feels by the end of the text, like the 'obvious' conclusion.

As I read the text, the sensation is similar to walking in the country beside someone who has the map and can read it expertly. The author(s) are able to convince me, with the minimum of fuss, that they know the countryside and where they are going, pointing out things of interest *en route*, with no getting lost, back-tracking, repetition. I feel safe in their company, as they expertly translate the 'real' world into a pattern of symbols and ideas that enhance my understanding of the area, steadily leading me to an end point.

Mapping agreed structures

This is relatively simple under Paradigm A, above, which is predicated upon a clearly defined view of the real world, agreed systems for symboliz-ing or making sense of that world, and a reasonably clearly defined and accepted way of reporting the sense-making. I started my academic life as a cognitive/developmental psychologist – well versed in experimentation, test theory, statistics and other ways of translating the 'real world' into numerically based symbols. This is, of course, the predominant way of interpreting the world (at least in the west) and it has its own mores and language for reporting such interpretations.

To some extent adopting the scientific method facilitates the whole process of researching and writing about it. There is an accepted struc-ture, whether the outcome is an academic paper or a doctorate. The research question can more easily be derived from previous ones, and from the work of others. The appropriate structure is laid down in the annals of custom, and 'quality', as discussed above, is the handmaiden of conformity to the ideals. This seems to me to be an eminently sensible way of progressing if, and when, the underlying structure, the geography of the place, is known and agreed and research is about better mapping.

In 'real life', however, as in Paradigm B, the metaphorical geography is not always known and agreed. Occasionally most of the parts are known, but the way in which they fit together, the overview, the larger structure, is a matter for debate. Sometimes only a few parts are known, and the challenge is to approximate the structure and map the parts in a way that best indicates the larger structure. More disturbingly, sometimes the very act of mapping changes the geography; the act of watching changes the group dynamics; the act of researching changes the outcome, the act of writing changes the map.

Mapping contended structures

So, 'map reading' shifts from naming and labelling to influencing the being and becoming; from capturing what is to creating what might be. There is little pre-existing structure to lend certainty and few mores to lend the essential patina of 'quality'. The desire for quality remains the same, but it is harder for author(s) to provide structure, rigour, relevance, clarity of purpose and direction, and so on, when translating the 'real world' into linguistically based symbols, particularly when there is no irrefutable agreement about either the symbols or the underlying structure that they might represent.

Under these circumstances authors have to apply the trademarks of 'quality' to the creation of their structure, the process of drawing their map, as well as to its contents. It is here that the development of the research question comes into play. In my opinion quality research is that which creates its own framework, and generates its own believable world. In order to do this it needs to meet the reader half way, to give some context to the reader so that he or she will agree to travel with the author.

Such context, of course, is not restricted to the content. It could be about the process. Perhaps it says 'I wish to take you blindfold along this path, so you pay particular attention to the sounds and smells as we go, and I shall explain it all as we finish'; or perhaps 'X says that it is best to go to the left, and T will try and take you to the right, but if you come with me I will explain how they are both wrong, and why my path is best'; 'walk this way and I will help you understand what we see', or even 'Come with me to the top of this hill, and I will describe all that is below'.

Conclusions and key learning points

I initially included 'world domination' in the title of the previous section as a joking reference to Michael's statement that with the guidance of the map he will rule the world – but is this not what happens – conceptually, if not physically? It is those who create the most persuasive structures, the most believable maps of our existence, the most (politically?) correct descriptions of our organizational lives that become the gurus. They are the people we wish to follow or walk beside as we travel, those who lead the way whilst helping us go with them, the people who have strong influence upon the area and who are recognized as 'world experts'. It is their persuasiveness that makes us believe them, and it is this phenomenon that moulds our understanding of 'quality'.

Quality is also about caring for the reader on the journey, providing signposts, allowing the reader to assess how far they have travelled and the distance yet to go. It is about providing conceptual links that strengthen and reinforce the believability of the structure and the 'authority' of the author. Finally, it is about showing the path that has been travelled, the meaning of the journey and, possibly, how the geography has been influenced by the act of travelling. The persuasiveness of quality only comes about because of the clarity and direction in the writing – those aspects that come from and are helped by seizing the moment as the research question emerges.

I hope I have illustrated, therefore, that identifying the 'right' research question is, indeed, central to 'good' research, but that it is not a formulaic process whereby one smoothly follows a set of apparently logical instructions and out pops the answer. Instead, the process is both complicated and complex (by which I mean that the sum is greater than the parts, in the Gestalt sense). The process is often made even harder by those who promulgate the assumption that regardless of area of investigation or personal style or situation, it should be a straightforward matter of 'stages' and that those who do not fit into this pattern are failures.

A very common example of this can be found in a pattern derived from the 'hard' sciences and applied to the other areas in the belief that it is right – namely the system towards standardization in many universities by which MPhil students are expected to do a literature review and from that derive their research question and outline their proposed research prior to being upgraded to PhD students. There obviously needs to be a sieve by which those who are capable of doing PhDs are identified, but a sieve of this form denies how 'research' actually happens; mitigates against experimentation with alternative methods; limits the researchable areas; and blankets development in the field.

Perhaps the most important point that I wish to emphasize from this is that research is confusing, just as life is confusing, and that it is OK as a researcher to be confused: the skill is not in ignoring the confusion and pretending that the world is simple, but in taking that confusion and working with it to present it in a form that is simpler, but still true to 'life'.

Note

Parts of the penultimate sections of this chapter are modified from Lee (2000).

1 This was conducted as part of the Duke of Edinburgh Award Scheme, in which teenagers/young adults have to fulfil four criteria, one of which is adventurous and independent expeditions.

References

Adams, D. (1995) *The HitchHiker's Guide to the Galaxy – A Trilogy in Five Parts*, London: Heinemann.

Briggs Myers, I. (1987) *Introduction to Type*, Palo Alto, CA: Consulting Psychologists Press.

Burrell, G. and Morgan, G. (1979) *Sociological Paradigms and Organisational Analysis: Elements of the Sociology of Corporate Life*, London: Heinemann.

Flick, E. (1998) *An Introduction to Qualitative Research*, London: Sage.

Gray, R. (1996) *Archetypal Explorations: an Integrative Approach to Human Behaviour*, London: Routledge.

Jung, C.G. (1964) *Man and His Symbols*, London: W.H. Allen.

Jung, C.G. (1971) *Collected Works. Vol. 6, Psychological Types* (Hull, R.F.C. (ed.), revised translation), Princeton, NJ: Princeton University Press.

Krebs Hirsh, S. and Kummerow, J. (1987) *Introduction to Types in Organisational Settings*, Palo Alto, CA: Consulting Psychologists Press.

Kuhn, T. (1969) *The Structure of Scientific Revolutions*, Chicago: University of Chicago Press.

Lee, M.M. (2000) 'Aspects of quality and world domination', *Human Resource Development International Vol. 3.2*, 139–42.

Mills C.W. (1959) *The Sociological Imagination*, Oxford: Oxford University Press.

Mitroff, I.I. and Kilmann, R.H. (1978) *Methodological Approaches to Social Science: Integrating Divergent Concepts and Theories*, San Francisco: Jossey-Bass.

Reason, P. (1981) '"Methodological approaches to social science" by Ian Mitroff and Ralph Kilmann: an appreciation', in P. Reason and J. Rowan (eds) *Human Inquiry: a Source Book of New Paradigm Research*, Chichester: Wiley, 43–51.

Ritzer, G. (1980) *Sociology: A Multiple Paradigm Science*, Boston: Allyn and Bacon.

Rowan, J. (1981) 'A dialectical paradigm for research', in P. Reason and J. Rowan (eds) *Human Inquiry: a Source Book of New Paradigm Research*, Chichester: John Wiley, 93–112.

PROBLEMS OF METHOD IN HRD RESEARCH

Company-based lifelong learning and 'longitudinality'

Jim McGoldrick, Graeme Martin and Judy Pate

Aims and contribution

In this chapter we aim to achieve two important contributions. First, we aim to report on some aspects of current research work, which is focused on lifelong learning, career development and the psychological contract at work. The research discussed here is part of a larger body of work, which has been going on over a considerable period of time (see Martin and Riddell 1996; Martin and Beaumont 1999; Martin *et al.* 1999; Pate *et al.* 1999 and Martin *et al.* 2000). This raises the second contribution, which is to offer some reflections on the research process more generally in the area of HRD. This is partly encapsulated by our concern to make sense of a number of episodes of engagement with the same company over a period of some eight or nine years and to critically reflect on our findings from different times. We originally framed this around an idea of 'reverse longitudinality' to see if there was a pattern of any kind to our findings. For example, we have noted above our interest in lifelong earning and the psychological contract, which derives in part from consideration of a fairly recent and current literature. For this chapter we could also easily have chosen to discuss the issue of knowledge transfer and the psychological contract. Similarly, we could also have focused on more HRM and employee relations themes as we have data on all of these. However, we are particularly interested to develop our understanding of the processes of organizational change and to reflect on our long-term involvement with the company and consider how our research themes help us to address 'big' questions such as understanding 'success' and 'failure'. We will return to these points and discuss them more fully in our reflections on methodology and the framing of research questions later in the chapter.

The context to our current work has two dimensions. First, the impact of global competition, technological change and new models of organizational design have led to the increased incidence of corporate restructuring, downsizing and employee displacement in Western economies. Second, learning organizations and knowledge management have increasingly been seen as an essential means of competing in such conditions (Scarborough, Swan and Preston 1998). These developments have recently brought education and training back on to the agenda and they have also influenced governments to promote the principles of *lifelong learning*.

The specific contribution of our research is to explore the influence of a long-standing company-based programme of lifelong learning on individuals' careers, salaries and on the organizational pay-off as measured by more positive psychological contracts. In doing so, we hope to add to the debate on whether such human or intellectual capital strategies yield significant returns to employees and their employers. The company in question is subsidiary of a major US multinational enterprise (MNE) and is a world leader in the design and manufacture of financial services equipment. The programme, called Education-for-All (EFA), has a broad and long-term focus on education, qualifications and the accumulation of intellectual capital rather than the short-term focus on competence and skills development. However, the current strategic situation in the US-based corporation as a whole has focused attention on the pay-off from investment in HRD and the accompanying internal 'soul-searching' has provided the impetus for our investigation.

This chapter draws upon the findings of an earlier study (Martin, Pate and McGoldrick 1999; Martin *et al.* 1999) and involves questionnaire data from a cohort analysis of 114 participants who began the EFA programme in 1995. We use these data to examine the career and salary movements of participants and some of their perceptions of key aspects of their psychological contracts.

The chapter begins by establishing the theoretical context through a review of some existing literature and evidence on whether training and career development pays under current market conditions and career expectations. This analysis is used to formulate four key questions related to the impact of lifelong learning programmes. Following this we discuss our methods and research design and briefly report some of our main findings. Finally, we analyse and evaluate our data and analyse the limitations of the work, and evaluate our contribution to theory and practice.

Theoretical context

The debate on lifelong learning, career development and psychological contracts

There are two main schools of thought concerning the pay-off of education and training for employees and organizations under the new market and organizational conditions of the 1990s and beyond. From the employees' perspective, the problem has been constructed as one of a breakdown in the 'old deal' of job security, a fair day's pay and career development in

Table 3.1 Past and present forms of psychological contract

Characteristic	Past form	Emergent form
Focus	Security, continuity, loyalty	Exchange, future, employability
Format	Structured, predictable, stable	
Underlying basis	Tradition, fairness, justice, socio-economic class	Market forces, saleable abilities and skills, added value
Employer's responsibilities	Continuity, job security, training, career prospects	Perceived equity, reward for added value
Employee's responsibilities	Loyalty, attendance, satisfactory performance, compliance	Entrepreneurship, innovation, enacting changes for improvement
Contractual relations	Formalized, mostly via collective bargaining	Individual's responsibility to barter for their skills internally or externally
Career management	Organizational responsibility, in-spiralling careers planned and facilitated through HR	Individual's responsibility, out-spiralling careers by personal reskilling and retraining

Source: Adapted from Hiltrop, J.M. (1995) 'The changing psychological contract', *European Management Journal*, 13(3): 286–94. Copyright 1995 Elsevier Science. Reproduced with permission

return for loyalty, commitment and, at least, a fair day's work (Guest 1998; Herriot 1992; Hiltrop 1995). Instead, they are being offered a 'new deal' (see Table 3.1) involving less security but the chance to make themselves more employable in the future.

From the perspective of organizations, the question concerning the economic returns on education and training is often framed in terms of measuring the contribution of returns on intangible assets versus tangible assets. Recently, the contributions of resource-based theories of competition, learning organizations and knowledge management have converged to provide a greater role for HRM and HRD in organizational success (Scarborough, Swan and Preston 1998).

Two schools of thought

The 'new deal' literature

There is not the space to review the 'new deal' literature in full (for an outline and critique see Herriot, Hirsh and Reilly 1998). However, part of the argument is that whilst market and organizational change has occurred during the 1980s and 1990s in the UK (see Gallie *et al.* 1998) the organizational career philosophy has yet to catch up in all but the most 'enlightened' organizations which are attuned to current and future trends (Arthur and Rousseau 1996; Rousseau and Arthur 1999). In its more extreme form, this is sometimes referred to as the 'end of career thesis' or 'boundaryless career', that is there is a new transactional contract or new deal of employability currently being offered by some employers. For example, Adamson, Doherty and Viney (1998) have recently argued that 'most organizations are now talking not of opportunities for advancement and/or progression but of opportunities to improve *marketability* and *employability*' (p. 255). They outlined key changes in career philosophy that were predicated on the breakdown in long-term employer–employee relationships and future time orientation of careers. Thus, they foresaw that career progression was no longer likely to involve upward hierarchical movement in the one organization but is more likely to involve lateral development. They argued that, given the current economic and competitive climate, 'from both the organizational and individual perspective, it is no longer so apparent how a logical, ordered and sequential career might evolve' (p. 255). The metaphors underlying much of this line of argument is of balancing 'agency' (individual and organizational freedom of choice) with 'community' (social relations) (Rousseau and Arthur 1999). It is also about 'career lattices' (Thomson *et al.* 2001) or 'jungle gyms' (Gunz, Jalland and Evans 1998) in which individuals scramble over 'upwards, sideways, downwards, diagonal, or in any direction that the jungle gym allows' (p. 22).

Echoing Handy's (1989) comment that lifetime employment represents 'bad economics and bad morals', much the same argument has been put forward by Cappelli (1997, 1998) in the US. He has argued that the 'old deal' and the recent attempts by some well-known US firms to recapture its features was in complete *denial* of the current market situation in the post-Business Process Re-engineering (BPR) era. This strategy, at least according to Cappelli, was unlikely to succeed and may even result in companies, particularly those which operate in knowledge-based industries, losing out in competitive labour markets. A common theme in these works is of employees' requirements to display 'career resilience' and to participate in the management of their careers by taking greater responsibility for their learning (Thomson *et al.* 2001). For example, Hall and Moss (1998) have argued that the myth of old style organizational career contracts in the US is dead (and, in effect only applied to about 5 per cent of the workforce). Instead, they offer the concept of the 'protean career' (see Table 3.2) in which

> the person, not the organisation, is managing. It consists of all of the person's varied experiences in education, training, working in several organisations, changes in occupational field, etc. The protean person's own personal career choices and the search for

self-fulfilment are the unifying or integrating elements in his or her life. The criterion of success is internal (psychological success) not external.

(p. 25)

Whilst some of these arguments may have their attraction we need also to ask what UK evidence exists to support them? In a recent large-scale survey, Gallie *et al.* (1998) pointed to some paradoxical findings. On the one hand there is clear evidence that employers have been investing in training and development over the last five years, that employees perceived that their jobs required more skills and that they have received more training than five years ago. This finding was particularly connected with the widespread adoption of new technologies (p. 292). On the other hand, one of the most notable of their findings was that employees were less likely to believe that their future careers lay in their current organizations, especially given the evidence of delayering and lack of career promotional prospects in their organizations. A more contextualized account of careers by Gunz, Jalland and Evans (1998) has identified from case-study evidence that different kinds of career logic and patterns can be found in different situations. Such conclusions implying key sectoral and

Table 3.2 The protean career contract

The career is managed by the person, not the organization	The ingredients for success change from: • know how to learn how • job security to employability • organizational career to protean careers, and • from 'work self' to 'whole self'
The career is a lifelong series of experiences, skills, learning, transitions and identity changes (career age not chronological age counts)	The organization provides: • challenging assignments • developmental relations, information and other development resources
Development is: • continuous • self directed • relational, and • found in work challenges but is not necessarily • formal training • retraining, or • upward mobility	The goal is psychological success

Source: Hall, D.T. and Moss, J.E. (1998) 'The new protean career contract', *Organisational Dynamics*, Winter, 22–37. Copyright 1998 Elsevier Science. Reproduced with permission

occupational differences have drawn further support, for it would appear that specific sectors of employment and industries have changed more than others in career patterns and in psychological contracts. Thus for example, young male workers have been particularly hard hit (Gallie *et al.* 1998), whereas the financial sector has been at the forefront of this so-called 'enlightened employer' approach. Rajan (1997) offered evidence from a survey of the financial services sector that 60 per cent of organizations in his sample claimed to have replaced traditional security by a policy of employability (at least to some extent) over the last three years. Furthermore, the study of managers' development by Thomson *et al.* (2001) found some evidence of career resilient behaviour among individual managers and firms, predicted in large part by the level of qualifications of managers (AMBA graduates) and whether the firms had policies on management development. Finally, a representative study of 1,000 employees by Guest and Conway (1997) offered a more mildly optimistic conclusion concerning careers since 55 per cent of respondents believed that their organizations broadly kept their 'promises' about careers and 70 per cent believed that 'promises' on job security remained intact.

Investment in HRD and careers pays

Alongside the more apocalyptic predictions of the new deal (which, admittedly, have received some empirical support), there has been an upsurge in studies investigating the relationship between high performance work practices, including investment in HRD, and positive organizational outcomes in the US and UK (Huselid 1995; Pfeffer 1994; Purcell *et al.* 2000). Although the HRM literature draws on various sources for its predictions, the strongest theoretical justifications for such a connection lie in four main areas. First, in resource-based theories of firm, in which competitiveness is seen to be based on control of unique and inimitable resources such as knowledge and intellectual capital (Bartlett and Ghoshal 1993; Mintzberg, Ahlstrand and Lampel 1998; Pfeffer 1994). Second, in the learning organization literature (Easterby-Smith 1997; Senge 1990; see also the special edition of *Organisational Dynamics*, Autumn, 1998 on Organisational Learning Revisited). Third, in the knowledge management literature (Nonaka and Takeuchi 1995; Scarborough, Swan and Preston 1998). Fourth, in the recent work on the links between HR policies and positive psychological contracts or 'balanced' employer–employee relationships (Guest and Conway 1997; Guest 1998; Tsui *et al.* 1997). Although these bodies of literature varied in the emphasis they placed on HRD, a common theme was the positive relationship between investment in HRD, careers and knowledge creation on the one hand and competitive success on the other hand, especially in knowledge-based companies.

The empirical evidence confirming HRD as a significant driver of change and high performance, however, is a little patchy. From a practitioner perspective, case-study and anecdotal evidence has hinted at enormous returns on HRD investment, when it has actually been measured (Pfeffer 1994; Torraco 1999). Paradoxically, however, not many organizations have attempted to measure the returns on HRD and even organizations such as Motorola admit to having no systematic evaluation of their training (Pfeffer and Veiga 1999). However, there is some evidence available to suggest that there is a link between an expectation of promotion or improved remuneration as a result of participation in some form of organized learning. Thomson *et al.* (2001) have been more positive about the individual returns on management development, pointing to a 40 per cent differential between MBA qualified managers and non-MBA qualified managers. However, and leaving aside the problems of measurement and causality in such research, they have noted that this differential only accrued to those managers who gained their qualification and then left their jobs for another employer. The pay-off for those managers who qualified and then chose to remain with their employers appeared to be much lower and in the region of 10 per cent. With respect to blue collar workers, Gallie *et al.* (1998) have pointed out that little is known about the impact of HRM and HRD on employees' experience of work, such as job satisfaction, motivation and commitment. On the other hand, in the same study, employees reported receiving more training and such upgrading in skills appeared to be linked to reports of higher earnings among these employees.

The research is more positive concerning the pay-off for firms. For example, in one of the few studies to attempt to operationalize 'hard' indicators, Winterton and Winterton (1997) found a significant relationship between adoption of the MCI management standards, personal development and individual and business performance. In terms of 'soft' indicators, case-study evidence has demonstrated positive links between training and improved organizational climate (Cannon 1995) and culture (Mabey and Mallory 1994). Finally, in connection with employer pay-off, the notion of positive psychological contracts has become fashionable as a measure of HR success (see the special issue of the *Journal of Organisational Behaviour*, vol. 19 for an excellent review and discussion of the value of psychological contracts). For example, Guest and Conway (1997) and Guest (1998) have built a theory around the relationship between the causes, content and consequences of the psychological contract (see Table 3.3). In this model employees' perceptions of fair treatment, trust in their employers and of delivery of what was promised (including career development) were deemed to have significant consequences for organizational commitment, job satisfaction, organizational citizenship and effort. Although not using the language of psychological contracts, one of the best studies that could be treated as an indirect test of this theory was of the relationship between career development, training and job security and key organizational outcomes by Tsui *et al.* (1997). These researchers found that one particular form of *balanced* organization–employee relationship (in the

Table 3.3 A model of the psychological contract

Causes	Content	Consequences
Organizational culture/climate		Job satisfaction
Human resource policies and practices	Fairness	Organizational commitment
Expectations of job security		Sense of security
Experience of redundancy	$\rightarrow$ Trust $\rightarrow$	Employment relations
Chances of alternative employment		Motivation
Involvement climate	Delivery of the 'deal'	Organizational citizenship Absence Intention to quit

Source: Adapted from Guest, D.E. (1998) 'Is the psychological contract worth taking seriously?', *Journal of Organisational Behaviour*, 19: 649–64. Copyright 1998 John Wiley and Sons Limited. Reproduced with permission

sense that both parties understood and accepted their obligations) appeared to be superior to other possible configurations of balanced and unbalanced relationships. This superior form was of 'mutual investment', in which a commitment to HRD and job security was associated with greater organizational citizenship behaviour, higher levels of affective commitment and employee performance.

In conclusion, there are at least two views on the potential for encouraging firms to invest in HRD investment strategies based on lifelong learning programmes. The first view is that traditional investment in HRD and old style careers may be inconsistent with current market realities, the adjusted expectations of employers, and the new protean careers of employees in many industries, particularly involving high technology or 'high velocity environments' (Eisenhardt 1989). The second view is that HRD, particularly when coupled with high levels of job security and promises of career development that are actually delivered, pays off in positive psychological contracts and key organizational outcomes. This is especially likely to be so in knowledge-based organizations (Kamoche and Mueller 1998). However, the returns to individuals, at least as measured by salary improvements, is less certain and may be related more to market circumstances and moves within the external labour market.

Framing the research questions

Drawing from the above analysis, we are able to formulate some key questions that we use to interrogate and evaluate our case-study data. The outcomes of which have significant implications for companies investing in programmes of lifelong learning, for employees participating in such programmes and for the universities and colleges providing input into these programmes.

*Question 1. To what extent has participation in the programme of
lifelong learning (EFA) had a positive influence on employees'
career perceptions and internal career moves?*

The literature on psychological contracts would suggest a positive influence,
where perceived 'promises' have been delivered and where expectations
of psychological growth, career moves and/or salary enhancement have
been met.

*Question 2. What were employee expectations concerning career
orientations, especially in the context of decreased job security
in the organisation, and what evidence was there of
the protean career contract?*

We were interested to see if there was evidence that employees were more
concerned to manage their career, learn how to become more employable, seek psychological growth rather than external success and be less
concerned with organizational careers and work self.

*Question 3. To what extent was participation in the lifelong learning
programme (EFA) associated with positive perceptions of salary
enhancement and with a differential between participants and
non-participants?*

The evidence on the returns to individuals from lifelong learning points
to small or negative returns. Thus we might expect to find no participant/
non-participant differential. This is particularly likely in a situation where
employees have to invest significant amounts of time in their learning, thus
'crowding out' alternative career-enhancing behaviour in the internal labour
market. On the other hand, the literature on protean careers and on
psychological contracts suggests that salary will be less of an issue but only
become important where perceptions of promises have not been met.

*Question 4. To what extent did the existence of the programme and/or
participation in it have a positive influence on employee perceptions of
their psychological contracts, as measured by their perceptions of the
content of the contract and the consequences of the contract?*

One the one hand, because all employees were likely to perceive this as part
of a mutual investment relationship in which everyone has had the chance
to participate, we might expect to find no differences between participants
and non-participants in their perceptions of their psychological contracts.
On the other hand, positive psychological contracts were likely to be
recursively related to participation on the EFA programme, in other words,
the *explanas* might have been influenced by the *explanadum* and vice versa.

Table 3.4 The key principles of lifelong learning

1	A continuous and wide-ranging commitment to learning for all employees
2	Ensuring that education and training become a normal and accessible aspect of all employees' careers
3	Placing employees at the centre of the learning process

Source: Adapted from Rainbird (1998)

Empirical context

The case of NCR (Dundee) and Education-for-All

The case study is of NCR (Dundee), a Scottish subsidiary of a major US-owned MNE. The Dundee plant is a world leader in the design and manufacture of automatic teller machines (ATMs) and has won a number of awards for its exporting and manufacturing performance (Wheatley and New 1997). In the early 1990s, the Scottish plant's senior management began Education-for-All to produce significant organizational change and achieve the Dundee company's strategic objectives of growth through continuous innovation, customer-focus and cost-competitiveness.

The EFA programme, which has been in operation for nine years, embodies the principles of lifelong learning set out in Table 3.4. EFA has committed the company to learning for all employees with a broad focus on education rather than training in skills development for a selected few. Education has been made available through easy access to well-stocked flexible-learning centres in the company and through close links with local universities and colleges. The company has encouraged self development through a well-developed career management system and courses in career development for employees, by paying the fees for any education course broadly related to the company's business and by giving employees time off work to undertake such courses.

The take-up on courses has been impressive with participation in education courses rising from 9 per cent of all employees in 1991 to 20 per cent in 1998. Such courses have included an introductory electronics certificate for all shopfloor staff, an extensive engineering degree programme designed to upgrade technicians, participation in a consortium masters programme and support for doctoral programmes.

The context for change in psychological contracts

After a decade of mass redundancies during the 1970s, the NCR plant has experienced nearly twenty years of growth in sales and profits largely associated with the market for ATMs. From the mid-1980s onwards, with the exception of only a few years, it has been the global market leader in the design, development and production of ATMs.

At the same time as investing in employees through EFA, NCR have been one of the reducing number of firms that have traditionally attempted to maintain long-term, high-trust relationships with employees through committing themselves to job security (Martin and Riddell 1996; Tayeb 1998). Currently, the Dundee plant employs some 1,500 managers, design and development engineers and assembly workers. In 1997, however, a change in corporate direction towards a 'solutions' strategy resulted in significant outsourcing and in the recent sale of world-wide manufacturing facilities. These changes have had a clear impact on the Dundee plant, which remains one of the few integrated design *and* manufacturing operations in the NCR Corporation, and on the EFA programme. Following these changes in strategy a general air of uncertainty has pervaded the plant. Moreover, for the first time since 1980 and despite record sales, order books and production, 200 redundancies out of a total head count of 1,500 employees were announced in March 1998 following decisions to outsource aspects of production in Dundee. One of our main arguments in this chapter is that EFA has had a positive influence on psychological contracts in the plant. However, our previous research (Martin, Pate and McGoldrick 1999) suggested that the recent changes in job security, acting as a potential trigger of psychological contract breach, may have affected employee perceptions of the EFA to create a new 'transactional contract'.

Methodological issues

In the introduction to this chapter we indicated an interest in exploring some of the broader problems of method in HRD research. All researchers to varying degrees operate on the basis of a personal or shared worldview of where their research fits into a specific body of theory and a more general body of knowledge. We indicated our interests at the start of this chapter and particularly our concern with what we have called 'reverse longitudinality'.

Longitudinal research in organizations in recent years has been primarily concerned with analysing the process of change (Pettigrew 1990; Van de Ven and Huber 1990). In particular, longitudinal research systematically studies the process of change over discrete periods of time. A set of research questions are generated, a mode of data gathering decided, analysis undertaken and then repeated at different points of time. This is perhaps an oversimplified description of the process but it captures the essence. The great strength of this approach lies in the design of the original research questions and the ability to negotiate access to organizations for times in the future.

Our research is also longitudinal but in a slightly different way. Our work involves an analysis of a set of common themes over a number of 'research episodes'. The common themes in our work are the psychological contract and company-based lifelong learning but specific research questions emerge from our particular analysis of other research and literature and reflect concerns with other issues that run alongside the core themes. So the difference between our research and classic longitudinal research in organizations is that our research questions themselves change, adapt and are modified with each episode of involvement with the company. Thus whilst we can track the processes of change over time, we do not do so in a *linear* way. In this chapter, our focus is on *career development* but other extant work we are involved with focuses on *issues of knowledge transfer and process epistemology*. The commonality of our work lies in our methods. These in turn are influenced by a number of contingency factors not least the exigencies of having access to the organization and maintaining good working relationships with our 'client'. We have the freedom to pursue our own research interests but have an obligation to provide useful knowledge for the company. Therefore, our model, which we might describe as 'negotiated freedom', is not pure as judged by the strictures of 'proper' field research but rather is flexible and adaptable and we would argue successful.

Later in the chapter, we describe specific data gathering and method analysis that we adopt. These are fairly conventional, using a questionnaire supported by interviews and documentary analysis where appropriate. However, in line with aims of this book, these also reflect philosophically informed choices. In 1979, Burrell and Morgan popularized the dichotomy in organizational research between positivist and subjectivist approaches, which still exist. We, however, are attracted to what Bryman and Burgess (1995) call 'methodological pragmatism'. Our position could perhaps be described as being akin to *post-positivism* (Trochim 1999) in that we acknowledge the blurring of what were once distinct and opposed epistemologies. This blurring of epistemological boundaries can lead to a perspective closer to *critical realism* (Sayer 2000) whereby, whilst we embrace elements of post-positivism, we are concerned to acknowledge the importance attached to interpretation and understanding. We are also particularly sympathetic to the critical realists' concern with *meaning*.

Another area of potential criticism of our work and with several other chapters in this volume concerns the limits of a case-study approach. These arguments are well rehearsed (Yin 1994). We fully acknowledge the limit of generalizability of our work but the case-study method, allied to a critical realist perspective on research, yields a depth and richness of texture to balance this. Our work in NCR addresses issues of validity and rigour through multiple evidence sources, variations on research themes and variations in methods and techniques. We are comfortable that this provides a workable and realistic approach to triangulation. In this sense we share the perspective of writers such as Dawson (1994) on the contingent nature of organizational research and acknowledge the processual dimension of the research itself.

Data collection – survey and sampling method

Notwithstanding the larger problems of process epistemology and philosophical positions, our work exemplifies the methodological pragmatism dictated by prosaic issues such as funding, negotiating access and maintaining a working relationship that permits ongoing access to the company. The specific data used for this chapter was collected over the period May – July 1999 and is drawn from a survey of a cohort of employees who participated in at least one EFA course beginning in 1995. The data from this survey has been compared with a matched sample of employees who undertook no EFA course during the period to provide benchmarks for career movements, salary differentials and perceptions of psychological contracts. This control group were matched as closely as possible for age, grade and department.

The cohort of participants who were surveyed numbered 114 and exactly the same number was surveyed in the control group. These people completed self-report questionnaires during group sessions that were arranged in working time, individual 'drop-in sessions' for those who could not make the groups sessions and, finally, e-mailed questionnaires to the remainder. This three-pronged approach resulted in response rates of 63 per cent and 55 per cent for the EFA group and control group respectively.

The characteristics of the EFA respondents (hereafter referred to as the 'sample') and the control group respondents ('control group') were very close in gender and in age. Educationally, as might be expected, the control group had a greater preponderance of people with only school qualifications, whilst people with HNDs and postgraduate qualifications were much more evident in the sample. However, the two groups were closely matched in terms of first degree level qualifications.

The research

Results

It is not our intention to report the detailed findings of the research, but rather to analyse some of our key findings in relation to the four research questions derived from the review of the literature and other research.

Question 1. To what extent has participation in the programme of lifelong learning (EFA) had a positive influence on employees' career perceptions and internal career moves?

In relation to our first research question we found some interesting results concerning career perceptions. For example, participants reported undertaking EFA primarily for career development with personal satisfaction and improved earning potential ranked second and third respectively.

Interestingly, we found that improving work performance as a prime reason for undertaking EFA ranked low from participants.

We also found that in responses to questions concerning the impact of EFA on subsequent career development, that EFA was perceived as having a significant impact on participants' subjective assessments of career development and an even greater one on their job performance. These data are all the more impressive since the company was not perceived to have fully put into practice its rhetoric on career development. Some 60 per cent of the sample group and 57 per cent of the control group had claimed not to have had a career development interview over the past two years, even though it was company policy for most of those surveyed. Also two thirds of the sample claimed their managers took only a little or no interest in their studies. One further point of note, however, to which we shall return later in the discussion, is that 48 per cent of respondents claimed that EFA had influenced their expectations of career development that as yet *had not* been met.

With respect to internal career movements we found that the career pattern in NCR did not correspond with the 'end of career' thesis discussed above. The data on job change showed that 54 per cent of the sample group had changed jobs at least once since 1995 and more than half of these reported vertical promotion in their existing or new department. The pattern of job changes was of a 'contractor' type (Gunz, Jalland and Evans 1998) in which employees appear to build themselves careers based on a variety of experiences and by working in a number of different departments.

However, we also found that vertical promotion involving salary increases were the most common form of job movement for the sample who reported job changes since undertaking their first EFA course. There were significant differences between the sample and control group in the pattern of changes with the sample group significantly more likely to report vertical promotion for any job change, especially to a new department.

Question 2. What were employee expectations concerning career orientations, especially in the context of decreased job security in the organisation, and what evidence was there of the protean career contract?

In relation to the second research question, a number of other questions emerged concerning the career orientations and motivations of people undertaking lifelong learning. Did they see the old deal as dead and was their career contract essentially with themselves and their work (Hall and Moss 1998)? Was there any evidence that employees were more concerned to manage their career, learn how to become more employable, seek psychological growth rather than external success and be less concerned with organizational careers and work self? If so, what are the implications for the employer and was there any evidence that they were less organization-ally oriented in career terms than the control group?

Whilst we had not set out to provide a direct test of these questions, we have sufficient data to suggest that there was some evidence of protean career contracts, although these data also provide some inconsistency over what is claimed and actual career patterns. The first point worth making is that the fact that these people had chosen to invest time and effort in education, perhaps knowingly sacrificing short-term career gain and incurring significant family costs. This may suggest that success for such individuals is measured in terms of learning *how* rather than learning *what* and also in terms of psychological success rather than material or external success. Moreover, the reported reasons for undertaking EFA courses sup-port such a conclusion, with career development and personal satisfaction ranking much more highly that other reasons, including salary or promo-tion. In further indirect evidence, the sample group ranked knowledge of theory and interpersonal skills ('learning how') much higher than the technical skills ('learning what') as the most useful learning that they derived from their courses.

A second point concerns perceptions of who was mainly responsible for career development and whether there was a change towards individuals accepting responsibility. There was little perception of shared responsibil-ity (19 per cent) with an overwhelming 81 per cent of the sample claiming that the way in which the career development system worked in the com-pany meant that they themselves had the responsibility for managing their own careers.

The third point, concerning promotion as a criterion for success, was not seen as a major reason for undertaking an EFA course. Moreover, it is clear that the sample group had experienced and presumably sought lat-eral and vertical job changes, as predicted by the protean career concept. However, it is also evident that, despite claiming promotion was not a major issue, the sample group had experienced significantly more vertical movement than the control group.

A fourth point concerns employability. Although we did not ask ques-tions in the survey on job security, we know from previous work in the company and from group discussions with the sample group, that most employees perceived that they were less secure than previously in their jobs. Given the recent memories of redundancy, this may not be surpris-ing. We also found that for the first two job changes at least, the sample group were significantly more likely to report that employability (internal and external) had been a more significant consequence of the change than salary. It appears that perceptions of a significant increase in salary resulted from the third job change or beyond. It is also at the third job change or beyond that any significant difference can be found between the sample and control group in reports of greater internal or external employability.

Employees' perception of the organization's management of the new career contract was also considered. Employees believed that the main reason that the company engaged in EFA was to 'improve the knowledge and skills of its workforce' (followed a long way behind by 'improving performance'). This indicates a genuine belief in the long-term outlook of company policy and in providing development opportunities. The data on career moves, for the sample and control group, indicates that the organization provided developmental opportunities for all with 54 per cent and 74 per cent respectively having changed jobs at least once since 1995. The data on boredom, job variety and job satisfaction seems to indicate relatively high levels of challenging assignments, with the sample group significantly less likely to report boredom being the only difference between the two groups.

The organization's managers, however, seem to be perceived as having provided mixed support to EFA participants. Both groups claimed that their managers placed a great deal of value on education and encouraged them to take the courses, whilst 66 per cent of those on EFA claimed that their managers took little or no interest in their progress on their studies. The provision of the learning centre was not seen to be a particularly significant resource with less than a fifth of the sample agreeing that it had been a big help in their learning.

Question 3. To what extent was participation in the lifelong learning programme (EFA) associated with positive perceptions of salary enhancement and with a differential between participants and non-participants?

In response to our third research question there are two points to note at the outset. First, as we recorded earlier, salary improvement was not a major factor in encouraging the sample to undertake EFA; furthermore we have established that the sample exhibited many of the characteristics of protean career contracts, in which psychological growth was paramount. Second, however, there is a notorious unreliability in the reporting of salary increases. In this study, for example, there was no significant relationship between the number of reported increases in salary bands since 1994 and individuals reporting significant increases in salary as a result of these job changes. Third, there is no obvious causal connection between participating in EFA and job moves; indeed, the control group was more likely to report job changes although these were more likely to be lateral rather than vertical.

Our analysis suggests that it was not until the third job change and beyond that the small number of participants (approximately 10 per cent of the sample) reported receiving significantly different salary increases from the control group. Whilst the majority indicated improvements in salary of some kind, there were no significant differences in reported increases between the sample against the control.

Question 4. To what extent did the existence of the programme and/or participation in it have a positive influence on employee perceptions of their psychological contracts, as measured by their perceptions of the content of the contract and the consequences of the contract?

In relation to our final research question there are two possible findings that we might expect. The first is that since EFA is open to all, awareness of the programme and awareness of high participation rates and the continuation of the programme would have positive effects on all psychological contracts of the kinds identified by Tsui *et al.* (1997). This would be likely to result in little or no differences between the sample and control groups. The second possibility is of a recursive relationship in which participation in EFA and positive psychological contracts are mutually related and reinforcing. If this were to hold, then we might expect to find significant differences in how the sample and control group perceived their employer in terms of overall fairness and trustworthiness. It may also have shown in their psychological contracts, in terms of factors such as perceptions of career development and fair rewards. It may also have been expressed through a judgement of whether what was perceived to have been promised in these areas had been delivered (Guest 1998).

In relation to perceived 'promises' made on career development, the results were generally positive. For even within the control group, 63 per cent who had not taken a course, reported that they would do so in the future. Moreover, everyone in the control group was aware of EFA. They generally accounted for their lack of participation in the programme to date in terms of factors over which they had a degree of choice, such as 'other commitments' (24 per cent). However, since 'time pressures' (30 per cent) was the largest overall explanation for not participating, it might be interesting to explore if this employer-related reason was associated with perceived breaches of contract. Nevertheless, the overall conclusion is that *access* to career development through EFA had been delivered.

The question remains, however, as to whether or not employee expectations of career development have been met. Three points are relevant here.

- Just under three fifths of the sample experienced at least a significant effect of participation in the programme on their careers, with about one fifth reporting an insignificant or no effect. This data suggests that what was promised in terms of career development was actually delivered.
- The sample were asked if career development had been their main objective, how successful had it been? Forty-five per cent reported success whilst only 11 per cent reported lack of success.

- The sample was asked if EFA had influenced their expectations of career development that, as yet, had not been met. Fifty-two per cent responded with unmet expectations, but given that only 41 out of the 72 members of the sample responded to this question, this corresponds to only 29 per cent of the sample with possible perceptions of a breach of their contracts in this area. Even then, one has to question the extent to which any breach might be treated seriously enough to be a contract 'violation' (Morrison and Robinson 1997).

There is not room to report all of the data on the perceptions of fairness, trust and delivery of the deal here. Instead, the following points should be noted.

- EFA was statistically likely to have increased the perception of the company as a good employer for both groups.
- The impression gained from the analysis was that both the sample and control groups were relatively committed to the organization. There were no significant differences in this respect.
- There were no significant differences between the two groups in overall scores of scales measuring perceptions of fairness, trust and cynicism.
- There were, however, significant differences in continuance commitment in that EFA was seen to make the sample more likely to remain with the company for the foreseeable future.

Critical analysis

The overall pattern of results provides general support for the argument that this programme of investment in lifelong learning for employees has paid off in positive career experiences and positive psychological contracts. Thus, within the limitations of a single case study, we hope that the research has provided some evidence that investment in HRD and careers pays off. Following Tsui *et al.* (1997) we suggest that a mutual investment relationship of the kind generally found in this case study will provide important benefits to employees and their employers.

Following the line of questioning of our evaluation framework, we found that there are four broad sets of implications:

1   That career development was the prime reason and expectation for undertaking EFA and, by and large, their subsequent experience of career development had been a positive one, as measured by perceptions and job moves. The company had played its part in creating a mutual investment relationship by providing a context of relative job security and lateral and vertical career pathways. The reality, however,

did not fully match company policy, particularly in relation to career development interviews and managers taking an interest in the courses that participants were following. Moreover, there was evidence that a significant minority were dissatisfied with their career progression and feel frustrated by expectations not being met. The extent to which these frustrated expectations can be treated as a breach of their psychological contract is less certain. Indeed, it is likely that such circumstances may have led to the development of different kinds of career orientations as described in the next paragraphs (which would be an interesting line of enquiry for the next stage of this research).

2   There was evidence that participants in the programme were developing protean career contracts, perhaps engineered by the company's policy of encouraging self-development and individual responsibility for career management. Participants reported 'psychological growth' as their main goal and were concerned with employability, managing their own careers and learning how rather than what. They appeared less committed to 'work self' and to organizational careers, evidenced by their taking time out of managing the politics of their careers. Such pay-off for political career behaviour is, perhaps, evidenced by the control group experiencing more overall career movement, but not so much vertical movement in the latter stages.

3   The data on salaries are ambiguous but in line with the emergence of protean career contracts and with the predictions of those writers pointing to small or even negative economic returns resulting from lifelong learning and time out for education. Salary increases were not claimed to be a major factor among the sample (or control group) and, indeed, other data confirmed such a view. For example, responses to a question as to whether the offer of a bit more money elsewhere would encourage people to leave produced no strong desire to change employers. There were no significant differences in the reported increases in the number of salary bands between the sample or control group since 1995. Nor were there any significant differences between the groups in reporting a significant increase in salary resulting from job changes.

Although we did not ask about satisfaction with salary and with job security in this study, the overall pattern of data on the psychological contract shows a positive relationship. The exceptions to this were shown in responses from two questions on whether respondents believed 'managers treated workers fairly' and whether they would act in the future as if 'managers treated workers fairly'. In both cases there were significant differences between the sample and control group, with the former less likely to report fair treatment of employees. These data suggest an interesting line of enquiry for future factor analysis to determine if there are a significant group of EFA respondents for whom contract breach has been their experience.

4　The pattern of responses to the scales measuring the state of the psychological contract and the items on career development show that EFA had produced a positive effect on both groups' expectations and delivery of career development. Moreover, since there were few significant differences between the sample and control groups in their reporting on the trust, commitment and cynicism scales, we can conclude that either EFA had had no significant effect on psychological contracts or that its effect had been uniform throughout the company.

The only significant differences between the sample and control groups were in the greater likelihood of continuous commitment on the part of the sample and the greater perceptions of fairness among the control group.

Indeed, reading these data in conjunction with our earlier work which examined the whole workforce (Martin, Pate and McGoldrick 1999), we can speculate that EFA has had a particularly positive and localized effect on that aspect of the employer–employee relationship where one would have expected it to – career development. However, we also found a more generalized but less strong positive effect on all other aspects of the psychological contract. In this sense it has helped to create a sense of balance in the organization–employee relationship, which, as Tsui et al. (1997) have pointed out, is likely to be associated with performance outcomes.

Conclusions and key learning points

We believe our case study has made some contribution to the employee relations literature generally and to the claims made by HRD scholars. These data provide some support for the thesis that HRD investment strategies pay, especially if they come in the guise of programmes of lifelong learning and continuous professional development that allow people to become more employable and grow psychologically. In contributing to the literature, we also believe that HRD practitioners can take some comfort from this study in supporting their efforts to provide lifelong learning to their colleagues. However, as Rousseau and Arthur (1999) argue, HR practitioners in this firm may have to pursue agency strategies as well as these community strategies. These might include offering (a) choices to individuals in designing their employment terms, jobs and career patterns to give them more discretion, and (b) designing employment terms and career opportunities that maximize employees' external, as well as internal, visibility. In doing so, they enhance individuals' employability and thus become a real employer of choice (Cappelli 1998).

We recognize the limitations of this study, which is restricted to a single case study. Nevertheless, the next stages of our research, which involve more statistical analysis and in-depth interviewing, will be to follow up the lines of enquiry generated by these data. We are also engaged in a similar programme of research with another company, and we are confident that this will help verify our findings and assist us in a broader generalization of our findings.

Earlier on we reflected on the specific approach to longitudinality adopted in this chapter. The classic approach to longitudinal research, which would look at an organization in real time, is not always available to us. However, if as in our case, the research questions changed with the different research episodes, then perhaps a means of assessing the overall impact of the change we are analysing could utilize what Leonard-Barton (1995) describes as 'retrospective questioning'. There may be some interesting lessons for organizational researchers with this approach. Inviting contemporary members of an organization to 'think back' and restructure the past generally in the light of the questions of the present (see Chet Miller, Cardinal and Glick 1997). This might go full circle with the interests and concerns of some researchers on HRD with critical reflection. This is an area worthy of further consideration by those involved in HRD research.

Our reflection is that the common thread to our work in NCR is change: that is what we have observed and have reflected in our writings. As Van de Ven and Poole (1995: 159–60) argue, most studies of change have been retrospective case histories conducted after the outcomes were known. This does not apply in our work, rather we have used the questions of today to interrogate in a different way the experience of the past.

References

Adamson, S.J., Doherty, N. and Viney, C. (1998) 'The meaning of career revisited: implications for theory and practice', *British Journal of Management*, 9(4): 251–60.

Arthur, M.B. and Rousseau, D.M. (eds) (1996) *The Boundaryless Career: a New Employment Principle for a New Organisational era*, New York: Oxford.

Bartlett, C.A. and Ghoshal, S. (1993) 'Beyond the M-form organisation: toward a managerial theory of the firm', *Strategic Management Journal*, 14: 23–46.

Bryman, A. and Burgess, G.M. (1994) *Analysing Qualitative Data*, London: Sage.

Burrell, G. and Morgan, G. (1979) *Sociological Paradigms and Organisational Analysis*, London: Heinemann.

Cannon, F. (1995) 'The role of education and training in organisational climate change: a case study', *Journal of Professional Human Resource Management*, 1, October 10–18.

Cappelli, P., Katz, H. and Osterman, P. (1997) *Change at Work*, New York: Oxford University Press.

Cappelli, P. (1998) *The New Deal at Work: Managing the Market-Driven Workforce*, Boston: Harvard University School Press.

Chet Miller, C., Cardinal, L.B. and Glick, W. (1997) Retrospective reports in organisational research: a re-examination of recent evidence. *Academy of Management Journal*, 40(1): 189–205.

Dawson, P. (1994) *Organisational Change: A Processual Approach*, London: Chapman.

Easterby-Smith, M. (1997) 'Disciplines of organisational learning: contributions and critiques', *Human Relations*, 50(9): 1085–113.

Eisenhardt, K.E. (1989) 'Making fast strategic decisions in high velocity environments', *Academy of Management Journal*, 32: 543–76.

Gallie, D., White, M., Chen, Y. and Tomlinson, M. (1998) *Restructuring the Employment Relationship*, Oxford: Oxford University Press.

Guest, D.E. (1998) 'Is the psychological contract worth taking seriously?', *Journal of Organisational Behaviour*, 19: 649–64.

Guest, D.E. and Conway, N. (1997) 'Employee motivation and the psychological contract', *Issues in People Management*, 21. Wimbledon: IPD.

Gunz, H.P., Jalland, R.M. and Evans, M.G. (1998) 'New strategy, wrong managers? What you need to know about career streams', *Academy of Management Executive*, 12(2): 21–37.

Hall, D.E. and Moss, J.E. (1998) 'The new protean career contract', *Organisational Dynamics*, Winter: 22–38.

Herriot, P. and Pemberton, C. (1996) 'Contracting careers', *Human Relations*, 49(6): 757–90.

Herriot, P. (1992) *The Career Management Challenge. Balancing Individual and Organisational Needs*, London: Sage.

Herriot, P., Hirsh, W. and Reilly, P. (1998) *Trust and Transition: Managing Today's Employment Relationship*, Chichester: Wiley.

Hiltrop, J.M. (1995) 'The changing psychological contract', *European Management Journal*, 13(3): 286–94.

Huselid, M. (1995) 'The impact of human resource management practice on turnover, productivity and corporate financial performance', *Academy of Management Journal*, 24: 689–713.

Kamoche, K. and Mueller, F. (1998) 'Human resource management and the appropriation-learning perspective', *Human Relations*, 51(8): 1033–60.

Leonard-Barton, D. (1995) 'Building theories from case study research', in G.P. Huber and A.H. Van de Ven (1995) *Longitudinal Field Research Methods: Studying Processes of Organisational Change*, Thousand Oaks, CA: Sage, 65–90.

Mabey, C. and Mallory, G. (1994) 'Structure and culture change in two UK organisations: a comparison of assumptions, approaches and outcomes', *Human Resource Management Journal*, 4(2): 1–18.

Martin, G. and Beaumont, P. (1999) 'Co-ordination and control of HRM in multinational firms: the case of CASHCO', *International Journal of Human Resource Management*, 10(1): 21–42.

Martin, G. and Butler, M. (2000) 'Comparing managerial careers, management development and management education in the UK and the US: some theoretical and practical considerations', *International Journal of Training and Development*, 4(4).

Martin, G., Pate, J., Beaumont, P. and McGoldrick, J. (1999) 'Company based life long learning: what's the pay-off?', *British Academy of Management Annual Conference* (1–3 September), Manchester.

—— (2000) 'Lifelong learning and knowledge transfer to the workplace: a longitudinal case study', *Academy of HRD Annual Conference* (8–12 March), Raleigh-Durham.

Martin, G., Pate, J. and McGoldrick, J. (1999) 'Do HRD investment strategies pay? Exploring the relationship between lifelong learning and psychological contracts', *International Journal of Training and Development*, 3(3): 200–14.

Martin, G. and Riddell, T. (1996) 'The wee firm that decked IBM: "manufacturing" strategic change and leadership in the "cash"', *Journal of Strategic Change*, 5(1): 3–26.

Mintzberg, H., Ahlstrand, B. and Lampel, J. (1998) *Strategy Safari*, Hemel Hempstead, Herts: Prentice Hall.

Morrison, E.W. and Robinson, S.L. (1997) 'When employees feel betrayed: a model of how contract violation develops', *Academy of Management Review*, 22(1): 226–57.

Nonake, I. and Takenchi, H. (1995) 'The knowledge-creating company', *How Japanese Firms Create the Dynamics of Innovation*, New York: Oxford University Press.

Pate, J., Martin, G., Beaumont, P. and McGoldrick, J. (2000) 'Company-based lifelong learning: what's the pay-off for employers?', *Journal of European Industrial Training*, 24(2/3/4): 149–57.

Pettigrew, A.M. (1990) 'Longitudinal field research on change: theory and practice', *Organisation/science*, 1(3): 267–92.

Pfeffer, J. (1994) 'Competitive advantage through people', *California Management Review*, 36(2): 9–23.

Pfeffer, J. (1998) *The Human Equation*, Boston MA: Harvard Business School Press.

Purcell, J., Kinnie, N., Hutchinson, S. and Rayton, B. (2000) 'Inside the box', *People Management*, 26 October, 30–8.

Rajan, A. (1997) 'Employability in the financial sector: rhetoric vs reality', *Human Resource Management Journal*, 7(1): 67–78.

Rainbird, H. (1998) 'Skilling the unskilled: access to work-based learning and the lifelong learning agenda', in T. Lange (ed.) *Skilling the Unskilled: Achievements and Under-achievements in Education and Training*, Aberdeen: The Robert Gordon University.

Rousseau, D.M. and Arthur, M.B. (1999) 'The boundaryless human resource function: building agency and community in the new economic era', *Organisational Dynamics*, Spring 7–18.

Sayer, A. (2000) *Realism and Social Science*, London: Sage, 17–18.

Scarborough, H., Swan, J. and Preston, J. (1998) *Knowledge Management and the Learning Organisation: the IPD Report*, Wimbledon: IPD.

Senge, P. (1990) *The Fifth Discipline: The Art and Practice of the Learning Organisation*, London: Doubleday.

Tayeb, M. (1998) Transfer of HRM practices across cultures: an American company in Scotland. *International Journal of Human Resource Management*, 9(2): 332–58.

Thomson, A., Mabey, C., Storey, J., Gray, C. and Iles, P. (2001) *Management Development in Practice*, Oxford: Blackwell.

Torraco, R.J. (ed.) (1999) 'Performance improvement: theory and practice', *Advances in Developing Human Resources*, No. 1, Academy of Human Resource Development, San Francisco, CA: Berrett-Koehler.

Trochim, W.K. (1999) 'Positivism and Post-positivism. Research Methods', *Knowledge Base* (2nd ed.), http://trochim.human.cornell.edu/Kb/positivism.htm

Tsui, A.S., Pearce, J.L., Porter, L.W. and Tripoli, A.M. (1997) 'Alternative approaches to the employee-organisation relationship: does investment in employees pay off?', *Academy of Management Journal*, 40(5): 1089–122.

Van de Ven, A.H. and Huber, G.P. (1990) 'Longitudinal filed research methods for studying processes of organizational change', *Organisation Science*, 1(3): 213–19.

Van de Ven, A.H. and Poole, M.S. (1995) 'Explaining development and change in organizations', *Academy of Management Review*, 20(3): 510–40.

Wheatley, M. and New, C. (1997) 'AT & T global information solutions', *Management Today's Guide to Britain's Best Factories*, London: DTI/Management Today/ Cranfield University.

Winterton, J. and Winterton, R. (1997) 'Does management development matter?', *British Journal of Management*, 8(2): S65–S76.

Yin, R.K. (1994) *Case Study Research. Design and Methods* (2nd edn), Thousand Oaks, CA: Sage.

4

THE TOOLS OF FREEDOM AND THE SOURCES OF INDIGNITY

John Hamblett, Rick Holden and
Denise Thursfield

Aims and contribution

This chapter is about science and morality. In his Preface to *Reclaiming Reality*, Bhaskar (1989) signals his intent to borrow Locke's (1959) notion of philosophy as under-labourer. The work of the under-labourer, we are told, is to clear 'the ground a little' and to remove 'some of the rubbish that lies in the way of knowledge' (ibid.). Bhaskar's aim is to use his philosophical under-labourings to aid the human sciences that they might 'illuminate and empower the project of human self-emancipation'. It is our aim, in turn, to use the work of Bhaskar (op. cit.) and others for the task of clearing away some of the obstacles that lie in the way to knowledge, understanding and human self-emancipation in the field of HRD.

A word that we will use often in what follows is 'praxis' (Roberts 1999). We use that concept as a term of art, as an expressive piece of shorthand employed to focus the reader's attention on a specific view of human agency. Through our usage, praxis is meant, first, to highlight both the theoretical and practical continuity of human productive activity, or *labour*. Second, it serves to define labour not merely as the 'key to understanding the determinations inherent in all forms of alienation', but also as the central activity in a 'practical strategy aimed at the actual suppression of capitalistic alienation' (Meszaros 1979: 88). In a recent paper Panitch and Gindin (1999: 13) have offered a concise exposition of this notion:

> Ontologically work is a stand-in for the specifically human capacity to conceive of that which does not exist and then to effect its realisation. Conceived in historical terms, the use of that capacity to create our material reality through work is intimately linked to the dynamics of social change. And in the specific context of capitalism, the organisation of work provides a defining contradiction of the social system, and a foundation for working class politics.

We have sought to anchor our discussion firmly in the substantive issues generated within the topical debates on lifelong and workplace learning. In particular, we will be concerned to examine the perceived links between learning, work and democracy (e.g. DfEE (1998)), which arise as a result of the debates concerning EDAP-style employee-led development schemes (hereafter ELD).

Although philosophical in kind, the importance of this endeavour does not reside solely, or even primarily, in the sphere of theory. As indicated by Bhaskar above, the significance of the work should be measured by the extent to which it supports the practical project of self-emancipation. For, as Chomsky (1991) has argued, at this point in history, 'in advanced industrial society the rational and human use of resources and technology provides the possibility to free people from the role of tools of production in the industrial process' (1991: 32).

This is how our argument will be ordered. Our first job in the section that follows this introduction will be to set before the reader what we have referred to above as the moral core of our position. Because our case is controversial we will follow this sketch by anticipating and refuting a number of objections which might emerge from what we have defined elsewhere (Hamblett and Holden 1998) as the orthodox account of HRD. We hope that a consequence of our decision to lead on the moral position will be a greater degree of expositional clarity in those portions of our chapter wherein we discuss methodological issues. Next, we will develop in finer detail the props and planks of our theoretical framework. As suggested above, our major guide in this endeavour will be the already cited work of Roy Bhaskar (see also Bhaskar 1989a; Sayer 1992; Collier 1994; Archer 1995). 'Critical realism' describes our position more or less accurately. By way of an introductory comment on the philosophical framework in question we can say that Bhaskar's critical realism is one instance of that class of philosophies referred to generically as naturalism. Callinicos (1989: 97), with his customary precision and brevity, offers three theses upon which naturalism rests. These are as follows:

1   man [sic], as primarily a physical and biological being, is a dependent part of nature;
2   the methodological principles relevant to the formulation and evaluation of theoretical discourses are the same in both the natural and social sciences;
3   the concepts and propositions of the natural sciences provide the social sciences with a model for their own procedure.

Through our methodological discussion we want to highlight three points. First, as already noted, we want to demonstrate the indissoluble link between scientific explanation and human freedom. This is posited in contradistinction to the 'fact–value dichotomy' native to positivism, which inverts the 'objective', or 'value-neutral' function of science. Second, we want to show that for Bhaskar, in opposition to contemporary hermeneutics, 'the main part of the work of emancipation is not cognitive, but consists in toil, and trouble, conflict, changes in power relations, the breaking up of some social structures, and the building up of others' (Collier op. cit.: 191). Third, we want to offer Bhaskar's idea of the 'depth investigation' as the major means by which researches into the development of human agency might aid, practically, the project under debate. Our final task prior to the conclusion will be to present some supplementary remarks on Realist principles of investigation before relating these to two case studies. These cases will not be used as examples of best practice in the conventional manner. Rather, we will employ them as the raw material necessary for the kind of self-criticism identified as a necessary component of progressive social science by Bhaskar.

In our conclusion we will draw together the key learning points. These will relate to the following propositions. First, we want to say that those who research human resource development (HRD) initiatives may only claim to make meaningful and true statements concerning such initiatives if they locate their investigation within a realist, social scientific framework. Second, we want to say that because there is an unbreakable link between the project of science and human emancipation, research into HRD issues is, of necessity, research into the conditions of human emancipation in work. Third, we want to say that insofar as the project of HRD is concerned with the realization of human agency within the workplace, it cannot be contained within the existing, exploitative social relations definitive of the capitalist mode of production. Fourth, we want to say this implicates the HRD researcher in a potentially conflictual relationship with employers and other powerful, vested interests who fund research activity, stand guard over points of access to research subjects, and who support the status quo. Finally, we want to say that because authentic social scientific research into HRD issues is a theoretically complicated and politically difficult business, a highly developed propensity to, and facility for self-critique is necessary.

Theoretical context

In order to make our position as transparent as possible we will offer the outline of the moral core of our position in the form of six propositions. Following this, in order both to demonstrate what is at stake in the argument and why it is controversial we will represent the case in a more natural form of words. First, then, the propositions and what they mean.

1   The development of a just and egalitarian social order is a desirable goal;
2   the development of such an order is a real historical possibility;

3 such an order can only be created by the intentional efforts of those
   who have a material interest in its development;
4 efforts so described pre-suppose agents with wisdom and moral acumen
   sufficient to make rational choices on the basis of the best available
   evidence;
5 a necessary though not sufficient condition for the development of
   wisdom and moral acumen is that agents subscribe to a process of
   lifelong learning;
6 those who take the task of promoting, investigating or facilitating
   lifelong learning initiatives are required to evaluate their activities
   according to the contribution such activities make to the development
   of human agency along the lines set down by (1) to (5).

These propositions can be translated in the following terms: we simply take it as given that the pursuit of social justice, freedom, self-determination, call it what you will, is a good thing. Similarly, we take it for granted that the eradication of the terrible gulf separating the rich from the poor, the majority who suffer the consequences of exploitation from a minority who profit from exploitation is a goal worthy of human agents. We take also the lesson from history that shows us how no amount of moral advocacy or ethical pleading will ever be sufficient to effect such a transformation. And it is an argument for transformation that we are intent on developing. Amelioration within existing structures will not deliver a just and egalitarian social order.

Transformation is properly the work of those who suffer exploitation, discrimination and so on. These agents have a shared, material interest in the generation of non-exploitative, non-discriminatory, truly human structures. As noted in the introduction, for short, though not without the risk of confusion, we refer to such transformational activity as 'praxis'. The ability of human agents to engage in a genuinely transformative practice, however, is limited as a result of being subject to exploitative and discriminatory social structures and their attendant relations. A necessary (though not sufficient) condition for the development of praxis is continuous education in the broadest sense.

The workplace represents the capital on which these processes converge. The qualitative transformation of work and of workplace relations is fundamental to the project under consideration. Relations within the workplace provide the dominant pattern for social relations within the broader society. The education of employees within work is, then, of the greatest significance for the process of transformation. And because there must be voices, organized, powerful and informed enough to pose such challenges in a meaningful way, the necessary work should

> be done with some thought for the social and material conditions of attaining any given ideals, the means of and agencies for

attaining them, *the social interests and movements* that can conceivably be coupled with or become attached to the ideals and imperatives in question.

(Geras 1990: 16–17, emphasis in original)

In the paper quoted earlier, Panitch and Gindin (op. cit.) make this same point. They argue that those who argue for a reformist programme aimed at 'changing the nature of the capitalist firm' misapprehend the nature of the problematic. In particular what such a 'negative utopia' fails to recognize is 'the social power of capital and the oppositional politics necessarily involved in changing it'. The 'social interests and movements' identified by Panitch and Gindin centre on the trade unions, the workers' organizations. It is on the unions' 'potential as sites of capacity-building and democratisation' that we should concentrate (ibid.: 17). In addition to 'aggressively fighting for traditional demands', they argue, new demands linked to the project of developing members' 'overall political and administrative capacities' are required.

In Bhaskar's terms this point regarding the identification of 'social movements and interests' suggests three things of significance with respect to the necessary conditions for emancipation. First, we are alerted to the fact that 'all values must be immanent' (Bhaskar 1989: 113). All agents are engaged in a practice prior to the intervention of research. Those practices 'secrete values'. The motive and the warrant for both the theoretical intervention and the practical transformation must reside in those values. So, for example, and as the quotations taken from Panitch and Gindin above indicate, the practices developed by trade unions secrete values which speak of the democratic regulation of work. However, it is worth mentioning here that the absence of trade unions does not entail the abandoning of the project of self-emancipation. Our research in SMEs (Hamblett and Holden 1999) suggests that in such non-union environments ELD schemes serve to strengthen the bonds of informally constituted work-groups. Theoretically it is feasible to suggest that such developments may constitute the first step to more formal self-organization within a trade union. Whether or not such an outcome materializes, however, is an empirical question that cannot be settled by resort to theory.

Second, the critique offered must be 'internal to its object' (ibid.). If a critique is to contribute to a *real* transformation it must emerge from the society of which it is a critique. This point comprises two practical elements: (1) because work in capitalist societies is exploitative and oppressive, and because, as we shall argue, science is necessarily emancipatory, the researcher must ally herself or himself with the oppressed; (2) this is very difficult because 'research' is also 'work' and that which is true for workers generally is true for researchers as workers. Thus, the critique must incorporate 'self-critique'. This point has been made for sociology most constantly by Pierre Bourdieu (1988, 1993). Finally, because Bhaskar's concept of emancipation is only partly cognitive, a necessary condition for emancipation is that agents *feel* a need for change. This is as much of our argument as we need to explicate at present. We will return to it, below. Let us move to examine a number of objections that might emerge from those who hold to the orthodox view.

Perhaps the easiest way to fix the objections that arise is to go right to the heart of the argument. That point of reference is given by our third proposition, which states that a just and egalitarian social order can only be 'created by the intentional efforts of those who have a material interest in its development'. By scrutinizing this proposition it is possible to identify four major objections. We would not claim that this set is exhaustive, merely that they represent the *strongest* objections available to the orthodoxy.

The first objections concern the concept of 'unintended consequences'. The second objection refers to a particular theory of knowledge, highly influential within contemporary social science, that we will refer to as 'perspectivism'. Third, we will examine the question of 'rationality' as it is posed by the orthodox account, and its entailment for the treatment of 'social structure'. The fourth objection met will concern the knotty question of 'interests'.

It will be evident to the reader that these objections are intimately related each to the other. The root of this relationship grows from the common soil of 'methodological individualism'. There are two elements of methodological individualism that are particularly significant for our discussion. First, for those who share this doctrine, events, states of affairs and so on can only be explained by reference to the behaviour of individuals. Second (and consequently), according to this doctrine, 'social structures are the unintended consequences of individual human action' (Callinicos 1995: 4). This said, let us move to the objections.

Unintended consequence

The first thing our opponents might wish to claim is that there is no royal road that leads from intention to outcome. This is a particularly critical objection where that intended outcome is something as complex as a 'just and egalitarian social order'. Crucially, the objection would run that what our proposition does not allow for are the *unintended consequences* of human action.

This Weberian notion feeds into the current debate on lifelong learning in a number of ways. Some of it surfaces in the commonsense *angst*, which denies the possibility of any certainties in a modern world defined in terms of uncertainty and a radical openness. Most powerfully, perhaps, it provides the causal context for the learning project (e.g. Fryer 1997). For, change, it seems, is the *only* certainty. If agents, organizations, communities and even nation-states are to prosper in the new millennium they *must* learn to embrace change.

So, on this count the best that the HRD project can hope to achieve is the development of a human resource sufficiently robust and flexible to deal with constant exposure to the 'new'. How are we to answer this objection? We cannot begin by denying the notion of 'unintended consequences'; it is beyond doubt that this concept represents a significant dynamic in social reality. We might, however, begin by asking if it is *necessarily* the case that an acceptance of the emergence of 'unintended consequences' leads to the frustration of *all* social planning? Whilst this very strong objection might be held by libertarians of the extreme right, it is not a position that is open to the orthodox advocates of HRD for the obvious reason that the HRD project presupposes an element of social planning. Our advocate may wish to argue that it is not social planning *per se* that is ruled out by a recognition of the fact of unintended consequences, but rather the planning of something so grand as a just social order.

Although this weaker objection appears to be more plausible it may be refutable on two counts. Both of these concern how 'planning' is thought of within the orthodox discourse. First, a strong implication of this objection is that the creation of a 'just and egalitarian social order' is a once-and-for-all act, and that the 'thing' thus created is an object of the greatest imaginable purity and integrity. 'Planning', here, is equivalent to 'wish fulfilment'. This is to base one's objection on a hopelessly idealistic representation of our argument. It is no part of our case to suggest that such a social formation can (or ought) to be created out of the blue and all of a piece. However, as Geras (op. cit.: 8) shows it is one thing to argue that 'perfection' is beyond our present grasp, it is another thing to plead that we are incapable of developing radical changes of the desired kind.

The second count is suggested by the first. For the orthodox the existing social division of labour is a given. Within that division the 'planning process' is the legitimate labour of 'experts', state appointees and managers, whose work it is to define the shape and content of future societies and institutions. From this perspective 'democracy', then as now, would be 'about' the development of the relevant kind of 'institutions' by 'experts' on behalf of the majority. As Collier (op. cit.: 202–4) demonstrates such views are intimately entangled with notions of 'one-level sovereignty'. The idea, that is, that the 'firm' is the relevant unit of analysis, that beyond the firm are 'relations of the market' and within its bounds, 'relations of management'. Yet, as Collier proceeds to argue,

> The myth of sovereignty – of the nation state or of the economic firm may . . . be no more than an instance of the same epistemic 'idol' (in Bacon's sense) as the discredited one-level metaphysical systems. . . . And the vision of a pyramid of democratic loci of political and economic power, from the street and the shopfloor meeting to the planetary plan, may have no inherent impracticability

– only the uphill task of overturning the vested interests that oppose it.

(Op. cit.: 204)

The orthodoxy might salvage some of its objection if it can demonstrate that developments within contemporary capitalism both facilitate and set the bounds for the measures they propose. We, however, follow Pantich and Gindin who argue that the presumption

> That neo-liberal prescriptions of efficiency are compatible with social justice is the contemporary expression of what Bloch (1986) designated as one of the key hallmarks of ideology – 'the premature harmonization of social contradictions' within the confines of existing social relations.

(Op. cit.: 4)

Another way of phrasing this same point would be to suggest that the HRD project as envisioned by the orthodoxy is imbricated in the 'power-saturated ways in which we normally interact' (Blaug 1999: 148). It is an idealism of the worst kind, a Utopian discourse that fails to recognize itself.

Perspectivism

The second objection concerns the role of the researcher and the legitimate goals of research. This objection turns on a particular theory of knowledge, which we can refer to as 'perspectivism'. Although the theory is expressed in a plurality of ways, the central tenet has been adumbrated most concisely by one of its fiercest critics, John Searle, for example:

> [W]e have no access to, we have no way of representing, and no means of coping with the real world except from a certain point of view, from a certain set of presuppositions, under a certain aspect, from a certain stance. If there is no unmediated access to reality, then, so the argument goes, there is really no point in talking about reality, and indeed, there is no reality independent of the stances, aspects or points of view.

(1999: 20)

The upshot of this position, it is supposed, is that researchers can claim no privileged access to 'reality', or 'truth'. It cannot, therefore, be any part of the researcher's brief to superimpose their worldview over the top of the worldview articulated by their research subjects. An entailment of this is that questions concerning the 'way things ought to be' are ruled out of court.

Our opponents may wish to extend and strengthen this objection by arguing that we are guilty of compounding our error by confusing ends

72

with means. For, although methodological individualism depends on a conception of human agents as 'rational actors', capable of rational evaluation and planning, 'rational', here, refers to *means*. Agents behave rationally when they select the means most appropriate to achieving a given end. In other words, actions must be judged rational where they represent the best possible route to achieving an end that is possible *within the prevailing state of affairs*.

By cleaving to such a position, the orthodoxy aligns itself with the dominant tradition in contemporary philosophy. However, as Searle (op. cit.) shows such arguments rest on a matching pair of *non sequitur*. First, to propose that one can only know reality from a 'perspective', or a 'point of view' is perfectly reasonable. The mistake is to presume that 'knowing reality directly as it is in itself requires that it be known from no point of view' (op. cit.: 21). Another way of phrasing this in more technical language would be to say that 'perspectivism' confuses epistemic relativism (or, the view that all perspectives are socially produced) with judgemental relativism (or, the view that all perspectives are equally valid).

The second problem also begins with an unremarkable proposition. That proposition maintains that language is a medium necessary for the formulation of facts, and any statement concerning states of affairs. The mistake resides in the next move. This says that because language is necessary to describe or state facts, the facts described or stated do not have an independent existence beyond language. For Searle,

> It is a use-mention fallacy to suppose that the linguistic and conceptual nature of the *identification* of a fact requires that the *fact identified* be itself linguistic in nature. Facts are conditions that make statements true, but they are not identical with their linguistic descriptions. We invent words to state facts and to name things, but it does not follow that we invent the facts or the things.
>
> (Op. cit.: 22, emphasis in original)

To claim that some explanations are closer to the truth than others is to claim that such explanations describe more accurately the 'facts of the matter'. This, it must be admitted, sets us a new problem which looks like this: how is one to judge between two conflicting theories when both of the theories in question are able to point to a body of supporting, empirical evidence? The answer to this dilemma provided by Sir Karl Popper's successor at the London School of Economics, Imre Lakatos, is elegant and powerful. The name Lakatos gave to his methodology is 'sophisticated falsification'. Sophisticated falsificationism can be differentiated from 'naïve falsificationism' thus:

> For the naïve falsificationist a theory is *falsified* by an . . . 'observational' statement, which conflicts with it . . . For the sophisticated

falsificationist a scientific theory T is *falsified* if and only if theory T^1 (1) T^1 has excess empirical content over T: that is, it predicts *novel* facts, that is, facts improbable in the light of, or even forbidden, by T; (2) T^1 explains the previous success of T, that is, all the unrefuted content of T is included . . . in the content of T^1; and (3) some of the excess content of T^1 is corroborated.

(1995: 32)

This is a dense and difficult paragraph. Let us unpack and supplement its meaning in a more leisurely way. The first point to make is that, for Lakatos, conflicting scientific explanations are never conflicts between one theory, another theory and a single piece of evidence. Rather, as Callinicos explains, for Lakatos, 'The history of the sciences is characterized . . . by the existence of series of theories forming scientific research programmes' (1989: 124).

Scientific research programmes consist of a 'hard core' around which is constructed a 'protective belt of auxiliary hypotheses' (Lakatos op. cit.: 48). Lakatos maintains that:

The negative heuristic specifies the 'hard core' of the programme which is 'irrefutable' by the methodological decision of its proponents: the positive heuristic consists of a partially articulated set of suggestions or hints on how to change, develop the 'refutable variants' of the research programme, how to modify, sophisticate, the 'refutable' protective belt.

(Op. cit.: 50)

What we are looking at, here, is a set of methodological rules, precisely defined, which allow us to differentiate between what Lakatos refers to as 'progressive' and 'degenerating' research programmes. As suggested by the first of our quotations above (op. cit.: 32), for Lakatos a research programme is progressive 'if it results in some corroborated excess empirical content; that is, as long as its theoretical growth anticipates its empirical growth, i.e. as long as it keeps predicting novel facts with some success; it is *degenerating* when it does not' (Bhaskar 1989: 32, emphasis in original).

The significance for us of Lakatos' methodology of scientific research programmes is that it provides a sophisticated means by which to evaluate the 'relative merit of theories by virtue of their success in explaining the world' (Callinicos op. cit.: 125). This methodology, as Bhaskar makes clear, implies realist ontology: 'For to say that two theories conflict, clash or are in competition presupposes that there is something – a domain of real objects or relations existing and acting independently of their descriptions – *over* which they clash' (Bhaskar 1989: 32, emphasis in original). Callinicos makes this same point a little differently. 'It is only from the standpoint of

our sentences' truth or falsity', he says, 'which depends not on our preferences but the state of the world, that a methodology such as Lakatos'
makes sense' (Callinicos 1989: 125).

Rationality and social structure

This brings us to the question of rationality. Again, here as previously,
there is an element within the objection that is unrefutable because it
represents 'truth content'. In this instance we have the claim that agents
are 'rational actors'. Although left largely unexplicated in the majority
of accounts, this belief is central to the orthodox HRD project, as a
moment's reflection would serve to confirm. The difficulty arises with the
way in which the boundaries of the 'rational', conventionally, are set.

The orthodox, in line with a basic tenet of methodological individualism, and as suggested above, offer a one-dimensional understanding of
'rationality', an 'instrumental rationality' that underpins a utilitarian theory
of action. As Callinicos points out, 'the utilitarian theory of action has had
an enormous influence on modern social theory' (1995: 114).

An illuminating, contemporary critique of this view can be found ranged
across the work of the North American, neo-Hegelian philosopher, Charles
Taylor (see, e.g., Taylor 1964, 1994, 1996). A key feature of Taylor's presentation of the 'modern identity' is that 'the life of production and reproduction, of work and the family, is the main locus of the good life' (1994:
23). Taylor refers to this as the 'affirmation of ordinary life', and conceives
of this in contradistinction to what were, for earlier ages, the 'dominant
distinctions of our civilisation' (ibid.). So,

> The notion that there is a certain dignity and worth in this life
> *requires contrast*; no longer, indeed, between this life and some
> 'higher' activity like contemplation, war, active citizenship, or heroic
> asceticism, but now lying between different ways of living the life
> of production and reproduction.
>
> (Ibid., emphasis added)

Crucially, this ability to contrast between 'the higher, admirable life and
the lower life of sloth, irrationality, slavery or alienation' (ibid.) is seen by
Taylor as an irreducible aspect of human nature. He refers to this as the
definitively human capacity to make 'strong evaluations' (see also Taylor
1996, esp. ch. 1). Taylor contrasts 'strong evaluation' with the notion of
'weak evaluation'. For Taylor,

> In weak evaluation, for something to be judged good it is sufficient
> that it be desired, whereas in strong evaluation there is also a use
> of 'good' or some other evaluative term for which being desired is
> not sufficient; indeed some desires or desired consummations can

be judged as bad, base, ignoble, trivial, superficial, unworthy, and so on.

(Op. cit.: 18)

Taylor refers to the 'weak evaluator' as a 'simple weigher of alternatives' for whom the process of reflection, 'terminates in the inarticulate experience that A is more attractive than B'. The strong evaluator, however, has the 'beginning of a language in which to express the superiority of one alternative'. For the strong evaluator: 'Motivations or desires do not only count in virtue of the attraction of the consummations but also in virtue of the kind of life and the kind of subject these desires properly belong to' (1996: 24–5). The point, here, is that the orthodox reduce, illegitimately, the concept of rationality to fit the notion of 'weak evaluation'. Human agents as strong evaluators, however, conceive of their engagement with the world of work *contrastively*; that is to say, in terms of 'how things ought to be'. This can be seen directly in the case of ELD schemes and in two significant ways. We will have more to say about this below. For the moment we must move to say something on the subject of 'structure'.

Its finest exponent, Sir Karl Popper (e.g. Popper 1972), most precisely defined the central tenet of methodological individualism. For Popper and those who have followed him,

> The task of social theory is to construct and to analyse our sociological models carefully in descriptive or nominalist terms, that is to say, *in terms of individuals*, of their attitudes, expectations, relations, etc. – a postulate, which may be called methodological individualism.

(1972: 136, emphasis in original)

The point at issue is highly significant. It is illuminated by Bhaskar (1989: 70) who quotes Jarvie as recording that, ' "army" is just the plural of "soldier" and all statements about the army can be reduced to statements about the particular soldiers comprising it' (1959: 57). To talk, then, about 'objective interests' or the 'causal efficacy of structures' is to misapprehend, fundamentally, the nature of agents and the world which agents inhabit. We will deal with the question of interests below. Here, we will offer some comments, which will suffice to counter the objection concerning social structures. Let us begin with a thought experiment. Imagine you are a researcher. Your job is to evaluate an ELD scheme in a large organization. In pursuit of that goal you are to undertake a series of interviews. Today you are to interview an employee, a young woman, who has declined to participate in the scheme. How will you begin to explain this reluctance?

Her refusal to participate does not appear to be the product of any physical or mental disability. You learn that she is an avid reader of

76

novels and newspapers, that she has a number of hobbies, and that her experience of school was, on the whole, positive. From her personnel file you have discovered that she has two small children of school age. You ask her whether being a 'working mother' makes participating in the scheme difficult. She agrees that this is the case; all the learning activities have to be undertaken outside working hours, and she sees little enough of the children as it is. This fits the bill; this is your explanation. You have explained the social event, '*in terms of individuals,* of their attitudes, expectations, relations, etc.'. This particular employee does not participate in the scheme because by doing so she would see still less of her children.

It is not, however, a strong explanation. It is a response that uncovers certain important features of an explanation; the desires of agents and the interpretations of states of affairs they make represent elements of an irreducible significance within social scientific explanation. However, to leave the matter there is to leave too much *un*-explained. In order to strengthen the explanation we must move to a consideration of *social relations.* These are not simply the structures of power within the woman's home, family and local community; nor even all of these plus the division of labour within her place of work, but in addition the broader set of gender relations by means of which women's role in society is enforced. We might lengthen this list, but the point is made: there are structural and relational features of the explanation, which are closed to the methodological individualist. Bhaskar makes this point well and is worth quoting at length:

> Society provides the means, media, rules and resources for everything we do. Far from it being the case that, in Mrs. Thatcher's dictum, society doesn't exist, the existence of society is a transcendentally necessary condition for any intentional act at all. It is the unmotivated condition for all our motivated productions. We do not create society – the error of voluntarism. But these structures which pre-exist us are only reproduced or transformed in our everyday activities; thus society does not exist independently of human agency – the error of reification. The social world is reproduced or transformed in daily life. All social structures . . . depend upon or presuppose social relations. . . . The relations into which people enter pre-exist the individuals who enter into them, and whose activity reproduces or transforms them; so they are themselves structures. And it is to these structures of social relations that realism directs our attention – both as the explanatory key to understanding social events and trends and as the focus of social activity aimed at the self-emancipation of the exploited and the oppressed.
>
> (1989: 4)

Interests as real things

The final objection takes issue with the idea of '*material* interests'. This description seems to suggest that 'interests' have an objective existence (e.g. Balbus 1971; Meyerson 1991), an existence beyond the desires and aspirations expressed by individual agents. This allows for the possibility that agents can be wrong about matters concerning their interests. From this point, it is but a short step to the idea of 'false consciousness'. In the eyes of the orthodoxy this is an untenable position.

'The point of the concept of interests', argues Callinicos, 'is to relate an agent's wants to the objective environment on which his or her opportunities for realising those wants depend' (1995: 123). The problem, as the orthodoxy see it, with the view that agents can be mistaken on questions concerning their interests is that such a proposition appears to break 'the connection between wants and interests' (ibid.). The significance of this objection for our argument can not be overemphasized. Our argument for transformation depends upon 'the move or transition from unneeded, unwanted and oppressive to needed, wanted and empowering sources of determination' (Bhaskar 1989a: 6). However, as generations of orthodox commentators have pointed out such a transformation has not, historically, formed a significant part of employees' articulated agendas.

For Kelly to argue in such a way, however, is to miss the obvious point:

> Let us take the familiar argument that most workers are highly motivated to obtain high and steadily rising earnings, job security, and an optimum degree of job satisfaction based on the exercise of skill and self-direction. The salience of these preferences is beyond dispute, having been confirmed in many attitude surveys, and manifested in collective bargaining and strike demands.
>
> (1988: 299–300)

The problem for the orthodoxy, as Kelly makes clear, is that as a result of competitive accumulation a capitalist economy is unable to satisfy these desires for the majority of employees throughout their lives. 'In other words', argues Kelly,

> The inevitability of industrial restructuring by individual firms, and of periodic economic crises, in a society where no agency has the incentive as well as the power to promote 'full employment', will conflict with workers' own preferences for job and income security.
>
> (Ibid.)

We want to say that Kelly's argument suggests an objective conception of interests. This is because, as they are articulated above, they presume 'wants' but the definitive point concerns not the wants as such but the potential for their *realization* within a given set of circumstances. Particularly it points to the contradictions within the mode of capitalist competitive accumulation, which makes impossible the satisfaction of these desires over time. Thus, it can be argued that employees have 'an interest in a type of economic system from which unplanned restructuring and periodic economic crises have been eliminated' (ibid.). By turn, agents' ability to achieve such an end depends on their, 'structural capacities, that is, on the powers they derive from their position in the relations of production' (Callincos 1995: 129). Thus, although we may talk meaningfully only about individuals as having 'wants', and while individual agents may articulate different 'wants', 'their ability to realize them will depend on their shared position in the relations of production' (ibid.).

Methodological issues

'What connections, if any,' asks Bhaskar (1989: 89), 'exist between the human sciences and the project of human emancipation?'. We opened this chapter by positing an indissoluble link between these two. We then moved to offer a sketch of that which we identified as the moral core of that proposition. Following that, and in order to strengthen our case, we examined some possible objections to that set of claims. It is time, now, to draw together our remarks on Bhaskar's philosophy, and where necessary, to expand upon them. The story we will tell represents an abbreviated version of that recounted through Bhaskar's philosophical work. It is not a synopsis or a summary of that work. Rather we will train our attention on that line which Bhaskar articulates, carefully, and which draws together in a single enterprise the goal of scientific enquiry and the project of human self-emancipation.

The social sciences offer us accounts of society that their authors claim to be true. In this, the social sciences are no different to the natural sciences. This is not to claim, however, that the substance of the object studied by social and natural sciences is the same. For the social scientist, society is the object of investigation; this implicates the social scientist, necessarily, in the study of ideas. This is so because the structure of social relations which comprise any society is dependent on the 'skilled accomplishments of active agents' (Bhaskar 1989: 4). This is not to argue that social structures are reducible to the ideas agents have about them; they always have a material dimension. It *is* to argue that whether they are nation-states, churches, workplaces, or whatever, the extent to which social structures are either reproduced or transformed depends upon the ideas agents hold concerning such structures, or their consciousness of them.

It is the case, frequently, that the ideas agents have about some aspect of society and the ideas social scientists have about that aspect conflict. For example, many managers (and the occasional researcher) explain the reluctance of employees to participate in training and development activities by suggesting that workers are lazy, or that they lack commitment, motivation, ambition or self-confidence, or that they have got out of the habit of learning. A realist social scientist, while careful to examine the content of such beliefs would want to include in his or her investigation of this phenomenon an account of such things as the division of labour within the workplace and beyond, the structure of social relations within which the employees and their managers were imbricated and so on. By so doing, the social scientist may well arrive at a different explanation to that offered by the manager.

The point, here, is that the social sciences are defined by what Collier identifies as an 'irreducible, but corrigible, hermeneutic moment' (1994: 178). That is to say, that while the social scientist cannot 'get started' without an understanding of the 'meanings actions had for their agents' it must be allowed that those meanings may represent 'systematic delusions' (ibid.). And that is the case because the social world 'may be opaque to the social agents upon whose activity it depends' (Bhaskar 1989: 4).

Because the social world may be opaque, and because some false beliefs are functional for the continued reproduction of oppressive structures, our realist social scientist cannot be satisfied with offering an explanation that conflicts with another; he or she will be compelled to explain the existence of the false belief in question. As a consequence we may argue, also, that because, *ceteris paribus*, agents who believe that which is true are more free than those who believe that which is false, those institutions that generate and are sustained by false beliefs stand in need of replacement by those that cause true beliefs.

We have gone some way toward establishing the veracity of our claim that social scientific explanation stands in a necessary and irreducible relationship to social emancipation. We must, however, go further. Agents are not only unfree as a result of cognitive ills. Thus, the role of social science is not reducible to the exposure of false beliefs. The 'manifest' of the social sciences must include also

> The explanation of the 'practical ills' of ill-health, misery, repression, and so on; and in between such ills and the cognitive ones, what might be called the communicative ills of deception (including self-deception), distortion and so on.
>
> (Bhaskar 1989: 106)

Two points may be drawn from this quotation. First, the identification of 'practical ills' calls forth the need for 'practical projects' aimed at the resolution of those ills. As Collier (op. cit.) argues this is not simply a matter of 'technical imperatives coming into play'. Rather, the social scientific critique 'may ground *assertoric imperatives*, i.e. *since* you need this, remove that obstacle thus' (1994: 183, emphasis in original). Second, the notion of 'communicative ills' (particularly, though not exclusively self-deception) serves to highlight the need for 'personal liberation'. This is where 'the work of personal liberation is a work of transforming one's emotions by means of an explanatory critique of them' (ibid.). So, emotion and reason, fact and value are inextricably linked theoretically, and practically.

In order to demonstrate more fully the emancipatory potential of this idea, Bhaskar develops a model of depth-rationality, where the levels 'may be regarded as so many ratchets of reason' (1989: 102). Before identifying and discussing these levels it is important to note that they share a common structure. Each conforms to the dictum that to 'explain an event or a regularity is to bring it under a new scheme of concepts, designating the structures, generative mechanisms or agents producing it' (op. cit.: 90). Theory works on pre-existing practices and the ideas associated with them. Because each level shares a common structure each level holds 'emancipatory implications'.

The first two levels Bhaskar defines as 'technical rationality' and 'contextually-situated instrumental rationality'. The first of these refers to the fact that human sciences, like any others, may be used to 'achieve (more or less consciously formulated and justified) ends'. It is, thus, the only kind of rationality recognized by positivistic science. As such it conforms to that identified earlier, after Taylor, as 'weak evaluation'. However, Bhaskar wants to argue that even at the level of instrumental rationality, the human sciences 'are not symmetrically beneficial to the parties involved in relation to domination' (op. cit.: 103). There are two reasons advanced by Bhaskar for this. First, 'explanatory knowledge increases the range of real (non-Utopian) human possibilities which may mean of course decreasing the range of assumed or fancied ones' (ibid.). Second, because knowledge 'appears as a necessary condition for rational emancipation', the 'dominated, exploited . . . or whoever have an *interest* in knowledge' (ibid.).

Level three Bhaskar refers to as 'intra-discursive (non-explanatory) critical rationality'. Here, Bhaskar wants to maintain that all 'the sciences . . . are intrinsically critical, and so evaluative' (op. cit.: 104). The point is made by approving reference to the work of Roy Edgley (1976). The point upon which this claim turns is this: if I accept theory T I am denying the efficacy, validity, or whatever, of other theories that purport to explain the same state of affairs. And, I am denying the validity of those *practices* that are upheld by conflicting theories.

With levels four to six we move toward the kind of explanatory rationality we have discussed above with respect to the manifest of the social sciences. At level four, the level of 'explanatory critical rationality', we have reiterated the view that the specificity of the human sciences is not that they make 'judgements of truth or falsity on beliefs about their object domain', but that for the social sciences that object domain includes beliefs about that domain. Whether or not five and six represent qualitatively distinguishable levels is debatable (Collier op. cit.: 188–9).

It is more likely, as Collier suggests, that these represent 'special cases' of 'explanatory critical rationality' (ibid.). So, level five 'depth-explanatory critical rationality' is illustrated by reference to Marx's *Capital* which has the 'Structure of a triple critique: of theories, of practical consciousness such theories reflect and rationalize, and of the conditions explaining such consciousness' (Bhaskar 1989: 109).

Level six represents an account of the form a 'depth investigation' might take. This is worth dwelling on for a moment. For, although it appears to be fashioned from the practice of psychoanalysis, Bhaskar claims that this idea of a 'depth investigation' is 'a transcendental condition for any human science and hence (at a remove) for any science at all' (op. cit.: 112). We will deal with the special inference one can take from the final clause in the above quotation in a moment. First let us look at the form of investigation advocated by Bhaskar. The rudimentary form that Bhaskar offers is that where two agents conspire in order to arrive at an understanding of a frustration suffered by one of them, and a remedy for it. Thus,

> A depth-investigation may be defined generally as any co-operative enquiry, which includes the agent, into the structure of some presumed set of mechanisms, constituting for that agent an unwanted source of determinations . . . with a view to initiating, preserving or restoring the agent's ability to act and think rationally.
>
> (Op. cit.: 111)

There are two inter-related points of great significance to be emphasized, here. First, the outcome of enlightenment of the kind suggested, here, may be *dissonance* rather than *emancipation*. Second, this is because cognitive emancipation is 'necessary, but insufficient, for full emancipation'. This is demonstrated by 'the example of the slave who knows very well that she is a slave, but remains a slave, unfree' (op. cit.: 112). So, 'cognitive emancipation will in general depend upon non-cognitive (and extradiscursive) conditions' (ibid.).

Why is the 'depth investigation' a 'transcendental condition' for 'any science at all'? The answer to this lies at the heart of our debate. For Bhaskar, science is, first, *work*. It is work undertaken by men and women who have undergone special training, who learn to use dedicated equipment, who develop special skills. It is work done, also, by men and women who have to earn a living by selling their capacity to deploy those skills to an employer. It is work done by men and women who are, therefore, subject to hierarchical managerial relations, who compete for jobs and resources with other men and women engaged in similar pursuits within other scientific establishments, or 'firms'. In short, science is made within the set of social relations inscribed by the same political, economic and ideological pressures as those that define all work within capitalism. Therefore, social scientific investigations into the causal context of discovery are a necessary feature of research work.

These points illuminate the important distinction between arguments and explanations concerned with the 'ameliorations of states of affairs' and 'those concerned with the transformation of structures'. Emancipation-enhancing ameliorations are not difficult things to imagine. Through participating in an ELD scheme, an employee learns to speak Spanish. As a result of knowing the language she experiences a greater sense of freedom on her annual holiday in Spain; in addition this raise in the stock of her knowledge serves to increase her self-confidence; moreover she is encouraged to exercise this enhanced self-confidence through a greater level of participation in the trade union which she has come to recognize as instrumental in winning the ELD scheme for her and her colleagues. By participating in trade unions sponsored education activities she comes to see more closely the oppressive nature of her workplace experience.

She is not, however, emancipated. She is in a position analogous to that of the 'slave who knows very well that she is a slave, but remains a slave, unfree'.

Empirical context

There is no one method of realist enquiry. Any realist methodology must, however, encompass certain principles that have their origins in the realist ontology described above. Development of a realist methodology in the field of HRD must also confront the primary objective of research: to facilitate self-emancipation through the recognition of objective interests on the part of employees. We begin this section with an outline of some basic principles of realist enquiry. Using evidence from research carried out in two very different organizations we will illustrate the model and develop some aspects of a self-critique. This last, important point will be taken up, again, in our concluding section.

The aim of realist enquiry is to identify and explain the causal powers inherent in social objects and to show how these powers generate particular effects. The key to this process is the use of abstract modelling. We will offer a rudimentary model of this process. In sum, real social objects consist of a variety of emergent properties, each of which can be separated out and examined through abstract thought. These abstractions can then be merged back into concepts that embody the concrete nature of the object from which it has been abstracted, and which illuminates the causal powers that emanate from concrete objects.

There are, however, a number of sub-issues concerning the process of abstraction that must be borne in mind. First, the nature of an object and its causal powers are internally related. If the nature of the object changes, then so will its powers. It is for this reason that realist social theory is concerned with explanation rather than prediction. Second, because of the stratified nature of the social world, abstract realist modelling is multi-layered. To identify the causal processes that link phenomena it is necessary to explore the interplay between the emergent powers of both structures and agents. Third, because the causal powers of a social object amount to more that the sum of its parts, that is because social systems are more than an aggregation of individual members, it is necessary to ensure that abstraction does not entail desegregation at the conceptual level.

A final issue concerning realist abstract modelling is the need to explain the relationship between the concrete object and its theoretical abstraction, specifically between empirical and rational claims to truth. According to the realist position the world consists of real objects, which possess real causal powers. These objects and causal powers exist independently of our knowledge of them. Independent reality is, therefore, the primary generator of knowledge. The realist position also states, however, that social objects possess real causal powers regardless of our knowledge or understanding of them. In order to describe these powers we must invoke theoretical concepts. Thus, realist social theory must adjudicate between the empirical and the theoretical. An effective way of doing this is to draw on Sayer's (1992) distinction between real objects and thought objects. He suggests that to overcome the dichotomy between empiricism and rationalism we must ensure that thought objects contain empirical statements. Thus, when constructing an abstract model of social reality we must ensure that theoretical concepts are grounded in concrete reality.

To illustrate the process of abstract realist modelling, the chapter draws on previous research carried out by the authors of this chapter. This research investigated the effects of ELD programmes on participants' attitudes to learning in two case-study organizations. The evidence thus meets the realist principle of comparison between different social contexts. By isolating the causal powers of ELD schemes in specific organizations we can best identify how such schemes might constrain and/or facilitate self-emancipation through the recognition of objective interests on the part of employees.

In order to interrogate the extent to which ELD programmes can facilitate this process we must first identify the emergent properties of various schemes and the causal powers they engender. We begin this process by describing the key concrete features of ELD programmes, which are then combined into internally related concepts that form the basis of the abstract theoretical model. The key features identified from previous research refer to three significant dimensions: (1) the formal aims and objectives of programs; (2) the involvement of a range of stakeholders; (3) the range of learning activities included in the scheme.

The formal aims and objectives put forward by employers range from 'giving something back to employees', fostering loyalty and commitment, overcoming resistance to training and engendering a 'learning culture'. In the majority of organizations, these aims and objectives are mixed and a variety of rationales for adopting this approach are articulated. While holding to Bhaskar's proposal that all learning aids the oppressed it is, nevertheless, possible to conceptualize these rationales into those that give most benefit to the organization and those that give most benefit to the employee.

The involvement of stakeholders refers to the balance of management, personnel and trade union representatives on steering committees, and whether the scheme coordinators are located in managerial or non-managerial sectors of the workforce. It is the structure of the social relations within which the scheme is enmeshed. Abstraction of these concrete features allows us to conceptualize schemes as either management led or genuinely employee led. Finally, the scope of learning activities allowed for by the schemes range from an open/inclusive model wherein any activity (excluding sport) which is not work-related is permissible, to a closed/exclusive model. As with aims and objectives, these concrete features can be conceptualized in terms of their bias towards the organization or the employee.

Running parallel to the emergent properties of ELD programmes is the agency of participants. When discussing participants we stress the definition of agency put forward earlier in the chapter. That is, a conceptualization of agency as 'praxis' which is invoked by humans who possess the capacity to reflect on not only their actions, but also on their motives. As suggested above, this conception of agency draws on Taylor's (op. cit.) distinction between weak and strong evaluation. There is also a requirement here to bring the notion of interests into our analysis. We have argued that actors have objective interests that result from their relationship to social structures. So, the aim of any investigation into the causal powers of agency should interrogate how agents evaluate their wants and desires in the context of objective workplace interests.

The first ELD case study is a small to medium-sized healthcare insurance company. Situated in a northern city which has twisted in the sharp wind of what is often referred to, euphemistically, as 'industrial re-structuring', this is a modern firm, which attempts to portray an image of a 'caring company'. The architecture of the place speaks a modern language of 'open-ness'. The open-plan office space is separated from the corridors by floor to ceiling glass walls. The firm uses a variety of equally modern-sounding techniques to reinforce this claim such as 'team development days' and 'employee development days'. There is no trade union. Our fieldwork, here, comprised a one-to-one interview with the group planning manager (GPM) and a planned series of three group-discussion sessions with participants in the scheme. As with all such group discussion we undertake, these were conducted on a semi-structured basis. Our optimum number of participants in such groups would be six to nine. Each group member would be briefed via an invitation to attend which would outline the nature of the subjects we wished to discuss with them. In fact, here (not unusually) our groups were reduced to two in response to the 'pressures of work'.

Responsibility for staff development lies with the GPM who is well versed in the discourse of 'holistic management techniques' and who communicates a serious attitude towards professional staff development. All talk of creating a desire for learning and personal development masks, however, a desire to use ELD to bring about a specific set of business benefits. This bias towards the organization becomes more pronounced when the menu of sanctioned learning activities is taken into account. The company allows only two activities, Tai Chi and Italian. The former activity is deemed to benefit the business because it helps staff overcome the high-pressure nature of their work. The latter activity, it is believed, will benefit the firm if and when it moves into European markets. The involvement of stakeholders in ELD at this firm is limited. The scheme is run by the GPM who also acts as co-ordinator.

The generative effects of the above emergent properties have been to create a prescriptive 'top-down' scheme of which participants have little ownership. The scheme is, quite obviously, not employee-led and it runs contrary to the ethos of ELD. Participants do not associate the scheme with notions of personal development, and the majority expresses a total ignorance of the principles of ELD. Many believed the term 'ELD' refers to, specifically, Tai Chi and Italian. The distorted version of ELD at this firm generates perceptions amongst staff that ELD is simply another management initiative aimed at increasing their motivation and commitment.

It would be tempting to argue, in conclusion, that the scheme does nothing to promote workplace democracy (although this was never really the aim). In a formal sense this would be true. However, by employing Bhaskar's model of depth rationality we are able, conceptually, to rescue the good without sugaring the pill. In particular, we would draw the reader's attention to Bhaskar's contention that the processes through which knowledge is generated 'are not symmetrically beneficial to the parties involved in relation to domination'. We would highlight two points with respect to this insight. First, although the ELD programme in question did not heighten, directly, the level of social control the participants were able to exercise over their work activity, the impact of the learning on individual participants was positive for them insofar as it expanded the bounds of their knowledge. Second, their participation in the scheme as constituted by their GPM, and their subsequent participation in the focus group discussion may well have served to facilitate a clearer-eyed view of the real motivations for the introduction of the scheme. Such a conclusion, though speculative, is warranted *theoretically* on acceptance of Taylor's conception of 'strong evaluation'. Such a conclusion also serves to undermine the orthodox notion of 'mutuality' that pictures all learning as mutually beneficial to both employers and employees. As suggested above, it may cast, also, a long shadow across associated fancies concerning the so-called 'motivational effects' of ELD schemes.

The second organization is a Labour-run city council. The council serves a small northern city. Historically the city has been protected from the level of unemployment suffered by some of its near neighbours by the particular configuration of industry within its bounds. Most recently a burgeoning tourist trade has offset the worst effects of recession. Here, ELD is open to employees in lower-level manual, craft and administrative grades. The formal objectives of this scheme are biased towards the employee, and are articulated as 'encouragement of individuals to take control of their own learning', 'to continually develop', 'to increase self-esteem and self confidence', and 'to create a culture of lifelong learning'. This bias towards the employee is further reflected in the views of the scheme's administrator who suggests that it be also aimed at encouraging 'citizenship' amongst employees. The structure of our fieldwork, here, was as follows: one-to-one interviews with 'expert witnesses' were run alongside group discussions, some comprising participants and others for managers. One novel method employed at city council was the 'post-cards from the learning zone'. We used these in order to encourage participants, unaccustomed to communicating through the formal medium of writing, to say something personal and meaningful about their learning experience.

A variety of stakeholders are involved in the city council's ELD programme. A steering group comprising representatives from personnel, Unison and learning advisers run the scheme. This last group represents a potentially significant force within the scheme. Identified on the basis of their communication skills, their knowledge of the workplace and the workforce, and their commitment to learning, these learning advisers are deemed to offer an impartial, alternative source of advice and guidance to that available via line management. The employee-oriented demeanour of this programme is further enhanced by the open/inclusive interpretation of learning that includes any non-sporting activity that is not work-related.

The combined effects of these emergent properties of the city council's ELD programme have been to generate an inclusive and employee-led scheme. The involvement of those managers charged with a responsibility for running and developing the programme has been geared toward facilitation rather than control. The benefits to the city council are ambiguous and diffuse. In part this is due to the factors internal to the scheme that have been adumbrated above. We must also, however, make reference to a broader range of factors.

The impact of organizational restructuring that resulted from the council's switch to unitary status and the fears and uncertainties this process generated cannot be discounted. Indeed, this restructuring and its entailments can be seen to feed more or less directly into a process of strong evaluation. Even among those who elected to participate there was a more or less precisely articulated concern regarding an employer who speaks of 'cuts' and leaves vacant positions unfilled and so on, and who, on the other hand is willing, apparently, to give away money for all manner of odd-sounding activities. Surely, the message seemed to be, this is not how things ought to be?

On the positive side empirical evidence, generated especially via the postcards, seemed to indicate strong evaluation of a different kind with respect to the learning experience. Thus, at the outset of their chosen course of study, many participants expressed feelings of apprehension:

> First session – nervous, hadn't done any further education for years.

> Before I started my course I felt a little apprehensive. After I felt much more confident and relaxed.

> Everybody knew someone on the course. Several were 'old hands' so I felt a bit out on a limb. Have never done pottery before so I found I needed to concentrate, but I find this beneficial to me.

> Before the session I felt excited and a little nervous.

That they persevered in the face of uncertainty and discomfort indicates a commitment to a particular view of that which is 'good', 'worthwhile', 'worth striving for' and so on. This indicates, by turn, that agents are thinking contrastively and, hence, in terms of strong evaluation. And, the benefits of this for participants are evident from postcards posted post-learning:

> The exam was easier than I thought, a real feel good factor, and great for my children to see *me* having exams as well as them. Made me feel confident to apply for a management job.

> It has given me a lot more confidence and I feel much happier in myself.

> The one thing that sticks in my mind about the course is the sense of satisfaction and accomplishment I felt.

> Felt like my employer was taking an interest in my development.

The question for employers is what to do with this enhanced self-confidence, this willingness to learn and participate in the organization? Our experience suggests that this is where amelioration runs up against the tyranny of structure. For, the very fanfare which signals, proudly, the requirement to produce a different type of employee is played on the same instrument which calls for a reduction in labour costs, for 'efficiencies', for 'out-sourcing' and 'downsizing'. Thus, the newly knowledgeable, clear-sighted and confident employee is contained within the familiar grip of a low-status, low-skill, low-pay job. The two things that seem to have increased are the levels of uncertainty with regard to the future, and the degree of effort required to exhaust one's responsibility to the employer. Thereby, the first step is taken in a process wherein the lay (or proto-scientific) discourse of 'us versus them' to which these workers have long had intuitive access is raised to the level of theoretical understanding. And, by such means are the sources of indignity re-forged into the tools of freedom.

Conclusions and key learning points

If research into HRD is not a scientific endeavour, then what kind of enterprise is it? If the narratives that researchers generate make no 'truth claims' then what *is* their currency? If they represent nothing other than the 'good news stories' required, with good reason, by the powerful élites who have a vested interest in the stability of the status quo, how do they differ from propaganda pure and simple? If, on the other hand, they claim to be something other than 'good new stories' we need to know how analysis proceeds in the absence of rational, scientific criteria. If it is difficult to imagine how systematic analysis is possible under such conditions, it is well nigh impossible to conceive of a constituency who would take seriously the prescriptions born of studies that renounce all claims to scientific rigour. Our argument has been that investigations into the development of human agency within the workplace can and ought to be carried out in a scientific fashion. And, we have tried to make plain what this means in theory and practice.

Given that, for the adherents of positivism appeals to scientificity are synonymous with claims to value-neutrality, we opened our account with an attempt to demonstrate the internal, irreducible connection that holds between fact and value with reference to what we referred to as the moral core of our position. The key idea, here, is that of 'human, self-emancipation'. We used the short-hand term 'praxis' as a means of *denaturalizing* the notion of 'work'. We did this in order to make clear the fact that human emancipation is not a mystical, other-worldly, or 'higher' activity in the first instance; rather, it is work as fully conscious activity. It is the work of transformation. We have argued, therefore, that research into HRD issues is, of necessity, research into the conditions of human emancipation in work.

Why is praxis the 'work of transformation'? The answer to that question is simple to articulate: because emancipation cannot be achieved within existing structures. Poverty, homelessness, chronic unemployment, tedious and uncertain work, exploitation and generalized oppression are not the contingent effects of an 'unrestrained' or 'liberal capitalism', they are integral to capitalism *per se* (Barratt Brown and Radice 1996). One cannot hope, rationally, to transcend the impact of oppressive structures through reforms dictated by the logic of those structures.

The recognition of these propositions does not mark, necessarily, a happy realization for the researcher in HRD. For, such recognition implicates our researcher in a potentially conflictual relationship with employers and other powerful, vested interests who fund research activity, and stand guard over points of access to research subjects. There is, then, an imperative on the researcher to make alliances, to develop research agendas and practices which take into account, in Geras' words quoted earlier, 'the *social interests and movements* that can conceivably be coupled with or become attached to the ideals and imperatives in question'.

Authentic social scientific research into HRD issues is not merely politically difficult; it presents, also, theoretical complexity of a high order, and significant problems of an empirical kind. We have said something about this last pair above. Here, we want to emphasize these points which emerge from reflection on Bhaskar's idea of the 'depth investigation'. Such an investigation, the reader will recall, is one which is concerned to expose, 'an unwanted source of determinations . . . with a view to initiating, preserving or restoring the agent's ability to act and think rationally' (1989: 111). We can divide these 'unwanted determinations' into two broad categories, the psychological and the sociological. Given that in cases concerning HRD issues it is probable that determinations of both types will be involved, interdisciplinary research teams ought to be the order of the day. Our own research demonstrates the limitations of working in single discipline teams.

The reader will recall, also, that such investigations represent 'co-operative enquiry, which includes the agent' (ibid.). Obviously, a co-operative endeavour of this kind requires the careful building of high levels of trust. Such trust does not come cheap, either in effort or resources. Our empirical work, again, provides an example of the boundaries one encounters when empirical work is time constrained. We have been limited, mostly, to one shot group work conducted within the workplace. Thus, we have been unable to move beyond the orthodox 'researcher/subject' model. Moreover, the physical location of the encounter is, for agents, the site of 'power-drenched relationships'.

Some indication of the possibilities, which emerge when empirical studies of this kind are developed, can be gained from the work, already cited, by Sennett and Cobb in the northern United States (Sennett and Cobb 1997). Other examples of work which witnesses the rewards of high-trust research relationships would include that undertaken by Paul Willis among young working-class males (Willis 1977) and the seminal study of the coal community by Dennis *et al.* (1969).

That, then, is our argument and the sum of that which we hope you will take from it. As a parting salute we offer you the following quotation. It is an extension of the extract from Noam Chomsky we included in our introduction, and it goes like this:

> This, then, is the real challenge of the twentieth century . . . : to create social forms that will realize the humanistic conception of Man [*sic*]. And it is the responsibility of teachers, of citizens, and

of ourselves, to liberate the creative impulse and to free our minds
and the minds of those with whom we deal from the constraints of
authoritarian ideologies so that this challenge can be faced in a
serious and open-minded way.

(1991: 32)

References

Ainley, P. and Rainbird, H. (1999) *Apprenticeship: Towards a New Paradigm of Learning*, London: Kogan Page.

Archer, M. (1995) *Realist Social Theory: the Morphogenetic Approach*, Cambridge: Cambridge University Press.

Balbus, I. (1971) 'The concept of "interest" in Pluralist and Marxian analysis', *Politics and Society*, 1(2).

Barratt Brown, M. and Radice, H. (1996) *Democracy Versus Capitalism: a Response to Will Hutton with Some Old Questions for New Labour*, Nottingham: Spokesman.

Bhaskar, R. (1989a) *Reclaiming Reality: a Critical Introduction to Contemporary Philosophy*, London: Verso.

—— (1989b) *The Possibility of Naturalism: a Philosophical Critique of the Contemporary Human Sciences (2nd edn) Hassocks*, Hemel Hempstead: Harvester.

Blaug, R. (1999) 'Outbreaks of democracy', in L. Panitch and C. Leys.

Bloch, E. (1986) *The Principle of Hope*, Cambridge, MA: MIT Press.

Bourdieu, P. (1988) *Homo Academicus*, Cambridge: Polity Press.

—— (1993) *Sociology in Question*, London: Sage.

Braverman, H. (1974) *Labor and Monopoly Capital: the Degradation of Work in the Twentieth Century*, New York: Monthly Review Press.

Callinicos, A. (1989) *Marxism and Philosophy*, Oxford: Oxford University Press.

—— (1995) *Making History: Agency, Structure and Change in Social Theory*, Cambridge: Polity Press.

Chomsky, N. (1991) 'Towards a humanistic conception of education and work', in D. Corson (ed.) *Education for Work: Background to Policy and Curriculum*, Clevedon: Multilingual Matters.

Collier, A. (1994) *Critical Realism: an Introduction to Roy Bhaskar's Philosophy*, London: Verso.

Dennis, N., Henriques, F. and Slaughter, C. (1969) *Coal Is Our Lives: an Analysis of a Yorkshire Mining Community*, London: Tavistock Publications.

DfEE (1998) The *Learning Age: a Renaissance for a New Britain*, London: HMSO.

Edgley, R. (1976) 'Reason as dialectic', *Radical Philosophy*, 15.

Fryer, R.H. (1997) *Learning for the Twenty-First Century: First Report of the National Advisory Group for Continuing Education and Lifelong Learning*, London: DfEE.

Geras, N. (1990) *Discourses of Extremity: Radical Ethics and Post-Marxist Extravagances*, London: Verso.

Hamblett, J. and Holden, R. (1998) 'To boldly go? Questioning orthodox accounts of employee development', *Human Resource Development International* (July) 1: 2.

Hamblett, J. and Holden, R. (1999) 'Workplace learning: our mutual friend?' *Employee Relations Review*, 9 (June).

ILO (International Labour Organisation) (1996) 'Women swell ranks of working poor', Press Release, ILO/96/25, Geneva.

Jarvie, I. (1959) *Universities and Left Review.*

Kelly, J. (1988) *Trade Unions and Socialist Politics*, London: Verso.

Lakatos, I. (1995) *The Methodology of Scientific Research Programmes: Philosophical Papers, Vol. 1*, J. Worrall and G. Currie (eds), Cambridge: Cambridge University Press.

Locke, J. (1959) *An Essay Concerning Human Understanding*, New York: AC Fraser.

Meszaros, I. (1979) *Marx's Theory of Alienation*, Manchester: Merlin Press.

Meyerson, D. (1991) *False Consciousness*, Oxford: Clarendon Press.

Panitch, L. and Gindin, S. (1999) 'Transcending pessimism: re-kindling socialist imagination', in L. Panitch and C. Leys.

Pantich, L. and Leys, C. (eds) (1999) *Necessary and Unnecessary Utopias: Socialist Register 2000*, Rendlesham: Merlin Press.

Popper, K.R. (1972) *The Poverty of Historicism*, London: Routledge and Kegan Paul.

Resnick, M. (1997) *Turtles, Termites and Traffic Jams: Explorations in Massively Parallel Microworlds*, Cambridge, MA: MIT Press.

Roberts, J. (1999) 'Philosophising the everyday: the philosophy of praxis and the fate of cultural studies', *Radical Philosophy* 98 (November/December).

Sayer, A. (1992) *Method in Science: A Realist Approach*, London: Routledge and Kegan Paul.

Searle, J. (1999) *Mind, Language and Society: Philosophy in the Real World*, London: Wiedenfeld and Nicholson.

Sennett, R. and Cobb, J. (1977) *The Hidden Injuries of Class*, Cambridge: Cambridge University Press.

Taylor, C. (1964) *The Explanation of Behaviour*, London: Routledge and Kegan Paul.

—— (1994) *Sources of the Self: the Making of the Modern Identity*, Cambridge: Cambridge University Press.

—— (1996) *Human Agency and Language: Philosophical Papers, Vol. 1*, Cambridge: Cambridge University Press.

Webb, R.K. (1955) *The British Working Class Reader 1780–1848*, London: George Allen and Unwin.

Willis, P. (1977) *Learning to Labour*, London: Saxon House.

5

TOWARDS EVIDENCE-BASED HRD PRACTICE

Bob Hamlin

Aims and contribution

This chapter is about the expertise that HRD practitioners require to maximize their contribution to organizational effectiveness. It presents arguments in support of an evidence-based approach to HRD practice and promotes the idea that HRD practitioners should endeavour to use evidence derived from good research to inform, shape, measure and evaluate their professional practice. A case is also presented for closer collaboration between HRD scholars and HRD practitioners as a means to achieve mutually desired research goals and to create research-informed HRD interventions that not only improve and enhance the practice of HRD in organizations, but also advance the field of HRD knowledge. For this purpose (and in accordance with the thinking of McLagan (1989), Marsick and Watkins (1994) and Swanson (1995) in the USA, of Simon and Streumer (2001) in the Netherlands and of the University Forum for HRD (1995) and Walton (1999) in the UK) the concept of HRD has been taken as comprising four key components. These are as follows: 'training and development', which includes management training and development; 'career development'; 'organisation development'; and 'learning', which includes organizational learning. It is assumed that the majority of readers are actively engaged in some way with organizational change and development. It is also assumed that readers will be engaged in academic research, possibly as part of a Master's degree in HRD or HRM or other field of study within the broad subject area of organization and management, whilst many more readers may be doing research without knowing it.

Theoretical context

What is meant and understood by 'evidence-based' HRD practice?

A first requirement is to set out what is meant and understood by the term 'evidence-based' practice within the field of organization and management in general and HRD in particular. This understanding has been influenced strongly by the developments over the past eight years or so of the theory and practice of *evidence-based medicine* (EBM). Most medical schools now train physicians in the skills of evidence-based practice. EBM originated in the UK in the early 1970s as part of an agenda first propounded by Cochrane (1972) for improving the effectiveness and efficiency of medical practice in Britain. This agenda was taken up by the McMaster Medical School (1992) in Ontario, Canada, who coined the term 'evidence-based medicine'. Its Evidence-Based Medicine Group (1996) has since defined EBM as 'the collection, interpretation, and integration of valid important and applicable patient-reported, clinician-observed, and research-derived evidence . . . to improve the quality of clinical judgements and facilitate cost-effective health care' (see Tanner 1999).

Another important influence has been the fact that an evidence-based approach is now seen as relevant to and well established in most of the other professions and client groups comprising healthcare provision in Britain besides medicine, including therapy, nursing, mental health and child health (see Bury and Mead 1998).

Sackett *et al.* (1996) define evidence-based medicine as the 'conscientious, explicit and judicious use of current best evidence in making decisions about the care of individual patients'.

In the context of EBM the term 'judicious use' means balancing the risks and benefits of alternative sources of evidence including research evidence, clinical expertise, beliefs and values of therapists and patients, clinical assessment of the patient and the patient's preferences. Hence evidence encompasses a wide range of information sources of which research evidence is just one. However, the use of the term 'best evidence' primarily refers to scientific evidence derived from research which Gray (1997) describes as falling into two categories, namely:

1   that which increases the understanding of health, ill health and the process of healthcare;
2   that which enables an assessment of the interventions used in order to try to promote health, to prevent ill health or improve the process of healthcare.

The former concentrates on the development of the knowledge base from which new ideas can be created for evaluation using the second category of research. It also provides contextual information against which the evidence arising from the latter should be interpreted. The second category of research is primarily concerned with the evaluation of ideas in practice. In America the clinical practice guidelines issued by the Agency for Health Care Policy and Research (AHCPR) have been designed 'to assist practitioner and patient decisions about appropriate health care for specific clinical conditions'. The guidelines suggest that best evidence should basically consist of either the 'findings from research of varying designs and thus of varying scientific strength ranging from, for example, a "meta-analysis" to an individual descriptive study, or the consensus of experts' (Stetler *et al.* 1998). Consensus is recognized as a lower form of evidence compared to empirical research and thus of lower strength, but it is evidence none the less. In Britain the type of evidence used in the practice of EBM can vary in scientific strength ranging typically from 'a systematic review of multiple well designed randomized controlled trials' to 'the opinions of respected authorities based on clinical evidence, descriptive studies or reports of expert committees' (Sackett 1997). However, Gray (op. cit.) argues that 'qualitative or survey study designs' can be more appropriate for answering many of the research questions associated with evidence-based practice in the other areas of healthcare provision. Furthermore Popay and Williams (1998) present very strong arguments for using evidence derived from qualitative research which they claim 'make important and unique contributions' to evidence-based healthcare.

Having explored the various debates and interpretations Bury and Mead (1998: 11) provide a working definition which they consider more helpful to therapists applying evidence-based practice in the broader field of healthcare, as follows:

> Evidence-based practice is the conscientious, explicit and judicious use of current best evidence in making decisions about the care of individual patients, integrating individual clinical expertise with the best available external clinical evidence from systematic research.

From an American perspective on the application of evidence-based practice and the role of nursing leadership in a particular healthcare setting, Stetler *et al.* (1998: 48–9) found that often 'the best evidence of well-established research findings was not available to substantiate various clinical, managerial or educational decisions'. Hence, in a similar way to Bury and Mead, they have produced a helpful summary definition 'as part of [*their*] realistic goal to enhance professional, evidence-based nursing practice' as follows:

> Evidence-based nursing de-emphasizes ritual, isolated and unsystematic clinical experiences, ungrounded opinions and tradition as a basis for nursing practices ... and stresses instead the use of research findings and, as appropriate, quality improvement data, other operational and evaluation data, the consensus of recognized experts and affirmed experience to substantiate practice ... inherent to evidence-based practice are critical thinking and research utilisation competencies ... and the ability to use research as a process.

Just as Stetler *et al.* view evidence-based practice as applying to managerial and educational decisions as well as to clinical decisions, Bury and Mead (1998) claim evidence-based healthcare in Britain goes beyond

EBM. Its scope includes evidence-based commissioning/purchasing, evidence-based policy, evidence-based patient choice and evidence-based management.

Various calls for evidence-based management have been made in the British literature. For example, although evidence-based medicine can draw on more clear-cut scientific research than that available in the field of management, Rosemary Stewart (1998) argues it is still desirable to practice evidence-based management. To her, evidence-based management is an attitude of mind that:

- thinks in terms of evidence for decisions and about the nature of the evidence;
- asks questions such as: what is happening?; how is it happening?; why?; and what are the consequences?;
- is aware of the potential limitations of the different answers; and
- is interested in research to try to find the answers or at least to reduce the ignorance.

She suggests managers need to build a questioning approach into their everyday management practice and encourage the creation of a research culture. However, to develop a research culture requires at least one senior manager to act as a role model.

Axelsson (1998) points out from a broader European perspective that many physicians in many healthcare organizations where large-scale organizational and managerial changes have taken place, have started to ask for empirical evidence on the efficiency and effectiveness of the different organizational models introduced. Drawing on the work of Ham *et al.* (1995) he notes that many healthcare managers and politicians are starting to ask for more scientific knowledge upon which to make their decisions on organizational design. Hence he strongly promotes the idea of an evidence-based approach to healthcare management in order to improve its practice as well as to stimulate research on the organization and management of healthcare. Referring to the work of Altman (1994) he draws attention to the fact that the practice of EBM has exposed various gaps in the medical knowledge base, with a large proportion of published medical research lacking either relevance or sufficient methodological rigour to be reliable enough to answer clinical questions. However, the identification of such gaps has been helpful in cumulatively generating new medical research which has continuously improved the practice of medicine. Encouraged by this he claims that the evidence-based approach can be applied to the practice of management in general and to healthcare management in particular. However, there needs to be some modification in approach for two main reasons. First, because there are important methodological differences between medical research and management research: the former can be seen as being quantitative and empirical in character with the latter being more qualitative and pheno-menological. Second, because of the significant differences and variability in the educational and professional backgrounds of managers compared to physicians. Taking these differences into consideration Axelsson (op. cit.: 313) takes evidence-based management as meaning that managers should examine the scientific basis for their practice by learning to search and critically appraise empirical evidence from management research as a basis for their decisions. This means they should be asking questions such as the following. What do we know empirically about different aspects of organization and management? What is the scientific state of this knowledge? What is the effectiveness and efficiency of different models of management? What is the experience of these models from different organizations?

These questions are similar to those posed by Rosemary Stewart and have important implications for both management practice and manage-ment research. Recognizing the practice of evidence-based management needs time and that many managers may say they have no time to spare for it, Axelsson also points out that that is what many physicians said when EBM was first introduced. However, they found very soon that 'they could improve the quality of their decisions so much [by adopting an EBM approach] that it was well worth the time and effort'. Today evidence-based practice is a widespread feature of medical and healthcare practice in the USA, Canada, Britain and many other European countries, and is beginning to be applied also in healthcare management and healthcare education. This being the case it should be possible for an evidence-based approach to be used to improve the practice of management in general, and also human resource development in particular.

The need for an evidence-based approach in HRD, together with ex-amples of the benefits to be derived from practising various forms of it, are set out in subsequent sections of this chapter. At this juncture it seems appropriate to provide a working definition for evidence-based HRD taking account of the definitions given above for evidence-based medi-cine, healthcare and healthcare management respectively. This seems justified given that modern day HRD professionals operate very much in the role of internal or external consultants, as do physicians and thera-pists. Additionally they are concerned professionally with most aspects of organization and management and many also perform in managerial roles. Furthermore, HRD as a function and process is necessarily a key strand in the practice of management and an important component of the role of the line manager.

Based on what is happening in healthcare and healthcare management, the suggested definition for evidence-based HRD is as follows:

Evidence-based HRD is the conscientious, explicit and judicious use of current best evidence in making decisions about the

97

development of individuals, groups and organizations, integrating individual HRD practitioner expertise with the best available external evidence derived from systematic research.

(Adapted from the Bury and Mead definition of
evidence-based practice in healthcare)

For EBM, best evidence is based on a combination of three dimensions, namely 'research'; 'clinical experience' and 'patient preferences'. Similarly for evidence-based HRD, best evidence could be viewed as being derived from a combination of good-quality research; consensus of recognized professional experts and/or affirmed professional experience that substantiates practice; quality improvement, operational or evaluation data; and the systematic feedback of opinions or preferences of client managers.

For many HRD practitioners the application of evidence-based HRD even at the lowest strength of scientific evidence will likely be an unrealizable goal for reasons outside their control. However, this does not mean they cannot be 'research minded' and build a 'research orientation' into their professional practice. They can and many do adopt what is termed a 'research-informed' approach to practice. A suggested definition for research-informed HRD is as follows: 'Research-informed HRD is the conscientious and explicit use of research findings and the research process to inform, shape, measure and evaluate professional practice' (see Hamlin and Ash 2000). With these in mind, the question begging to be asked is the following: Is there a compelling need for either an evidence-based or research-informed approach to HRD practice? It has been argued elsewhere that evidence-based and/or research-informed practice should be key features at the forefront of initiatives for revitalizing HRD for the new millennium (see Hamlin, Reidy and Priddey 1998). It has also been argued that HRD lacks a sound and sufficient empirical base; that many organizational change and development programmes fail because change agents omit to use the findings from empirical research or to engage with research as part of their change agency practice; and that a gap exists between research and practice (see Hamlin and Stewart 1998). These arguments support the contention that there is a compelling need to move towards evidence-based approaches to HRD practice.

The need for evidence-based and research-informed approaches to HRD practice

Much HRD practice, particularly in the field of management development (MD), is based on little analysis of empirical research into the conditions prevailing in particular organizational contexts. Furthermore, despite a significant body of qualitative research on managerial work that has been reported in the management literature, little has been used to inform management development. This has led to few organizations achieving a proper return on their investments in management development activities, whether conducted off-the-job or on-the-job. As West and Patterson (1998) reveal, in many organizations the HR function (including HRD and MD) has had little impact on the bottom line with managers perceiving it merely as part of the 'tinsel rather than the trunk of the organisational tree'.

Mumford (1997) argues there is a continuing failure on the part of many HRD academics and practitioners, both in business schools and management development training centres, to define and implement their offerings in terms of what managers actually do. Rather, they continue to base their programmes predominantly on the views of classical theorists and modern day management 'gurus', and tend not to adopt or be influenced by the empirical research findings of writers such as Stewart (1982), Mintzberg (1975) and Kotter (1982). Hence much management development is based on inappropriate or obsolete models of management. This view appears to be reinforced by research from the Zenger Miller Group in the USA whose consultants observed 'interesting shifts in practice – although not in theory' (Russ-Eft *et al.* 1996).

Even when management research has been used to inform the content and processes of management development, the studies have often been small-scale and the results 'thin'. For example, although Rosemary Stewart collected diary data from over 100 managers for her work on 'the choices managers make', Mintzberg and Kotter observed and interviewed only small numbers of managers for their respective research studies on the 'fundamental features of managerial life' and the 'realities of what managers do'. As Mumford (op. cit.) claims 'little really is known about management other than generalized statements of managerial work' and that what managers need to be able to do 'is more likely to be specific and contingent than easily generalisable'.

Compared to the American management literature there is in Britain a dearth of reported empirical research into the 'particularities' of management, whether in the private, public or voluntary sector. Thus, in the teaching of management and the development of managers, there has been an over reliance on what is known about management as derived from research carried out in America. For example research carried out and reported in the mid to late 1980s by the author on the criteria of managerial effectiveness within UK secondary schools found reported in the British and American literature only ten directly comparable empirical studies across all other sectors in the British and American literature (see Hamlin 1990; Hamlin and Stewart 1990). Of these, only one was of UK origin, and even this had been a small-scale project. Since that time several household-named organizations in the UK, including BP and NatWest, have carried out research into effective and ineffective management using similar research methods. But few organizations release their research findings into the public domain, and even those that do tend to reveal scant details. Of the small number of empirical research studies that have been added to the British management literature base most have been concerned predominantly with the effectiveness of top managers as opposed to senior, middle and junior managers. (For example see the work of Spurgeon and Flanagan (1997); Alimo-Metcalfe and Alban-Metcalfe (2000, 2001) in the healthcare sector.)

An analysis of more than 100 of the most recent USA leadership studies completed as part of the Zenger Miller empirical research programme into 'what leaders do' at grass roots level, showed that despite its importance there was little agreement on what constitutes leadership (see Russ-Eft *et al.* 1996). Furthermore, a review of five general competency studies carried out by the Zenger Miller researchers revealed no common identification of leadership behaviours. Of the three studies that examined leadership competencies, each defined leadership differently. Moreover, most of the studies were concerned with senior management only, excluding examination of leadership embedded in the roles of middle, junior and first line supervisory managers. From this one can conclude that even in the USA there has been a general lack of empirical management research into the vast majority of management and leadership roles within organizations below senior management level. It is suggested the same applies in the UK and other countries worldwide. This suggestion is supported by Axelsson (1998) who has carried out a wide-ranging review of the history of management research. He concludes that after nearly a hundred years of research on organization and management, the practical knowledge in the field seems to be back almost on the same (*very low*) scientific level as when the research started.

The argument that HRD lacks a sound and sufficient empirical base appears to apply to the much promoted government inspired 'competency approach' to management development in Britain. This approach, spearheaded by the Management Charter Initiative (MCI), has been much criticized (Jacobs 1989; Burgoyne 1990; Stewart and Hamlin 1992, 1993; Tate 1995; Mumford 1997; Woodall and Winstanley 1998). Various commentators have questioned the soundness of the research and the research methods used to derive the competencies (Bates 1995; Stewart and Sambrook 1995; Tate op. cit.). Referring in particular to the MCI management competencies Mumford (op. cit.) argues strongly that insufficient (research) effort has gone into deriving their content. This is supported by Woodall and Winstanley (1998). Highlighting the fact that in general most organizations adopting the competency approach 'find they have to adapt a generic description of competency to their own needs', they stress 'the importance of involving staff in the process of identifying competencies in order to develop ownership and commitment', and suggest 'the language must be that used by managers in every day usage and this is something that needs to be addressed from within the organisation'. But to identify such organization-specific competencies requires some form of internal research. However, this needs to be relevant, robust, and of sufficient academic rigour to secure the 'ownership' and 'commitment' of people within the organization. According to Woodall and Winstanley, 'ownership' and 'commitment' are of paramount importance.

Turning to the organizational development (OD) component of HRD practice, considerable evidence suggests that failure to use 'best evidence' derived from 'good research' in order to influence decision making in professional practice can account for failure in attempts at bringing about beneficial organizational change and development. It appears that the majority of 'down-sizing' and 'delayering' exercises tend to be unsuccessful with few ever achieving the aimed-for goals (Wyatt and Co. 1994; de Meuse, Vanderheiden and Bergamann 1994; Howard 1996; Hussey 1997). Furthermore the majority of TQM and BPR programmes are also unsuccessful with 50 per cent to 70 per cent failing to yield the required improvements or benefits claimed (Schaffer and Thomson 1992; Hammer and Champney 1993, Kearney 1994; Hamel and Prahalad 1994; Wilkinson *et al.* 1993; Coulson-Thomas 1996; Nelson and Coxhead 1997). Regarding culture change the situation is even more bleak with the failure rate running at over 80 per cent in the UK (see IRS 1997). Additionally research suggests that many organization change initiatives fail badly, resulting in unintended consequences that seriously damage the organization and the people within it. (See Marks 1994; Devine and Hirsch 1998; Worrall and Cooper 1997, 1998, 1999, 2000.)

Various commentators have put forward reasons as to why OCD programmes fail. Most causes appear to come from within the organization itself, stemming from what is a general lack of change management know-how and skill on the part not only of many managers, but also of many trainers and developers. In particular, as will be demonstrated, it appears they tend not to take heed of 'received wisdom', or follow 'best practice approaches', or adopt an 'evidence-based/research-informed approach' to managing organizational change and development. However, when they do, as will also be demonstrated later, their change agency is enhanced.

A 'distillation' of 'best practice' relating to the management of change, derived from the change management models offered by a wide and various range of experts, has been extracted (Hamlin 2001a) and presented in the form of a 'Generic Change Management Model', illustrated in Figure 5.1.

Although most change management models described in the management literature are basically sound and have high face validity, in many cases the simplified diagrammatic/summary formats of the models similar to Figure 5.1 can appear overly simplistic and just plain commonsense. Herein lies a potential weakness of change management 'models' and 'prescriptions'. They can be subjected to oversimplification in use, resulting either in the skipping of important steps or a general lack of rigour in the application of each step. From the literature it also appears that a

Stage 1   Diagnose/explore the present state and identify the required future state
Stage 2   Create a strategic vision
Stage 3   Plan the change strategy
Stage 4   Secure ownership, commitment and involvement including top
          management support
Stage 5   Project-manage the implementation of the change strategy and
          sustain momentum
Stage 6   Stabilize, integrate and consolidate to ensure perpetuation of the change

Figure 5.1 A generic change management model
Source: Adapted from Hamlin (2001a)

general lack of change agency expertise is exacerbated by one or more of
the following 'managerial failings'.

Failing 1: Not knowing the fundamental principles of change management

Complacency and ignorance appear to be two of the most significant factors
that contribute to the failure of organizational change programmes. For
evidence of this see, for example, Hammer and Stanton (1995) commenting upon the situation in the USA, and the Royal Society of Arts (1995)
reporting on 'The Role of Business in a Changing World' within the UK
context.

Failing 2: Succumbing to the temptations of the 'quick-fix' and 'simple solutions'

The management literature contains considerable anecdotal and research-
based evidence of this failing. Attention is drawn particularly to the writings
of Kilman (1989), Hussey (1996), Kotter (1996) and Gamblin (1997).

Failing 3: Not fully appreciating the significance of the leadership and cultural aspects of change

Beckhard and Pritchard (1992) discuss in some detail the interdependence of what many expert commentators consider to be the three most
important factors in a fully functioning organization, namely 'leadership',
'culture' and 'the management of change'. Other writers including Hammer
and Stanton (1995), Warrick (1995) and Kotter (1996), commenting from
an American perspective, have demonstrated that failing to give sufficient
attention to the 'leadership' and 'cultural' factors leads to failure. European examples of major transformational change programmes failing because
of insufficient attention being given to the cultural issues have been well
documented. See for example Brooks and Bate (1994), Boonstra and Vink
(1996) and the Industrial Relations Service (1997).

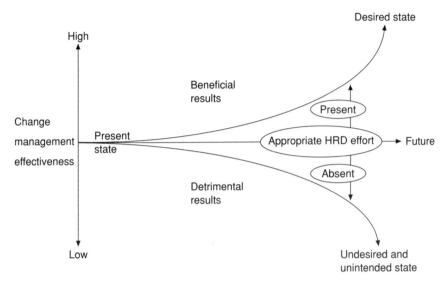

Figure 5.2 The critical contribution of appropriate HRD effort to change
management effectiveness

Source: Adapted from an original model by Stewart and Hamlin (1990). Published also in
Hamlin, B., Keep, J. and Ash, K. (2001) *Organizational Change and Development*, Financial
Times/Prentice Hall. Copyright 2001 Pearson Education Limited. Reprinted by permission
of Pearson Education Limited

*Failing 4: Not appreciating sufficiently the significance of
the people issues*

This can be inferred from the range of undesired, unintended and damaging consequences resulting from badly implemented OCD programmes as the work of Marks (1994) and Worrall and Cooper (1997, 1998, 1999, 2000), suggest. For other evidence see also Hammer and Stanton (1995), Alexander (1991), Hussey (1996), Skilling (1996) and Devine and Hirsch (1998).

*Failing 5: Not knowing the critical contribution that
the Human Resource Development (HRD) function can make to
the management of change*

Implicit in all change is the need for people either to acquire new knowledge, attitudes, skills and habits (KASH) or to redistribute the existing know-how. Clearly this process is an HRD issue. The scale and nature of the HRD effort built into OCD programmes will determine whether or not they succeed. Change can either be brought about beneficially with the organization reaching its desired future state, or detrimentally with the organization suffering unintended, damaging consequences and ending up in an unwanted state, as illustrated in Figure 5.2. For managers to be in control of change they need to be in control of the KASH issues associated with change itself. This means giving sufficient time and attention to the 'soft' HRD (and HRM) aspects of managing the change process. (See Stewart and Hamlin 1990; Stewart 1993 and 1996; Hamlin and Stewart 1998.) More recent writers also claim that HRD is an integral component of change and growth that lies at the heart of managing change. (For example, see Bennett and O'Brien 1994; Grundy 1997; Bruce and Wyman 1998; Walton 1999; Thornhill et al. 2000.)

Unfortunately the failure to incorporate appropriate HRD effort into many change management programmes comes about because of the way trainers and developers are perceived by line managers (for example see Holland and Aitken 1999), and how they perceive themselves. Historically most have operated in roles and positions widely considered of 'lower status' than those of other functional specialists in, for example, finance or marketing. Generally they have lacked 'credibility' in the eyes of line managers. This has not been helped by being part of personnel departments also lacking in credibility because of the dominant focus on administration (Hussey 1997; Herriot 1998; West and Patterson 1998).

Hence many trainers have had little or no access to top management, or experience in positions of significant strategic influence. In many cases the constraints or barriers experienced have been self-induced due to their own narrow understanding of HRD. For over a decade calls have been made in the UK for trainers to become more managerial in orientation, and to develop themselves for roles with strategic influence (Coopers and Lybrand 1985; Barnham, Fraser and Heath 1988; Phillips and Shaw 1989; Stewart and Hamlin 1990). It is encouraging to note that strategic HRD is now emerging as a significant and discrete field of scholarship complementing that of strategic HRM (Thomson and Mabey 1994; Mabey and Salaman 1995; Harrison 1997; Rothwell and Kasanas 1989a and 1989b; Walton 1999; Wilson 1999). However, the majority of trainers and developers will continue to find themselves operating at the margins of organizational life unless they improve their 'credibility' in the eyes of line managers. But this means managers overcoming the five OCD 'failings' outlined above.

As discussed earlier, traditional approaches to manager and management development do not adequately address these 'failings'. In many organizations the management climate is not conducive for trainers and developers to operate strategically as internal management and organization development consultants. This precludes the development of appropriate management development initiatives that could, perhaps, help managers to overcome their 'failings'. Within the field of management and organization development there appears to be a 'vicious circle' in play where the five OCD 'failings' of managers contribute to the 'credibility' problems of HRD practitioners. This leads to a lack of 'appropriate' HRD effort in OCD programmes that fail to trigger managers to question the 'inappropriateness' of the MD programmes on offer, which in turn leads to failure in managers being helped to overcome the five OCD 'failings'.

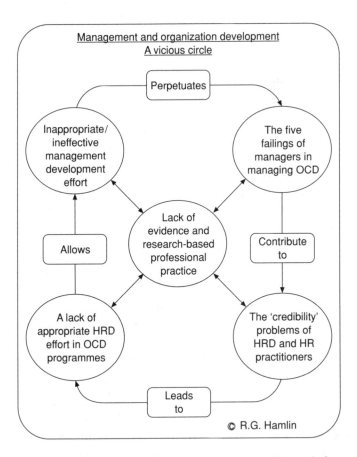

Figure 5.3 Management and organization development: a vicious circle
Source: Bob Hamlin in Hamlin, B., Keep, J. and Ash, K. (2001) *Organizational Change and Development*, Financial Times/Prentice Hall. Copyright 2001 R.G. Hamlin. Used with permission of Pearson Education Limited

And so the 'vicious circle' goes on as illustrated in Figure 5.3. At the heart of this vicious circle is a perceived lack of sufficient evidence-based or research-informed professional practice on the part both of line managers, trainers, developers and other HR professionals.

Evidence suggests those 'evidence-based' approaches to practice, or at least 'research-informed' approaches, need to become essential features of the process of managing organizational change and development if maximum success is to be assured. As Quirke (1995: 175 and 214) observes, 'the use of internal research as an instrument on the corporate dashboard' provides 'continual feedback that allows greater responsiveness' and helps 'to speed up the changing behaviour within organizations'. Several other UK writers have argued the case for research-informed approaches to

HRD including management development and organizational change and development (Jacobs and Vyakarnam 1994; Davies 1996). Similar arguments have been made in the USA. For example, Swanson (1997) exhorts HRD professionals to advance their professional practice by becoming truly expert practitioners through what he calls 'back yard' research, whilst Jacobs (1997) calls for collaborative partnerships between HRD practitioners and HRD scholars for integrating research and practice. Their views are strongly supported by Russ-Eft *et al.* (1997) who present telling arguments encouraging HRD practitioners to use the results of current HRD research in order to enhance their professional practice. Reflective research-informed HRD, enhanced by collaborative partnerships between managers, trainers and developers on the one hand and HRD scholars on the other for producing good internal research, will become increasingly important in the drive for excellence and expert practice in the field of change management.

Implications for HRD/OCD practice

As can be inferred from the foregoing, managers, trainers, developers and all other HR professionals with responsibilities for bringing about organizational change effectively and beneficially, whether or not in collaborative partnership, need to be appropriately skilled to perform the tasks of the change agent. Invariably these are to:

1 diagnose, understand and make sense of the organization;
2 formulate appropriate change strategies;
3 implement these strategies effectively and beneficially;
4 critically evaluate the effectiveness of their own contribution;
5 draw lessons by reflecting upon their own professional practice.

A detailed discussion of these five tasks have been presented elsewhere (Hamlin and Davies 2001), but it suffices here just to acknowledge the fact that these tasks of the change agent are complicated by virtue of the increasing complexities, contradictions and paradoxes associated with organizational life and the processes of organizational change. Hence change agents need to be very selective in the theoretical approaches they use to inform and shape their practice, and they need also to build into their organizational change and development programmes sufficient time for review and reflection. From such reflection new theoretical insights may be gained as to why particular aspects of change programmes either succeed or fail. Furthermore, new ways of approaching the problems of change may emerge through the development of new 'ideas or theories' informed by the practice. Additionally, as change agents they need to incorporate research activities as part of their professional practice for the purpose of better informing, shaping and evaluating what they do. Conducting internal research is itself a process which can help make change occur. It can, when conducted with appropriate academic rigour, lead to fundamental issues concerning the effective functioning of the organization being brought to the surface and being confronted. As a result people are more likely to admit in public both the effective and ineffective features of organizational life including their own individual performance or behaviour deficiencies, and to advance personal 'theories', reactions and opinions which otherwise would not be revealed. Such research gives HRD/OD practitioners the evidence required 'to hold a mirror up to the organization' that will 'reflect accurately' the truth and realities of organizational life (see also Bruce and Wyman 1998).

However, the question needs to be asked as to how evidence-based and research-informed approaches might become commonplace features of HRD practice, particularly in the area of strategic organizational change.

Implementation of evidence-based and research-informed HRD practice

For reasons already discussed, it is unlikely that an 'evidence-based' approach to HRD can ever emulate the model of Evidence-Based Medicine. However, it should at least be possible to emulate the various evidence-based approaches successfully and beneficially applied in healthcare and healthcare management. At best this might mean that 'best evidence' for HRD is limited to the findings of good quality empirical research based solely on qualitative methodologies, which is an approach that is becoming increasingly legitimized within various areas of healthcare. At worst, but still desirable, evidence-based HRD practice might just mean practitioners building into their every day practice the 'questioning approach' advocated by Rosemary Stewart or using 'best evidence' of lowest strength in the hierarchy of scientific evidence. It needs to be recognized that there are many HRD professionals who have had experience of carrying out rigorous research as part of a Master's degree and have since become research-minded and reflective. Although not strictly 'evidence-based' in practice they are certainly 'research-orientated'. In terms of the strength of scientific evidence this approach falls short of the minimum requirements to be considered as 'evidence-based', but even so it needs to be recognized as a desirable feature of professional practice. Encouraging this approach would be a significant development leading to evidence-based practice.

What follows are a few recent real life examples of how the 'evidence-based' and 'research-informed' approaches have been used in practice by various HRD practitioners and others. These examples are drawn partly from personal experience, partly from the experiences of other reflective practitioners, and partly from the literature. They indicate that the notion of research-informed and evidence-based HRD is not rhetoric but a reality. They also provide pointers that give direction to ways of enabling and expanding the implementation of research-informed and evidence-based practice.

Organizational change and development: 'reflections on practice' pointers towards research-informed and evidence-based HRD practice

In their recent book Hamlin, Keep and Ash (2001) provide various practical insights and perspectives on 'what makes for effective and successful organizational change and development'. Many of these are based on the 'narratives', 'stories' and 'lessons' offered by various reflective research-informed change agents, including managers, trainers and developers, who have been successful in bringing about beneficial organizational change either in their own organization or in host organizations. A detailed analysis of these various 'reflections on practice' by Hamlin (2001b) reveal several common lessons from which a number of generalized insights and conclusions have been drawn regarding effective change agency in practice. The critical factors pertaining to most of the case histories reinforce various aspects of the 'Generic Model of Organisational Change Management' referred to earlier in this chapter which was derived from 'best evidence' reported in the management literature. Other critical factors common to many of the 'reflections on practice' demonstrate the benefits of knowing the common failings of managers when managing change, and the importance of avoiding them. The key insights gained include:

- the significance placed on 'communicating with all stakeholders for the purpose of securing common ownership, commitment and involvement';
- the pivotal importance of 'securing the active commitment, involvement and participation of senior to middle managers' and particularly 'top management';
- the need to be 'clear, consistent and open with regard to what you are seeking to achieve, setting clear strategic objectives and sharing the vision';
- the importance of 'recognizing and addressing the real problems or root causes of problems, including the cultural dimensions';
- the importance of 'giving enough time for the OCD programme to take root and succeed';
- the importance of the 'contribution that the HR function can make and the strategic role it can play in bringing about transformational change';
- the need to recognize 'the role of learning in the change management process and the need for a no blame culture';
- the value of 'being reflective';
- the emphasis and importance placed on 'the value of conducting internal research as part of change agency practice'.

The latter two insights are particularly significant. For most of those who contributed the case histories, reflection was a legitimate component of their change agency practice which they made an integral and explicit part of the change process. Furthermore, many wished they had spent even more time up front of their change projects carrying out research to understand better the organizational context, particularly the cultural aspects, in order to form a stronger foundation upon which to build their change programmes and developments.

Quality in healthcare

Enabling the implementation of evidence-based practice

This example relates to the world of nursing and healthcare management (Kitson, Harvey and McCormack 1998). Some of the case studies presented in this work relate strongly to change management, facilitation and learning issues in contexts, settings and situations similar to those faced by managers and HRD practitioners in other types of organization. At heart it is the belief that 'the implementation of good quality research is likely to have improved outcomes for patients and is therefore important for quality patient care'. The conceptual framework presented by the authors suggests that 'successful implementation of research into practice is a function of the relation between the nature of the evidence, the context in which the proposed change is to be implemented, and the mechanisms by which the change is facilitated'. As much attention needs to be given to preparing the context and choosing the facilitation method as to testing the evidence. Four case studies are presented of varying degrees of quality from low to high relating to the evidence, the context and the facilitation respectively. The most successful implementation seems to occur when evidence is high; when the context is receptive to change with sympathetic cultures and appropriate monitoring and feedback mechanisms, and when there is appropriate facilitation of the change, using in a complementary way the skills of both external and internal facilitators. The framework could be used as a tool by HRD practitioners for implementing research findings or engaging in research activities as part of their change agency practice. Additionally it provides a useful reminder of the importance of giving sufficient attention to the process issues of change which call for high levels of facilitation skill and change agency expertise.

Research-informed and evidence-based HRD through professional partnerships

As already mentioned various authors in the UK have called for more research informed approaches to human resource development and management development (Jacobs and Vyakarnam 1994; Davies 1996; Hamlin and Davies 1996). Others have argued the case for more internal research in support of organizational change programmes and organizational learning (Quirke 1995; Stewart 1996; Hamlin and Reidy 1996 and 1997; Hamlin, Reidy and Stewart 1997; Denton 1998; Easterby-Smith and Araujo 1999). In the USA Swanson (1997) advocates that HRD professionals should 'advance their professional practice by becoming truly expert practitioners' through what he calls 'backyard research'. Jacobs (1997) strongly advocates HRD collaborations between organizations and universities. However, these should be 'professional partnerships' in which the 'partners' recognize that HRD scholars and HRD practitioners enter such partnerships with their own respective goals. Thus, in 'HRD professional partnerships', there is a dual goal to advance the HRD field and improve the organization through the findings and application of rigorous internal research. Building upon the ideas of Jacobs, and a number of tentative ideas shared by a group of HRD academics and practitioners attending the 1997 Annual Conference of the University Forum for HRD, a 'conceptual framework' has been devised to illustrate the connection between 'HRD professional partnerships' and the 'HRD research–practice gap' (Figure 5.4).

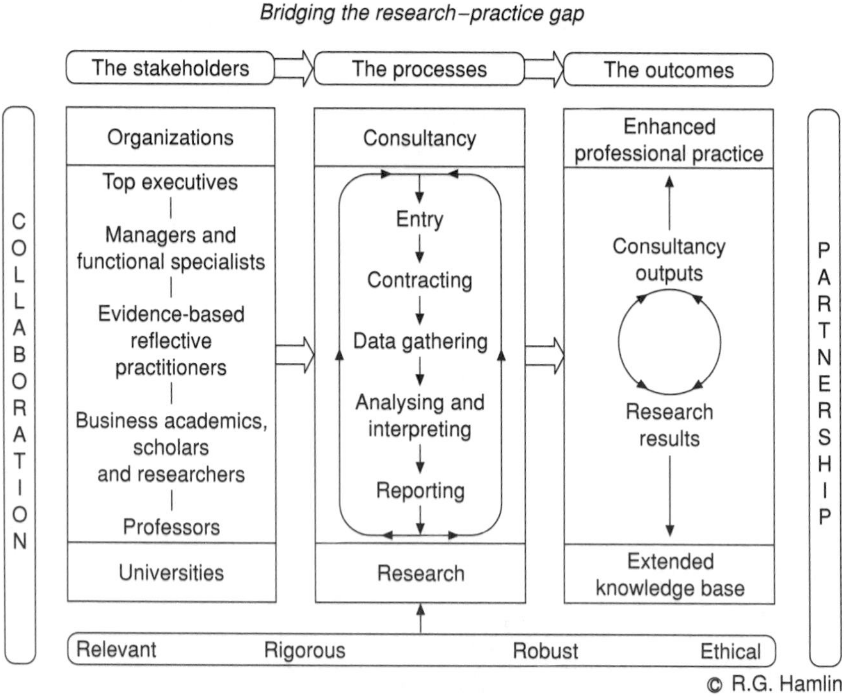

Figure 5.4 Closing or bridging the HRD research–practice gap through HRD professional partnerships

Source: Bob Hamlin in Hamlin, B., Keep, J. and Ash, K. (2001) *Organizational Change and Development*, Financial Times/Prentice Hall. Copyright 2001 R.G. Hamlin. Used with permission of Pearson Education Limited

The narrow outside 'boxes' to the left and right of the model are there to remind us that the joint research effort is not a 'service contract' but a 'collaborative partnership'. The narrow outside boxes at the top and bottom of the model illustrate the connection between the respective 'stakeholders' who are jointly involved in the active 'processes' of research and consultancy. These need to be relevant, rigorous, robust and ethical if they are to lead to 'outcomes' of maximum value to the interested parties. The large box to the left of centre of the model endeavours to illustrate 'professional partnerships' in which HRD scholars from universities, in partnership with HRD practitioners, conduct internal organizationally related research to academic standards. At the centre of this box is the notion of the 'reflective research-informed/evidence-based' practitioner. The large box at the centre of the model draws attention to the cyclical nature of the processes for conducting internal research and consultancy respectively. These are similar and follow a 'common' sequence of stages from entry to reporting. The outcomes from the research/consultancy activities as illustrated in the large box to the right of centre of the model are perceived as being mutually reinforcing. At the outset of an HRD intervention the reflective research-informed/evidence-based HRD practitioner uses 'best evidence' to support his or her decisions. This might mean building a 'research' component into the HRD strategy for the specific purpose of using empirical evidence from internal organizational research to further inform, shape and measure the required HRD intervention and thereby enhance the professional practice. Building sufficient rigour into the research with the help of an HRD scholar in a professional partnership arrangement will give the necessary 'academic credentials' required to ensure the credibility and acceptance of the research by people inside the organization, and also impart value in terms of its contribution to the advancement of knowledge.

This concept of collaborative 'professional partnerships' for generating internal partnership research, and the processes involved, bear similarity to the notion of 'co-operative research' as advocated and practised within the healthcare sector (Sang 2000). To get 'research into practice' Sang draws attention to a 'virtuous cycle' of co-operation that needs to exist from beginning to end of the research process involving the initiators, commissioners, designers, planners, implementers and evaluators.

An HRD professional partnership in practice

Case-study example: HM Customs and Excise (Anglia Region)

This HRD professional partnership was set within the Anglia Region of HM Customs and Excise (HMCE), which at the time was one of fourteen executive units comprising HMCE within the UK. The partners in this instance included Dick Shepherd, the regional head of 'Anglia', Margaret

Reidy his internal research officer/HRD consultant, plus the author and Professor Jim Stewart from Nottingham Trent University.

The aim of the partnership was to help bring about radical change in the management culture of the organization through HRD initiatives based on the findings of rigorous internal academic research. The research programme included, amongst other activities, an extensive 'ethnographic' longitudinal case study on the changing culture of the organization. It also comprised a complementary empirical research study into the criteria of managerial and leadership effectiveness using critical incident technique and statistical analytic methods for processing the data.

The partnership comprised two strands, the one concerned with the 'ethnographic' research, the other with the study of managerial effectiveness. The 'ethnographic' research became coincidentally the focus of a PhD/MPhil study programme undertaken by the research officer. Hence this strand of the partnership was partly contractual for the doctoral studies component and non-contractual for all of the other aspects. The managerial effectiveness strand to the partnership differed from the 'ethnographic' strand in that it was wholly voluntary and non-contractual with each partner entering the 'partnership' with quite different yet complementary goals. It should be mentioned that in the 'Anglia partnership' the internal HRD practitioner, Margaret Reidy, carried out most of the field research, but the other stages of the research programme were done jointly.

At the time of his appointment as regional head of Anglia in 1991, Dick Shepherd found himself in a region which, whilst productive, was working with a 'command and control' style of management. However, to reflect the changing organizational environment where year on year demands to deliver more for less were being made by the department, the management style needed to be changed. Furthermore, to cope effectively with the various change programmes he anticipated would be imposed 'top-down' from above, and those he intended initiating himself, he concluded a new cultural infrastructure was required. He found though that change was slow to happen due to the effects of 'cultural lag', a term first coined by Bate (1996). He realized he needed to understand better the resilient but no longer relevant culture of his organization so as to know how best to change it. Hence he commissioned an ethnographic longitudinal research study from Margaret Reidy on culture and cultural change that was designed to help inform, shape and measure the changes he had set his mind to bring about. In the main his early change initiatives were a success in terms of changing the organizational structure. However, the desired changes in the management culture were only partly achieved as revealed by the ethnographic study. A large proportion of managers persisted in managing in the traditional ways of the Civil Service.

At the beginning of 1995, Shepherd decided to address again the issue of changing the management culture. However, he wanted to know with a greater degree of certainty the type of managerial behaviours that were proving particularly effective within the changing organization which therefore needed to be encouraged and promoted, and conversely those behaviours that were least effective which needed to be discouraged or eliminated. Furthermore, he and Margaret Reidy were curious to know whether a different research methodology would substantiate the longitudinal 'ethnographic' research findings. Hence a second strand of the HRD professional partnership was formed focusing on a complementary research programme into managerial and leadership effectiveness. This latter research, and its application to inform and shape the range of HRD interventions used to bring about significant change in the management culture of 'Anglia', has been published in some detail elsewhere (see Hamlin and Reidy 1997; Hamlin, Reidy and Stewart 1997, 1998 and 1999). In summary, the initial research revealed six 'positive' criteria relating to managerial effectiveness within 'Anglia', and twelve 'negative' criteria relating to managerial ineffectiveness.

The criteria are rich and robust in that they are underpinned by behavioural statements which are relevant in terms of the inherent language and culture of 'Anglia', and have been piloted and tested through a number of diverse tools. A further research study was carried out focusing specifically on team leaders with the purpose of identifying criteria of leadership effectiveness. It was based on twenty of the 'positive' leadership-specific behavioural statements obtained from the managerial effectiveness research, and used the same data processing methods.

Dick Shepherd presented the preliminary findings from the critical incident stage of the research to his managers at his 1995 Annual Management Conference. The results were well received with people agreeing that the identified behaviours did exist. These were then discussed in syndicate workshops with some of the revealed behavioural problems being addressed. Various managers and team leaders carried the results back to their offices, and ran similar workshops with their own people in order to address those problem issues affecting them. Subsequent monitoring of the culture changes that had taken place as a result of the research-based HRD interventions revealed marked increases in the incidence of 'positive' managerial behaviours, and reductions in the 'negative'. However, many problems remained with certain managers still exhibiting attitudes and behaviours associated with ineffective management as defined by the 'negative' criteria. Hence it was concluded additional effort was required to effect further change in the management culture. The reasons why the initial findings had not had a bigger impact was that some people did not relate the 'negative' behaviours to themselves, although they accepted that in general such behaviours were a major problem for the organization. The strict codes of confidentiality and anonymity as applied when conducting the research meant none of the observed critical incidents and behaviours reported in the findings were attributed to any persons in particular. Hence it was too easy for some people to believe that other managers elsewhere in the organization were the ones exhibiting the negative behaviours. Some managers were obviously reluctant to analyse their own behaviours in relation to the research findings. This created a barrier to further cultural change. Therefore a different approach was needed that would encourage and enable managers and team leaders in the organization to relate the 'positive' and 'negative' criteria to their own behaviours. The approach used was based on the concepts of self-analysis, 360-degree feedback and action learning, using a range of 'framework tools' focusing on different criteria and problem issues identified by the managerial and leadership effectiveness research. Team-effectiveness workshops were set up for particular team leaders (managers) and their respective teams, and these were facilitated initially with the help of Margaret Reidy. Through the process of action learning, participants at the workshops were helped to translate and transfer to themselves not only the positive findings of the research, but also the negative findings that required personal remedial action as revealed by the 360-degree feedback process. This team effectiveness/ action learning workshop approach enabled people to obtain feedback from colleagues without risk of compromising their positions or relationships within the organization. It allowed them to work through problems in a supportive climate and learn from them, and led to meaningful change on a personal, team and organizational level. Subsequent workshops became self-generating and self-facilitating.

The research-informed/evidence-based HRD practice outlined above, which took place between 1995 and 1998, was highly successful in engaging the active interest and commitment of 'Anglia' people to the process of strategic change. Managers went much further in their thinking than had been the case with previous organizational change programmes. In the past 'Anglia' people had not always responded well to certain organizational change initiatives, particularly those involving consultants using external research or adapted 'off the shelf' OD instruments that failed to 'ring true'. In this case they were willing to move forward with cultural change brought about through the strategically led and research-informed/ evidence-based HRD interventions initiated by Dick Shepherd. This was because the internal research findings presented an accurate picture of the actual realities of managerial life as it existed, and also 'struck a chord' with people. But the perceived value of this research-informed/evidence-based HRD practice stemmed particularly from the attributes of the research resulting from the 'Anglia' HRD professional partnership, namely its academic rigour and credentials, the strict codes of anonymity and confidentiality that were applied, its relevancy and the sense of ownership it engendered. In the case of the 'Anglia' cultural change programme the contribution of the internal research was pivotal and of crucial importance. As Dick Shepherd said, 'it was of enormous value in bringing about the culture change, and gave me the confidence and courage to proceed with the change programme'.

Conclusions and key learning points

Several lessons can be drawn from the examples outlined above. There are strong arguments that strategically led research-informed/evidence-based HRD practice can become a central plank of any HRD strategy for helping to bring about beneficial organizational change and development. However, this is unlikely to become commonplace if most HRD practitioners remain constrained at the margins of the organization, rather than at its centre. The question is how might HRD professionals become centrepiece players on the organizational stage? Certainly this will not happen unless and until line managers overcome the five OCD 'failings' outlined earlier in this chapter, and unless and until HRD people increase significantly their competency and credibility. Herein lies a major challenge for those who educate and train managers, trainers and developers, particularly university academics who teach on professional qualification programmes such as the MBA and Master's degrees in HRD and HRM. They should be making key contributions towards such developments as:

1   Ensuring that the organizational/business leaders and managers they teach do fully understand the significance of investing in appropriate HRD (and HRM) effort when initiating and implementing organizational change programmes. This might mean changing the way HRD/HRM is taught in business schools. Greater emphasis should be placed on helping practising managers recognize not only the importance to themselves of becoming more skilled as change agents and research-informed/evidence-based reflective practitioners, but also on the value of co-operative or partnership research and professional partnerships.
2   Ensuring HRD practitioners develop the skills required to operate effectively and with competence, confidence and credibility at strategic levels within organizations. This includes helping them develop expertise as internal consultants, change agents, strategic organizational facilitators, and as research-informed/evidence-based reflective practitioners.
3   Doing more applied research themselves, focused towards enhancing professional HRD practice as well as advancing the field of HRD knowledge.
4   Working collaboratively with their current and past students and other research-active HRD practitioners, preferably within HRD professional partnerships and other co-operative or partnership research arrangements.
5   Recognizing the potential of such partnerships for generating academically rigorous HRD research that can be of relevance and interest to HRD practitioners.

A key message for those readers who are HRD practitioners is the need at least to become a reflective research-informed professional; and then to embark upon a journey towards becoming an evidence-based practitioner, emulating what other professionals do in the healthcare professions. HRD professional partnerships or co-operative research arrangements with HRD academics are one means of enhancing professional HRD practice through research.

There is also an important message to be drawn from the above examples for top managers and business/organizational leaders. They need increasingly to recognize the value of research-informed/evidence-based HRD for bringing about beneficial organizational change and development. However, as an HRD-orientated manager, trainer, or developer it may fall to you, the reader, to ensure this message 'strikes home' at the top of your own organization. This may prove an essential requirement if you are to maximize your contribution to organizational effectiveness and helping to bring about beneficial organizational change and development.

Acknowledgements

In writing this chapter I have drawn upon previous publications jointly authored with Gron Davies, Margaret Reidy and Jim Stewart respectively, and significant parts of the chapter are published also in B. Hamlin, J. Keep and K. Ash, *Organisational Change and Development*, Financial Times/ Prentice Hall, 2001.

References

Alexander, L. (1991) 'Strategy implementation: nature of the problem', in D. Hussey (ed.) *International Review of Strategic Management*, Chichester: Wiley.

Alimo-Metcalfe, B. and Alban-Metcalfe, R. (2000) 'Heaven can wait', *Health Service Journal*, 12 October, pp. 26–9.

—— (2001) 'The development of a new Transformational Leadership Questionnaire', *Journal of Occupational and Organisational Psychology*, 74(1): 1–23.

Altman, D.G. (1994) 'The scandal of poor medical research', *British Medical Journal*, 308: 283–4.

Axelsson, R. (1998) 'Towards an evidence based health care management', *International Journal of Health Planning and Management*, 13(4): 307–17.

Bate, S.P. (1996) 'Towards a strategic framework for changing corporate culture', *Strategic Change Journal*, 5: 27–42.

Bates, I. (1995) 'The Competence Movement and the National Qualification Framework: the widening parameters of research', *British Journal of Education and Work*, 8(2): 5–13.

Barnham, K., Fraser, J. and Heath, L. (1988) *Management for the Future*, Ashridge Management College/The Foundation for Management Development.

Beckhard, R. and Pritchard, W. (1992) *Changing the Essence: the Art of Creating and Leading Fundamental Change in Organisations*, San Francisco: Jossey-Bass Publishers.

Bennett, J.K. and O'Brien, M.J. (1994) 'The 12 building blocks of the Learning Organisation', *Training*, 31: 41–8.

Boonstra, J. and Vink, M. (1996) 'Technological and organizational innovation: a dilemma of fundamental change and participation', *The European Journal of Work and Organisational Psychology*, 5(3).

Brooks, I. and Bate, P. (1994) 'The problem of effecting change within the British Civil Service: a cultural perspective', *British Journal of Management*, 5: 177–90.

Bruce, R. and Wyman, S. (1998) *Changing Organisations: Practising Action Training and Research*, Thousand Oaks, CA: Sage.

Burgoyne, J. (1990) 'Doubts about competency', in M. Devine (ed.) *The Photo Fit Manager*, London: Unwin.

Bury, T. and Mead, J. (1998) *Evidence-Based Healthcare: a Practical Guide for Therapists*, Oxford: Butterworth-Heinemann.

Cochrane, A.L. (1972) *Effectiveness and Efficiency: Random Reflections on Health Services*, London: Nuffield Trust.

Coopers and Lybrand Associates (1985) *A Challenge to Complacency: Changing Attitudes to Training*. A Report to the Manpower Services Commission and the National Economic Development Office. Sheffield Manpower Services Commission.

Coulson-Thomas, C. (1996) 'Business Process Re-Engineering and Strategic Change', *Strategic Management Journal*, 5(3): 165–78.

Davies, G. (1996) 'Research methods and HRD', in J. Stewart and J. McGoldrick (eds) *Human Resource Development: Perspectives, Strategies and Practice*, London: Pitman Publishing, pp. 280–302.

de Meuse, K., Vanderheiden, P. and Bergamann, T. (1994) 'Announcing layoffs: their effect on corporate financial performance', *Human Resource Management*, 33(4).

Denton, J. (1998) *Organizational Learning and Effectiveness*, London: Routledge.

Devine, M. and Hirsh, W. (1998) 'Mergers and Acquisitions: getting the people bit right', Roffey Park Research Report, Roffey Park.

Easterby-Smith, M. and Araujo, L. (1999) Organizational learning: current debates and opportunities', in Mark Easterby-Smith, John Burgoyne and Luis Araujo (eds) *Organizational Learning and the Learning Organization*, London: Sage Publications, pp. 1–21.

Gamblin, C. (1997) 'Why the paradigm shift approach rarely works: in search of the magic bullet', *Organisation and People – The Quarterly Journal of AMED*, 4(4): 97–108.

Gray, J.A.M. (1997) *Evidence-Based Healthcare: How to Make Health Policy and Management Decisions*, Edinburgh: Churchill Livingstone.

Grundy, T. (1997) 'Human resource management: a strategic approach', *Long Range Planning*, 30(4): 507–17.

Ham, C., Hunter, D.J. and Robinson, R. (1995) 'Evidence-based policy making', *British Medical Journal*, 310: 71–2.

Hamel, C. and Prahalad, C. (1994) *Competing for the Future*, Boston, MA: Harvard Business Press.

Hamlin, R.G. (1990) 'The criteria of managerial effectiveness within secondary schools', *Collected Original Resources in Education*, 12(1).

—— (2001a) 'A review and synthesis of context and practice', in B. Hamlin, J. Keep and K. Ash (eds), pp. 13–38.

—— (2001b) 'Towards Research Informed Organisational Change and Development', in B. Hamlin, J. Keep and K. Ash (eds), pp. 283–96.

117

Hamlin, R.G. and Ash, K. (2000) 'Towards evidence-based organizational change and development', paper presented at the NHS-P Research into Practice Conference. Birmingham, England, 13 January.

Hamlin, R.G. and Davies, G. (1996) 'The trainer as change agent: issues for practice', in J. Stewart and J. McGoldrick (eds) *Human Resource Development: Perspectives, Strategies and Practice*, London: Pitman Publishing, pp. 199–219.

—— (2001) 'Managers, trainers and developers as change agents', in B. Hamlin, J. Keep and K. Ash (eds), pp. 39–60.

Hamlin, R.G., Keep, J. and Ash, K. (eds) (2001) *Organisational Change and Development: a Reflective Guide for Managers, Trainers and Developers*, London: Financial Times/Pitman Publishing.

Hamlin, R.G. and Reidy, M. (1996) 'Effecting changes in the management culture of an executive unit of HM Customs and Excise through visionary leadership and strategically led research-based OD interventions', paper presented at the 1996 Annual Conference on the Strategic Direction of HRM, Nottingham Trent University.

Hamlin, R.G. and Reidy, M. (1997) 'Effecting change in management culture', *Strategic Change Journal*, special edition, December: 435–50.

Hamlin, R.G., Reidy, M. and Priddey, L. (1998) 'Evidence and research-based HRD practice through HRD professional partnerships', paper presented at the 27th International Federation of Training and Development Organisations (IFTDO) World Conference-Revitalising HRD for the New Millennium, Dublin, Ireland.

Hamlin, R.G., Reidy, M. and Stewart, J. (1997) 'Changing the management culture in one part of the British Civil Service through visionary leadership and strategically led research-based OD interventions', *Journal of Applied Management Studies*, 6(2): 233–51.

—— (1998) 'Bridging the HRD research-practice gap through professional partnerships', *Human Resource Development International Journal*, 1(3): 273–90.

—— (1999) 'Effecting management culture change through research-based management development: a British case study', *Management Development Forum* (Empire State College, State University of New York) 2(1): 21–47.

Hamlin, R.G. and Stewart, J. (1990) 'Approaches to management development in the UK', *Leadership* and *Organisation Development Journal*, 11(5): 27–32.

—— (1998) 'In support of evidence-based human resource development practice', Lancaster–Leeds Collaborative Conference: Emergent Fields in Management – Connecting Learning and Critique, Leeds University.

Hammer, M. and Champney, J. (1993) *Re-Engineering the Corporation: a Manifesto for Business Revolution*, London: Nicholas Brealey.

Hammer, M. and Stanton, S. (1995) *The Re-Engineering Revolution: a Handbook*, New York: HarperCollins.

Harrison, R. (1997) *Employee Development*, London Institute of Personnel and Development.

Herriot, P. (1998) *Trust and Transition: Managing the Employment Relationship*, Chichester: John Wiley.

Holland, N. and Aitken, A. (1999) 'HR, Line and IS as business partners in IT-related change: will you, won't you, join the dance', *AMED News*, April/May: 10.

Howard, C. (1996) 'The stress on managers caused by downsizing', *The Globe and Mail*, 30 January.

Hussey, D. (1996) *Business Driven Human Resource Management*, Chichester: John Wiley.

—— (1997) 'Strategic management past experiences and future directions: Part 1 – Why do so many organizations suffer strategic failure despite their processes of strategic management?' *Strategic Change Journal*, 6(5): 261–71.

Industrial Relations Service (1997) 'Cultural change', *IRS Management Review*, 11(4).

Jacobs, R. (1989) *Assessing Management Competences. Report of a Survey of Current Arrangements in the UK for the Assessment of Management Competences*, Berkhamstead: Ashridge Management Research Group, April.

Jacobs, R.L. (1997) 'HRD partnerships for integrating HRD research and practice', in R. Swanson and E. Holton III (eds) *Human Resource Development Research Handbook: Linking Research and Practice*, San Francisco: Berret-Koehler, pp. 47–61.

Jacobs, R. and Vyakarnam, S. (1994) 'The need for a more strategically led research-based approach in management development', *BPS Occupational Psychology Conference*, Birmingham, UK.

Kearney, P. (1994) 'Business process re-engineering', *Training and Development*, March: 14–17.

Kilman, R.H. (1989) *Managing Beyond the Quick Fix*, San Francisco: Jossey Bass.

Kitson, A., Harvey, G. and McCormack, B. (1998) 'Enabling the implementation of evidence-based practice: a conceptual framework', *Quality in Health Care*, 7: 149–58.

Kotter, J. (1982) 'What effective general managers really do', *Harvard Business Review*, November/December.

—— (1996) 'Leading change: why transformation efforts fail', in J. Champy and N. Nohria (eds) *Fast Forward: The Best Ideas on Managing Business Change*, Boston, MA: Harvard Business Press.

Mabey, C. and Salaman, G. (1995) *Strategic Human Resource Management*, Oxford: Blackwell Business.

Marks, M.L. (1994) *From Turmoil to Triumph: New Life After Mergers, Acquisitions and Downsizing*, New York: Lexington.

Marsick, V. and Watkins, K. (1994) 'The learning organization: an integrative vision of HRD', *Human Resource Development Quarterly*, 5(4): 353–60.

McLagan, P. (1989) *Models for HRD Practice*, Alexandria, VA: American Society for Training and Development.

McMaster University, Evidence-Based Medicine Working Group (1992) 'Evidence-based medicine: a new approach to teaching the practice of medicine', *JAMA*, 268: 2420–5.

Mintzberg, H. (1975) 'The manager's job: folklore and fact', *Harvard Business Review*, July/August.

Mumford, A. (1997) *Management Development: Strategies for Action*, London: Institute of Personnel and Development.

Nelson, T. and Coxhead, H. (1997) 'Increasing the probability of re-engineering culture change success through effective internal communication', *Strategic Change Journal*, 6(1): 29–48.

Phillips, K. and Shaw, P. (1989) *A Consultancy Approach for Trainers*, Aldershot: Gower.

Popay, J. and Williams, G. (1998) 'Qualitative research and evidence-based healthcare', *Journal of the Royal Society of Medicine*, 91(35): 32–7.

Quirke, B. (1995) *Communicating Change,* Maidenhead: McGraw-Hill.

Rothwell, W.J. and Kasanas, H.C. (1989a) '*Strategic Human Resource Development*', Englewood Cliffs, NJ: Prentice Hall.

—— (1989b) *Human Resource Development: a Strategic Approach,* revised edition, Amherst, MA: HRD Press.

Royal Society Of Arts (1995) *The Role of Business in a Changing World,* London: RSA.

Russ-Eft, D. *et al.* (1996) 'Updating the meaning of leadership: a grass roots model for the new workplace', in Zenger Miller, M2021 V.1.1 (7/96), Zenger Miller, Inc.

Russ-Eft, D., Preskill, H. and Sleezer, C. (1997) 'Human Resource Development Review: Research and Implications', Thousand Oaks, CA: Sage.

Sackett, D.L. (1997) 'Evidence-based medicine', *Semin Perinatol,* 21(1): 3–5.

Sackett, D.L., Rosenberg, W.N.G., Gray, J.A.M., Haynes, R.B. and Richardson, W.S. (1996) Evidence-based medicine: what it is and what it isn't', *British Medical Journal,* 312: 71–2.

Sang, B. (2000) 'Co-operative research-working with users', paper presented at the NHS-P Research into Practice Conference, 13 January 2000, Birmingham, UK.

Schaffer, R. and Thomson, H. (1992) 'Successful change programs begin with results', *Harvard Business Review,* 70(1): 80–89.

Simon, R.-J. and Streumer, J. (2001) 'Position statement on HRD', Second International Conference on HRD Research and Practice across Europe: 2001 University of Twente, The Netherlands.

Skilling, D. (1996) 'Beyond the quick fix: how to manage more effectively in the heart of change', *Industrial and Commercial Training,* 28(4): 3–7.

Spurgeon, P. and Flanagan. H. (1997) *Public Sector Managerial Effectiveness: Theory and Practice in the NHS,* Buckingham: Open University.

Stetler, C., Brunell, M., Giuliano, K., Morsi, D., Prince, L. and Newell-Stokes, V. (1998) 'Evidence-based practice and the role of nursing leadership', *Journal of Nursing Administration,* 28(7/8): 45–53.

Stewart, J. (1993 and 1996) *Managing Change through Training and Development,* first and second edns, London: Kogan Page.

Stewart, J. and Hamlin, R.G. (1990) 'The management of change: what contribution can training make?' *Training and Development,* August: 11–13.

—— (1992) 'Competence-based qualifications: the case against change', *Journal of European Industrial Training,* 16(7).

—— (1993) 'Competence-based qualifications: a way forward', *Journal of European Industrial Training,* 17(6).

Stewart, J. and Sambrook, S. (1995) 'The role of functional analysis in national vocational qualifications: a critical appraisal', *British Journal of Education and Work,* 8(2): 93–106.

Stewart, R. (1982) *Choices for the Manager,* Maidenhead: McGraw-Hill.

—— (1998) 'More art than science?' *Health Service Journal,* 26 March, pp. 28–9.

Swanson, R.A. (1995) 'Performance is the key', *Human Resource Development Quarterly,* 6(2): 207–13.

Swanson, R. (1997) 'HRD research: don't go to work without it', in R. Swanson, R. and E. Holton III (eds) *Human Resource Development Research Handbook: Linking Research and Practice,* San Francisco: Berrett-Koehler, 3–20.

Tanner, C.A. (1999) 'Evidence-based practice: research and critical thinking', *Journal of Nursing Education,* 38(3): 99.

Tate, W. (1995) *Developing Managerial Competence: A Critical Guide to Methods and Materials*, Aldershot: Gower.

Thomson, R. and Mabey, C. (1994) *Developing Human Resources*, London: Butterworth-Heinemann.

Thornhill, A., Lewis, P., Millmore, M. and Saunders, M. (2000) *Managing Change: A Human Resource Strategy Approach*, Harlow: Financial Times/Prentice Hall.

University Forum for HRD (1995) *Emerging concept of HRD – a position statement*, London: UFHRD.

Walton, J. (1999) *Strategic Human Resource Development*, Harlow: Financial Times Prentice Hall.

Warrick, D. (1995) 'Best practices occur when leaders lead, champion change and adopt a sound change process', *Organisation Development Journal*, 13(4): 91–102.

West, M. and Patterson, M. (1998) 'Profitable personnel', *People Management* January 1998, Institute of Personnel and Development, pp. 28–31.

Wilkinson, A., Allen, S. and Snape, E. (1993) 'Quality and the manager', *Institute of Management Report*, London: Institute of Management.

Wilson, J. (1999) *Human Resource Development*, London: Kogan Page.

Woodall, J. and Winstanley, D. (1998) *Management Development: Strategy and Practice*, Oxford: Blackwell.

Worrall, L. and Cooper, G. (1997, 1998, 1999, 2000) *The Quality of Working Life: 1997, 1998, 1999, 2000 Surveys of Managers' Changing Experiences*, London: Institute of Management.

Wyatt and Co. (1994) *Best Practices in Corporate Re-structuring*, Toronto, Ontario.

6

RESEARCHING HRD IN SMALL ORGANIZATIONS

Rosemary Hill

Aims and contributions

If this volume is an axiomatic recognition of the need for a serious examination of research in the specific field of HRD, then this chapter recognizes an equally demanding need – that of HRD enquiry into small and medium-sized enterprises (SMEs). In accepting the arguments that smaller organizations are not scaled-down versions of large ones (Westhead and Storey 1996) and that the majority of the HR literature in the UK derives from large organizations (Harrison 1997) it would seem sensible to want to address such a potentially serious omission through an understanding of how the research process in SMEs might inform both the ontology of HRD and the epistemological issues in researching it. Proposals for a new body – the Small Business Service (SBS) – 'to act as a voice for small business at the heart of Government' (DTI 1999: 1) recognize the importance that the UK government places upon the contribution of small organizations to the nation's socio-economic infrastructure.

Against this academic and commercial rationale, the chapter examines an episode of case-study research into HRD in three small organizations located in the Wirral, in the north-west of England. In the chapter, the theoretical context of HRD and the smaller organization is explored and the research context explained; but its main focus is to describe the case-study methodology used. This it does in two ways: first, by discussing case-study research from a conceptual perspective; and second, by describing the data collection and analysis techniques adopted. A critical analysis of issues raised by the research and how the characteristics of the small organizations studied may have shaped the casework design and analysis techniques in practice is then offered. The chapter proceeds with a comparison of the different HRD approaches found in the three cases, and closes with a discussion of research conclusions and implications.

Theoretical context

The issue of small organization 'smallness'

Definitions of what constitutes a small organization do vary within the literature and defining it is no easy task. Those used in the research align with the European Commission's definition of SMEs summarized at Table 6.1 – essentially organizations employing less than 250 people. The terms 'SME' and 'small organization' are used interchangeably in the chapter, as both are equally applicable to the three cases studied (although it is recognized that 'small' is positioned specifically within the data at Table 6.1 as pertaining to organizations with less than 50 employees). The most significant point here is, perhaps, that because the term 'SME' encompasses such a broad church, it is important to define its constitution and application within a particular piece of research or writing.

Stanworth and Curran (1976: 7–8) report that the Bolton Committee saw the small organization as a socio-economic unit displaying the characteristics in Box 6.1. This conceptualization may, however, be criticized. For example, small organizations frequently create niche markets (Bradburd and Ross 1989), thus achieving quite a large, if not always obvious, market

Table 6.1 European Commission's definitions of SMEs

Number of employees	Defined as:
0–9	Very small (micro) firms
10–49	Small firms
50–249	Medium firms
250 +	Large firms

Source: Compiled from TUC (1997), originating in a Commission of the European Communities publication of 3 April 1996

Box 6.1 Small firm characteristics as reported by the Bolton Committee

1 Economically, a small firm is one that has a relatively small share of its market.
2 Managerially, the small firm is administered by its owners or part-owners in a personalized way, rather than through the medium of formalized management structure.
3 It is independent in the sense that it does not form part of a larger enterprise and owner-managers are free from outside control in taking their principal decisions.

Compiled from: Stanworth and Curran (1976). Copyright 1976 Blackwell Publishers share. In contention of point 2, Storey (1994: 150) suggests that 'once small firms exceed between ten and twenty workers, they begin to employ individuals to act as managers or supervisors', reflecting an overall pattern in the relationship between non-owning manager recruitment and small-firm growth. The matter of independence at point 3 is also interesting and contestable. For instance, such reasoning may extend to larger organizations that operate within a framework of autonomous units in an effort to enhance flexibility, responsiveness and entrepreneurialism (Handy 1995; Harrison 1997; Osborne 1995; Stanworth *et al.* 1989) – typically believed to be small-organizational traits (Storey op. cit.). Are such business units 'small' organizations in their own right? Or must the essence of small-firm operation inherently and constitutionally incur absolute freedom from the encumbrance or comfort of large-firm endorsement? Several SMEs encountered early on in the research whilst seeking access to case-study organizations were either wholly reliant upon a single large customer (and thus seen as extensions of these customers' businesses), or functioning as an independent franchise of a larger organization. These small organizations were, however, still regarded by the local Training and Enterprise Council (TEC) as part of the region's SME populace – thus offering a perspective on the above speculation about the essence of 'small-firm operation'.

Watson and Everett (1993) suggest that a non-quantitative approach to small business definition is preferable to one where, typically, figures relating to size of workforce or annual turnover are quoted. They do, however, acknowledge that there are difficulties in applying qualitative methods to include the need for consistency of measurement processes across different industry sectors. Certain sectors appear to contain a proliferation of small organizations. For instance, Curran and Burrows (seen in Storey op. cit.: 17) located almost 90 per cent of all UK businesses employing between one and twenty-four workers in the construction and service industries; whilst Keeble *et al.* (1992) report that service industries in general are typified by an above-average share of small organizations.

The main point in all of this discussion is that small-organization 'smallness' is a multi-dimensional concept which may not always be judged from a size perspective alone and that, perhaps, there is no such thing as a 'typical' small organization.

HRD and the small organization

If there is no such thing as a typical small organization, then it may also follow that there is no such thing as an approach to HRD that is 'typical' of small organizations – empirical findings of this study seem to indicate so. Vickerstaff and Parker (1995: 60) report: 'Case-study-based work has revealed a high degree of unplanned and informal training activity in small firms, where there is typically unlikely to be a dedicated personnel manager or training officer.'

Other literature – for example, Cosh, Duncan and Hughes (1998), DfEE (1997), Gibb (1997), Harrison (1997), Lane (1994), Metcalf, Walling and Fogarty (1994) and Westhead and Storey (1996) – supports this and a sibling argument that in many small organizations training does not take place at all. It is also worth adding here that where training does occur in SMEs, not only is it more likely to be reactive and informal but it tends to be short term and almost exclusively directed at the solution of immediate work-related problems rather than the development of people. Sadler-Smith, Down and Field (1999: 375) cite research that points to 'training interventions in smaller firms being less sophisticated than those in larger firms'. Collectively, such factors suggest that HRD in small organizations focuses on training that is predominantly job-skill related, delivered simply on the job as part of the job (rather than training taking place away from the workplace in a more formal setting). It is seen by the small organization not so much as 'proper training', but instead regarded as 'part of everyday life' (Joyce, McNulty and Woods 1995: 19). In this sense, 'the job' in an SME may be conceived of as an HRD intervention in itself. These arguments indicate that the characteristics of HRD in small organizations concur with much that is characteristic of SMEs themselves – essentially informal, uncomplicated and action-oriented, with a tendency to ground policies and activities in values of 'business as usual'. They also imply that the dynamics of HRD in small organizations could be very different from those in larger enterprises (Joyce, McNulty and Woods 1995).

'Working' interpretation of HRD for researching in the small organization

First, it is acknowledged that HRD comprises an intricate web of issues and activities as demonstrated by a wealth of writers such as French and Bazalgette (1996), Garavan, Costine and Heralty (1995), Harrison (1997), Stewart and McGoldrick (1996) and Weinberger (1998). One HRD activity is the training and development of people in a work organization.

Whilst recognizing that the individual activities of 'training' and 'development' may hold separate and differing connotations for the overall philosophy and practice of HRD – as advanced by Buckley and Caple (1990) and Harrison (1997), for example – 'training and development' (TandD) is applied here in its aggregate form, in keeping with composite definitions of TandD such as that offered by IIP UK (1996: 27):

> any activity that develops skills and/or knowledge, and/or behaviour. Activities may range from formal training courses run internally or externally, to informal on the job training by a supervisor. Also includes other activities such as shadowing, coaching, mentoring etc.

Box 6.2 How the term HRD was used in the research

> In the research, the term HRD was used in a descriptive sense, in that it (HRD) may be thought of as a series of activities carried out in a work organization – aimed at the training and development of individuals and teams, and the development of the organization itself – rather than as an abstract and perhaps rhetorical construct.

Harrison (1997: xiii) defines the term 'training' as 'shorthand for planned instructional activities, and sometimes for wider developmental activities and processes', and assigns 'development' to 'all learning experiences whereby growth occurs'. She then goes on to say that when development is 'used in conjunction with "training" it is in order to distinguish wider learning experiences from narrowly focused, planned, job-related events'. There are similarities in the definitions advanced here by IIP UK and Harrison. Each informs us that TandD activities engage both formal and informal processes, for example. Combined, the two infer that training is a more formal and narrowly focused activity designed to impart or improve upon specific knowledge and skills. Development is aimed inherently at the realization of growth and a capability to think, behave and perform differently – changes invoked through planned or emergent learning experiences (Megginson 1996).

In discussing the concept of HRD, Stewart and McGoldrick (1996) argue that whilst there is no definite view of what constitutes HRD, it is both strategic and practical. They also suggest that HRD is implicit in organizing and managing, and is concerned with leadership, culture, organizational learning and development, and change. There are also many interpretations of HRD which have been located in various theories and practices relating to the subject over several decades. Weinberger (1998) helpfully summarizes a range of HRD definitions offered by a variety of authors over the period 1970 to 1995. For purposes of the research described in this chapter, HRD is used descriptively/practically rather than conceptually, as that seemed a more pragmatic and, therefore, appropriate application of the term in the context of studying small organizations. Box 6.2 explains.

The interpretation at Box 6.2 explicitly exhibits key components of TandD and organizational development (OD), and strongly implicates performance improvement and learning capability. Furthermore, for empirical investigations HRD was organized within three primary 'branches', as depicted in Figure 6.1. As suggested by the figure, TandD activities constitute the dominant component in this interpretation of HRD, whilst the learning and development processes and underpinning theories associated with OD (see for example, French and Bell 1990; Stewart 1996)

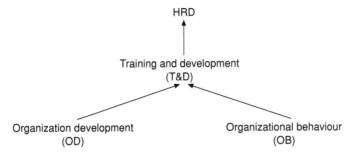

Figure 6.1 Branches of HRD

and organizational behaviour (OB) (see for example, Davis and Newstrom 1972; Robbins 1997), feature as subordinated but significant contributors.

Whilst Figure 6.1 might imply clear demarcations between TandD, OD and OB, in reality there exists a blurring of the boundaries between them and an effective HRD researcher or practitioner, arguably, should be able to call upon all three as and when necessary.

So where does all this leave the notion of researching HRD in small organizations? The research described in the chapter has mainly concentrated upon what TandD activities were carried out in the cases studied. Having said that, the project's total involvement with HRD was much deeper and wider than merely an investigation into what TandD was, or was not, being done. For example, research activities included the design and facilitation of team-building and role analysis interventions in one of the case-study organizations, development of an appraisal proforma in another, and mentoring owner/managers to some degree in all three cases. Achieving close involvement and reciprocity (in the form of offering some hands-on 'expert help') with research respondents, and making observations and drawing conclusions about the wider issues of HRD as discussed above were, therefore, inevitable consequences of the research.

The empirical context

The multiple case study was the primary research strategy of a four-year doctoral programme aimed at examining the effectiveness of UK national HRD (N/HRD) in small organizations using the Investors in People (IIP) standard and process as the paradigm case for N/HRD. Data were collected intermittently in the three organizations between October 1996 and June 1998, with a follow-up visit made to two of the cases in mid-1999. The casework was preceded by a preliminary survey of 350 small organizations in the Wirral over the first half of 1996. The survey was supported by the local TEC and aimed at surfacing employers' views about IIP. It was conducted in two phases: phase one comprised a postal questionnaire;

Table 6.2 The case-study organizations

Organization	Nature of work	Approx. nos. employees (at time of selection)
Case 1:	Light engineering: design and build machines for mainly the automotive industry; trading as a limited company; single site; international trade	19
Case 2:	Install/maintain security and telecommunications systems; trading as a PLC; several sites over the UK; national trade	70
Case 3:	Youth and community project work in the voluntary sector; single site; a registered charity serving the local (Wirral) community only	6

and phase two featured a series of semi-structured interviews with the owner/managers of twenty-three of the surveyed organizations. As a secondary research strategy, the preliminary survey had two basic components: access and prehension. 'Access' is meant in a literal and practical sense – that is access as being a 'way in' to the case-study organizations. 'Prehension' is used within the context of Kolb's (1984) writings about experiential learning in that the survey provided an initial insight into characteristics of the local small-business community. It is also a useful glimpse into some of the problems, experiences and opinions of owner/managers, and invaluable bedrock of data to inform the subsequent case fieldwork (prehension). In discussing their methodology for managing a particular multiple case study, Miles and Huberman (1994: 31) refer to the principle of conducting a large survey prior to casework as 'nesting'. The survey and casework were supplemented by literature and Internet searches, and interviews with several people prominent in areas of expertise relevant to the study.

Overview of the case-study organizations

Table 6.2 presents an overview of the three case-study organizations. They were selected because the survey interviews had been mutually pleasant, achieving a 'feel-good' factor and, in each case, researcher and research respondent felt that they would be able to collaborate effectively together, over a sustained period of time, towards the realization of independent goals and mutual benefits. This may have added a potential weakness to the research design in that such factors could be atypical of the SME sector and that the research relationship could, perhaps, be perceived as overly cohesive. However, given the well-known problems of access

(Easterby-Smith, Thorpe and Lowe 1993), such potential weaknesses were judged acceptable. The three cases had the advantages of providing a contrasting and complementary mix of industry types, and based upon the impressions gained in the interviews, they also offered a contrasting and complementary mix of management styles, organizational structures and cultures, markets and ambitions.

Case 1, being a specialist engineering operation with an expanding overseas market, presented an opportunity to study the effect of design innovation and growth on the way it viewed HRD. As an organization at a cross-roads with regard to the direction of its current market position and national growth, Case 2 demonstrated an interesting blend of trade and service aspects and, therefore, training and development needs and activities. In complete contrast, Case 3 operated locally (to the Wirral) in a 'pure' service environment in the voluntary sector. As an organization focused on bringing together the separate agendas of individual and community development through the progression of a live project, Case 3's *modus operandi* reflects the principles of action learning as advanced by McGill and Beaty (1992) and Revans (1983): the volunteers being the action learners, the community project serving as the action learning problem, and Case 3's field officers operating as facilitators of learning for the volunteers and a project result for the community. Congruent with Case 3's primary 'product' – the facilitation of people- and society-based learning – research findings revealed that this organization naturally exhibited a more developmental infrastructure and focus than the other two cases.

Methodological issues

Overview of research methodology

The case-study design, analysis and ongoing data interpretation were based upon the discussions about case-study research by Yin (1994), with the analysis techniques advanced by Bryman and Cramer (1990, 1997), Easterby-Smith, Thorpe and Lowe (1993), Feldman (1995), Miles and Huberman (1994) and Riley (1990) being used to broaden Yin's arguments. For example, Bryman and Cramer's (1990) and Easterby-Smith, Thorpe and Lowe's (1993) discussions of quantitative research methods helped to inform management of the preliminary survey, to include the construction of questionnaires and the ordering and analysis of the data collected. The qualitative analysis techniques described by Miles and Huberman (1994) were particularly useful with regard to the case-study data in terms of explaining how to: design data collection documents; write up and code case field notes; and engage data analysis techniques such as pattern coding, memoing, interim case summaries and data displays. Feldman's (1995) discussion of semiotic analysis was adopted in the development of a technique of cross-case comparison and analysis, described later in the chapter as 'from metaphor to model'. The majority of case data were acquired by means of semi-structured and informal interviews, telephone conversations and site observations: typically, all three cases preferred flexibility and informality of contact and reporting – a reflection of small organizational operating values.

Case-study research – a conceptual perspective

Is the case study a method or an approach? Yin (1994: 13) argues that the case study:

> comprises an all-encompassing method – with the logic of design incorporating specific approaches to data collection and analysis. In this sense, the case study is not either a data collection tactic or merely a design feature alone . . . but a comprehensive research strategy.

In exemplification of how the case study is something 'bigger' than just a method or an approach, Yin (1994) suggests that case studies may collect any mix of quantitative and qualitative data through a variety of evidence collection mechanisms – direct observation, interviews, questionnaires and surveys, for instance – over either a sustained or a short period of time. Essentially, the case study provides an adaptable framework for application in a number of research contexts and environments that may be conducted through a range of sub-strategies that seek to explore, describe or explain the phenomena under scrutiny. It was thought that these prime factors (comprehensive and adaptable) rendered the case-study method/ approach particularly suitable for researching in SMEs as it allowed for a good deal of intra-case individualism and flexibility – in order to meet each small organization's particular set of needs – within the framework of a visibly consistent and rigorous inter-case process.

Whatever a particular set of needs a case study may have, Yin (op. cit.) stresses the importance of developing a *quality* of research design aimed at maximizing: construct validity (establishing correct operational measures for the concepts being studied); internal validity (for explanatory studies only – establishing a causal, as distinguished from a spurious, relationship); external validity (establishing the domain to which a study's findings can be generalized); and reliability (demonstrating that the operations of a study can be repeated, with the same results). Yin (ibid.: 18) defines a research design simply as:

> *an action plan for getting from here to there*, where *here* may be defined as the initial set of questions to be answered, and *there* is some set of conclusions (answers) about these questions. Between 'here'

Box 6.3 Case-data collection methods

Semi-structured interviews	Participant observations
Unstructured interviews	Non-participant observations
Group interviews	Informal telephone interviews
Questionnaires	Informal observations and 'overhearings'
Reviewing organizational documents	

and 'there' may be found a number of major steps, including the collection and analysis of relevant data.

The journey 'between here and there' in the three case-study organizations is now discussed.

Data collection

Case data were collected over two main phases. The first phase, from October 1996 to April 1997, explored what HRD policies and practices were in place in the three cases and to what extent N/HRD encouraged and supported their efforts: during the second phase, from May 1997 to June 1998, the research focus changed conceptually from an *exploration* of content to an *explanation* of why N/HRD had or had not been adopted in the cases. Further contact was attempted with all cases during April/May 1999 in order to review site activities twelve months on, and generally tidy up loose ends. At this time, it transpired that Case 1 (the engineering company) had gone into receivership in late 1998 and had ceased trading. Box 6.3 summarizes the case-study data collection methods utilized which captured a mix of both quantitative and qualitative data so that the quantitative versus qualitative distinction was 'not seen as a dichotomy, but as a continuum, with mixed methods at the midpoint of scale' (Martin 1990: 31).

Interviews and questionnaires

Semi- and unstructured interviews were the mainstay of the casework. Semi-structured interviews were managed by means of a prepared topic guide, but it was not unusual for a semi-structured interview to evolve into an unstructured one. For instance, as Case 1's technical manager (the main respondent in this organization) shared an office with the MD and the financial manager, much unscheduled and unstructured group debate ensued during site visits. It was common for other managers and shop-floor employees to wander in and out of the management office and interrupt or join in with discussions: the presence of a researcher was apparently not perceived as a barrier to the assortment of jokes, arguments, work and personal issues presented to the MD and/or technical manager by those who 'dropped in'. It was also common for either the MD or the technical manager (or both) to disappear for a while during an interview to accompany a caller back to the shopfloor to deal with an urgent matter. The informality and spontaneity of such phenomena were taken to be significant examples of small-organization behaviour, and regarded as opportunities to observe first-hand site activities and the interactions of managers with managers and managers with employees. The research role in these scenes seemed to slip randomly and naturally between that of participant and non-participant observation.

Interviews in Case 3 too mostly digressed into unscheduled and unstructured discussion, as the management respondent was difficult to keep focused on the planned subject matter and liked to use the research process as a reflective mechanism to bounce ideas off. On the other hand, Case 2's sales and marketing director (the main respondent) appeared content to forgo control over the content and flow of information – interviews with him invariably assumed a question and answer scenario, and were rarely subject to interruption. Interestingly, Case 2 was the largest and most structured of the three cases. The main point here is that, even though consistency in data collection across the three cases was *planned* for, in reality a pattern of data-collection technique unique to each case emerged naturally over time. Researching in these small organizations proved to be an organic process that required a relaxed and flexible style of interaction, to include the researcher's personal demeanour and dress mode. However, whereas it was necessary to permit a substantial amount of freewheeling during the bulk of the casework, there came a point when a structured intervention was needed to 'force' a particular construct ('formality', for instance) into a context in order to ensure consistency and rigour of data collection/interpretation across cases. It was found that two questionnaires delivered some twelve months apart served this need. This approach – structured (but sparing and timely) intervention in the observation of predominantly naturally-occurring organizational processes – worked well and was effective, as it reflected a balance between informality and structure that small organizations seem to achieve, or gravitate towards, naturally.

Informal telephone interviews

These were mostly 'opportunist' and conducted during telephone conversations with case respondents for purposes of scheduling/postponing/rescheduling site visits, clarifying information, and just generally keeping in touch. This type of informal contact was, however, invariably useful and as such worthy of reflection and recording in case notes.

Reviewing organizational documents

Organizational documents were reviewed both on and off site during the case fieldwork. A total of 22 documents from Cases 2 and 3 were catalogued as off-site items – about 50 per cent related directly or indirectly to HRD matters. Nothing was collected off-site from Case 1, although on site, product information and technical drawings relating to product at various stages of design were frequently offered up for scrutiny. The scarcity of the off-site document collection (given three organizations and the longevity of the study) was seen as yet another sign of SME informality.

Informal observations and 'overhearings'

These were also opportunist in nature, but could be powerfully meaningful in content. This 'technique' basically entailed keeping eyes and ears open and being attuned to what might be happening outside of the planned scope of a particular contact. Feldman (1995) relates how semiotic analysis may be used in the interpretation of qualitative data. Drawing upon the work of Eco, she (ibid.: 21) describes semiotic theory as 'a unified approach to every phenomenon of signification and/or communication. Semiotics is concerned with everything that can be taken as a sign. A sign is everything which can be taken as significantly substituting for something else'. The data gained through informal observations and overhearings lent themselves particularly well to the principles of semiotic analysis. The practice of reviewing organizational documents (above) also holds significance for the process of semiotic analysis, whereby the relevance of a document's content can become secondary to the relevance of the document's ontological status and the context and manner in which it is regarded by the respondent and offered up for scrutiny. For instance, the tendency by Case 1 respondents to offer only documents relating to product design may be taken as a sign of the high regard that this organization placed on its design innovation capability; a valuable insight that in turn helped shape understanding of other organizational beliefs, values and HRD perspectives.

Data analysis framework – 'Seeing the wood for the trees?'

Data analysis and interpretation were carried out continually throughout the fieldwork by way of writing up, coding and repeated reading of case notes. It was also helpful to periodically develop a written summary, or focus sheet from case notes. Miles and Huberman (1994: 77–8) refer to this analysis as the production of an 'Interim Case Study', and describe the practice as 'the first attempt to derive a coherent, overall account of the case'. There was a period of concentrated effort to bring together all the issues identified from all organizations over the final six months of the

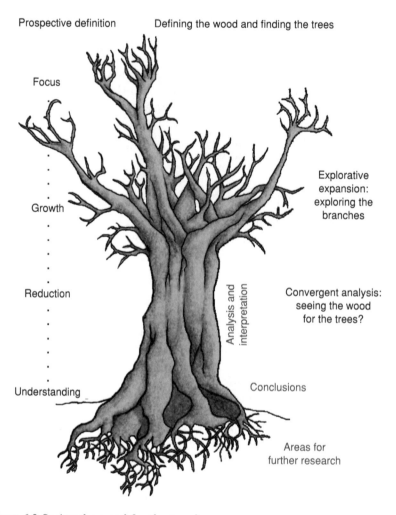

Prospective definition   Defining the wood and finding the trees

Focus

Explorative
expansion:
exploring the
branches

Growth

Convergent analysis:
seeing the wood
for the trees?

Reduction

Analysis and
interpretation

Understanding

Conclusions

Areas for
further research

Figure 6.2 Seeing the wood for the trees?
Source: Graphic design by David Llewelyn, Spryte

research project, when it became necessary to design a convergent analysis framework to manage and 'reduce' (Miles and Huberman 1994) the vast and varied amount of data and information gathered. A way into the development of this framework was to summarize and describe the research design diagrammatically. The display at Figure 6.2, entitled 'Seeing the wood for the trees?' depicts this, metaphorically, as a tree.

The research was seen to comprise three broad phases:

- **Prospective definition** (Defining the wood and finding the trees)
- **Explorative expansion** (Exploring the branches)
- **Convergent analysis** (Seeing the wood for the trees?)

Box 6.4 Three phases of the research

Prospective definition phase: (Defining the wood and finding the trees)
Key word: FOCUS

Activities in this phase included the development of a project statement, research objectives, conceptual framework and key concepts in order to determine and define the scope of the study ('defining the wood'). The preparatory survey is also positioned within this phase because it prospected for: (a) an initial empirical understanding of the world of the SME; and (b) organizations for subsequent casework ('finding the trees'). This phase was very much one of experiential learning (Kolb 1984), whereby perspectives and ideas were continually being framed and re-framed.

Explorative expansion phase: (Exploring the branches)
Key word: GROWTH

Having defined the wood and found the trees, the case fieldwork involved an expansive phase of gathering data from within the thick of the trees' branches. This was a time of great excitement and increasing confidence as relevant empirical data were captured and skills and techniques, such as those of taking and writing up case notes, were honed or acquired. It was also a time of frustration due to a tendency to become distracted by a myriad of interesting, but peripheral, issues in the case-study organizations.

Convergent analysis phase: (Seeing the wood for the trees?)
Key word: REDUCTION

As the branches of a tree are connected by its trunk to a hidden root system, so research data may be interpreted through a process of convergent analysis designed to probe beneath their surface. Immediately where the trunk of a tree grows into the ground, it tends to thicken slightly for stability and for protection of its roots. As research data filters through a convergent analysis process, two things tend to happen. First, new insight and perspectives may become apparent; and second, new questions may emerge. The former may then be offered as research conclusions, and the latter suggested as areas for further research and clarification. Thus, as a tree draws upon its roots through its trunk for growth, so does the research process attempt to understand the 'truth' through a convergent mechanism in order to 'grow' a particular body of knowledge.

Whilst it is difficult to locate time-scales and particular activities precisely within these phases, Box 6.4 provides a summary.

The model at Figure 6.2 led to the development of a convergent analysis framework (CAF) at Figure 6.3 that enabled a cohesive exploration of the project's main concepts and constructs, and a more focused explanation of findings. In keeping with Yin's (1994) arguments about maximizing the quality of case-study design to address matters of validity

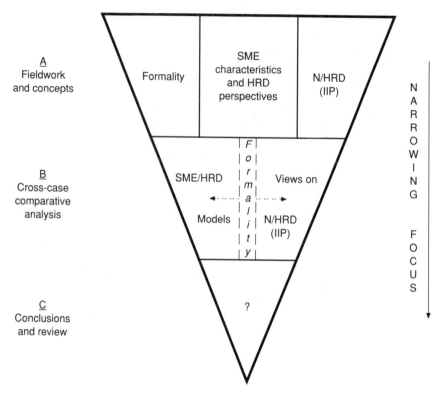

Figure 6.3 Convergent analysis framework (CAF)

and reliability, the CAF (Figure 6.3) was constructed so that it drew from and related to the research objectives and conceptual framework. The CAF depicts a continual dissemination of data from several conceptual and empirical sources into a narrowing focus of cross-case examination and analysis and an ultimate focal point for research conclusions and review.

Data analysis – individual cases

Data from each case were analysed and interpreted within the consistent framework engendered by the CAF. As well as the common constructs examined (organizational formality, HRD approaches, and owner/manager perspectives on N/HRD), and in order to inject an element of rival theory (Yin 1994), each case was assigned a particular SME characteristic as an additional focus in this process (innovation in Case 1, evolution and growth in Case 2, and leadership in Case 3). An outcome of the individual case analyses was a set of three 'organisational metaphors' as follows:

Case 1: 'Against the background of making the product'
Case 2: 'Connecting with contextual criticality'
Case 3: 'Pulling from the front as not yet up and running'

These 'metaphors' were derived from the language frequently used by principal research respondents, and other signs and symbols located in discussions with employees and organizational documents. If a sign is a significant substitution of something else (Feldman 1995) characterized by detachment from the item it substitutes, then a symbol system may be thought of as a significative theme constructed through signs (Berger and Luckmann 1991). In this sense, signs and symbols co-exist within a system of shared meaning. It is argued that a work organization too has a system of shared meaning, sometimes called 'organizational culture' (see, for example, Robbins 1997). So, if we live in a world of signs and symbols that help shape and interpret the shared meaning of a work organization, then it would seem logical to understand organizational phenomena through an exploration of its signs and symbols. As management respondents illustrated personal and organizational perspectives with description and stories grounded in both reality and metaphor, each of the above three organizational metaphors was deemed to be symbolic of its respective organization's primary culture.

Cross-case comparisons and analysis – 'From metaphor to model'

The use of organizational metaphor was extended into the cross-case analysis process by engaging an epistemological principle advanced by Nonaka (1996). He (ibid.: 23) argues that the conversion of tacit knowledge to explicit knowledge 'means finding a way to express the inexpressible', and that 'it is often the very conflict that metaphors embody that jump starts the creative process' (ibid.: 25). In suggesting how the imagery of a metaphor can lead the creative process to the logic of a model, Nonaka (ibid.) further comments:

> But while metaphor triggers the knowledge-creation process, it alone is not enough to complete it. The next step is analogy. Whereas metaphor is mostly driven by intuition and links images that at first glance seem remote from each other, analogy is a more structured process of reconciling contradictions and making distinctions. Put another way, by clarifying how the two ideas in one phrase are actually alike and not alike, the contradictions incorporated into metaphors are harmonised by analogy. In this respect analogy is an intermediate step between pure imagination and logical thinking.

The basis of Nonaka's argument is that movement from 'pure imagination' (metaphor) to 'logical thinking' (model) is too great without an

'But the universe is even more talkative ... it speaks not only of ultimate things (which it does always in an obscure fashion) but also of closer things, and then it speaks quite clearly.' (Eco 1992)

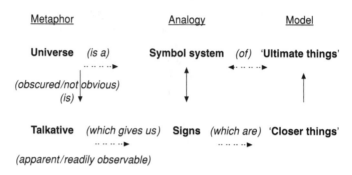

Figure 6.4 From metaphor to model

intermediary step – analogy, whereby an enquiry into how the elements of a metaphor are similar and yet different facilitates a more structured analysis. But the process begins with the imagery of metaphor.

As metaphor is rich in signs and symbolism which managers tend to use to 'articulate their intuitions and insights' (Nonaka 1996: 23), and that the analysis of research data is inherently concerned with the passage of knowledge from tacit to explicit state, then the principle of 'from metaphor to model' is appropriate in the analysis process here. This principle also captures the spirit of owner/manager conversations and disclosures encountered in the research, which by and large were colourful, and often metaphorical, recollections of everyday events. Figure 6.4 illustrates how a metaphor from a passage by Eco (1992: 24) was abstracted to build into a model conceptualizing the principle of 'from metaphor to model' used in the cross-case analysis process.

In Figure 6.4, the 'universe' is depicted as a symbol system – obscured and 'ultimate' – that exudes more obvious ontological signs by 'being talkative'. An exploration of these signs ('closer things') may lead to a discovery of what is hidden in the higher system ('ultimate things'), which in a work organization tend to gravitate towards issues allied to values, beliefs, culture and management perspectives. Two observations are made here. First, that Figure 6.4 is an axiomatic illustration of 'from metaphor to model', in that Eco's metaphor led to the development of the model (Figure 6.4). Second, that as the metaphor used to extrapolate the model is epistemologically grounded, the model provides a fitting framework to analyse research findings.

To move the data underpinning the three organizational metaphors (above) from metaphor to model was a two-stage process. First, a listing was made of the principle characteristics of each case as suggested by the metaphors. Then a semiotic analysis based upon principles of analogy (Nonaka 1996) and opposition (Feldman 1995) was carried out to organize and compare the data within a matrix. Two questions were asked in this process: 'How are the cases alike?' and 'How are they different?' The result was an understanding of how the cases compared culturally to feed into further cross-case analyses of the constructs contained in the CAF (above). Findings from the cross-case comparison of HRD approaches are now discussed.

The research findings

Table 6.3 compares the HRD 'planning', 'doing' and 'evaluating' activities in the three cases. The statements at the top of the table are summaries of the three HRD approaches extracted from the individual case analyses.

It may be observed from the table that each HRD approach differs from the other two, with Case 1 most closely matching the conventional SME paradigm. Whilst all three organizations demonstrate little formality in their HRD processes, Case 3 shows a focused determination to explore TandD at organizational, team and individual levels – a probable reflection of its industry and operational focus. Whereas Cases 1 and 2 appear more internally focused, Case 3 demonstrates an external perspective through participation in programmes and activities such as the New Deal, National Vocational Qualifications (NVQs) and foreign exchanges. The semiotic cross-case analysis technique advanced above (asking how are the cases alike, and not alike?) revealed a similar pattern, with Cases 1 and 2 more culturally akin to each other than to Case 3. Other data suggested that, in all three cases, HRD concentrated upon developing the organization to meet the particular demands of its own operating environment and circumstances: engineering and product development needs in Case 1; to a reasonable sufficiency and balance in Case 2; and attention to issues concerning both society and enterprise in Case 3. There was also evidence to suggest that the cases directed HRD effort at organizational level first and at individual employee level second – or not at all. For example, Case 1 focused its innovative energy on the development of new technology aimed at enhancing organizational product design and manufacturing capability; Case 2's managing director interviewed all employees under the auspices of an appraisal system in order to enhance his own (and, therefore, according to his self-conceptualization, his organization's) knowledge base without reciprocity in the form of employee development; and even Case 3 seemed to concentrate more upon the development of formalized organizational structures and systems over the development of individuals.

If, then, small organizations pursue organizational development before, or to the exclusion of, individual development, the extent of HRD (in

Table 6.3 Comparison of HRD approaches in the three cases

	Case 1: design and build engineering	Case 2: security and telecommunications	Case 3: youth and community projects
Summary	Within the limits of individual capability and responsibility against the background of making the product	'Ad hoc', or developed to a 'reasonable sufficiency' to instill/retain customer confidence; balanced against a need to limit corporate risk and disruptions to work	Focused upon developing the organization. T&D is eclectic but gradually becoming more integrated. Delivery is creative, resourceful and opportunistic, reliant upon external funding and provision for individuals
Planning	No formal HRD planning. HRD not planned in the context of its plans for growth. Tended to employ qualified people who need little or no training. Planned to introduce ISO 9001 which does require some formality in T&D	HRD has been considered in the light of recent organizational changes. No organizational T&D plan in place. Individual training plans were discussed with the MD but not developed. Plans to do job descriptions put off	T&D planning is informally, but regularly, discussed during team and individual performance meetings with the DM. More formal planning now being put in place as a result of the organization becoming a 'supplier' to the New Deal programme. Would like to implement IIP (or industry specific equivalent) and more formalized HRD processes in general
Doing	1 traditional apprentice. Workforce training *ad hoc* and dependent upon informal sharing of information and skills with peers. No management development. Management apparently happy with the level of T&D undertaken, although some managers recognize the need for more diverse management skills	1 Modern Apprentice (MA). Management team have undertaken formal off-job development. No evidence of training being carried out according to T&D plans. Workforce training is reactive and sporadic. Staff appraisal system in place	Designed and implemented its own behaviourally based selection process. Employee exchange visit to Hong Kong. Team building taken place to examine team roles and responsibilities. Individual performance reviews/coaching sessions with development manager take place regularly – output is documented. Staff development with NVQs and other external programmes
Evaluating	Evaluation occurred as part of feedback on on-the-job errors. No internal HRD expertise	Informal through annual appraisal system. The MA's progress is evaluated under the overall modern apprenticeship scheme by the college and on-the-job feedback on errors. No internal HRD expertise	Informal evaluation takes place during reviews and team meeting. The need for more specific evaluation of learning is appreciated. Development manager is familiar with business planning and HRD processes

its broader sense) in small organizations may be misunderstood and under-estimated. As much of the literature on the subject appears to converge upon the TandD of individuals, this point may be valid. However, differing rationales in each case for developing organization over individuals were determined. For instance, Case 1 preferred to employ qualified craftsmen and saw individual development as the responsibility of individuals; Case 2's MD felt that TandD was lost time; and the development manager in Case 3 recognized a need for personal intervention in the development of employees, but saw the augmentation of formality and work projects as more pressing and immediate priorities for the needs of the organization.

Critical analysis

In focusing upon small organizations, the data presented in the chapter raise some important issues for the conceptual and practical development of HRD, and for researching it. In particular, the data question the relevance of 'conventional' HRD thinking and practices to SMEs. Whereas the underpinning concepts and theories of HRD may just as readily apply to people in small organizations as to those who work in large ones, HRD *approaches* in small organizations are individualistic and reflect small-firm, not large-firm, logic. Based upon the three cases studied, the importance of trying to discover what each organization's logic might be, cannot be underestimated, undercut or undervalued. Academics and practitioners of HRD may also have to concede that a particular SME's chosen logic could be not to 'do' HRD at all – or, perhaps, do it in ways that are not obviously located in some form of externally recognized theory or practice. Furthermore, if as already argued the issue of organizational 'smallness' is a multidimensional concept not determined exclusively by size, then the disposition and delivery of HRD within autonomous business units of large enterprises may be better served by small- not large-firm logic and perspectives.

With regard to issues surrounding the theory and practice of conducting research in SMEs, the study suggests that a cohesive pattern of short, uncomplicated, intermittent interventions, that do not interfere with organizational direction, pace and fluidity, forms the basis of an effective research methodology. This would position longer-term casework more acceptable to small organizations than, for example, a disjointed battery of surveys. Interestingly, the argument for research continuity and cohesion here is antithetical of much that is characteristically attributed to SMEs. It may be, however, that 'dipping in and out' in a sustained and loosely structured manner appeals to a small organization's tendency towards 'informal formality'.

As it was relatively difficult to locate literature specifically about *researching* HRD in SMEs, the programme of work was initially designed to emulate 'purist' case-study tradition. However, within that framework, field practices and interactions with respondents were shaped considerably by the characteristics of small organizational life and the idiosyncrasies of owner/ managers. For instance, it soon became apparent that small organizations do not relate well to planned research schedules, systematic data collection, and formal reporting: and although extremely willing to share their views and experiences, owner/managers do not tolerate what they perceive as interference rather than help. They like to tell, and be listened to. During the initial visit to Case 1, for example, the technical manager explained in no uncertain terms what the role of 'consultants in small companies' should be. However, he was keen to hear how the 'learning organization', which he described as a 'black hole', could be of tangible value to a small organization. This remark presented an interesting challenge, but more importantly it offered a valuable lesson.

The data analysis technique 'from metaphor to model' mirrors small organizational life, as it is has strong visual impact located in practical contexts. The technique was especially useful in extrapolating and articulating organizational phenomena in a 'language' that connects with the SME – that is a language of everyday activities and problems, and things you feel you want to know more about.

Conclusions and key learning points

First, it must be said that to present in detail the entire project's main conclusions would be inappropriate in the context of the chapter. So a single finding of most significance (to the chapter) is featured here. As case respondents have indicated that small organizations need to focus on critical issues to survive, that survival is about connecting with critical markets and customers, and that everything must be done against the background of the product, then it is not unreasonable to believe that product/service capability might inevitably seem more crucial to a small organization than the individual capabilities of those who work there. Their development, it seems, is considered best left (either permanently or temporarily) to occur 'naturally with the job'. If, as the research concludes, HRD in small organizations is more instinctively directed at the development of the organization than at the training and development of those who work there, this poses a potentially significant barrier to the traditional notion of HRD, and N/HRD, in SMEs, which mainly appears to focus upon the training and development of individuals.

It is also possible that the small and, perhaps, predominantly introverted world of the SME may cause it to suffer the effects of individual subjective realities and industry habitualizations (Berger and Luckmann 1991) more acutely than larger organizations. This creates a self-reinforcing position that may considerably inhibit the likelihood of effective external intervention and receptiveness to alternative HRD perspectives and credible (genuine and appropriate) 'help' – to include collaborative research approaches.

Given the validity of all this, it may be sensible that the HRD profession should concentrate its SME effort on helping owner/managers in the following ways. First, to intervene more deliberately and effectively in their business systems and processes, thus organically building upon existing but intuitive skills and capabilities (the HRD function supporting with process, rather than content intervention). Second, to step outside of their often solipsistic existences to interact and learn with and from their people. Third, to create more effective ways of positioning the job as the HRD intervention for individuals. There is little point in talking to an owner/manager about the virtues of 'training plans', 'lifelong learning', or any other 'HRD-speak'. Evidence from the research suggests that the language of the SME is grounded in notions of activity, energy, pace and having to find ways out of problems rather than planning for them to happen – 'being in it', as one case respondent put it. To be perceived as a credible and worthwhile endeavour, HRD in an SME is best located conceptually and practically in what is currently critical to the organization. Above all, it must achieve an immediate and highly visible payback to the business. Informality and simplicity of HRD delivery in this context need not equate to inadequacy: again, short, uncomplicated interventions that complement and work *with* an SME's pace, fluidity and direction seem acceptable and effective.

Finally, the research has highlighted some interesting areas for further research; notably those concerning the knowledge-development and learning processes in small organizations, and a perceived lack of clarity about the impact of HRD on SME capability and performance (see, for example, Cosh *et al.* 1998 or Storey 1994). It may be that the two issues are connected, and that notions of tacit knowledge (Nonaka 1996; Spender 1996) and related ideas on 'informal' and 'incidental' learning (Marsick and Watkins 1997) hold the key to analysing and understanding HRD processes in small organizations and how to study them.

References

Berger, P.L. and Luckmann, T. (1991) *The Social Construction of Reality: a Treatise in the Sociology of Knowledge*, Harmondsworth: Penguin.

Bradburd, R.M. and Ross, D.R. (1989) 'Can small firms find and defend strategic niches? A test of the Porter hypothesis', *Review of Economics and Statistics*, LXXI(2): 258–62.

Bryman, A. and Cramer, D. (1990) *Quantitative Data Analysis for Social Scientists*, London: Routledge.

—— (1997) *Quantitative Data Analysis with SPSS for Windows: a Guide for Social Scientists*, London: Routledge.

Buckley, R. and Caple, J. (1990) *The Theory and Practice of Training*, London: Kogan Page.

Cosh, A., Duncan, J. and Hughes, A. (1998) *Investment in Training and Small Firm Growth and Survival: An Empirical Analysis for the UK 1987–95*, DfEE, Research Report RR 36.

Davis, K. and Newstrom, J.W. (1972) *Human Behaviour at Work* (eighth edn), USA: McGraw-Hill Series in Management.

DfEE (1997) *TECs and Small Firms Training – Lessons from Skills for Small Businesses*, DfEE, Research Report RR 27.

DTI (1999) *The Small Business Service* (online). Available at: www.dti.gov.uk/sbs (accessed 19 July 1999).

Easterby-Smith, M., Thorpe, R. and Lowe, A. (1993) *Management Research: an Introduction*, London: Sage.

Eco, U. (1992) *The Name of the Rose*, London: Minerva.

Feldman, M.S. (1995) *Strategies for Interpreting Qualitative Data*, Thousand Oaks, CA: Sage.

French, R. and Bazalgette, J. (1996) 'From "learning organisation" to "teaching–learning organisation"?', *Management Learning*, 27(1): 113–28.

French, W.L. and Bell, C.H. Jnr. (1990) *Organisation Development: behavioural science interventions for organisation improvement* (fourth edn), Englewood Cliffs, NJ: Prentice Hall.

Garavan, T.N., Costine, P. and Heraty, N. (1995) 'The emergence of strategic human resource development', *Journal of European Industrial Training*, 19(10): 4–10.

Gibb, A.A. (1997) 'Small firms' training and competitiveness. Building upon the small business as a learning organisation', *International Small Business Journal*, 15(3): 13–29.

Handy, C. (1995) *The Age of Unreason*, London: Arrow Books.

Harrison, R. (1997) *Employee Development*, London: Institute of Personnel and Development.

IIP UK (1996) *Investors in People the Revised Indicators: advice and guidance for practitioners*, London: IIP UK.

Joyce, P., McNulty, T. and Woods, A. (1995) 'Workforce training: are small firms different?' *Journal of European and Industrial Training*, 19(5): 19–25.

Keeble, D., Bryson, J. and Wood, P. (1992) 'The rise and role of small service firms in the United Kingdom', *International Small Business Journal*, 11(1): 11–22.

Kolb, D.A. (1984) *Experiential Learning*, Englewood Cliffs, NJ: Prentice Hall PTR.

Lane, A.D. (ed.) (1994) *Issues in People Management No. 8: People Management in Small and Medium Enterprises*, London: IPD.

McGill, I. and Beaty, L. (1992) *Action Learning: a Practitioner's Guide*, London: Kogan Page.

Marsick, V.J. and Watkins, K.E. (1997) 'Lessons from informal and incidental learning', in John Burgoyne and Michael Reynolds (eds) *Management Learning: Integrating Perspectives in Theory and Practice*, London: Sage, 295–311.

Martin, J. (1990) 'Breaking up the mono-method monopolies in organisational studies', in J. Hassard and D. Pym (eds) *The Theory and Philosophy of Organisations*, London: Routledge, 30–43.

Megginson, David (1996) 'Planned and emergent learning: consequences for development', *Management Learning*, 27(4): 411–28.

Metcalf, H., Walling, A. and Fogarty, M. (1994) *Individual Commitment to Learning, Employers' Attitudes*, Sheffield: Employment Department, Research Strategy Branch.

144

Miles, M.B. and Huberman, A.M. (1994) *Qualitative Data Analysis* (second edn), Thousand Oaks, CA: Sage.

Nonaka, I. (1996) 'The knowledge creating company', in Ken Starkey (ed.) *How Organisations Learn*, London: International Thomson Business Press, 18–31.

Osborne, R.L. (1995) 'The essence of entrepreneurial success', *Management Decision*, 33(7): 4–9.

Revans, R. (1983) *The ABC of Action Learning*, Bromley: Chartwell-Brant.

Riley, J. (1990) *Getting the Most from Your Data*, Bristol: Technical and Educational Services Ltd.

Robbins, Stephen P. (1997) *Essentials of Organisational Behaviour* (fifth edn), Englewood Cliffs, NJ: Prentice-Hall.

Sadler-Smith, E., Down, S. and Field, J. (1999) 'Adding value to HRD: evaluation, Investors in People and small firm training', *Human Resource Development International*, 2(4): 369–90.

Spender, J.C. (1996) 'Competitive advantage from tacit knowledge', in B. Moingeon and A. Edmondson (eds) *Organisational Learning and Competitive Advantage*, London: Sage, 56–73.

Stanworth, M.J.K. and Curran, J. (1976) 'Growth and the small firm – an alternative view', *Journal of Management Studies*, 13: 95–110.

Stanworth, J., Stanworth, C., Granger, B. and Blyth, S. (1989) 'Who becomes an entrepreneur?' *International Small Business Journal*, 8(1): 11–22.

Stewart, J. (1996) *Managing Change Through Training and Development* (second edn), London: Kogan Page.

Stewart, J. and McGoldrick, J. (eds) (1996) *Human Resource Development: Perspectives, Strategies and Practice*, London: Pitman.

Storey, D.J. (1994) *Understanding the Small Business Sector*, London: Routledge.

TUC (1997) *The Small Firms Myth*, TUC, Economic and Social Affairs Department.

Vickerstaff, S. and Parker, K.T. (1995) 'Helping small firms: the contribution of TECs and LECs', *International Small Business Journal*, 13(4): 56–72.

Watson, J. and Everett, J. (1993) 'Defining small business failure', *International Small Business Journal*, 11(3): 35–48.

Weinberger, L.A. (1998) 'Commonly held theories of human resource development', *Human Resource Development International*, 1(1): 75–93.

Westhead, P. and Storey, D. (1996) 'Management training and small firm performance: why is the link so weak?' *International Small Business Journal*, 14(4): 13–24.

Yin, R.K. (1994) *Case Study Research Design and Methods* (second edn), Thousand Oaks, CA: Sage.

7

EVALUATING THE IMPACT OF MANAGEMENT DEVELOPMENT ON PERFORMANCE

Jonathan Winterton and Ruth Winterton

Aims and contribution

This chapter describes a research project, undertaken for the UK Department for Education and Employment, which investigated the impact of management development upon performance in sixteen organizations. The aim is to contribute to debates both on the role of HRD in improving performance and on ways of evaluating HRD impacts. While much of the literature on measuring the impact of HRD on performance is from the USA, the debates take on a particular significance in the UK context because it has long been recognized that UK managers are inadequately trained and qualified in comparison with those of competing nations.

As post-war demand for managers increased (Clements 1958: 158), British industry was handicapped by a shortage of suitably qualified managers (McGivering, Matthews and Scott 1960: 79). The general lack of qualifications among senior managers in the UK has been reiterated over the years (CBI 1989; Legatt 1972; Mangham and Silver 1986) and reinforced by recent work completed for the UK Government's Skills Task Force (Johnson and Winterton 1999).

The background to the study described in this chapter was rooted in policy initiatives designed to remedy deficiencies identified in successive reports on management education and training during the 1980s and 1990s. In 1987 two reports were produced as part of a review of management education and training, prompted by the recognition that the UK still lagged behind other industrialized nations in terms of its formal management education (Constable and McCormick 1987; Handy *et al.* 1987). A few years later, the Cannon and Taylor Working Party Reports (IoM 1994), arising out of the 1992 Institute of Management review of management development, noted that the challenges of organizational changes, especially contracting out, de-layering and empowerment, made the need for management development particularly acute. The situation was

146

exacerbated by persistent structural unemployment, competitive pressures from low-wage economies, rapid technological change and standards in education that were inappropriate to the needs of employers.

The Handy Report recommended that a group of top companies form a Charter Group and establish a charter of good practice for management development (Constable 1991). From these origins, the Management Charter Initiative (MCI) was established in 1988 as the operating arm of the National Forum for Management Education and Development and by the end of 1991 had the support of over 800 companies. Following the adoption of a competence-based approach to vocational training in the UK, MCI was recognized as the lead body for management and developed a generic set of occupational standards relating to areas of activity in which managers need to be competent (Miller 1991). In 1994, with renewed concern over developing the UK managerial workforce, the Employment Department (now the Department for Education and Employment, hereafter simply 'the Department') decided to appraise the use of the Management Standards developed by MCI. The subsequent study that we undertook for the Department investigated the business benefits that could be attributed to competence-based management development in a range of sixteen organizations.

The *Growth, Competitiveness, Employment* White Paper from the European Commission (1994) argued that skills must be raised at all levels if European enterprises were to compete in global markets. At the same time the *Teaching and Learning* White Paper (European Commission 1996) stressed the need to provide opportunities for continuous development in order to achieve this. The arguments resurfaced in successive Competitiveness White Papers in the UK during the 1990s and, after the Labour victory of 1997, in the work of the *Skills Task Force* and the emerging framework for life-long learning. For UK managers, the need to increase the volume and quality of development is particularly acute given the dramatic changes taking place in the external environment and in organizations (Winterton *et al.* 2000).

The study was therefore stimulated both by the need to increase management development and to evaluate the effectiveness of development that was competence based, the approach promoted under the reform of vocational education and training in the UK (Winterton 2000). If performance improvements could be identified and attributed to management development, managers would be more likely both to engage in development themselves and to make opportunities available for their subordinates. Moreover, if tangible benefits to business could be identified from the competence-based approach, more managers might use the NVQ/SVQ route to accredit their competence, thereby raising the overall level of managerial qualification.

After this brief introduction, the remainder of the chapter is organized into six sections. The conceptual and theoretical underpinning of the

147

study is first considered in relation to the literature on the role of HRD in general, and management development in particular, in improving performance. The third section outlines the empirical context, explaining the logic of the research design and briefly describing the sixteen organizations involved. The fourth section takes up this discussion of methodological issues, elaborating the design of the case-study protocol and the fieldwork that was involved. The next section describes the main findings of the research in relation to the five hypotheses articulated at the design stage. The critical analysis that follows highlights the significance of the findings. Clear performance benefits were identified from management development, and these were more evident where management development was linked with organizational strategy and where HRD systems and processes adopted a coherent set of competence statements, such as the Management Standards. The concluding section draws out the significance of both the substantive research findings and the procedural methodological issues that together represent the key learning points of the study.

Theoretical context

There is an extensive literature supporting the crucial role of human resources in improving organizational performance and sustaining competitive advantage (Arthur 1994; Carter and Lumsden 1988; Coopers and Lybrand 1992; Cutcher-Gershenfeld 1991; Downham, Noel and Prendergast 1992; Huselid 1995; MacDuffie 1995). Snell and Dean (1992) showed that effective management of human capital, especially in relation to building employee skills and commitment, was the key factor in releasing the productive potential of advanced manufacturing technology. Where organizational strategies have focused on replacing employees with physical capital, the effect of human activity on organizational performance is correspondingly minimized (Zuboff 1988). However, investment in human resources as the ultimate source of competitive advantage (Barney 1991; Pfeffer 1994) is more plausible in the context of globalization, which weakens the advantages deriving from economies of scale and access to product markets and capital (Reich 1991). Therefore, the optimum human resources policy, and the potential role of human capital, is contingent upon the relative importance of cost, quality and flexibility imperatives in the manufacturing strategy adopted (Youndt et al. 1996: 841).

Nevertheless, there is insufficient robust evidence concerning the effect of HRD on organizational performance, because relatively few organizations bother to evaluate the impact of training and development beyond the reaction level as defined in Kirkpatrick's (1967) typology. The paucity of evaluation of HRD initiatives is often explained by the difficulty of attributing causality: 'at best, management development and training must always be an act of faith' (Peel 1984: 35). Not only is it difficult to identify operational results that are amenable to improvement through training and development, causality is difficult to establish because often 'no single factor, including training, could by itself have brought about the change that has taken place' (Robinson and Robinson 1989: 275). The problem is compounded by 'political' considerations which deter proper evaluation because of vested interests in demonstrating the effectiveness of MD opportunities for which individuals are responsible or to which they have committed time or money (Fox 1989; Currie 1994; Easterby-Smith 1994). Because of these practical difficulties in measuring the effects of developing people (Harrison 1992), reported benefits are often anecdotal and confined to a single aspect of performance.

Not only is the cumulative body of knowledge under-developed, it also lacks a coherent conceptual framework and an accepted structural model (Becker and Gerhart 1996). In one of the pioneering contributions to the HRD and performance literature, Rummler and Brache (1992) distinguished three different levels of analysis: individual; process; and organization. In the influential *Analysis for Improving Performance*, Swanson (1994) adopted the same framework of analysis, which was perpetuated in subsequent work (Lynham 1998; Holton 1999; Swanson 1999).

This division of individual, process and organizational levels of performance has created conceptual confusion because it neglects the team or group level in the structure and conflates structures with processes. Performance at the team level links individuals with the organization and therefore plays a pivotal role in translating individual performance improvements into bottom line results (Katzenbach and Smith 1992; Magjuka and Baldwin 1991; Sundstrom, De Meuse and Futrell 1990). Team level activities are important in facilitating the transfer between individual learning and organizational learning through the development of shared mental models (Kim 1993) and the adoption of routines that improve existing practices to develop core competence (Barney 1991; Grant 1991). However, as Russ-Eft (1996) has argued: 'We need more research on defining and measuring team performance.'

Individuals, groups and the organization as a whole represent different structural levels, whereas processes (along with capacities and accomplishments) exist at each of these levels, as Fisher and Sleezer (1999) recognized. In advance of commissioning the research described here, the Department established an expert group to identify an appropriate methodology for assessing the business benefits of the Management Standards. From the outset, the study group drew a clear distinction between *levels in the organisational structure* and *work processes* at each of these levels in exploring appropriate methodologies for tracing and measuring the business impact of management development, particularly that which was competence-based (Leman *et al.* 1994). Given the causal ambiguity concerning the mechanisms by which human resource practices translate into improved business performance, the expert group recognized that rigorous methods of analysis would be required (Barney 1991).

The literature provided the expert group with some indication of the nature of performance benefits to be anticipated from management development. At the individual level, the literature demonstrates above all else the difficulties of measurement and attribution associated with identifying performance improvements arising from management development. In relation to team performance, the key message is the importance of developing collective knowledge so that when individuals change jobs, organizational capacity is not adversely affected (Brooks 1994). With organizational performance, the literature links the achievement of critical success factors to the management capability of organizations (Berry 1990). Strategies that recognize core competence as a key resource for gaining competitive advantage are prevalent in the recent literature (Barney 1995; Campbell and Sommers Luchs 1997; Hussey 1988, 1996; Prahalad and Hamel 1990; Thurbin 1995; Tobin 1993). Clearly, if the development of core competence, including managerial competence, is a crucial determinant of improved organizational performance (as represented by competitive success), then improved performance of individuals and teams ought to be intervening outcomes.

The need to link management development with organizational strategy (Taylor and Thackwray 1995) is also prominent in recent literature, as is the need to justify individual development in terms of benefits to the organization (Mitrani, Dalziel and Fitt 1992). There is evidence that organizational performance is enhanced when there is a good fit between organizational strategy and employees' competences, whether employees are developed in line with strategy (Wright and Snell 1991) or strategies are designed to match employees' competences (Snow and Snell 1993). Finally, recent literature contains claims that management development is more effective where HRD systems and procedures have adopted the MCI Standards (King 1993).

Having considered the literature alongside the evaluation needs of the Employment Department, the expert group proposed five testable hypotheses:

- Management development improves individual performance.
- Management development improves team performance.
- Management development improves organizational performance.
- Improvements in individual, team and organizational performance are more likely if management development is linked to organizational strategy.
- Improvements in individual, team and organizational performance are more likely if HRD systems and processes are based on a common, coherent integrated set of competence statements (such as the MCI Standards).

The expert group recommended to the Department that these hypotheses could best be tested using a case-study approach in a range of organizations.

The group drafted a preliminary case-study protocol identifying the evidence to be assessed in relation to the processes and performance outcomes to be investigated at each level. The draft protocol was included as part of the specification for the project when the tender was awarded to us with colleagues at PriME Research and Development of Harrogate.

Empirical context

In order adequately to test all five hypotheses, it was necessary to include 'counterfactual cases'. We needed organizations that did not use the Management Standards as well as users, and to include organizations in which management development was not linked with organizational strategy as well as those where there was a clear link. For each of the four categories defined by these two variables, the objective was to identify five organizations suitable for case study. Information therefore had to be gathered from potential case organizations *before* any fieldwork took place in order tentatively to allocate them to one of the four categories. Contenders for study were identified from discussions with MCI, the Department Steering Group, and from previous research. The organizations were to be drawn from a range of different economic sectors, and it was intended that one third of the organizations studied would be SMEs (fewer than 200 employees).

The MCI supplied details of twenty-five organizations known to have adopted the Management Standards and a second tranche of eighteen organizations, known to practise competence-based management development but not thought to be users of the occupational standards, was also identified. Initially, a letter was sent to each organization by the Department, which the researchers followed up by telephone to arrange a meeting with senior managers and negotiate access. Difficulties in achieving access, particularly with SMEs, made it necessary to approach further organizations and out of a total of 126 organizations approached sixteen cases were selected for detailed study from those that agreed to collaborate.

The sixteen cases were tentatively allocated to the four categories on the basis of preliminary discussions with the contact in each organization, and the cases appeared to be weighted in favour of Standards users, and especially in favour of those claiming that management development was closely linked with organizational strategy. There were early indications that using the double dichotomy as a basis for categorizing cases was an oversimplification and would prove less useful than intended. Each dimension was really a spectrum, with cases located somewhere along each continuum. Differentiating cases according to whether management development was linked to organizational strategy was especially problematic, since most respondents believed that development was linked to strategy. Clearly management development could be integrated with organizational strategy in some respects and not in others and the difficulty in establishing

151

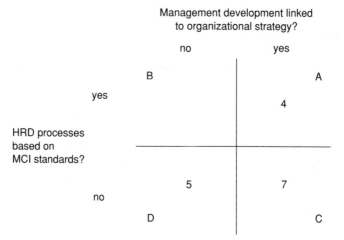

Figure 7.1 Achieved cases by type

the extent to which the two were integrated was reflected in the different perspectives of individuals in the same organization.

It was feared that these problems would impose limitations on the extent to which the first conditional hypothesis (concerning the impact of linking management development with organizational strategy) could be tested. Differentiating cases according to whether the organizations had adopted the Standards appeared less problematic, and cases were provisionally labelled as users and non-users (of the occupational standards developed by MCI). However, the case studies demonstrated that some organizations that were ostensibly users of the Standards had not, in fact, adopted them comprehensively.

The case reports and written evidence were evaluated by independent consultants and validated against the criteria established by the expert group. The cases were re-classified on the basis of this evaluation, producing the achieved cases shown in Figure 7.1. In this final classification, only four cases were defined as type A, while five were viewed as type D, and the remainder type C. Type B, in which HRD systems were based on the Management Standards but management development was not linked to organizational strategy, proved to be an empty cell. This finding confirmed empirically, for the cases studied, what, with the benefit of hindsight, might have been assumed *a priori*: that an organization is unlikely to adopt the Management Standards and not link its management development to organizational strategy.

The sector, size and final classifications of the sixteen cases that were involved in the study are shown in Table 7.1 and detailed information is provided in the extended account of the case studies (Winterton and Winterton 1999a). In terms of sectors involved, the cases were drawn from:

Table 7.1 Characteristics of collaborating cases

Case	Sector	Size	Category
01	mining	200	D
02	galvanizing	103	A
03	retail	410	A
04	oil	4,000	C
05	engineering	3,500	C
06	civil service	68,000	C
07	insurance	260	A
08	charity	2,300	D
09	law courts	560	A
10	newspapers	3,200	C
11	NHS Trust	1,400	C
12	aeroplane components	274	C
13	NHS Trust	7,000	D
14	clothing	170	D
15	footwear	167	C
16	NHS Trust	1,400	D

primary (2); manufacturing (5); private services (3); public services (3); and the health service (3). In terms of the size distribution (by number of employees), the cases were drawn from: < 201 (4); 201–499 (3); 500–1,999 (3); 2,000–3,999 (3); and > 3,999 (3).

Methodological issues

The Employment Department study group considered a variety of methodologies and recommended an embedded, multiple case-study approach to investigate the impact of CBMD and the adoption of the Management Standards.

The case study offers a distinct advantage in examining 'a contemporary set of events, over which the investigator has little or no control' (Yin 1984: 20). Case studies, whether exploratory, descriptive or explanatory, are by definition empirical inquiries that investigate a contemporary phenomenon within its real-life context, when the boundaries between phenomenon and context are not clearly evident, and in which multiple sources of evidence are used (Yin 1981). Given appropriate research design, a series of case studies may be generalized to theoretical propositions, not to a universal population, as is the goal with statistical generalization from a sample. In recommending a case-study approach, the expert group recognized that observation would play a minor role in data collection and that case-study reports should be kept concise and focused on the issues relating to the hypotheses outlined above.

A multiple case-study approach was identified as most appropriate for this research. Multiple case studies offer the advantages associated with replication when cases are selected to offer either literal or theoretical replication, the theoretical framework establishing the conditions under which a phenomenon should be, and should not be, found. It was recognized that the research design for the case studies would have to embody the theoretical and conceptual underpinnings of what was being studied. As the elements of the design were developed, so the theory was more clearly articulated. In formulating the research design, five areas were addressed:

- The research question to be explored: how does management development or the adoption of the Management Standards developed by MCI improve performance?
- Propositions or hypotheses: such as the hypotheses that management development improves both individual and team performance.
- Unit of analysis: the primary unit of analysis was the organization, but within this sub-units such as functional areas and individuals were defined.
- Logic linking data to propositions: such as evidence of improved performance following the adoption of the Management Standards.
- Criteria for interpreting a study's findings: it was necessary to establish criteria to assess what constitutes a significant improvement in performance.

After the initial theory development stage, the cases for study were selected and the hypotheses operationalized by defining appropriate measures and identifying methods of data collection. An embedded design (involving more than one unit of analysis) was most appropriate for this research since each case involved a consideration of different functional areas and different levels of analysis. Each case was a self-contained study, and each case report sought to establish conclusions concerning the propositions to be tested. The cross-case analysis aimed to explain convergence and divergence between cases in terms of *a priori* predictions made as part of the replication logic at the design stage.

The expert group offered a tentative case-study design including the data collection protocol that specified the written evidence required and recommended detailed interviews with key respondents in each organization. This initial case-study protocol was operationalized, piloted and refined by the authors once the research was commissioned. The protocol defined the written evidence to be examined in relation to each hypothesis and the range of measures of performance to be considered. It also comprised interview schedules that were to be used for in-depth, semi-structured interviews with senior strategic managers (chief executive, finance director and head of human resources), line managers and junior managers. The full case-study protocol is contained in the official report of the study (Winterton and Winterton 1996).

As a minimum in each case, face-to-face interviews were conducted with the three senior strategic managers, four line managers and four team members. Multiple sources of evidence were collected to increase the reliability of data through triangulation and interlocking questions in the interview schedules were designed to test for consistency between the views of managers at different levels. Details of improvements in performance and of HRD systems and processes were collected through an extensive range of written evidence. Managers' job specifications gave an indication of the extent to which responsibility for management development was a feature of their role, while company accounts were examined as evidence of improvements in organizational performance.

A dossier was compiled of written evidence and interviews for each organization studied, and a case report was written in accordance with the protocol. The case reports provided background details of the organization, details of the organizational strategy, the HRD systems and processes, and the evidence of improvements in individual, team and organizational performance attributed to management development by respondents. Each case report was validated with two senior managers in the organization and revised before being evaluated and used in the cross-case analysis.

To test the five hypotheses, a team of independent consultants was asked to rank the cases according to three criteria:

- the extent of improvements in individual, team and organizational performance attributable to management development;
- the degree to which management development was linked to organizational strategy;
- the extent to which the Management Standards had been adopted in HRD systems and processes.

The evaluation was co-ordinated by a consultant who had been involved in developing the Management Standards and had participated in the original expert group but had not been involved in the case studies; she was therefore familiar with the protocol but was not biased by knowledge of particular cases. The rank order of the cases according to the three performance measures and the two defining characteristics was used to structure the cross-case analysis. The rankings made it possible to test for any correlation between the defining characteristics and performance improvements measured at the three levels, as well as correlation and concordance between the three performance measures. In addition to the case-study evidence, therefore, the hypotheses were examined using robust non-parametric techniques. The results of the statistical tests are reported in the concluding section.

The research

The dossiers for each case study were too extensive to be included in the official report of the research (Winterton and Winterton 1996) although abbreviated case reports are included in the extended account of the study (Winterton and Winterton 1999a). A selection of the evidence is considered below in relation to the hypotheses outlined above.

In the cases demonstrating the most robust evidence of improvements in individual performance, the central importance of management development was demonstrated through written evidence and corroborated interviews. The improvements included increased personal confidence, awareness of potential and continuous development of general managerial skills and competences. Managers reported having a better understanding of both organizational objectives and their individual responsibilities. A range of efficiency gains were attributed to management development, such as better planning and time management, more effectiveness in running meetings, and improvements in project management, change management and problem solving. Increased competence in managing people was also cited, especially through raising skills in communications, presentation, leadership and motivation. Middle management mentioned empowerment, faster individual career advancement and a more methodical approach to developing others.

Improvements in individual performance were clearly associated with the use of the Management Standards and the implementation of NVQs, which provided criteria for performance, facilitated best practice benchmarking and promoted new ways of conceptualizing work tasks. With the Standards, individuals take responsibility for, and can track, their own development, and this is associated with increased commitment and motivation.

In the organizations providing less robust evidence of improvements in individual performance, there were nonetheless examples of specific improvements attributed to management development activities. In other organizations, isolated examples of individual performance gains were cited, but these were more a consequence of *ad hoc* initiatives than the result of operating a coherent management development framework. Towards the lower end of the ranking, there was ambiguity in relation to reported improvements, difficulties of measurement and of attributing improvements to management development. In particular, there were difficulties in separating individual and team performance measures, and systematic measurement and evaluation was thought to be too costly. It was also noted that the outcomes of development vary between individuals and that the effects are difficult to isolate when other major changes are taking place.

Where there was most evidence of improvements in team performance attributed to management development, these typically related to process issues such as quality of service, better focus on customer needs, reduced queues, better telephone standards and improved customer relations. Managers in some organizations cited evidence of more strategic behaviour and identified better procedures and monitoring of actions. Cost reductions, efficiency gains and more effective debt control were also reported. Other examples of improved team performance arising from management development included improved procedures for controlling and handling materials as well as the identification of potential areas for improvement in the future such as new information systems.

Improvements in team performance attributed to management development initiatives designed to promote team working included greater flexibility, awareness of team responsibilities and more effective team working. Both interpersonal and interdepartmental relations improved as a result of better communications, and individuals were also said to demonstrate increased commitment and motivation. In one case, managers identified improved team performance, such as more 'flexibility and commitment', as a result of management development introduced to support business process re-engineering. In another case, improvements in team performance as a result of management development initiatives were visible in the changes in team behaviour, including performance and the dynamics of work-groups.

Major difficulties of measurement of team performance and of attributing improvements to management development were encountered, especially where the same measures were used for individual and team performance, or where team performance was regarded as a function of a manager's performance. Equally, team performance was difficult to separate from organizational performance and was affected by extraneous factors.

The organizations which were ranked highest in terms of organizational performance improvements displayed quantified, written and corroborated evidence and respondents were unequivocal that management development had contributed to all prime measures of business efficiency. In such organizations, managers emphasized increased turnover and profit, sales and revenue growth, increased market share and competitiveness. Productivity, efficiency and quality gains were important factors, as was decreased unit costs. Other benefits reported were reductions in arrears and stock holding, shorter waiting times and queues, and reduced staff turnover.

In cases ranked lower than the best, evidence was provided of specific business benefits, which were largely attributable to management development activities. Where improvements in organizational performance were identified, the extent to which these were attributed to management development initiatives varied from the unequivocal cases where they would have been impossible without management development, to cases where the contribution of management development was implicit. Other cases showed how management development was the major, but not the only, contribution to success, or how management development was a necessary factor, in conjunction with other changes.

Problems of measurement of organizational performance were most serious in the weaker cases, and largely arose from the interaction of other factors affecting bottom line results. Difficulties of attribution were a consequence of being unable to produce counter-factual evidence as to what outcomes might have been expected in the absence of management development initiatives. In cases where improvements could not be attributed unambiguously to management development, few attempts had been made to measure its impact.

In the cases where written evidence and corroborated interviews showed how organizational strategy and management development were interrelated, the links between the two were pervasive and demonstrated in a variety of ways. Typically, management development was shown to be an intrinsic part of the business plan, and to support strategic priorities. Business objectives were shown to be linked to strategy through defined competences, strategic objectives were mapped onto performance standards, and personal development plans related to business plans. Roles and responsibilities for management development were devolved to individuals and their line managers, with only limited HR intervention, thereby embedding management development within OS.

Major changes provided both the opportunity and necessity of linking management development to organizational strategy, and management development initiatives responded to changes in the organization's environment. Extensive restructuring or business process re-engineering provided opportunities for linking management development to organizational strategy and focused attention on the competences required to achieve the organizational transformation. Throughout, the MCI Standards and NVQs were seen to provide a structure for the links.

Even where the links between management development and organizational strategy were less clear, there was some evidence of management development initiatives to support specific aspects of organizational strategy. In other cases, problems were identified in establishing the link; for example difficulty in identifying which competences would improve organizational performance. Also, management development was found invariably to lag organizational strategy where this was dynamic, and immediate priorities inevitably took precedence over longer-term strategic management development. An apparent paradox was also highlighted between devolving responsibility for management development and linking it to organizational strategy, since much management development is focused on the needs of the individual, not the organization.

In four organizations, the Management Standards were comprehensively adopted in HRD systems and processes. In these organizations, all or most management development activities were competence-based. The Management Standards were central to appraisal, training and development, although they were used less extensively in job descriptions, recruitment and remuneration. Written evidence and corroborated interviews demonstrated the ways in which the Standards were adopted and the benefits of building management development initiatives around the MCI Framework.

The major benefit identified from adopting the Management Standards was the coherent structure that they provided for training, management development and personal development. Gaps in competence, for example, are more readily identified through appraisal, training and development needs are specified more precisely in relation to the competences required for individuals to meet the needs of the organization, and there are clear criteria for human resource planning and career succession. In addition, management development is linked to a qualifications framework.

In three cases, the Management Standards had been partially adopted, and were used to a limited extent in some HRD systems and processes. The remaining nine organizations had either not attempted to adopt the Management Standards or had only made limited progress in this direction, so that they were regarded as non-users. The research identified some limitations to the adoption of the Management Standards both in the extent to which they had percolated through an organization and in the range of HRD systems and processes involved. The main limitations were that the Standards were not extensively used in recruitment and selection, other than in relation to job profiles, and reward and remuneration systems were rarely linked to the achievement of competences defined in the Standards. Additional criteria were sometimes used alongside the Standards, especially in relation to specific technical competences, and familiarity with the Management Standards was less extensive outside the HR specialists.

Critical analysis

The sixteen organizations provided very positive and highly significant results demonstrating performance improvements as a result of management development. Despite the difficulty of measuring performance, and especially team performance, the three measures of performance were significantly correlated. The overall coefficient of concordance between the rank orders of individual, team and organizational performance was significant at the 1 per cent level (Kendall's $\omega = 0.796$), showing that the rank position of an organization in terms of one performance measure was similar to its rank position for another performance measure. Moreover, as Table 7.2 shows, each pair of performance measures correlated at the 5 per cent level or better, especially in the case of individual and organizational performance (Spearman $R_s = 0.797$). Of the three performance measures, organizational performance was the most problematic, but the significant rank correlation coefficients suggested that team performance could be 'captured' adequately by individual and organizational performance measures.

Significantly, the results of the rank correlation also provided support for the conditional hypothesis that management development was more likely to improve performance when linked with organizational strategy.

Table 7.2 Spearman rank correlation coefficients

Factor	TP	OP	OS	HRD
IP	0.635	*0.797*	*0.863*	0.611
TP		*0.650*	(0.411)	(0.170)
OP			*0.658*	0.548
OS				0.575

Key:
IP = rank in terms of evidence of individual performance improvements attributed to management development
TP = rank in terms of evidence of team performance improvements attributed to management development
OP = rank in terms of evidence of organizational performance improvements attributed to management development
OS = rank in terms of evidence of link between organizational strategy and management development
HRD = rank in terms of evidence that HRD systems and processes are based on the management standards
Statistical note:
For 14 degrees of freedom, $R_{S(0.01)} = 0.645$; $R_{S(0.05)} = 0.456$
In the table, *correlation coefficients in italics are significant at 1 per cent*; others are significant at 5 per cent (results in brackets are not significant at the 5 per cent level)

The Spearman rank correlation coefficients between organizational strategy and both individual and organizational performance were significant at the 1 per cent level. There was no significant correlation between organizational strategy and team performance, which may reflect the difficulties of measurement and attribution already noted. In the case of individual and organizational performance, these results offer unambiguous support for the importance of linking management development to organizational strategy in order to realize business benefits.

The rank correlation also provided support for the conditional hypothesis that management development was more likely to improve performance when HRD systems and processes were based on the competence statements in the MCI Standards. The Spearman rank correlation coefficients between HRD and both individual and organizational performance are significant at the 5 per cent level, although again there is no significant correlation between HRD and team performance. In the case of individual and organizational performance, these results again offer support for the importance of designing management development around the Management Standards in order to improve organizational performance.

Conclusions and key learning points

The conclusions and learning points to be drawn from the research outlined above relate both to the substantive findings, which contribute to the debate on the role of HRD in improving performance, and the procedural aspects of the methodology developed to undertake the study.

In substantive terms, three policy implications follow from the above conclusions, relating to the performance measures that should be used to monitor the business benefits of management development, linking management development to organizational strategy, and adopting the Management Standards.

First, the most reliable performance measures for monitoring the business benefits of management development are individual and organizational performance, which correlate with, and therefore probably also incorporate, the less tangible organizational performance measures. The strength of the link between management development and both individual and team performance suggests that management development should be promoted with the message that *developing people contributes to business success.*

Second, performance benefits are more likely to arise from management development where this is strongly linked with organizational strategy. The link between management development and organizational strategy should be seen as complementary to the value of developing people since this is the mechanism through which the development of individuals contributes to business performance. In policy terms, these findings provide further support for the *Investors in People* approach, through which development is linked to organizational strategy.

Third, performance is improved additionally where organizations adopt the Management Standards as a framework for development within HRD systems and processes. The additionality is important and provides support for further promoting the *MCI Standards*, encouraging their adoption by organizations to provide coherence in management development and to support mobility within the managerial workforce.

In the context of this book, the key learning points are procedural ones, relating to the development of an appropriate methodology to test the hypotheses established at the outset. A detailed case-study protocol was developed to cope with the complexity of identifying performance improvements at individual, team and organizational levels in a wide range of different settings. In process terms, the protocol was also designed to investigate the nature of links between management development and organizational strategy and the ways in which HRD systems and processes incorporated competence statements.

A complex protocol was inevitable given the need to reduce causal ambiguity and to relate performance improvements to specific developmental events. However, the complexity operated as a barrier to entry in many organizations, creating major difficulties in negotiating access. The protocol was stretched to the limit in being applied to organizations in such different sectors, but it proved possible, by using generic terms and analogous measures, to translate into all sector contexts. The different sizes of organizations, however, proved most challenging; the methodology was less well suited to the largest case studied and proved unworkable in a very small firm that was removed from the final case list.

A case-study approach was necessary in order to capture qualitative information, including such 'soft' measures as perceptions of individuals, as well as exploring the relevant development and performance processes within organizations at different levels. In adopting such a methodology, however, there was a risk of marginalizing the findings because policy makers invariably seek 'hard' measures, with quantitative data that can be subject more easily to statistical tests. The challenge, therefore, was to devise a methodology that could permit hard conclusions from soft data.

By using a team of consultants to make independent comparative evaluations of the case reports (i.e. ranking them against established criteria), it was possible to employ non-parametric techniques and arrive at concrete statistical conclusions. In other words, the study demonstrated the potential for combining the richness of case-study research and subjective evaluation by independent experts with robust statistical methods capable of offering a quantitative measure of the extent of correlation between the factors being investigated.

References

Arthur, J.B. (1994) 'Effects of human resource systems on manufacturing performance and turnover', *Academy of Management Journal*, 37: 670–87.

Barney, J. (1991) 'Firm resources and sustained competitive advantage', *Journal of Management*, 17: 99–120.

—— (1995) 'Looking inside for competitive advantage', *Academy of Management Executive*, 9, 4: 49–61.

Becker, B., and Gerhart, B. (1996) 'The impact of human resource management on organisational performance: progress and prospects', *Academy of Management Journal*, 39: 779–801.

Berry, J.K. (1990) 'Linking management development to business strategies', *Training and Development Journal*, 44(8): 20–2.

Brooks, A. (1994) 'Power and the production of knowledge: collective team learning in work organisations', *Human Resource Development Quarterly*, 5(3): 213–35.

Campbell, A. and Sommers Luchs, K.S. (1997) *Core Competency-Based Strategy*, London: Thomson.

Carter, P. and Lumsden, C. (1988) 'How management development can improve business performance', *Personnel Management*, October, 49–52.

Clements, R.V. (1958) *Managers: a Study of Their Careers in Industry*, London: Allen and Unwin.

Confederation of British Industry (1989) *Towards a Skills Revolution*, London: CBI.

Constable, J. (1991) 'A management charter or a chartered manager?', in M. Silver (ed.) *Competent to Manage – Approaches to Management Training and Development*, London: Routledge, 228–32.

Constable, J. and McCormick, R. (1987) *The Making of British Managers*, London: British Institute of Management.

Coopers and Lybrand Associates (1992) *Meeting the Management Challenge*, CLA: London.

Currie, G. (1994) 'Evaluation of management development: a case study', *Journal of Management Development*, 13(3): 22–6.

Cutcher-Gershenfeld, J.C. (1991) 'The impact on economic performance of a transformation in workplace relations', *Industrial and Labor Relations Review*, 44: 241–60.

Department of Trade and Industry (1994) *Competitiveness: Helping Business to Win*, White Paper, Cm. 2563, London: HMSO.

—— (1995) *Competitiveness: Forging Ahead*, White Paper, Cm. 2867, London: HMSO.

Downham, T.A., Noel, J.L. and Prendergast, A.E. (1992) 'Executive development', *Human Resource Management*, 31(1–2): 95–107.

Easterby-Smith, M. (1994) *Evaluating Management Development, Training and Education* (second edn), Aldershot: Gower.

European Commission (1994) *Growth, Competitiveness, Employment: the Challenges and Ways Forward into the 21st Century*, White Paper, Luxembourg: EC Publications Office.

—— (1996) *Teaching and Learning: Towards a Learning Society*, White Paper, Luxembourg: EC Publications Office.

Fisher, S.R. and Sleezer, C.M. (1999) 'Bridging the gap with a multi-dimensional performance model', *Academy of Human Resource Development Conference*, Arlington, VA, 3–7 March 1999, Conference Proceedings Volume 1: 221–9.

Fox, S. (1989) 'The politics of evaluating management development', *Management Education and Development*, 20(3): 191–207.

Grant, R. (1991) 'The resource-based theory of competitive advantage: implications for strategy formulation', *California Management Review*, 33(3): 114–22.

Handy, C., Gordon, C., Gow, I., Maloney, M. and Randlesome, C. (1987) *The Making of Managers: a Report on Management Education, Training and Development in the USA, W. Germany, France, Japan and the UK*, London: National Economic Development Office.

Harrison, R. (1992) 'Developing people: for whose bottom line?', in R. Harrison (ed.) *Human Resource Management Issues and Strategies*, Wokingham: Addison-Wesley, 299–329.

Holton, E.F. III (1999) 'Performance domains and their boundaries', in R.J. Torraco (ed.) *Performance Improvement: Theory and Practice, Advances in Developing Human Resources*, 1: 26–46.

Huselid, M.A. (1995) 'The impact of human resource management practices on turnover, productivity and corporate financial performance', *Academy of Management Journal*, 38: 635–72.

Hussey, D.E. (1988) *Management Training and Corporate Strategy: How to Improve Competitive Performance*, Oxford: Pergamon.

—— (1996) *Business Driven Human Resource Management*, Chichester: Wiley.

Institute of Management (1994) *Management Development to the Millennium: the Cannon and Taylor Working Party Reports*, London: IoM.

Johnson, S. and Winterton, J. (1999) *Management Skills*, Skills Task Force Report 3, SKT8, Sheffield: Department for Education and Employment.

Katzenbach, J.R. and Smith, D.K. (1992) *The Wisdom of Teams: Creating the High-Performance Organisation*, Boston, MA: Harvard Business School Press.

Kim, D.H. (1993) 'The link between individual and organisational learning', *Sloan Management Review*, Fall, 37–50.

King, S. (1993) 'Business benefits of management development', *Management Development Review*, 6(4), 38–40.

Kirkpatrick, D. (1967) 'Evaluation of training', in R. Craig and L. Bittell (eds) *Training and Education Handbook*, New York: McGraw-Hill, 18.1–18.27.

Legatt, T. (1972) *The Training of British Managers: a Study of Need and Demand*, London: HMSO.

Leman, S., Mitchell, L., Sanderson, S., Sturgess, B. and Winterton, J. (1994) *Competence-Based Management Development: Methodologies for Evaluation*, Sheffield: Employment Department.

Lynham, S.A. (1998) 'The development and evaluation of a model of responsible leadership for performance: beginning the journey', *Human Resource Development International*, 1(2): 207–20.

MacDuffie, J.P. (1995) 'Human resource bundles and manufacturing perform-ance: organisational logic and flexible production systems in the world auto industry', *Industrial and Labor Relations Review*, 48: 197–221.

McGivering, I., Matthews, D. and Scott, W.H. (1960) *Management in Britain*, Liver-pool: Liverpool University Press.

Magjuka, R.J. and Baldwin, T.T. (1991) 'Team-based employee involvement pro-grams: effects of design and administration', *Personnel Psychology*, 44: 793–812.

Mangham, I. and Silver, M.S. (1986) *Management Training: Context and Practice*, London: Economic and Social Research Council.

Miller, L. (1991) 'Managerial competences', *Industrial and Commercial Training*, 23(6): 11–15.

Mitrani, A., Dalziel, M. and Fitt, D. (1992) *Competency Based Human Resource Man-agement*, London: Kogan Page.

Peel, M. (1984) *Management Development and Training*, London: British Institute of Management/Professional Publishing Limited.

Pfeffer, J. (1994) *Competitive Advantage through People: Unleashing the Power of the Workforce*, Boston: Harvard Business School Press.

Prahalad, C.K. and Hamel, G. (1990) 'The core competence of the corporation', *Harvard Business Review*, 68(3): 79–89.

Reich, R.B. (1991) *The Work of Nations: Preparing Ourselves for 21st-Century Capital-ism*, New York: Knopf.

Robinson, D.G. and Robinson, J.C. (1989) *Training for Impact*, San Francisco: Jossey-Bass.

Rummler, G.A. and Brache, A.P. (1992) *Improving Performance: How to Manage the White Space on the Organisation Chart*, San Francisco: Jossey-Bass.

Russ-Eft, D. (1996) 'Hurrah for teams or teams-schmeams: so, what is the impact of teams?' *Human Resource Development Quarterly*, 7(4): 305–9.

—— (1999) 'Research methods for advancing performance improvement', *Advances in Developing Human Resources*, 1: 68–82.

Snell, S.A. and Dean, J.W. (1992) 'Integrated manufacturing and human resource management: a human capital perspective', *Academy of Management Journal*, 35: 467–504.

Snow, C.C. and Snell, S.A. (1993) 'Staffing as strategy', in M. Schmitt and W.C. Borman (eds) *Personnel selection in organisations*. San Francisco: Jossey-Bass, 448–78.

Sundstrom, E., De Meuse, K.P. and Futrell, D. (1990) 'Work teams: applications and effectiveness', *American Psychologist*, 45: 120–33.

Swanson, R. (1994) *Analysis for Improving Performance: Tools for Diagnosing and Docu-menting Workplace Expertise*, San Francisco, CA: Berrett-Koehler.

—— (1999) 'The foundations of performance improvement and implications for practice', in R.J. Torraco (ed.) *Performance Improvement: Theory and Practice*, *Advances in Developing Human Resources*, 1: 1–25.

Taylor, P. and Thackwray, B. (1995) *Investors in People Explained.* London: Kogan Page.

Thurbin, P. (1995) *Leveraging Knowledge: the 17 Day Program for a Learning Organisation,* London: Pitman.

Tobin, D.R. (1993) *Re-Educating the Corporation: Foundations for the Learning Organisation,* Essex Junction, VT: Omneo.

Wild, R. (1993) 'Management development in a changing world', *Management Decision,* 31(5): 10–17.

Winterton, J. (2000) 'Social dialogue over vocational training in market-led systems', *International Journal of Training and Development,* 4(1): 26–41.

Winterton, J., Parker, M., Dodd, M., McCracken, M. and Henderson, I. (2000) *Future Skill Needs of Managers,* Research Report RR182, Sheffield: Department for Education and Employment.

Winterton, J. and Winterton, R. (1996) *The Business Benefits of Competence Based Management Development,* DfEE Research Series RS16, London: HMSO.

—— (1997) 'Does management development add value?' *British Journal of Management,* 8, S65–S76.

—— (1999a) *Developing Managerial Competence,* London: Routledge.

—— (1999b) 'Developing managerial competence: does it improve performance?' *Academy of Human Resource Development Conference* Arlington, VA, 3–7 March 1999, Conference Proceedings Volume 1: 620–6.

Wright, P.M. and Snell, S.A. (1991) 'Toward an integrative view of strategic human resource management', *Human Resource Management Review,* 1: 203–25.

Youndt, M.A., Snell, S.A., Dean, J.W. and Lepak, D.P. (1996) 'Human resource management, manufacturing strategy, and firm performance', *Academy of Management Journal,* 33: 836–66.

Yin, R.K. (1981) 'The case study crisis: some answers', *Administrative Science Quarterly,* 26: 58–65.

Yin, R.K. (1984) *Case Study Research: Design and Methods,* London: Sage.

Zuboff, S. (1988) *In the Age of the Smart Machine: the Future of Work and Power,* New York: Basic Books.

8

LEARNING FOR CHANGE BY
TELLING STORIES

Jeff Gold, Stuart Watson and Mike Rix

Aims and contribution

There has been intense attention given to HRD as learning at work in recent years. From traditional approaches to on/off-the-job or skills learning through team programmes to organization-wide initiatives aimed at creating learning companies and achieving Investors in People status, learning has become the factor that is considered essential for survival, sustainability and, where appropriate, competitive advantage. In addition, learning is usually seen as central to any large-scale change initiative such as TQM, BPR, culture change or simply the installation of new equipment. These views of the centrality of learning are replicated in other contexts beyond the boundaries of organizations. Thus professional bodies advocate learning within frameworks of continuous professional development and government agencies support 'lifelong learning' as a means of achieving a 'learning society'. It would seem that learning became the emblem of the 1990s, destined to continue into the new millennium. Indeed, the vast numbers who are now locked into the learning industry via processes, products, journals, books and conferences will ensure a long life for a notion that, as we will explore below, is rather tenuous. Indeed, many of the learning activities and initiatives referred to above side step the inherent difficulties of specifying exactly what is meant by learning, how it occurs or whether it has taken place, attesting to the ambiguity of the term and the plethora of possible meanings.

In this chapter, we will examine a collaborative approach to researching HRD based on a methodology adapted from Learning Histories (Roth 1996). We will first of all explore our conceptualization of the terms 'learning' and 'workplace'. In particular, both terms will be located within what are referred to as 'nets of collective action' (Czarniawska-Joerges 1993). Working with a social constructionist approach, we will explain the development and use of a reflective infrastructure as a methodology to research HRD during planned projects of change at work. We will highlight how such projects are subject to diverse interpretations which are held in place by the 'vicissitudes of social process' (Gergen 1985) which in turn affect whether learning occurs. We will argue that narrative knowledge is required to gain access to such understandings and meanings and will conclude that researching HRD has a vital contribution towards making learning work.

Theoretical context

Conventional views of HRD tend to focus on interventions at the level of the individual's potential to think or act more effectively and usually result from some perceived perturbation in the individual or their environment. Thus individualized versions of learners are placed 'in the centre of the learning discourse' (Gray 1998) and the responsibility for learning is passed to individuals, e.g. individual learning accounts, employee led development, learning styles, self-development, self-directed learning, learning contracts, and associated provision of support such as learning centres, CBL, learning packs, workbooks, etc. It is supposed that organizations can learn by developing individuals. That is, if individual learning refers to something a person thinks and does, then organizations must learn in a similar way. According to Weick and Westley (1996), this approach is the consequence of the difficulty in finding an experiential referent for the term organization so when it comes to learning, it may be easier to refer to individual learning as though this was evidence of organization learning. It might therefore be construed that the purpose of researching HRD is to capture the process and results of learning interventions at the individual level and perhaps the impact of this at the macro-organizational level.

An immediate problem, highlighted by Holmes (1998), is that it is difficult at any time to say how learning takes place. The verb 'to learn' may not refer to an activity performed by someone with the consequence that the term operates at a high level of abstraction and is used to cover a wide range of common processes which may not have anything in common at all. Second, individualized views of learning decontextualize and distort the importance of the social and cultural context of learning (Reynolds 1997). Thus, whatever performance that is called learning and how it occurs is never decided by individuals alone.

These problems highlight the importance and value of language and social process in the social construction of learning. Rather than the focus on individuals, learning occurs as part of an ongoing social process of sense making. Learning is mainly but not wholly linguistically constructed according to the discursive and narrative conventions of particular cultures (Harré and Gillett 1994). Whether such learning is concerned with a change in knowledge or skills or occurs through direct relationships with others or other forms of mediation, the result will be the adoption and structuring of practices which will serve to further relationships within a social-cultural context. Thus, to acquire a skill to perform in practice or make a claim to know relies on the presence of linguistic categories and understandings which form an interpretative context which only make sense as part of a social process of interchange and relationships between people.

Individuals are likely to live through many exchanges with others, directly or indirectly, in a variety of contexts during the course of time, often during the course of a single day, and these will all contribute to the positions adopted and identities that are formed. We are able to use different ways of talking and different practices in different contexts because we have acquired and draw upon different interpretative repertoires (Potter and Wetherell 1987). Thus whenever we speak, we draw upon the resources of a social language, a way of talking or discourse (Bakhtin 1981) that is specific to a group or community and whatever we do has to make sense in a context or risk being seen as nonsense. Because there is the potential for a vast range of exchanges and relationships which provide the basis for an ongoing construction of life at work, it may be better to understand organization or work as the process of construction of meanings which lead to collective action. Czarniawaska-Joerges (1993) refers to 'nets of collective actions' where meanings are constructed through exchanges between people and within which actions are taken based upon such constructions. To learn means to become a member of a net. Within any workplace, there may be a range of nets where: 'One net of collective actions is distinguishable from another by the kind of reality it constructs, as it is socially perceived. However, what is publicly acknowledged and recognised is just the tip of the iceberg' (ibid.: 61).

Seen in this way, it becomes evident why so many intentional efforts to make learning work or to bring about a change in practice, however minor, meet with difficulties, often fatal but certainly with unintended consequences for those who initiate such efforts outside the 'net'. It also emphasizes why, if we are to gain anything approaching an adequate understanding of learning, the working of relationships in the 'dark side' of organizations (Pedler and Aspinall 1996) need to be captured and understood. In this chapter, the ongoing processes that make and remake meaning within local contexts, 'nets of collective action', provide the unit of study for researching HRD. As argued by Czarniawska-Joerges: 'Any understanding of organizations thus requires an understanding of the meanings ascribed to and produced by a given net of collective action' (1993: 61).

Thus within any location called organization, there are likely to be a range of nets, each with a version of reality represented in the values and interests of its participants. For change agents, what they may be able to see and understand in nets outside their own, represents 'just the tip of the iceberg'. In such situations, change agents are likely to form an abstracted version of practice within nets, meaningful and sensible only within the context of their own net.

Nevertheless, armed with internally coherent and rational versions of their project of change, which can be presented to others as opportunities for learning, change agents are likely to struggle to deal with what Bruner (1991) refers to as 'the rich and messy domain of human interaction'. They are therefore more likely to resort to a physicalist conception of change or what Latour (1987) refers to as a diffusion model, whereby the claim for change can be attributed with its own 'energy', 'force', 'pressure' and 'momentum' as it moves toward a desired goal and others can be cast as 'resistors' to 'unfreeze, change and refreeze'. In contrast to this logico-scientific mode of reality construction, Bruner posits that human interaction can be better understood by narrative providing a representation of versions of reality but also contributing to the making of reality. Polkinghorne (1988) claims it is through personal stories, myths, fairy tales and novels that narrative can be seen as the 'primary form by which human experience is made meaningful'. Thus narrative is used to make ourselves intelligible to others, providing coherence to past and present events and a direction for the future. In local contexts, narratives provide the store of knowledge that must be referenced in ongoing activity and making sense of new situations. Further, since narratives concern people and their practice within a context, they will also be imbued with the value constructions of the context reflecting the desires, concerns and interests of a net of collective action. As claimed by Czarniawska (1997), in organizations, narratives 'are carriers of life itself' and, as we argue, the source of understanding in researching HRD by providing a complex portrayal of social situations and rich ingredients for study.

Empirical context

A significant project of change in the north of England forms the focus of our research. The project (N1), which began in autumn 1998, concerned an attempt by a local government agency, to encourage inter-organization learning among forty-eight companies via the creation of learning networks. All companies, having already achieved Investors in People (IIP) status, were considered ready for a more advanced approach to HRD. As described within the proposal for funding which was made during the summer of 1998:

> the overall aim of the project is to help companies embed the processes and practices developed during the recognition process (of IIP) while at the same time, establish the link between the development of a robust life-long learning culture and company growth and competitiveness.

The project sponsors proposed to provide a programme of leading-edge HRD workshops for managing directors and chief executives at

6-weekly intervals which would help them transfer appropriate practices and models to their own organizations. It was proposed that each workshop would be facilitated by the IIP advisers.

The project also proposed to develop further HRD ideas such as 'intercompany mentoring projects' and use electronic conferencing to create a virtual dimension to network activity.

It is important to add that N1's only existence at the time we became involved consisted of an approved funding document, a series of memos and varying degrees of enthusiasm among the change agent and two sponsors in the local government agency. In other words, N1 was hardly very real at all with no other hard facts to point to indicating that the change agent had a great deal of work still to do.

Methodological issues

Our approach to research was via Learning Histories, understood as attempts to assess projects of change by endeavouring to understand the value of learning within projects through the investigation of 'noticeable results' (Roth 1996). The approach is an attempt to elicit, capture and document data from 'multiple perspectives' with particular reference to 'controversial events' with the aim of representing the voices of different interests in an equitable manner in the form of 'story jointly told' (Kleiner and Roth 1997). In its most basic form, a Learning History is a narrative of a project of change as a learning intervention, earlier comments on the meaning of learning notwithstanding.

According to Roth (1996), there are three key purposes to a Learning History. First, it is a learning tool that promotes learning by allowing people to reflect as the project of change unfolds. Second, it provides an assessment in the service of future learning by providing the means for people in the project to assess their efforts in bringing about learning and change so that further learning can be planned. Third, a Learning History supplies a diagnostic lens, which help identify what is happening in a project and why barriers to learning may exist.

In addition, we see Learning Histories as a participatory approach to researching HRD by reconciling the differing traditions and values of academic and change agents through a process of partnering (Gold et al. 1999). This is accomplished first, by allowing researchers to collect data from many sources within the change, especially the interpretations of events made by different communities. Second, the data can be used to engender critical thinking among participants in the face of conflictive and paradoxical situations (O'Connor 1995).

A crucial part of our approach to the use of Learning Histories was the use of narrative analysis (Georgakopoulou and Goutsos 1997; Van Dijk 1997). As personal accounts of important events, narratives told as stories work in two connected ways. First, they have an epistemological orientation to provide a description that is a plausible and credible but contingent representation of reality. Second, storied accounts also have an action orientation in that they are seeking to do something as part of an inter-action with others (Potter 1996). That is, storytellers have an interest in their story which reflects their values, desires and prejudices and those of their local context although the teller may also seek to hide such inter-est via a range of linguistic and rhetorical devices. Stories will therefore rhetorically seek to establish a purpose and a valued endpoint. As data to be read as text, stories gathered become amenable to techniques of liter-ary, narrative and rhetorical analysis which reveal the valuational features of the local context and learning within nets of collective action. Data analysed can then be fed back to participants to allow the consideration of their situation and the possibilities for action.

The means to achieve data collection and critical thinking was a reflect-ive infrastructure. Controversies in projects of change arise from disputes about the meaning of what is going on (Schön and Rein 1994). Such disputes cannot be solved by appeals to fact or obvious truths because particular facts and truths will be selected to support the arguments and interests of different communities. The reflective infrastructure seeks data via a set of reflective devices such as logs and recordings relating to con-troversial events and issues and, at the same time, provides feedback via a range of devices, to participants involved. As well as the opportunity to observe meetings and interview individuals, the particular approach to reflection pays attention to the means by which sense is made through language in story-telling.

The research

Partnership arrangements were made for the collection of data from different participants and conditions for the working of the Learning History methodology agreed. In addition, we agreed to provide an inter-pretation and feedback of data gathered to participants to facilitate their reflection on key issues and so that they could consider alternative ways of proceeding.

In the project N1, we were first of all able to monitor the intervention through access to project documentation and interviews with the change agent and sponsors. Adopting space travel themes and language, N1's initial shape was set in its 'flight plan' to provide 'high energy to fuel . . . the formation of a Galaxy of Learning' which would be achieved by 'engaging warp engines' leading to a 'warp drive' followed by a 'chain reaction'! It was three months before this view was presented to others whose energy was sought to form a 'steering group' with the change agent and continue the translation of the version of change envisaged. This consisted of a group of five employers from the local area who, it soon became apparent, had their own interests which were very much at variance to the change agent's. We noted the particular attention given by the employers to the importance of the 'here and now' and the casting of the change agent and his sponsors as 'visionaries' with 'their esoteric stuff of the future'. The principal concern, which quickly found mutual agreement and co-ordination among the employers, concerned surviving the approaching recession (October 1998). Each was able to build up a version of current reality with a recession story – 'it's as bad as it could be'. We were able to observe the construction of an alternative reality, something much more 'real' and 'truthful' to the employers present. To them recession seemed 'unstoppable' – the markets, the trade figures, the value of sterling and high interest rates all said so.

The change agent and sponsors went back to reconsider and reshape the world that they had created. We were able to examine how the change agent had partly adapted to the situation through his storied account following the next meeting with the employers.

According to Gergen (1994), stories are 'saturated' with value, which are derived from the accepted realities and truths of a teller's context. By the selection and ordering of characters and events, the story moves towards a valued endpoint, working as a resource for particular purpose and this gives it rhetorical and argumentative qualities (Edwards 1997). The point of a story is shown by a range of linguistic devices which attempt to capture the engagement of the audience making the story 'tellable' (Labov 1972). As a personal story conveying feelings, emotions and values, the text becomes an 'affective device per se' (Georgakopoulou and Gousos 1997). Through the selection of events and the inclusion of particular characters, the story leads us towards a valued endpoint reflecting the interests and value constructions of the change agent and his sponsors.

The first paragraph provides a preamble which sets the context of the story:

> We had decided to produce chapters for the meeting as a result of the feedback (whinging) from last time. I remembered the innuendo that chapters are needed and that the group was uncomfortable with a completely open agenda. P, H and I arrived c.30 minutes early and went through the agenda and chapters. Everything was set, we were all very pleased with ourselves particularly the new brand image.

The overall plot appears to make progress in the meeting. While the teller is grudgingly conciliatory with respect to using feedback from the last meeting, producing chapters and having a less open agenda, a position is established that reflects the views of the change. This is the first 'we' which includes 'P, H and I'; the employers by contrast are positioned as 'whinging' and 'uncomfortable with a completely open agenda' (Davies and Harré 1990). A number of intensity markers (underline) emphasize, amplify or hedge feelings (Quirk *et al.* 1985). Thus 'Everything (emphasis) was set' and they were 'all very pleased (amplified) with ourselves'. We can see here the localized reality constructed by the advocates of change which is valued and based on a set of shared agreements. However, in the next paragraph, we see a challenge to this reality, centred on the 'new brand image' with which the change agent was 'particularly' pleased.

> The first to arrive was F followed by G and finally J. Everybody was late – very late – and it took 45 minutes to really get underway. We followed the agenda, the people from last time did seem to feel more comfortable. We presented the brand image that seemed to irritate G and he said so. It did not have the right feel or portray the right image, a funny thing seemed to happen – once G had declared he did not like the image the others seemed to join in. They seemed to want to hunt in a pack and they seemed to work themselves into a minor state over the model. Anyway after that they got stuck into the invitation letter. I was a bit fed up, we had put a lot of effort into the meeting and the brand and they seemed to be just picking.

In this paragraph, the valuational reality of the advocates of change works in two ways. First, it gives a positive status to certain meanings, talk and actions. Second, it limits the status of the meanings, talk and actions of others. Thus the teller is expecting his work to meet with approval; however the disapproval produces feelings of discomfort and anger. The rejection of the brand image and subsequent actions by the others (attacking 'the model', getting 'stuck into the invitation letter', 'picking') leads the teller to draw on what Edwards (1997) calls a 'repertoire of irrational mass reaction'. The others are compared to a metaphorical 'pack in a hunt' who 'work themselves into a minor state' and get 'stuck into the invitation letter'. The purpose of this seems to challenge the seriousness of the response of the employers. In the last line of the paragraph, the teller stands back from the action and highlights his feelings. He was 'a bit fed up' because they had put 'a lot (amplified) of effort into the meeting and the brand'. In this external evaluation of what happened, the value orientation of the change agent takes the form of an argument (Walker and Sillars 1990). The teller claims to be 'a bit fed up' because they 'had put a lot of effort' into their preparation for the meeting. The justification for such a view is that effort is a good reason for being fed up. In comparison, the employers are less serious; they are 'just picking'. The argument is being used rhetorically to persuade his audience of the justice of his position.

While later in the meeting, the change agent was able to establish sufficient common ground to set up a steering group of employers and change agents, the teller still had doubts:

When we closed the meeting everybody agreed to stay with the steering group, but I wonder, anyway we will see, this is an ambitious project which will take some getting going, the steering group experience is a valuable taste of things to come.

'We' now refers to the steering group who have acted together, although the teller expresses of feelings of uncertainty. By the end of the meeting, the steering group is an emerging net of collective action which through further activity together was able to move the project forwards although in a different shape to that envisaged by the change agent.

Two months later, N1 had progressed to its first key event, the 'official' launch of the project involving forty employers, represented mainly by managing directors and chief executives. The purpose was to launch the main idea of the project relating to the formation of learning networks among employers to operate over the next 18 months and beyond. Vital to this work was the energy of eight development agency advisers who would facilitate the working of the networks. It is important to note that the advisers already saw the forty employers as 'their clients'.

The change agent presented N1 to the advisers as a 'learning opportunity'. In particular, there was a need for advisers to adapt their practice so that they could take on a responsibility for facilitating the learning networks as they emerged. From the early documentation of the project, there is evidence of the change agent's expectations of the advisers:

> there will be new things to consider and learn such as action planning and facilitating networks . . . the project will initially cause some more work for advisers but this is an investment . . . the project can be crafted to ensure it eases their workload . . . in the longer term.

Preparation for the envisaged new role included three half day 'learning' sessions with the change agent before the official launch of the project at the first network event. It was at this first event, where there were a number of difficulties, that a narrative was collected from each adviser.

The advisers saw their identity as 'professional' advisers and 'experts'. They had 'pride' in their relationships with the clients whose representatives would form the learning networks and were concerned about others 'imposing' on their clients. After all, 'who knows our clients better than us'.

A particular value evident within the narratives was the importance the advisers attached to their achievement so far. In previous times, the advisers had been set challenges but had been able to meet them and this had created a shared view that 'we were made to win'. However, a crucial part of such practices was the way new challenges were presented to them. There was a concern for 'being in control' and 'developing commitment'. As one adviser commented: 'We can get excited about a vision if we are helped to define what it looks like.'

A further requirement for success was to 'be set down'. This phrasing was used by several advisers and refers to the point at which the advisers reached joint understanding concerning what to do, how to do it and how to assess it. This difficulty for the advisers was that none of these requirements had been settled with the consequence that they felt 'isolated'. The failure to meet the requirements for dealing with new challenges had left the impression that they 'had been rail-roaded'.

Such talk and accompanied pattern of practices can be seen as the background values and interests, the importance of which would be to limit attempts by others to require them to adopt new practices and change roles. The change agent would have to reference these existing patterns of talk in order to have any hope of persuading the advisers to change. Until such persuasion occurs, his interventions are likely to be seen as a 'deviation' from 'existing patterns of action' (Gergen 1995). The following extract from one adviser's narrative gives an indication of an attempt to discredit the change agent's work:

> We arrived at 2.00pm and went up to the reception area of the attic suite at the Hotel. There was a very tense atmosphere amongst everyone including R and G, the two people ultimately responsible for the running of the programme. Most of the Advisers were nervous, as this was the first event of this kind which they had been involved in as facilitators. We had plenty of experience of facilitation of issues with mainly internal co-ordinators although this was certainly new ground for us.

The first paragraph establishes the context and the narrator's connection to it. N1 is something of an unknown quantity and he is expressing some of his concerns about the expectation to adopt a revised identity of facilitator. He uses an intensity marker and a certain amount of hyperbole to highlight the '*very* tense atmosphere amongst everyone'. He goes on to tell us about his concern and the connection to his interests and the interests of others, his net of collective action. Thus while they had 'had *plenty* of experience', the explicative 'although' is used to emphasize the uncertainty of N1 which was '*certainly* new ground'.

In the next paragraph, the teller breaks the flow of the narrative to provide an external evaluation (Labov 1972) to press a point about R and G who are seen as 'ultimately responsible', a move which simultaneously attempts absolve the advisers from responsibility:

> I, for one felt a little disappointed and perturbed at the extreme nervousness of R and G. I didn't expect them to display superhuman qualities but did expect them to feel a little more comfortable with the event having lived and breathed it for some time (particularly R). The tension in the air was so thick you could cut it with an

oxy-acetylene torch (knife too blunt). The atmosphere amongst everyone was almost debilitating and we desperately needed some strong, confident leadership to give us an injection of confidence.

He emphasizes their '*extreme* nervousness' and uses negative encoding (Polyani 1985) such as 'I didn't expect . . . superhuman qualities but . . .', to highlight what he did expect from them, utilizing the emotional discourse of nervousness to rhetorically contribute to his version of events (Edwards 1997) and to blame others. R in particular is seen as more blameworthy who the narrator, working with the categorization of 'leadership' (Edwards 1991), assumes must be in control of events and have a large degree of certainty, after all, he had 'lived and breathed it for some time'.

The basic structure at work here can be seen as part of a three-part sequence where the narrator establishes an initial proposition which could be challenged: 'I, for one, felt a little disappointed and perturbed at the extreme nervousness of R and G.' He then offers a concession which includes evidence against the first proposition: 'I didn't expect them to display superhuman qualities.' The concession is then qualified as the narrator attempts to reassert the first proposition: 'but did expect them to feel a little more comfortable with the event having lived and breathed it for some time (particularly R)'.

As explained by Antaki and Wetherell (1999), the effect of this is rhetorical in seeking to provide exoneration from blame for the advisers and attributing it to the change agent (Antaki 1994). In this way, the story constructs R. as blameworthy for the difficulties described as an element its purpose. The categorization again provides an indication of the shared background knowledge and expectations of the advisers. However, not all projects are clear cut and N1 in particular was a project that had many possibilities but was also subject to many interpretations and the teller was not yet aware of this complexity.

In the event itself, there had been a disappointing turnout from the MDs and CEs and later in the narrative, there is some qualified consideration of the energy that the advisers can provide to N1: 'Perhaps we had not done the correct selling job on these companies in order to make them appreciate the importance of their attendance! Perhaps we were not given sufficient time to effectively sell the programme to our clients!'

Following the report of the above event, and in response to our interpretation of the story provided, the advisers' voices were heard and their experience acknowledged and, more importantly, valued. N1 continued, although not without further difficulties from often-unpredictable sources.

Critical analysis

The change agent and his sponsors referred to in this chapter frequently used key HRD terms of with good intentions to achieve an obviously good outcome. As we have observed and recorded, projects of change presented were 'opportunities for learning' and 'a chance for development' for individuals and organizations. However, it would be a very rare circumstance if the path of change could be guaranteed to match the intentions of change agents and their sponsors. Absorbed as they might be with visions of what should be learned, who should be developed and how organization should change, it was easy to neglect the importance of context and miss the variety of possible interpretations within contexts where, as explained by Gergen (1989), shared understandings are 'hammered out on the forge of daily relationships'. It has been part of the purpose of our research to employ narrative knowledge to capture the complex workings of such relationships and the versions of world constructed by them. However, what does such an approach to research do? Orthodox research practice is built on a real world assumption and that, as researchers we stand apart from the real world of our observing and data collecting to enable the production of knowledge that has the status of truth or a fact. In this process, we bring into play a range of ideas and practices that would apparently require us to follow rules of methodology already 'in place' (Hosking and Ramsey 1998). We could argue that our approach has, in particular, employed unconventional and non-HRD domains of knowledge, although discourse and narrative analysis are rather conventional fields somewhere else. We could still be accused of reinforcing a subject–object binary whereby the researcher as knowing subject positions others as objects to be known. The outcomes of our work can be seen as expert monologues. However, as social constructionists, we refute such a conception of research. Like all claims to knowledge, research is understood as a process of social construction, where findings do not serve as a picture of truth, reality or a world independent of the researcher. Instead, what we do, i.e. observe meetings, collect and interpret narratives, write book chapters, etc., is our attempt to make meaning. However, as so clearly stated by Gergen: 'If others do not recognisably treat one's utterance as meaningful, if they fail to co-ordinate themselves around such offerings, one is reduced to nonsense' (1995: 37).

Just as there is a precariousness in your response to this chapter, so it was with all feedback to participants in project N1. In other words, our findings from research had to be part of a process and unless supplemented by the responses of others, faced the very real prospect of making no sense at all. Always remembering that a process is not in our hands alone, we attempted to avoid such an outcome by attending to the use of our work within relationships of various kinds. We have reported in detail on such processes elsewhere (Gold *et al.* 1999; Rix and Gold 1999), however there seem to be two key features of such collaborations.

First, we acknowledge the differences between academic and change agent/business worlds but see these as differences in language which fail to co-ordinate temporarily rather than as a permanently fixed order with images of academic ivory towers separated by theory from the hurly-burly of everyday organization life in times of change. This separation produces dichotomies such as academic = theory and business/change = practice which, in our view, are false and unnecessary. Instead, both researchers from academe and change agents work with *praxis*, that is theory and practices, or ways of talking and going on, which are suited to context. Second, the opportunities, and especially the difficulties, presented by HRD interventions associated with projects of change provided sufficient space for conversation and dialogue between researchers and change agents to occur. By acknowledging our already existing background knowledge and our respective interests, what Shotter (1994) refers to as 'responsive ways of going on', a meaning between us could be made and sustained although we also recognize the contingent, temporary and unfinalized features of such arrangements.

Emerging from such considerations, it is incumbent upon researchers (and change agents) to be reflexive of their background knowledge and interests. In particular, as we indicate above, there is the danger that our research can be seen as the expert production, a privileged view of truth and facts which in turn can soon lead to some kind of power over others (Hosking and Ramsey 1998). Instead, as we believe we have shown throughout this chapter, it is possible to act in a reflexive way where, as explained by Ruby (1980), we 'deliberately, intentionally reveal . . . the underlying epistemological assumptions' of what and why we are researching and how we do it.

Conclusions and key learning points

This chapter has examined findings from our recent work in adopting a narrative approach to the study of HRD during a project of change. We have rejected mainly individualistic and cognitivist views of learning and aligned the term organization with ongoing processes of sense making and collective action within local contexts. We have argued that it is within nets of collective action that ways of working and co-ordinating are made meaningful in an ongoing social process of construction. Such meanings are always local and contingent but may, through continued use, embellishment and accompanying practices, become accepted and valued as the truth and the real. In this way, we can say that learning has occurred and continues to do so, forming the 'taken-for-granteds' of a local ontology which can also provide the resources to defend against the encroachment of others. It is access to such resources that has been afforded by our narrative approach to researching HRD.

We have shown how attempts to engender HRD through a project of change, for whatever progressive purposes claimed by the sponsors, can be understood as attempts by the meanings made in one context to interrupt locally accepted versions of reality in another. We have shown how such versions are likely to be highly valued and how a failure to achieve co-ordination provides the source for claims of frustration to change agents. This does not mean that the agents that make the nets of collective action set out to resist change and learning. Indeed, a key tenet of the social constructionist view is that change and learning are an ongoing and everyday achievement (Bass and Hosking 1998) even though there may be an appearance of stability. What is important is how ongoing and accepted processes are (re)produced and, in the face of the efforts of others to interrupt and impose their version of change, others are able to invoke a stock of already available narratives to provide the necessary resources to counter such efforts as required. However, such others do not just live by one narrative and a single set of values. Boundaries between nets are seldom impermeable and members of one net often practice in others. They are therefore able to reference the narratives from other contexts if necessary or desired and such narratives form part of a 'bricolage' to help them deal with difficult situations (Brown and Duguid 1991), as revealed by the valuational discourse within the project referred to in this chapter.

Boundary impermeability also provides some encouragement for change agents seeking to bring HRD from one net into another. The narratives and values of the nets of collective action revealed in this research provide a partial view of the stock of knowledge which must be referenced in any attempt by those outside to bring about change and learning within. Furthermore, change agents can become aware of the narratives that form the background knowledge in their own nets and others, seeking to build the bridges to cross the boundaries between nets (Van Looy et al. 1997). Indeed this is one of the purposes, and a key learning point, of researching HRD presented in this chapter. Learning Histories and the reflective infrastructure provide a framework for collaborative working between researchers and the business world providing the interests of each party is satisfied in a reciprocal chain of value.

Finally, we have shown how our adapted approach to Learning Histories has provided access to nets of collective action working below the 'tip of the iceberg'. By use of various devices in the reflective infrastructure, we have been able to discern the operation of valuational discourses which, we claim, are vital for understanding HRD interventions designed to bring about learning at work. It is accepted that this approach can only be partial, however by establishing partnership arrangements, we were able to gather multi-voiced data from within the project. As data was gathered, interpreted within a social constructionist meta-theory and then fed back to project participants, we could make no assertions with respect to the truth or moral authority of our claims, nor that others would learn from such efforts. That is, our own interventions could also be seen as a rhetorical move which, like all others, had no guarantee of success.

References

Antaki, C. (1994) *Explaining and Arguing*, London: Sage.

Antaki, C. and Wetherill, M. (1999) 'Show concessions', *Discourse Studies*, 1(1): 7–27.

Bass, A. and Hosking, D-M. (1998) *A Changed Approach to Change*, Aston Business School, Research Paper 9808.

Bakhtin, M. (1981) *The Dialogic Imagination: Four Essays by M.M. Bakhtin* (ed. M. Holquist), Austin, University of Texas Press.

Brown, J.S. and Duguid, P. (1991) Organisational learning and communities-of-practice: toward a unified view of working, learning and innovation, *Organisation Science*, 2(1): 40–7.

Bruner, J. (1991) The narrative construction of reality, *Critical Inquiry*, Autumn: 1–21.

Czarniawska, B. (1997) *Narrating the Organisation*, Chicago: University of Chicago Press.

Czarniawska-Joerges, B. (1993) *The Three-Dimensional Organisation*, Lund: Studentlitteratur.

Davies, B. and Harré, R. (1990) Positioning the discursive production of selves, *Journal for the Theory of Social Behaviour*, 20(1): 43–63.

Edwards, D. (1991) Categories are for talking, *Theory and Psychology*, 1(4): 515–42.

—— (1997) *Discourse and Cognition*, Sage: London.

Gergen, K.J. (1985) 'Social pragmatics and the origins of psychological discourse', in K.J. Gergen and K. Davis (eds) *The Social Construction of the Person*, New York: Springer-Verlag.

—— (1989) 'Warranting voice and the elaboration of the self', in J. Shotter and K.J. Gergen (eds) *Texts of Identity*, London: Sage.

—— (1994) *Relationships and Realities*, Cambridge, MA: Harvard University Press.

—— (1995) 'Relational theory and discourses of power', in D-M. Hosking, H.P. Dachler and K.J. Gergen (eds) *Management and Organization: Relational Alternatives to Individualism*, Aldershot: Avebury.

Georgakopoulou, A. and Goutsos, D. (1997) *Discourse Analysis: an Introduction*, Edinburgh, Edinburgh University Press.

Gold, J., Hamblett, J. and Rix, M. (1999) 'Telling stories for managing change: a business/academic partnership', paper presented to the EDINEB Conference, Bergen.

Gray, C. (1998) 'Against learning', paper presented to the Emergent Fields in Management Conference, Leeds University.

Harré, R. and Gillett, G. (1994) *The Discursive Mind*, Thousand Oaks, CA: Sage.

Holmes, L. (1998) 'Learning as a confidence trick: exorcising the ghost in the machine', paper presented to the 'Emergent Fields in Management Conference', Leeds University, July.

Hosking, D-M. and Ramsey, C.M. (1998) 'Micro-social processes in research', paper presented to the 3rd Conference on Organisational Discourse, Kings College London, July.

Kleiner, A. and Roth, G.L. (1997) *Learning Histories: a New Tool for Turning Organisational Experience into Action*, <http://www.sol-ne.org/res/>.

O'Connor, E.S. (1995) Paradoxes of participation: textual analysis and organisational change, *Organisation Studies*, 15(5): 769–803.

Labov, W. (1972) *Language in the Inner City*, Oxford: Blackwell.

Latour, B. (1987) *Science at Work*, Cambridge, MA: Harvard University Press.

Pedler, M. and Aspinall, K. (1996) *Perfect PLC?* Maidenhead: McGraw-Hill.

Polkinghorne, D.E. (1988) *Narrative Knowing and the Human Sciences*, New York: University of New York Press.

Polyani, I. (1985) *Telling the American Story: a Structural and Cultural Analysis of Conversational Storytelling*, Norwood, NJ: Ablex.

Potter, J. (1996) *Representing Reality*, London: Sage.

Potter, J. and Wetherell, M. (1987) *Discourse and Social Psychology*, London: Sage.

Quirk, R., Greenbaum, S., Leech, G. and Svartvik, J. (1985) *A Comprehensive Grammar of the English Language*, London: Longman.

Reynolds, M. (1997) 'Learning styles: a critique', *Management Learning*, 28(2): 115–33.

Rix, M. and Gold, J. (1999) ' "With a little help from my academic friend": mentoring change agents', paper presented to the Sixth Mentoring Research Conference, Cambridge, November.

Roth, G.L. (1996) *Learning Histories: Using Documentation to Assess and Facilitate Organisational Learning*, <http://www.sol-ne.org/pra/>, accessed 1/10/97.

Ruby, J. (1980) 'Exposing yourself': reflexivity, anthropology and film, *Semiotica*, 30(1–2): 153–79.

Schön, D. and Rein, M. (1994) *Frame Reflection*, New York: Basic Books.

Shotter, J. (1994) *'Now Can I Go': Wittgenstein and Communication*, <http://www.massey.ac.nz/~ALock/virtual/wittgoon.htm>, accessed 12/3/99.

Van Dijk, T.A. (ed.) (1997) *Discourse as Structure and Process*, London: Sage.

Van Looy, B., Debackere, K., Bouwen, R. and Heyrman, K. (1997) 'Innovation as crossing boundaries between communities: balancing between openness and closure', chapter presented to *Organising in a Multi-Voiced World*, Leuvan, Belgium, June.

Walker, G.B. and Sillars, M.O. (1990) 'Where is argument? Perelman's theory of values', in R. Trapp and J. Schuetz (eds) *Perspectives on Argumentation*, IL: Waveland Press.

Weick, K. and Westley, F. (1996) 'Organisational learning: affirming an oxymoron', in S. Clegg, C. Hardy and W. Nord (eds) *Handbook of Organisation Studies*, Beverly Hills: Sage.

9

LEARNING TO CHANGE, CHANGING TO LEARN

Case studies in the automotive sector

Penny West

Aims and contribution

Organizational learning and the 'learning organization' are human resource development concepts that are of growing interest in contemporary theoretical and practical management literature. The concepts and their contribution to the process of change are examined in the context of the automotive sector, a sector well known for innovative work practices and continuous change. The chapter offers an analysis of established theoretical perspectives connecting learning and change and continues with a discussion of comparative case-study research within two manufacturers, the Rover Group and Volvo, and two component suppliers, Creative Engineering and XZZ components. The conclusions that are drawn indicate that individual and organizational learning are human resource development processes that all the organizations are attempting to promote in order to deal proactively with change and to maintain competitive advantage and market share. Such interventions may appear to democratize the employment relationship and to be dependent upon the contribution and the continuous development of the individual. However, they may also be seen as part of an 'ongoing effort by managers to reassert their control as they seek to coax, inspire, demand or otherwise produce action in their organisations' (Alvesson and Willmott 1998: 28).

Theoretical context

Organizational learning and the learning organization

Over the past decade in particular, theorists have advanced a range of interpretations of organizational learning and what constitutes a 'learning organization' although clear definitions are imprecise and often subject to wide interpretation. Tsang (1997), for example, discusses not only the wealth of recent literature on the topics but also the growing dichotomy between two streams of research that he identifies as the descriptive (how does an organization learn?) and the prescriptive (how should an organization learn?). He further suggests that organizational learning and the learning organization are terms that are often used interchangeably which tends to complicate an understanding of both phenomena. Despite this element of confusion, promoting learning within organizations is increasingly seen to be vital for those that are keen to sustain competitive advantage. The emerging trend is seen as one in which strategic human resource management is less concerned with how to react over the long term but more focused on how to influence and create the environment in which the organization operates both now and in the immediate future. In other words, to be a learning organization capable of continuous proactivity, transformation and choice.

Hence, Tsang (op. cit.) identifies the interrelationship between the two concepts stating that a learning organization is one that is good at organizational learning *per se*. Leading from this then, what does the term organizational learning mean? A simple definition states that learning means getting everyone in the organization to accept and embrace change as an ongoing process (Stata 1989). To expand upon this notion, most theorists would appear to view organizational learning as complex and multidimensional, as a process that unfolds over time, and link it with knowledge acquisition and improved performance (Garvin 1993). Nevertheless, theorists appear to differ on a range of significant issues. For example, Fiol and Lyles (1985: 803) consider that 'organisational learning means the process of improving actions through better knowledge and understanding' while Argyris (1977) suggests that it is a process of detecting and correcting error. Huber (1991: 89) takes a systemic approach by stating that 'an entity learns, if, through its processing of information, the range of its potential behaviours is changed'. Stata (1989: 64) considers that organizational learning occurs 'through shared insights, knowledge and mental models and builds on past knowledge and experience, that is, on memory'.

From the variety of perspectives quoted, prescriptive theorists consider that behavioural change is required for learning, while those focusing on descriptive studies suggest that new ways of thinking are sufficient. Some indicate information processing as the mechanism by which learning occurs; others prioritize shared insights and organizational memory. Garvin (op. cit.) attempts to draw these streams of research together by suggesting that unless there are adjustments to the way work is organized and performed (that is, there is continuous improvement to established systems and practices), significant change and double loop learning cannot occur.

Garvin (op. cit.: 80) therefore presents a definition of a learning organization that acknowledges that new ideas are an essential starting point if organizational learning is to occur.

> A learning organisation is an organisation skilled at creating, acquiring and transferring knowledge, and at modifying its behaviour to reflect new knowledge and insights.

New knowledge creation can occur as a result of insight or inspiration from within the organization; additionally it can also be provoked from external influences by expanding and/or relaxing organizational boundaries. Whatever their source, such new ideas form the foundation for organizational improvement and learning. They alone cannot create a learning organization, however, unless there are accompanying changes to the manner in which the organization and the people within it perform and are developed and managed. In other words, it seems that while many organizations can develop skills in acquiring and creating knowledge, few seem to be successful in applying that knowledge to their own activities and behaviour. This connects with the view advanced by Beer and Eisenstat (1996) and other commentators on processual and emergent change. They suggest that for learning to be of relevance to the organization, there have to be simultaneous changes to structures, systems and behaviours to make it work and to take the organization somewhere better than it is now.

The key issue identified by early writers Pedler, Burgoyne and Boydell (1991) and more recently by Belohlav (1996) is organizational transformation or the ability of a company to recreate itself, to become a different organization to meet the new competitive realities it faces now and in the future. Hence the importance of understanding processes by which the organization can develop itself and can choose its course of action rather than being forced to change by outside intervention is elevated. The inference is that if the organization is recognized as an open system operating in a dynamic and non-linear environment, it also has a degree of control and choice over its own destiny if it so chooses (Burnes 1996; Morgan 1997; Stacey 1996).

On a practical level, writers (Coopey 1996; Garvin 1993; Hirschorn and Gilmore 1992; Nonaka 1991; Senge 1991) argue that learning organizations are basically skilled at a range of activities that enable them to develop and integrate their learning within and beyond the organization (see Figure 9.1). These include their capacity for the following:

1 systematic problem solving (which traditionally underlies much of the quality movement and is essentially focused on transformation in management, work practices and organizational activity);
2 experimentation, actively seeking and testing new knowledge, and learning from mistakes and encouragement of a 'no blame' culture;
3 drawing upon memory and past experience as vital sources of learning and unlearning;
4 learning from and with others;

5   communicating effectively within and beyond the organization;
6   systems thinking and developing shared ideas/models of the current organizational position in the wider context.

In connection with this final point, the interaction of groups/teams in terms of the organizational learning process becomes more significant, particularly in the area of enquiry, the automotive sector. Hendry, Arthur and Jones (1995) offer some useful insights relating to team learning in which they draw upon March and Olsen's (1975) model which describes three themes that contribute to the analysis of learning in terms of the individual, the organization and the environment:

- **Theme one** – individual learning occurs in successive foundation, formation and continuation stages. The foundation stage is concerned with

	Characteristics
Individual	People take an active role in identifying and undertaking self-development activities that lead to continuous learning and improvement in knowledge, skills, aptitude and performance
Group	Good communication, trust and understanding of shared meanings within groups in order to identify and solve problems and to experiment with measures for change and improvement
Departmental	Encouragement for self-development, experimentation and creativity within an environment that tolerates mistakes. Toleration of ambiguity and uncertainty and a good understanding of their contribution to the effective performance of the 'whole' organization
Organizational	The organization is unique in terms of its ability to promote and sustain the learning processes that are required for all stakeholders so that change is an ongoing process for both the individual and the organization in terms of its ability to promote further learning and change
Intra-organizational	Excellent communication between departments with celebration of 'difference and variety'. Avoidance of 'compartmentalization' with cross-fertilization of ideas, HRD and work approaches within the organization
Inter-organizational	Deliberate and continuous attempts to transfer learning and information between organizations by experimentation and sharing best practices through collaborative ventures and exchange of ideas, personnel and approaches to work organization
Extra-organizational	Continuous attempts to understand, anticipate and create environmental change and translate it to the advantage of the organization and all its stakeholders by undertaking and/or exploring contemporary practical and analytical research, learning from this and promoting any required changes or adjustments to work organization

Figure 9.1 Characteristics/levels of learning potential

basic readiness for learning; the skills needed to achieve learning, together with the experience of success and self-confidence through learning activities.

- **Theme two** – the formation stage focuses on the wider issues of self-development, independent learning and an understanding of role interdependence and teamwork.
- **Theme three** – the continuation stage is displayed by self-motivation and independence as a learner, the development of a questioning approach and an increasing level of autonomy on a group and individual level.

Hendry *et al.* (1995) continue their analysis by drawing a matching frame of reference at the level of the organization (see Table 9.1). They see this as involving dependency, transitional and independency phases:

- **The dependency phase** responds to people at the foundation learning stage by means of formal job training, remedial education together with a basic introduction to teamwork.
- **The transitional phase** attempts to respond to individuals at the formation learning stage by offering wider opportunities for job rotation and shadowing, wider industry training together with increased opportunities for teamwork and experiential learning.
- **The independency phase** responds to the continuation learning stage by offering linked career planning shared responsibility for production and investment goals and broad commitment to work group autonomy.

Table 9.1 Individual readiness to learn and the organizational response

Individual learning ability	*Organizational response*
Continuation stage The individual is self-motivated; has achieved independence as a learner; has developed a questioning approach; demonstrates autonomy at a group and individual level	Independency Organization offers linked career planning; shared responsibility for production and investment goals; broad commitment to work group autonomy
Formation stage Self-development; independent learning; role interdependence; interest in teamwork	Transitional The organization offers job rotation and shadowing; wider industry training; opportunities for teamwork; experiential learning
Foundation stage The individual is ready to learn; shows interest in acquiring the skills to learn; involvement in learning activities	Dependency The organization offers formal job training; remedial education; introduction to teamwork

They indicate, however, that for organizational learning to occur, much is dependent upon individual readiness to learn and also people's enthusiasm to join in shared learning efforts. The manner by which this team learning is translated into organizational learning is analysed in terms of the management of 'routines' – the translation of 'learning by doing' to 'remembering by doing' (Hendry *et al.* 1995: 184). These findings connect with Huber's (1991) analysis of organizational identity and memory discussed earlier and Zemke and Zemke's (1995) findings on adult learning that suggest that individuals are pragmatic in their approach to learning and do so only when they are convinced that it is in their own interests. Hence, the role of managers is significant in ensuring that people are offered appropriate and relevant data to enable them to make an informed choice to underpin their current and future actions and development.

Organizations and the people within them, therefore, are highly individualistic and will be driven by their own interpretation of the meaning of what it is to be a learning organization. In this way, organizational learning will not be static but will continuously adapt and evolve as individuals and groups within the organization are encouraged to develop skills, knowledge and a common sense of purpose to achieve shared (and often changing) goals and targets. The tension identified by Tsang (1997) is that the number of prescriptive texts on how to be a learning organization emerging in the 1990s ignore much of this complexity while the more rigorous, descriptive analyses of organizational learning often lack substantiation from empirical research and inevitably, accessibility for managers. The chapter therefore attempts to explore these issues through an examination of four case studies in the automotive sector. Research was undertaken from 1993 to 1997 and explores the approaches of the organizations in developing individual and organizational learning and how this affected the change process.

Empirical context

The automotive sector

The mass production of automobiles accounts for the largest manufacturing activity in the world. It incorporates a work system that to many has 'raised production, cut costs and reduced the judgement and skill needed by the average worker' (Kanigel 1997: 498). This system developed in the early part of the twentieth century by pioneers such as Ford and Taylor was to be globally emulated across a range of sectors. Since that time the automotive industry has been at the forefront of innovation in work organization and it continues to be one of the lead sectors for the advancement of new work practices and organizational forms. However, the trigger for profound change for Western companies in the sector (particularly over the past forty years) was the threat of their own collapse. Market maturity, overcapacity, outdated and inflexible factory work practices, poor employment relations and the increasing penetration of established markets by Japanese producers from the 1960s onwards posed severe threats to those established in the sector. Whilst Japanese approaches to work organization had evolved over time, this presented an immediate and major crisis for Western companies that forced them to re-invent themselves in order to remain competitive. Hence, established companies were confronted with two key challenges if they were to survive.

First, they needed to learn new skills that were associated with the new organizational forms developed in Japan incorporating 'lean' approaches. Lean production systems revolutionized the way that vehicles were built insofar as the approach allows the use of less resources within the context of a 'just-in-time' (JIT) framework, greater flexibility in product variety, improved quality and reduced lead times for new product development. In his analysis of lean production, Harrison (1994: 179) suggests 'the competitive advantages of lean manufacturers who can support low-cost, high accuracy products with short order-to-delivery times can be devastating in the marketplace. Lean manufacturers can use their superior design, production and delivery systems to reduce costs or increase variety, or both.' But its success is heavily dependent upon a skilled, flexible and highly motivated workforce that is geared towards achieving continuous improvement in a production environment in which the pace of work is often unremitting.

Lean production is also dependent upon integrated buyer-supplier relationships between organizations involved in production and assembly. It is likely that component suppliers and buyers will have close association at the research, design and assembly stage and will be involved in joint training and development needs identification and delivery. Preferred supplier status grants an element of security to the supplier in the relationship, as it signifies that the buyer is satisfied with levels of quality and performance and is confident of the organization's commitment to continuous improvement. The buyer, however, inevitably assumes a dominant role in the relationship and can exert considerable controls over the supplier, particularly in terms of monitoring, performance, delivery and pricing. It is the supplier that bears the brunt of the manufacturers' continuous drive for year-on-year cost reduction and increased productivity. Indeed Kenney and Florida (1993) consider that large manufacturers such as Toyota, Honda, Nissan and Mazda have used their resources and power in their American transplants to construct JIT complexes that have become a source of discipline and structure for the network of producers. Lean production is therefore dependent upon the flexibility of both workers and the manufacturing system itself (Boer 1994). Nevertheless, whilst the emergence of such developments appeared enlightened to existing players in the sector, they inevitably posed a threat to established Western organization and management systems *per se*.

If this was not enough, the second challenge that faced established companies in the sector was that if they were going to attempt to regain any form of competitive advantage they had to ensure that people would embrace and adopt the changes that lean production systems demand. Hence, the key for success in this environment was seen as the ability to learn and change continually; the key approach for achieving this has been the development of organizational learning, to become a learning organization capable of continual transformation in order to meet the challenge of change. For organizations in the sector, therefore, the focus has been both to introduce new work arrangements and to effect change through people by moving towards a team-based environment. Indeed, the emphasis on teamwork is considered by Womack, Jones and Roos (1990) to be at the core of modern production processes in the automobile industry.

The implications for management in a manufacturing environment are therefore significant. If continuous improvement is to be a realistic goal there has to be a sense of reciprocal obligation, in which workers respond positively if they feel that management values their skills, will go some way towards trying to keep them in employment and will delegate responsibility to the team. Sandkull (1996: 76), however, warns 'because lean production . . . is being introduced with little reference to the reality of particular cases . . . it readily becomes managerial rhetoric, a device to maintain established power structures, the inertia of which precludes learning'. Paradoxically, the risk is that what managers set out to implement may be jeopardized due to their inherent desire to preserve positional power, hence reinforcing an inability to learn and change.

Methodological issues

Background and research methods

The organizations selected as case studies for research are the Rover Group and Volvo (manufacturers and assemblers) and Creative Engineering and XZZ Components (component suppliers). They were selected because, with varying levels of success, they have been recognized within their sector as organizations that have attempted to deal with change by means of a learning approach. Indeed Schon (1989: 114) considers this learning approach to be 'an idea that has become in good currency in recent years for a variety of reasons mainly associated with environmental instability'. Hence, the linkages are drawn between continuous improvement, change and double loop learning (learning to learn) so that people have the opportunity to challenge the status quo and to modify existing methods and operating systems, if required.

The approach of each organization has been inspired and dictated by different internal and external factors prevalent within their task and contextual environments. It is acknowledged, however, that the sample is limited and biased towards those already established in the development of learning and change. Their relevance is such that they provide a source of interpretive investigation that may inform future studies in a wider sample of organizational settings. The ontological stance throughout the investigation was based upon gaining an understanding of people's knowledge, opinions, interpretations and the depth and complexity of their experiences of learning and change by means of interview and observation. Similarly, the epistemological position suggested that the most effective way of generating such information was to interact with people within the organizations, to ask questions and to listen to their responses and explanations.

The process of selection and elimination, with the final decision to confine research to one industry sector by means of the case-study approach, was justified on the basis that it was an attempt to achieve a degree of corroboration, validity, generalizability and reliability (Dey 1993; Mason 1996). Given the qualitative nature of the investigation, however, there is likely to be more emphasis on validity rather than reliability. Generalizability is approached from the concept of *possibility* in the occurrence and/or development of findings similar to those in the research sites, in other organizations (Perakyla 1997).

From a research design perspective the qualitative case-study approach was also selected for its flexibility and ability to reveal a range of perceptions surrounding organizational change, learning interventions and how those involved interpret them. As Cassell and Symon (1994: 5) observe 'only qualitative methods are sensitive enough to allow the detailed analysis of change. . . . With quantitative methods we may be able to assess that a change has occurred over time but we cannot say how or why.' Whilst concerns surrounding case-study research are recognized, the approach was considered to be the most useful research strategy because of its flexibility and ability to adapt to areas of original and emergent theory. Its selection, therefore, was considered appropriate given the dynamic and changing contexts in which organizations in the automotive sector operate, the nature of contemporary theoretical debate that seeks to provide analyses and evaluation of the phenomena and the comparative nature of the research.

Observation was conducted on the basis of a non-participant, overt approach and whilst this was appealing on ethical grounds, one of the limitations is that of reactivity whereby people's behaviour may be affected by the observers presence. An additional limitation is that observations are 'inevitably filtered through the interpretive lens of the observer' (Sapsford and Jupp 1996: 59) and what the researcher obtains can only be constructed as selected representations and interpretations of reality.

Interviews within the research sites were conducted by means of structured and unstructured approaches and were designed to provide a sample of views on the phenomena associated with learning and change. The process, however, is reciprocal insofar as the interviewer must develop skills in listening, hearing and sharing to successfully glean and record the required data. With the exception of Volvo (where I only interviewed group managers and shopfloor workers), interviewees spanned all levels within the organizations, including managing directors. It was, however, a requirement that interviewees came with a range of experience and length of service.

The epistemological shortcomings of interviewing are recognized, insofar as people's experiences can only be recounted and their perceptions can only be accessed by what the interviewee is prepared to reveal (Mason 1996). Moreover, relatively small numbers of respondents cannot be taken as representative, even if care is taken to produce a cross-section; and *social desirability* responding may occur when answers may be altered to show the respondent in a favourable light to the interviewer (Sapsford and Jupp 1996). Nevertheless, given that 'knowledge and evidence are contextual, situational and interactional' (Mason 1996: 40), organizational culture and the development of shared norms, meanings and rules are relevant to the enquiry and it is through the interview that attempts can be made to interpret and understand it. Within this approach, the interviewee was regarded as an active participant and attempts were made to develop the relationship as part of the research process and to build and connect explanations and analyses from qualitative data as a continuous process.

Nevertheless, reflecting on the research process, it is clear that the project posed a number of challenges predominantly associated with the fast moving daily pace of the industry itself. Given the difficulties of conducting interviews in a manufacturing environment, the demanding production schedules and targets meant that those people who took part in the interviews could not spend too long away from the shopfloor. A significant issue experienced during the research process was that regarding the length of time that elapsed between the decision to approach an organization as a potential case study and when access was actually gained. Implications for the researcher can be profound as intense activity can quickly turn into periods of frustration and despair, fearing that access may never be negotiated again. The difficulties in arranging convenient times to visit were not just confined to the researcher (part-time in my case), given the busy schedules of people within manufacturing environments as already mentioned. Also, the nature of the automotive sector always dictates that priority for attention rests with the customer and the production processes rather than the researcher, and, on occasions, appointments were cancelled or abandoned. Whilst this might be interpreted as a reflection of the perceived value of the research, there were fortunately few occasions when there was not an enthusiastic welcome into the research sites with the opportunity to interview a wide sample of employees.

Similarly, whilst there was always concern to preserve the confidentiality of the interviewees' responses, reporting back the progress of the research and any general findings was a useful exercise in establishing and maintaining relationships for continued access. Most often, contacts were members of staff involved in personnel/human resource management/ development functions who were interested in the perceptions of employees regarding the implementation of their own changes and initiatives. Other members of staff expressed an interest and curiosity with the research topic *per se* with one person asking why 'a woman would want to look at this sort of industry anyway?'

The development of the relationship during the interview was seen as an important issue and attempts were made to respond to the needs of the interviewee. Whilst the majority of interviews produced rich data, inevitably there were occasions when difficulties were encountered. On reflection, these could be classified as follows:

1   Throughout the research period it became clear that people responded to the interview in a variety of ways. Some wanted to find out a great deal about the research topic and the interviewer; others were keen to portray an inflated impression of their position and importance within the organization; and others were dismissive of any pre-existing knowledge and understanding on the part of the researcher. Whilst these observations might be analysed from a gender perspective, Rubin and Rubin (1995: 102) comment on the significance of 'the novice at the feet of the master' analysis which seems equally relevant in this scenario.

2   Missed opportunities on my part to take advantage of verbal cues for further avenues to pursue offered by the interviewee but not realized at the time of the interview.

3   Uncommunicative interviewees who were unwilling to give informa-tion – this seldom occurred but on those occasions when it did, it appeared that they were defensive about the nature of the questions and/or reluctant to take part in the research. From a researcher's perspective, this required a sensitive approach and an understanding that questioning needed to be open and non-threatening if any involve-ment was to occur. Another obvious consideration was the use of the information provided and issues surrounding confidentiality, as dis-cussed. It was important in all cases to ask permission to take notes (recording interviews was not feasible due to noise levels) during the interviews and to make it clear that sources would not be revealed.

4   Just as some interviewees were uncommunicative, more people were over-communicative and wanted to digress from the interview topic areas, providing tangential information that was not always useful to the study. Whilst this was not often discouraged, it was potentially problematic if a number of interviews were to be accomplished in a given time-frame.

5   Another form of interview was that of the group discussion which occurred spontaneously at one research site. This was an opportunistic

event that provided the exploration and description of a range of perspectives in a group context. On reflection, its disadvantages were that it did not provide any depth of response from the participants as there was little opportunity to pursue points with individuals; also that it was a difficult process to manage from the interviewer's perspective so that all group members were involved and/or heard. Its advantage, however, was that reactions of the individuals involved to the views of their peers was interesting to observe and record and provided an overall feeling of the mood of the group.

6   Finally, at the end of the empirical element of the research, sorting and analysing data into a coherent framework proved to be a considerable challenge. With the benefit of hindsight and the guidance of more experienced researchers and theorists, it seems useful (and indeed obvious) to conduct the collection, sorting and analysing of data as an ongoing, iterative process. Sadly, this was not always possible for a variety of reasons but the wisdom of embarking upon this as a systematic activity throughout the research exercise cannot be more strongly recommended.

Finally, Silverman (1993: 91) and many others suggest that interview subjects construct not just narratives but social worlds and for researchers 'the primary issue is to generate data which give an authentic insight into people's experiences'. Whilst some of the shortcomings of the research approach, together with my own experiences, have been identified, the intention throughout in recording and analysing the data collected was to represent the interviewees' views fairly and to portray them as consistent with their meanings. Inevitably, many of the conversations also offered interesting diversions from the research that warranted further (and possible future) avenues to explore, most notably issues surrounding the impact and continuity of leadership on the promotion and development of organizational learning. Also, the organizations (and the people within them) had clearly become immersed in the language and practice of continuous improvement and organizational learning and the point of entry for the research therefore positioned at a comparatively high starting point. How the approaches and concepts might be viewed in a sector/ organization with limited exposure to these ideas would therefore be an interesting project for the future.

The research

Main findings

The research organizations are involved in similar strategies to promote learning and development and the chapter affords only a limited opportunity for a selected sample of their approaches. Case study one, the Rover

Group, experienced a period of falling market share, product decay and poor employee relations during the 1960s, 1970s and 1980s. During this period characterized by crisis, reorganization and nationalization, it chose to address these issues by focusing simultaneously on changes to work practices and procedures, product regeneration through collaborative alliances with Honda and on the contribution of the individual and the group (Burnes 1996; Pilkington 1996). Most significantly, in order to demonstrate the Rover Group's commitment, both internally and externally, to its people and their learning and development, it established a separate business, Rover Learning Business in 1989. From its creation, the intention of Rover Learning Business was to assist the Rover Group in becoming a learning organization to effectively manage change. Its products and initiatives included a suggestion scheme for improvements to established practices and Rover Employee Assisted Learning (REAL) in which employees were funded to take on any learning and development that might assist in their performance at work but that need not be directly related to their job. This was intended to encourage people to return to learn and to enable them to gain confidence and positive experiences from the learning process. A further initiative was a company wide approach to assist people to manage change effectively. In 1996 after the sale of the company to BMW, senior management in the Rover Group decided to dissolve the company, considering that it had succeeded in its remit to establish learning as a fundamental process throughout the organization. Indeed BMW confirmed that there would be a continued commitment to promote individual and organizational development. The current uncertainty surrounding the future of the company following the recent sale of the Rover Group to the Phoenix consortium (led by former Rover Group managing director John Towers) may be attributed to a number of internal and external forces for change in the sector. However, it is still apparent that there is an overriding drive for survival that is characterized by an eagerness to adapt, learn and to reposition the company in the marketplace.

The second manufacturer, Volvo of Sweden, is an international transport equipment organization employing 70,000 people, with production in more than twenty countries. Since its formation in 1927 the company has experienced a series of changes that have threatened its future. By the end of the 1970s, industry analysts thought that small companies like Volvo (which captures only 1 per cent of the global market of passenger vehicle sales) were doomed. Models were outdated, exports had shrunk and home market shares had collapsed. The problems were compounded by increased costs in Sweden in 1975–76. Nevertheless, it has now become a niche player with an established reputation for vehicle safety, quality and consideration for the environmental impact of its products. In terms of work organization and management practices, Volvo has established itself as a leader since the 1970s when it began to move away from traditional methods of vehicle assembly and develop approaches that focused on work humanization and job redesign. Periods of experimentation with the removal of the traditional assembly line, the development of teamwork and the instigation of 'reflective production' techniques at the Kalmar, Uddevalla and Born plants are well documented (Berggren 1992; Burnes 1996; Karlsson 1996; Sandberg 1995). Recent developments following the collapse of a proposed merger with Renault saw Volvo embarking upon a joint venture with Mitsubishi in 1996 to produce co-operatively designed cars in Born, Belgium, in order to expand sales in Europe and America. Volvo has maintained an established reputation for vehicle safety and reliability and has moved on to produce a range that is stylish and techno-logically robust. The company's potential was identified by Ford who bought Volvo in 1999 in a move to expand its (Ford's) product portfolio and to fill the gap between the most expensive Mercedes and the lower end of the Jaguar range. It is anticipated that Ford's intention is to maximize Volvo's 'established image capital of vast amounts of unexploited value' by using Ford's own superior advertising strategies to penetrate and estab-lish products in niche markets (Bayley 1999). Thus, despite the varying degrees of internal and external pressures for change over a twenty-year period, Volvo has continually maintained a commitment to improving the quality of working life through an investment in a plurality of production concepts that attempt to promote individual learning and teamwork.

The third case study, Creative Engineering Limited, is now a well-established supplier of components to the motor industry, with a reputation for quality that is approaching world class. Its development has been characterized by distinct periods of decline and recovery, with its most recent success driven by a focused strategy to manage change through continuous learning and improvement through a variety of strategies. For example, there have been attempts to develop self-managing teams, to eliminate loss of production and breakdowns through a system of total productive main-tenance whereby all operators are responsible for checking and maintain-ing machines and equipment. Opportunities for learning occur within a centre that is equipped with computer based self-directed learning pack-ages. Again, there is acknowledgement within the company that the goal of becoming a learning organization is a constant, but often elusive, target that is well worth trying to achieve. In 1997 it was announced that Creative (in partnership with a United States company) would build an automotive chassis component plant in the US, demonstrating the company's commit-ment to the support of the globalization of the component industry and the needs of customers.

Case study four, XZZ Components, a Midlands-based company, is an organization that would appear to have commenced a transformation pro-cess over the past ten years through what managers believe to be a process of evolution rather than revolution. Similar to the Rover Group, XZZ was a traditional organization with many problems of resistance to change throughout the 1970s and 1980s. Its previous success had promoted an internal complacency that was difficult to erode and it was not until the failure of piecemeal changes (the introduction of new technology, robotics, etc.) that it became clear that more significant interventions were needed if it were to remain competitive.

The company was restructured and close links were forged with customers such as Nissan in order to improve quality and learn best practices from them. Internally, there were concerted efforts to develop a culture of learning and participation by increasing communication and promoting training and development for all employees. The company operates an apprentice scheme and workshop close to the shopfloor that replicates work procedures as closely as possible in order to provide an accurate impression of the work involved in component manufacture. Additionally, further opportunities for development are offered through the framework of National Vocational Qualifications (NVQs) which managers feel help to instil a sense of worth and achievement amongst those individuals who might have only negative impressions of prior learning and development experiences. Commentators now consider XZZ to be a good example of how traditional companies can orchestrate their own recovery through effectively developing the processes of learning and change. Notwithstanding this transformation, managers within the organization believe that there is much more that can be achieved and this will only occur within a framework that supports the ability to learn and change continually. The key approach for achieving this is seen by many players in the automobile industry as the creation of a learning organization. Whilst there is recognition of the validity of the concept within management at XZZ, there is a tendency to avoid the distraction of the label in the legitimization of new practices and procedures.

Critical analysis

While all the organizations have undertaken specific learning and development approaches to deal proactively with change as identified above, it is clear that they have achieved varying levels of success in the process so far. The Rover Group, contending with a history of poor industrial relations, inferior product quality and falling sales as a result of aggressive competition from Japanese producers, commenced a profound culture change that had as its central focus the intention to become a learning organization. Volvo's approach to dealing with a similar task, but contextually unique, environment was to embark upon a series of revolutionary changes in production systems that afforded an improved quality of working life for its employees.

Both the Rover Group and Volvo appeared to equip people with the necessary skills and abilities to function effectively in this environment by offering development opportunities that reflect the importance to adults of the self-directed nature of the learning process. In the Rover Group there are clear indications that such approaches enabled the organization to move into a transitional phase in the mid to late 1990s (see Table 9.1), with individuals prepared to take an increasing role in identifying and addressing their own development needs. In Volvo, however, where approaches are well established and strategically integrated with organizational culture and systems, it would appear that the emphasis is on process. Individuals are placed in an environment that encourages them to learn how to learn (double loop learning) rather than purely skills and knowledge acquisition and application.

Both the Rover Group and Volvo have chosen to approach the challenge of change from a learning perspective that is focused not only at individual and organizational levels, but also beyond the boundaries of the companies. As manufacturers and assemblers, they maintain positions of relative safety when compared to their component suppliers; to this extent, they are able to create their own environments by working closely with them, usually determining the terms on which the relationship is conducted.

Creative Engineering and XZZ Components also place considerable emphasis on the development of individuals at all levels of the organization. In their efforts to maintain their positions in the sector in which they operate, management consider that an investment in this function is unavoidable, not only because of expectation from industry partners, but also to remain competitive and innovative. There also seems to be a clear indication that the companies are pragmatic in their approaches to development, ensuring that people with attitudes that 'fit' the goals and cultures of the organizations are recruited before any investment is made.

In tandem has been an increase in upward and downward communication with people considering that they are more informed of their organizations' activities and performance. In XZZ Components, however, some employees interpret increased information as a subtle management tactic to scare and control workers. Nevertheless, it would appear that both companies have experienced profound changes to culture, work practices and the social organization of production since the late 1980s and that these aspects continue to evolve.

However, it is clear that the transformation is incomplete. In Creative Engineering, where teamwork has become established within the organization, training and development assumes a higher profile with more encouragement of interventions that promote creativity and problem solving. In XZZ Components, which retains a more traditional structure in which teams are beginning to be established, team and individual learning to complement the more structured training interventions based around national industrial schemes are gradually assuming a greater importance. Nevertheless, in both companies there are concerns surrounding the difficulties of releasing people for training in a manufacturing environment.

Similarly, many members of Creative Engineering consider that teamwork has led to the development of a learning culture while some managers are aware that the nature of the environment dictates that the company is far from achieving this state. Like the Rover Group, XZZ would appear to have achieved a significant transformation, but there remain those who cling to traditional assumptions of the employment relationship, indicating that culture change may be superficial compared to that in Creative Engineering.

Nevertheless, as a generic approach, all of the companies have invested substantially in developing the workforce and in changing systems, structures and processes in order to maintain competitive advantage. This has involved the development of individuals in team-based structures that allow the expression of ideas for continuous improvement in order that change can occur. But the shift to employee development and involvement was preceded in all the organizations by increased management intervention in order to re-establish management's right to manage. In Volvo, for example, despite the more egalitarian basis upon which the employment relationship was historically founded compared to that in the United Kingdom, management would appear to have driven the changes and maintained some of the more established hierarchical control mechanisms that allow innovative approaches to be explored. As Burgoyne (1993: 10) suggests, this type of framework preserves people as 'manageable commodities rather than unpredictable and self-willed agents'.

Similarly, when faced with industrial unrest, Japanese competition and out-dated approaches to work organization in the 1980s, it would appear that management in the Rover Group, Creative Engineering and XZZ Components adopted similar tactics. They assessed the changes that were occurring in the environment and exerted tighter controls over their workforces in order to introduce and establish new work practices. It was from this re-assertion of control that greater (but limited and/or restricted) autonomy and responsibility was gradually given to the workforce in return for an increased level of involvement and commitment framed within the lean production and organizational learning contexts.

On the basis of the research surrounding the activities and performance of the organizations therefore, the generic issues and key themes that emerge are as follows:

1   Management identification of the nature of change in the external environment and application of a top-down approach that establishes internal change in work organization in order that the company becomes proactive in dealing with change.
2   Management recognition that to be proactive, this will involve bottom-up approaches that lead to more emergent strategy making by the contribution of the wider organization through activity that leads to continuous improvement.

3 Dominant cultures are encouraged that support continuous improvement, through individual and team learning that challenges the status
   quo.
4 Individuals are encouraged to develop so that they can engage in
   learning and so that change can occur.

At the first level, barriers between the organization and the environment are relaxed, so that patterns of events can be detected, understood
and appropriate responses developed and/or anticipated. This is clearly
dependent upon leaders and managers having the capacity to learn and to
challenge the status quo so that new forms of action can emerge. This may
disrupt the fundamental principles upon which the organization is founded
and may involve the creation of a new vision for the future of the organization. Essentially, however, it is indicative of management's need to re-
establish some form of control over an unstable environment and clearly
requires flair and imagination in approach. Moreover, it is important that
managers are able to provide a conceptual framework that assists employees
in understanding the new reality that is the organization and its context.

Second, accurate interpretation of external change together with the
development of appropriate internal responses cannot be confined to
leaders but has to be seen as the responsibility of the wider organization.
This occurs within what writers (Hancke and Rubinstein 1995) identify as
a new social organization of car production that involves teamwork, commitment, training and development. This locates the explanation within
an organizational framework in which the importance of people is elevated. Individuals and teams act as buffers for, and champions of, change
strategies. This does not, however, imply that managers perceive their own
role as diluted. Rather, by offering individuals and teams the opportunity
to contribute, the knowledge base of the organization (together with the
commitment and motivation of the individuals to the organization and
their work) is potentially increased. Whilst it is clear that some individuals
may find this an uncomfortable process, again it is symptomatic of management attempting to exert greater control by adopting an approach that
includes, rather than excludes, wider learning and involvement.

That this form of control is clearly more subtle than that evident in
traditional work arrangements would appear to be indicative of the more
participatory nature of the employment relationship that managers believe
is required to maintain competitive advantage. Contribution from the
wider organization occurs within parameters that are defined by management (identified by one manager as 'tramline empowerment') and this,
in turn, is influential in terms of the depth and extent of learning that
can, or is likely to, occur. In organizations where traditional approaches to
managing people remain intact, the opportunities for transferring learning
within the organization and beyond are limited or prevented by failure
to fully exploit the process.

In terms of how far organizational cultures encourage established norms to be challenged by individuals and teams, it seems that for traditional organizations this represents a significant shift in approach that affects both management and workers. Whilst people in the organizations researched are offered more opportunities to question and debate work organization, and are more willing to contribute suggestions for improvement, there is little evidence to suggest that management control has been reduced or replaced. What is apparent is that management appear to make more use of the informal organization, embedded in the social interaction and team learning that occurs in the workplace, and that this is interpreted by workers both negatively and positively.

In the negative context, it would appear that there is little apparent overt resistance from workers who subscribe to the fundamental principles of developing organizational learning in order to manage change but they believe that it is yet another management tactic to control and exploit the individual. Some workers like strong management control mechanisms and are suspicious if managers try to appear relaxed and egalitarian. On a positive basis, there are those managers and workers who perceive the employment relationship to have profoundly changed, having been reestablished on more democratic terms. It would appear, therefore, that people within the organizations are increasingly aware that change is an ongoing process that cannot be resisted but how it can be accomplished is widely interpreted.

The final issue relates to the development of individuals so that they can contribute effectively to the performance of the organization. Research suggests that people within the organizations are generally enthusiastic to learn and recognize that by increasing their skill levels and involvement they will contribute more effectively to the organization. However, whilst for some individuals this represents a genuine interest in, and involvement with, the organization, for many it is pragmatic and borne out of feelings of job insecurity and uncertainty for their futures if they do not comply. Given economic and labour market conditions in the manufacturing sector that display high unemployment and job insecurity, management clearly have control over the terms on which people are recruited to, and are retained by, the organization. They can therefore insist that selected forms of learning and development are placed high on the agenda.

Conclusions and key learning points

The automobile industry is characterized by uncertainty, continuous change and innovation in technology, work practices and markets. Clearly, managing change effectively by encouraging innovation, learning and continuous improvement are purported to be the key issues that are essential in order to ensure survival in the sector. Some companies go so far as to espouse that their goal is to become a 'learning organization' with their commitment to this end actively demonstrated both internally and externally. But it is only by engaging the commitment of the people to such principles that their energy and learning can be harnessed for the benefit of the organization. Thus, a framework that encourages individual and organizational learning as an effective platform for change management is constructed but those involved must believe that this will lead them and their organizations to a better state.

The main issues that emerge from the research therefore concern the ability of senior managers to understand and articulate the nature of environmental change to the wider organization. From this frame of reference, they must then convey the 'picture' in a manner which people understand so that the company is able to construct and develop a shared impression of the current reality. Thereafter, the involvement and contribution of individuals and teams is sought so that existing orthodoxy is challenged and strategy emerges from the learning and contribution of the wider organization. For this to occur, the development of cultures that support this phenomenon must be promoted and this can only occur if the learning and development of individuals is encouraged by managers so that they have the skills, knowledge, confidence and the perceived 'right' to challenge. Similarly, managers in turn are prepared to encourage and develop a more democratic approach to the employment relationship in which openness and a 'no blame' environment is promoted.

Furthermore, whilst the organizational environment is characterized by change and instability, managers can, if they want, exercise choice and control in order to determine future survival and success. The form of control is subtler than that evident in traditional work arrangements and, through a limited analysis, would appear to represent an employment relationship that is indeed more participatory and inclusive than was historically the case. Parameters within the relationship, however, inevitably remain defined and controlled by management and this, in turn, seems influential in terms of the depth and extent of individual and organizational learning that may occur.

References

Alvesson, M. and Willmott, H. (1998) *Making Sense of Management: a Critical Introduction*, London: Sage.

Argyris, C. (1977) 'Double-loop learning in organisations', *Harvard Business Review*, September/October: 115–25.

Bayley, S. (1999) 'Swede smell of success', *Guardian*, 11 February, p. 15.

Beer, M. and Eisenstat, R.A. (1996) 'Developing an organisation capable of implementing strategy and learning', *Human Relations*, 49(5): 597–620.

Belohlav, J. (1996) 'The evolving corporate paradigm: corporate strategy of the future is reinventing business itself in search of competitive essence', *Business Horizons*, March–April, 39(2): 11–20.

Berggren, C. (1992) *The Volvo Experience*, London: Macmillan.

Boer, H. (1994) 'Flexible manufacturing systems', in J. Storey (ed.) *New Wave Manufacturing Strategies*, London: Paul Chapman Publishing.

Bower, D. (1993) 'The learning organisation: a Rover perspective', *Executive Development UK*, 6(2): 3–6.

Burgoyne, J. (1993) 'The competence movement: issues, stakeholders and prospects', *Personnel Review*, 22(6): 6–13.

Burnes, B. (1996) *Managing Change* (second edn), London: Pitman.

Cassell, C. and Symon, G. (eds) (1994) *Qualitative Methods in Organisational Research*, London: Sage.

Coopey, J. (1996) 'Crucial gaps in the learning organisation: power, politics and ideology', in K. Starkey (ed.) *How Organisations Learn*, London: Thomson Business Press.

Dey, I. (1993) *Qualitative Data Analysis*, London: Routledge.

Fiol, M.C. and Lyles, M.A. (1985) 'Organisational learning', *Academy of Management Review*, 10(4): 803–13.

Garvin, D. (1993) 'Building a learning organisation', *Harvard Business Review*, July–August, 78–91.

Hancke, B. and Rubinstein, S. (1995) 'Limits to innovation in work organisation?', in A. Sandberg (ed.) *Enriching Production*, Aldershot: Avebury.

Harrison, A. (1994) 'Just-in-time manufacturing', in J. Storey (ed.) *New Wave Manufacturing Strategies*, London: Paul Chapman Publishing.

Hendry, C., Arthur, B. and Jones, A. (1995) *Strategy through People*, London: Routledge.

Hirschorn, L. and Gilmore, T. (1992) 'The new boundaries of the boundaryless company', *Harvard Business Review*, May–June: 104–15.

Huber, G. (1991) 'Organisational learning: the contributing processes and the literatures', *Organisation Science*, February: 88–115.

Kanigel, R. (1997) *The One Best Way*, London: Little, Brown.

Karlsson, C. (1996) 'Radically new production systems', *International Journal of Operations and Production Management*, 16(11): 8–19.

Kenney, M. and Florida, R. (1993) *Beyond Mass Production*, Oxford: Oxford University Press.

March, J.G. and Olsen, J.P. (1975) 'The uncertainty of the past: organisational learning under ambiguity', *European Journal of Political Research*, 3: 147–71.

Mason, J. (1996) *Qualitative Researching*, London: Sage.

Morgan, G. (1997) *Images of Organization* (2nd edn), London: Sage.

Nonaka, I. (1991) 'The knowledge creating company', *Harvard Business Review*, November–December: 96–104.

Pedler, M., Burgoyne, J. and Boydell, T. (1991) *The Learning Company*, Maidenhead: McGraw-Hill.

Perakyla, A. (1997) 'Reliability and validity in research', in D. Silverman (ed.) *Qualitative Research: Theory, Method and Practice*, London: Sage.

Pilkington, A. (1996) 'Learning from joint venture: the Rover–Honda relationship', *Business History*, 38(1): 90–115.

Rubin, H.J. and Rubin, I.S. (1995) *Qualitative Interviewing*, Thousand Oaks, CA: Sage.

Sandberg, A. (1995) *Enriching Production*, Aldershot: Avebury.

Sandkull, B. (1996) 'Lean production: the myth which changes the world?', in S. Clegg and G. Palmer (eds) *The Politics of Management Knowledge*, London: Sage.

Sapsford, R. and Jupp, V. (eds) (1996) *Data Collection and Analysis*, London: Sage.

Schon, D.A. (1989) 'Organisational learning', in G. Morgan (ed.) *Beyond Method: Strategies for Social Research*, London: Sage.

Senge, P. (1991) *The Fifth Discipline: the Art and Practice of the Learning Organisation*, New York: Century Business.

Silverman, D. (1993) *Interpreting Qualitative Data: Methods for Analysing Talk, Text and Interaction*, Sage: London.

Stacey, R.D. (1996) *Strategic Management and Organisational Dynamics* (2nd edn), London: Pitman.

Stata, R. (1989) 'Organisational learning – the key to management innovation', *Sloan Management Review*, Spring: 63–74.

Tsang, E. (1997) 'Organisational learning and the learning organisation: a dichotomy between prescriptive and descriptive research', *Human Relations*, January, 50(1): 73–89.

West, P. (2000) *Organisational Learning in the Organisational Sector*, London: Routledge.

West, P. and Burnes, B. (2000) 'Applying organizational learning: lessons from the automotive sector', *International Journal for Operations and Production Management*, 20(10): 1236–51.

Womack, J.P., Jones, D.T. and Roos, D. (1990) *The Machine that Changed the World*, New York: Macmillan.

Zemke, R. and Zemke, S. (1995) 'Adult learning – what do we know for sure?' *Training*, June, 32(6): 31–7.

10

ANALYSING QUANTITATIVE RESEARCH

Darren C. Short and K. Peter Kuchinke

Aims and contribution

Professions are characterized by a body of specialized knowledge, and commonly this knowledge is the results of scientific research. As for other professional fields such as medicine, management, or education, research is critical for human resource development (HRD), and this is so for two major reasons. First, research yields new knowledge related to the many issues, questions, and problems in HRD, and second, research ensures a process for disseminating such knowledge when and if it is judged to be of high quality. Research, thus, has both a product and a process aspect, addressing substantive findings and the process of obtaining and reporting them. Research is the life-blood of HRD, aiming to advance our understanding and improve practice. In this chapter we will address one important type, quantitative research, introducing its major tenets, assumptions, methods, and evaluating its strengths and weaknesses.

This chapter differs in its topic and approach from others in this book because of its focus on a specific research method. Rather than focusing primarily on the results of a specific study or series of studies, we will take a look behind the scenes and describe how research is actually conducted, what reasoning lies behind certain choices, and what methods and tools are available. This will be done in the context of a published article that will allow us to explain the conventions for reporting research findings and guide the reader to better understand and critically evaluate published research.

The overall aim of this chapter is to provide an overview of the standard assumptions, methods, and conventions of quantitative research. The purpose is to educate the readers in this important method so that they may become more informed and confident users of such research and, perhaps, become enticed to develop their research skills in more depth through formal study. The chapter assumes relatively little prior knowledge of the research process. As an introduction to quantitative research, the chapter is limited in its scope and depth and will illustrate core principles and concepts but not cover them in depth.

Theoretical context

Research presents a specific way of obtaining knowledge that contrasts with other ways of knowing, such as tradition, faith, authority, or intuition. While the term is used rather loosely in everyday language (example: 'we need to research different brands of a product to find out which has the features we want'), in the professional world of HRD research refers to 'a systematic investigation including research development, testing, and evaluation designed to develop or contribute to generalizable knowledge' (University of Illinois 1999).

Research includes a family of methods, among them quantitative, that share the characteristic of disciplined inquiry. Disciplined inquiry, as Chronbach and Suppes (1969: 15) observed, 'has a quality that distinguishes it from other sources of opinion and belief. [It] is conducted and reported in such a way that the argument can be painstakingly examined'. This examination allows other members of the profession to evaluate the quality of the data, arguments and conclusion and form judgements over the validity of the findings (Shulman 1981). Only research that adheres to carefully developed standards related to the research process and reporting of findings is thought to yield trustworthy knowledge, that is knowledge that is solid enough to form the base for important practical decisions.

History of research and science

Research falls, very broadly speaking, into two categories, quantitative and qualitative, and there have been many long-standing debates and often-heated arguments over the merits of each. More recent thinking (for example: Shulman 1981; Hunt 1994; Morris *et al.* 1999) views them not as mutually exclusive but as complementary, each capable of answering specific questions but each also subject to important limitations.

Tracing the history of scientific research in a very cursory manner, we are led back to the British empiricist school of thought of Francis Bacon, David Hume and John Locke in the seventeenth and eighteenth centuries who expanded on the thoughts of the age of enlightenment and argued that all valid knowledge should be based not on faith or authority (as it had been during the Middle Ages) but on data available through the senses and open to observation and investigation by everyone.

Saint-Simon and Auguste Compte in nineteenth-century France built on these ideas and coined the term positivism, a philosophical position against metaphysics and theology that placed all human knowledge within the boundaries of science. Just as the scientific method had brought dramatic advances in the physical sciences, so would the application of science be able to improve the lot of humanity. 'Positivism in the nineteenth century was characterized by optimism about the benefits that the extension of the scientific method could bring to humanity. . . . It was hoped that the systematic study of human nature and human needs would provide, for the first time in history, a truly scientific basis for the reorganization of society' (Flew 1984: 283). The philosophy of positivism gave birth to the quantitative research methods addressed in this chapter. Although the hopes of reforming society through science did not come true, the scientific method and, in particular, quantitative research form a very important foundation of modern social science as applied in HRD and related fields.

Quantitative and related methods referred to as positivistic, post-positivistic, or realist science research are based on three core assumptions. First, that the social world under investigation exists independently from the researcher, that researchers can examine social phenomena, like leadership or motivation in organizations, in a manner similar to biologists who place a plant specimen under a microscope to investigate its structure and properties. Second, that there exists in the social world general laws and principles that explain human behaviour and make prediction possible. And third, that the research process in itself is value-free and neutral and that it is possible to measure social systems without altering them in a fundamental way.

Challenging these core assumptions and positing that the study of the social world differed in very fundamental ways from that of the physical world, qualitative approaches to research were proposed by German philosophers like Dilthey, Husserl, and Weber in the mid-1800s. These approaches differ drastically from quantitative methods and are based on the notion that not measurement and objective description but interpretation and subjective understanding are the most appropriate ways of comprehending social reality. The social world, they asserted, does not exist independently of the observer, and research is never value-neutral or objective. The very act of conducting research alters what is being observed in a fundamental way. Based on these convictions, a range of qualitative and interpretative approaches was developed and these are practised today.

Next to quantitative and qualitative methods, there exists a third group of approaches to research, namely critical or emancipatory research where the goal is neither observation nor understanding, but fundamental change of the social world and its institutions towards democratic ideals and freedom from oppression and injustice. Here, the roles of the researchers are decidedly partisan and their primary responsibility is to alleviate human suffering and create a more just and humane society for all.

While most researchers prefer one approach to research over another, many acknowledge that quantitative and qualitative research methods present complementary methods that illuminate different aspects of reality. Using mixed-mode approaches, for instance, many studies now include quantitative (or etic) and qualitative (or emic) aspects. Other researchers conduct series of studies alternating between emic and etic approaches.

It is widely recognized that the research method should be derived from the research question and that the primary selection criterion should be which method is better able to shed light on the question or problem under investigation.

The research process

Returning, then, to the central focus of this chapter we can describe quantitative research as an orderly process consisting of six major steps. The first step is the identification of a research question that needs answering. These questions may be very specific, such as 'what are the effects of outsourcing of HRD services on the quality of program delivery?' or more general, such as 'what factors contribute to employee motivation in the workplace?' Based on the nature of the question, research can be categorized as applied or as basic.

The next step consists of reviewing theories and past research reports related to the question. Research in HRD and in other social science fields is cumulative; each study builds upon previous work, either confirming, refuting, or expanding upon it. The review of related literature will inform the researcher of the state of knowledge related to the question, point to existing theories and research designs, and suggest measurement instruments and approaches that have been successful in the past. As a result of careful review of the existing literature, the researcher will often refine the original question, and formulate more specific research questions and, in many cases, hypotheses to be tested in the new study.

The third step consists of designing the study in order to collect data related to the research question. This includes decisions as to who should participate, how, when, and how often data should be collected, and what data collection instruments should be used. Research design must be done in a careful and deliberate manner so as to yield valid and reliable information to answer the research questions. The planning phase is critical and the quality of the research design determines the quality of the information and research results. At this stage, the researcher also decides whether the study will be descriptive or inferential, that is whether the entire population of interest can be accessed and described or whether a sampling plan is used whereby only a portion of the population participates in the study with the aim of generalizing the results.

The fourth step consists of implementing the research design and conducting the study to obtain information and data to answer the research questions. The fifth step is the analysis of the data using appropriate statistical techniques, and the sixth and final step consists of interpreting the results of the study and reporting the findings.

Hardly ever are important research questions answered in a single study, and researchers therefore conduct replications to test whether findings hold across different populations and circumstances. Even though this process appears slow and cumbersome at times, such replication is critical to ensure trustworthy knowledge and to rule out that the results of a single study are mere happenstance and artefacts of the specific research design.

The research process and important concepts and key terms are explained in more detail in the following section where we illustrate quantitative research by using a published research report.

Empirical context

Let us now turn to an actual example of quantitative research. In 1998, the second author of this chapter published an article in the refereed journal *Human Resource Development International (HRDI)*, entitled: 'The influence of leadership styles on subordinates' attitudes towards their leaders and towards performance: a comparison of US and German manufacturing employees' (Kuchinke 1998). The article was awarded the Outstanding Research award from the Academy of Human Resource Development in 1999. Having a copy of that article is not necessary for reading this chapter, although some readers may gain additional benefit from reading the two together.

As the title of Kuchinke's article suggests, the study was conducted in the US and Germany with the aim of better understanding leadership styles and cultural norms and values in the manufacturing sector. Using the classification introduced earlier, this research was applied, with the opportunity for the study arising from professional contacts between the researcher and senior management in that industry.

The context for the study was the acquisition of the German manu-facturing plant by the US parent company and the promotion of the plant director of one site to assume responsibility of a second US and the German sites. With the three sites reporting to the same manager, closer co-operation and co-ordination were required since all three sites produced very identical products using similar work processes and equipment. The three sites had previously operated quite independently and the need for closer collaboration now gave rise to questions about management and leadership styles and behaviours at each location, and about similarities and differences within each site and across the three sites. In addition, there was interest from both the US and German sites to learn about the results of specific forms of leadership to see what effects could be observed and what types of leadership behaviours might be effective. While the study arose from the need to learn something about this specific situ-ation, the results of the study also added to the knowledge base of the field. Because the findings were of interest to a broader audience, it was published in the journal. This dual aspect of specific application and broader inter-est is common to many studies in HRD.

With the general questions about leadership and culture in mind, the researcher reviewed existing literature and selected a set of theories and concepts that appeared to provide insight into the questions on hand. A process of negotiation with managers and employees at each of the three locations related to the fit between the company's culture and values and the proposed theories, concepts, and instruments resulted in the final research design that was implemented over a 3-month period. After data collection was completed, the data were analysed, the results interpreted, and the conclusions presented to the company in a series of meetings at each site. The presentation of results was followed by discussion and action planning to align the leadership styles among the sites and improve the outcomes from managerial and leadership action. The research results were then written up, disguising the identity of the organization to preserve confidentiality, and submitted to the journal. The review by the editor and four independent HRD scholars resulted in recommendations for improving the manuscript and refining the statistical analysis and final acceptance for publication. Throughout the review and revision process, which lasted about 8 months, the identity of the reviewers and the author was known only to the editor, a process called 'double-blind review'.

Methodological and research issues

Now we will guide you through the anatomy of the research article, looking in turn at each of the main components of published research with specific reference to the Kuchinke study.

Problem statements and research questions

Following the title and the abstract, which briefly summarizes the study, the purpose statement is usually the first component of published quantitative research, although in journal articles it frequently appears as part of a section entitled 'introduction' or 'background'. Its purpose, as Creswell (1994) noted, is to act as a signpost by establishing the central direction for the study, stressing the importance of the problem from a theoretical and/or practical perspective, and introducing the reader to the main variables and constructs. Where space is at a premium, as with conference papers and journal articles, summaries of research problems and purpose statements have to be relayed in as few as 300 words. In addition to being the first component of published research, the purpose statement is also frequently the first step in the research process. By clarifying the purpose of a study, a researcher can focus literature searches, specify questions to answer through study, and consider ways of designing data collection.

Before embarking on a research study, researchers tend to look to a number of sources to clarify the problem statement and purpose. The most usual sources are as follows: the researcher's personal interests and experiences; existing HRD theories that are tested, revised, or clarified; theories from disciplines other than HRD that the researcher is interested to develop or extend into an HRD setting; past studies that are repeated with a view to checking findings, validity with different subjects, trends over time, and results using different methodologies; and situations where previous research has produced contradictory results and clarification is being sought (McMillan 1992).

Specific research questions or hypotheses usually follow statements of research purpose. These are developed from the problem statement and from existing literature and theories, and are designed to focus the broadly defined problem down to specifics. Research questions are usually found in non-experimental research. Hypotheses, which are connected more with experimental research, provide tentative expectations about findings that are testable using research data. By testing hypotheses from a review of available literature, the researcher can confirm or disconfirm theories and develop explanations of relationships.

Kuchinke's research was designed to address the need for a better understanding of leadership in different countries at a time of increased globalization of business. It was a non-experimental and comparative study, the comparison being between the effects of different leadership styles on subordinates in the US and German manufacturing plants of one company. His three major research questions were as follows:

- What leadership styles and behaviours are prevalent among employees in Germany and in the United States? How do they differ by country and job category?
- What leadership outcomes are present among German and US employees and how do they differ by country and job category?
- How are leadership styles and leadership outcomes inter-correlated at the country and job category levels and what is the magnitude of these relationships?

As can be seen from these examples, research questions provide an insight to the main constructs and variables covered by the research. The terms *constructs* and *variables* are used to describe classes of objects or traits that vary, and in the Kuchinke study these were leadership styles, leadership behaviours, country where employed, job category and leadership outcomes. Some of those are considered *independent variables*, in that they precede or influence *dependent variables*, as with the relationship between the independent 'leadership styles' and the dependent 'leadership outcomes'. Research questions, as with Kuchinke's third, frequently seek to test the extent of relationships between independent and dependent variables.

The research questions also reveal that this particular study was non-experimental and correlational in nature, seeking to examine relationships between and among variables as they exist. This is in contrast to experimental methods where one or more variables would be manipulated in order to observe the consequences of these changes. Experimental designs are often conducted in laboratory settings while correlational studies predominate where researchers are working in existing organizational settings.

Literature review

The review of literature is an essential component of the research process and is the second major section of most research articles. During the quantitative research process, the literature review: (1) assists in refining research problems and hypotheses, specifically by identifying conclusions from past research, gaps in knowledge, and contradictions from past findings; (2) informs the choice of research methodology by identifying the approaches adopted successfully by past researchers, the instruments they have used, definitions, etc.; and (3) allows the research findings to be interpreted in the context of what is already known, which for the researcher enables the easier identification of new findings.

Readers of quantitative research literature reviews should therefore find that they answer at least four main questions:

- What do we already know or not know? That draws the reader's attention to the existing body of knowledge on the research topic, including gaps in understanding and contradictions;
- What do you need to know to understand the rest of the article? That provides the reader with sufficient background knowledge on the research topic to understand the specifics of the research being described;
- What methods are used in the research that can be justified by past use? That provides the reader with a justification for the research methods and instruments; and
- Why is this important? That provides the reader with an understanding of the significance of the research.

Literature reviews are usually based on material researched from several sources, and the thoroughness of the review, the types of publications cited, and the age of the material cited, all give readers an indication of the possible quality of the literature review. The main literature sources used by researchers are as follows:

- journal articles, particularly those publishing reports of empirical research, are a source of relatively current information on topics of interest. Refereed journals (check the 'notes for contributors' section in the publication) offer readers the knowledge that articles have been evaluated by external reviewers to check on significance, methodology, data analysis, and other criteria. Reference lists in journal articles also point readers to additional sources of information;
- books, although the information they contain is less timely given the lengthy period between writing a manuscript and books landing on

bookshelves. Nevertheless, they provide readers with a source of detail and depth not possible in single journal articles; and

- conference papers, most notably where conference papers are refereed and proceedings are published, as with the proceedings of the annual conferences of the Academy of Human Resource Development (AHRD), the University Forum for HRD, and the International Federation of Training and Development Organizations (IFTDO). Conference papers do not have the same academic standing as journal articles but they do contain the most timely information on current research and, like journal articles, offer a good guide to other papers, articles, and books of interest to researchers.

In the Kuchinke article, the literature review was divided between contextual material comparing US and German industry and leadership approaches, and specific material on transformational leadership theories and research. Among the points made by Kuchinke were the following.

- There are similarities and parallels between the US and Germany, not least because of the pre-eminent positions of both in the global economy, trade between the two countries, and organizations from one country with subsidiaries, affiliates, or branches in the other.
- There are profound differences in the underlying philosophy, history and regulation of each country's economies that could suggest the possibility of substantial differences in attitudes toward leadership.
- There are a number of different leadership theories, although leadership can be most generally defined as a complex interaction between the leader and the social and organizational environments.
- Leadership theory contrasts transactional and transformation styles: transactional leadership is a negotiation process based on contingent rewards and management-by-exception; transformational leadership consists of charisma, inspirational motivation, intellectual stimulation and individualized consideration.
- Past research has shown transformation leadership to be positively correlated with a variety of worthwhile outcome variables, whereas transactional leadership contributed less or had negative effects.

Kuchinke's article contained twenty-seven references to other publications, mainly journal articles and books. Among the journals were some of the most highly regarded in the field, such as *Human Resource Development Quarterly, Journal of Applied Psychology,* and *Leadership Quarterly.* Most of the literature was recent (mid-1990s).

Questions for evaluating quantitative research

- Does the literature review establish a basis for the research by describing: what is already known and not known; what the reader needs to know to understand the article; how research methods can be justified by past studies; and why the topic is important?

- Does the literature review appear comprehensive and appear to contain all-important past research?
- Are references recent and taken from recognized sources?
- Are past studies reviewed critically, identifying contradictions and flaws?

Research design and method

Types of research design

The term *research design* refers to the way information is gathered by the researcher. There are two broad types of quantitative research: experimental and non-experimental. *Experimental research* takes place in a controlled environment, usually a laboratory, where the factors or variables of interest can be studied without the influence of factors or variables that might interfere (known as *extraneous variables*). The aim of experimental research is to produce clear-cut answers to very specific questions but the artificial situation limits the extent to which the findings are applicable outside of the laboratory setting.

In *non-experimental research*, also called *field research*, data are collected in natural situations, such as in organizations. Most HRD research is non-experimental and thus it is impossible to control for all extraneous variables that may influence the findings. Consequently, findings are less clear-cut than for experimental research but have often-greater practical use. In published non-experimental research, readers should look for how the researcher sought to control for extraneous variables. Kuchinke for example, used three very similar sites from one organization, and thus any identified differences in leadership could not be explained by the surveyed employees working in different organizations or industries, nor could differences be due to different company policies or work processes and procedures. Those extraneous variables were therefore considered to be controlled for in the survey design.

The two main types of non-experimental research design are quasi-experimental and *ex post facto*. *Quasi-experimental* involves treating two or more groups differently and checking differences in the outcomes of those different treatments. Typically, it involves one group receiving something, such as a training course, and a second group serving as a control. In *ex post facto* research the researcher does not manipulate the variables being studied; instead collecting information on a subject of interest after the fact and considering reasons that may explain any differences found. The primary purpose is to investigate possible relationships between variables where an experiment is not possible. Kuchinke's research had an *ex post facto* survey design.

213

Sampling methods

Most quantitative HRD research involves studying a small group of people with the intention of using the results to make inferences about larger groups. That occurs at two levels: first, the researcher seeks to learn about some *target population*, such as all senior managers, by studying a *survey population* of senior managers at particular organizations; second, the researcher seeks to learn about the survey population by studying a *sample* of the selected organizations' managers. This path raises a number of potential concerns, not least the possibility that the sample does not reflect the survey population (that is, is *biased* in some way), and that the survey population does not reflect the target population (meaning the results are not *generalizable* beyond the organizations studied to a wider target population).

In the Kuchinke research, the target population was employees in Germany and the United States, the survey population consisted of the 5,400 employees at three manufacturing sites in Germany and the US of a Fortune 500 multinational telecommunications organization, and the sample consisted of the 3,540 employees sent a survey instrument. As this shows, the research was designed specifically to explore leadership in the single organization rather than to draw conclusions about leadership more widely in the two countries; the latter could only have been achieved by looking at many organizations that were somehow representative of those found in the two countries. As Kuchinke stated in his conclusions, 'the research setting was not selected at random . . . the findings of the study, therefore, lack external validity and do not generalize to other US or German organisations' (p. 305). This, of course, limits the strength of the findings and makes replication studies very necessary.

The purpose of sampling is to identify a sub-set of the survey population who are *representative* of that population. That can be achieved two ways: through probability sampling, where every member of the survey population has a known probability of being selected in the sample, or non-probability sampling. The four main approaches to probability sampling found in HRD research are as follows:

- *simple random sampling*, where each member of the survey population has an equal chance of being selected, and the sample is selected at random;
- *systematic sampling*, where members of the survey population are listed (say alphabetically) and every *n*th person is selected, beginning with a member selected at random from the first *n* in the list;
- *stratified sampling*, where the survey population is divided into homogeneous groups (known as strata) and a sample then selected at random from within each group. The sample selected from each stratum can either be *proportional* to the total number of survey population members in that stratum or can be *non-proportional*;

- *cluster sampling*, where the survey population naturally divides into groups and a random sample of whole groups is selected.

Non-probability sampling designs are used where it is not feasible or unnecessary to obtain a probability sample. *Convenience sampling*, for example, is based on easy access to a particular group, such as a class of students. However, the generalizability of results from such samples is usually poor, and they are found more frequently in qualitative HRD research than quantitative.

The size of the sample is an important consideration, and formal statistical techniques must be used to determine the ideal sample size. Generally, the larger the sample, the greater the confidence researchers have in the findings, although the benefits of large sample sizes have to be balanced against cost increases of collecting data from such samples. Consequently, sample sizes of between 100 and 1,000 are common in quantitative HRD research.

Kuchinke selected a stratified, non-proportional, random sample of 3,540 of the 5,400 employees on the three sites being studied. The population of employees was divided up into naturally occurring strata of the three sites and then, within each site, three job categories. There were therefore nine strata – management employees, engineers, and production-level employees at each of the three sites. A random sample was then selected from each stratum. However, the sample size for each stratum was not proportional to the stratum size as the number of members in some strata (management employees) was small, and Kuchinke wanted to ensure adequate representation of all groups.

Instruments and measures

Once the sample is selected, the researcher uses one or more means to collect data. There are four basic ways of collecting data: observation, surveys, interviews and review of existing documents. It is preferable to use more than one data collection method to avoid what is known as single-method bias. Further, it is wise to collect information from more than one source to avoid single-source bias.

Kuchinke's study, like many in quantitative HRD research, used a single data collection instrument, a *survey*, where subjects were invited to complete a written questionnaire, and this presents a limitation to the study because of the chance that the results are distorted by single-method, single-source bias. Two key concepts when considering data collection instruments are *validity* (whether the instrument measures what it claims to be measuring) and *reliability* (whether the measure yields consistent results). Users of quantitative research should pay attention to researchers' claims for the validity and reliability of their measures and be sceptical of those who avoid the topic in their work.

Kuchinke's survey instrument was created by adding demographic questions to a recognized leadership questionnaire (the MLQ5x – Avolio, Bass and Jung 1995). That questionnaire had been used previously in over seventy-five research studies in several countries, used in a variety of organizations for leaders with high and low levels of responsibility, and had been translated into several languages, including German. The questionnaire was considered to have very good reliability and validity and this strengthens the level of confidence in the findings.

Representativeness and bias

Of the 3,540 instruments administered by Kuchinke, 1,872 were returned completed – a response rate of 53 per cent. However, one concern with all surveys is whether the respondents are representative of the survey population – that is, whether the 1,872 people were different from those employees who did not complete a questionnaire in ways that would influence the research findings. If that had been the case, then the results would be biased.

To test whether those who returned completed questionnaires were representative of all employees on the three sites, Kuchinke completed a chi-squared test, which tests for differences between two sets of data. For Kuchinke, the two sets were as follows: the demographic data from the survey respondents (gender, age, level of education, and union membership); and the same information on all 5,400 employees as provided by the organization's personnel function. The numerical output from the chi-squared formula is compared by the researcher against a published table of results to determine whether a hypothesis of no significant difference between the two data sets is not rejected (that is, the survey respondents are not significantly different from the survey population) or rejected (they are not representative). In the case of the Kuchinke research, the hypothesis was not rejected, and there was therefore no reason to suggest that the respondents were unrepresentative of the survey population.

Questions for evaluating quantitative research designs

Users of HRD research may want to consider the following questions when reviewing published research designs:

- Are potential extraneous variables described and considered by the researcher (for example, could an external factor not considered by the researcher have caused the reported changes)?
- Where groups are being compared, are differences between the groups controlled for (for example, are there differences between the groups in terms of experience, age, location, or some other factor that could have caused the reported changes)?

- Are the target and survey populations clearly defined?
- Is it a probability or non-probability sample, and does the researcher justify the selection of the particular sampling method?
- Can the research design lead to unbiased and generalizable results?
- Is the sample of an adequate size to represent the population accurately?
- Where a stratified sample is used, does the researcher identify the characteristics used to stratify the survey population?
- Does the researcher describe the response rate and the results of tests on the representativeness of those who completed the survey?

Data analysis

In examining the common data analysis methods used by HRD researchers, we shall take advantage of the useful classification of tools produced by Holton and Burnett (1997), which is based on whether the researcher seeks to:

- describe the characteristics of some group or groups;
- compare two or more groups;
- check the association between two variables and the strength of that relationship;
- predict something in the future;
- explain why some outcome or phenomena occurs.

Description

Descriptive statistics are used to summarize the characteristics of a sample, the most common ones being the following:

- frequencies, which indicate how often each score or value or answer is given (and is often presented as a percentage);
- means, which are the most common measure of average used in quantitative HRD research, and are calculated as the arithmetic average of the obtained answers. Two other averages readers will sometimes come across are modes (the score, or group of scores, that occur most often) and medians (the middle score where one-half of the score fall above and one-half fall below it);
- standard deviations, which provide a measure of the spread of answers around the calculated mean – the larger the standard deviation, the more varied the answers given.

Kuchinke made use of each of these descriptive statistics:

- percentages, to describe the gender distribution of the sample; for example, 62 per cent of US production employees were male;

- modes, to describe the most frequently occurring age group and education qualification level of the sample; for example, most German managers had an education of a 5-year college degree;
- means, to report the average responses for each of the leadership style and leadership outcome variables; for example, the mean score on charisma was 2.31 and on motivation was 2.41 on a scale from 1 (low) to 5 (high);
- standard deviations, to describe the spread of answers given in response to questions on leadership styles and outcomes; for example the standard deviation for charisma was lower than for motivation (.84 against .93).

Comparison

Comparison analysis tools allow researchers to compare results for two or more variables to determine whether or not there is a *statistically significant* difference between them. Where data are collected from the whole population, such tests are unnecessary, as any difference is real: taking the example above from Kuchinke's study, if the charisma and motivation means had been calculated from data obtained from the whole population, then we could state that there was an actual difference between the two scores. However, where samples are involved, the means are not error-free and will vary depending on which survey population subjects are selected for the sample, and the amount of possible error will be greater with smaller samples than larger ones. HRD researchers therefore use statistical tests to determine whether differences between means are statistically significant, or could be due to the nature of the sample.

The two comparison tests most frequently reported in quantitative HRD research are as follows: *t-tests*, which test whether two groups are statistically different from each other using the values of those means and their standard deviations; and ANOVA (*analysis of variance*), and close relatives ANCOVA (*analysis of covariance*) and MANOVA/MANCOVA (*multivariate analysis of variance/covariance*), which test for statistical differences where more than two means are involved. Researchers then report the results of those tests, indicating where the results were statistically significant and stating the level of significance (such as Kuchinke's use of 0.001 to indicate 99.9 per cent confidence in the reporting of statistical significance or a 1 in a 1000 chance of error in the stated result).

Kuchinke made use of both types of comparison tests. For example, he used t-tests when checking whether leadership style and outcome scores were significantly different between the sites in the two countries. He also used ANCOVA to compare all three groups or employees at each site while statistically controlling for the effects that age, education and job tenure might have on leadership styles and outcomes.

Association

The main association question HRD researchers seek to answer is whether the scores of two variables are associated (which does not imply that one causes the other). *Correlation* is the measure of associated relationship between two variables, that is the extent to which one variable increases or decreases as a second changes.

The extent to which two variables are correlated is represented by a *correlation coefficient*, a number between −1 and +1 that indicates both the strength and direction of the relationship. The closer the coefficient to +1, the more positive the relationship so that one variable increases as the other increases; the closer to −1, the more negative the relationship so that one variable increases as the other decreases. Coefficients around zero suggest little or no correlation, that is no association between the two variables. As with comparisons, researchers can test whether a correlation coefficient is statistically significant from zero.

Kuchinke used correlation coefficients to measure the association between the variables of leadership style and outcome. Those showed that the three outcome measures were clearly positively correlated with the four transformational leadership scales and also with contingent rewards and were all negatively correlated with management-by-exception. Although Kuchinke did not report statistical significance of correlation coefficients in his HRDI article, they were reported in another article about this study (Kuchinke 1999), where 44 of the 55 reported coefficients were statistically significant from zero at the .05 level (that is, 95 per cent confidence).

Prediction and explanation

A next step on from correlation is to consider whether a dependent variable can be predicted for given levels of one or more independent variables. That occurs in the analytical technique of regression (multiple regression for more than one independent variable). Multiple regression analyses are often conducted to answer research questions related to the contribution of several independent variables to the dependent or criterion variable. While not included in the Kuchinke article, it might be, for example, interesting to determine what percentage of the dependent variable *extra effort* (measuring employees willingness to put in extra effort to the task when needed) might be explained by their age, gender, professional experience, tenure in the organization and various styles of leadership. Answers to this question would be valuable for organizations interested in raising the level of extra effort that employees exert, and multiple regression analyses would be the statistical technique to answer questions of this kind.

The highest level of research is explanation, where the aim is to establish the changes in one or more variables are caused by changes in another or others. This is referred to as establishing causality. The best approach is to conduct experimental research, and so HRD research is rarely at the explanation level. However, some non-experimental HRD research can be designed to infer causal relationships.

Questions for evaluating quantitative research analyses

- Did the data analysis provide results to answer the research questions?
- Was it clear that the researcher used appropriate statistical tests?
- Did the researcher identify where results were statistically significant, how that was determined, and the level of significance?
- Did the researcher discuss the suitability of the data for various statistical techniques?
- Did the researcher avoid suggesting there was a cause-and-effect relationship between variables (unless this had been determined experimentally)?

Conclusions and recommendations

The final section of published quantitative research is usually entitled conclusions, conclusions and recommendations, discussion or similar. Its purpose is to offer an interpretation of the results, a set of conclusions, and some recommendations for action and further research. Although the precise content varies between articles, most contain the following components (McMillan 1992):

- interpretation of results, specifically related to: the problem statement, research questions, or hypotheses; the research methodology; the measurement of variables; and (if experimental research) the experimental treatments. Some of the questions the researcher may address include: why did the results turn out how they did?; what may have affected the results?; and what is the meaning of the findings?;
- interpretation of statistical procedures, specifically in relation to the appropriateness of those procedures, and the importance placed on statistical significance and significant results;
- interpretation related to previous research, specifically covering how the results relate to the findings of the literature review with the intention of placing the results in the context of other research and exploring the contribution of the research to the body of knowledge;
- conclusions, which are summary statements of the results in relation to the research questions or hypotheses, and support for those statements;
- limitations to the conclusions, specifically in relation to characteristics of those in the sample, characteristics of the research situation (such as the setting and research context), timing of the study and limitations related to the treatment and to measures; and

- recommendations and implications, which are likely to address the practical implications of the research findings and the need for further research.

In Kuchinke's article, he titled the section 'conclusions' and included:

- a summary of the research focus and research design;
- main findings in relation to past research;
- implications for HRD practitioners;
- issues of validity and generalizability; and
- constraints of the study and suggestions for further research.

The main thrust of the findings were as follows: higher levels of charisma and inspirational motivation among the US sample; a higher level of satisfaction with leadership in the US, but no country-related differences in the other two outcome measures; analysis at the job category level showing that the samples in the two countries exhibited similar trends, with those lower in the organization experiencing lower levels of transformational leadership; correlation analyses showing a clear positive relationship between outcome measures and the four transformational leadership styles and positive reinforcement.

The implications were as follows: (1) transformational leadership is effective with a German population, although it should be modified to fit the German culture; (2) an increased emphasis on supervisory training for transformational leadership would offer the potential to increase levels of satisfaction, effectiveness and willingness to exert extra effort; and (3) charisma, inspirational motivation, intellectual stimulation and individual consideration are effective in creating desired behaviours above and beyond what transactional styles are able to achieve.

Questions for evaluating quantitative research concluding sections

- Do conclusions answer all the research questions?
- Are the research results interpreted appropriately in identifying the conclusions?
- Are limitations discussed, including the implications for the findings of those limitations?
- Do recommendations and implications flow from the conclusions?

Critical analysis

Every serious social science researcher is only too aware of the limitations of his or her work: in the process of designing, developing, implementing, analysing, and reporting research, numerous decisions have to be made and oftentimes these decisions present trade-offs between competing goals.

The selection of the study participants, for example, should be free of bias and random to ensure that findings are valid and generalizable to the population under examination. In reality, however, there are numerous threats to validity and reliability, both with respect to design and measurement.

One important threat to external validity is the fact that the vast majority of research in HRD is conducted with volunteers who may not represent the population at large. Obtaining information from non-respondents is often difficult and time consuming, and the benefits of seeking including non-respondents must be weighted against the goals of honouring people's decision not to participate, the need to complete the study and report the results in a timely fashion, and other considerations. Despite careful design and implementation, all research studies present compromises that limit the scientific value of the study but are, at the same time, unavoidable.

Ethical reporting of research findings, thus, includes an acknowledgement of the limitation of the study, and this does not diminish the stature of the researcher and the research report but rather attests to the integrity of the scholar to be aware of and openly discuss these limitations. Oftentimes the limitations of one study give rise to another study addressing the specific shortcomings of the first and thus rounding out the picture and adding to the body of knowledge in the field.

Pertaining to the Kuchinke study, the major limitations, as indicated in the manuscript, relate to response bias (the fact that only a portion of the sample decided to participate), to single-source/single-method bias (the fact that data were collected only by a written employee survey), and to the one-shot design (which lessens the confidence in the stability of the observed leadership behaviours which might have been the result of a host of situational factors). Finally, the study used an existing theoretical framework that might only partially fit with the context of the organization where it was used. By using an external set of leadership theories, the study likely failed to capture salient behaviours and information simply because the data collection approach and instrumentation were not set up to capture those. These limitations should be addressed in subsequent replications or follow-up studies related to leadership in an international context.

More broadly, there are important limitations related to quantitative research in general. First, quantitative research, built on the assumption that reality exists largely independent of the researcher, is prone to reification, that is the fixing in time of processes that might be highly situational, contextual and fluid. Processual events that depend on the social interaction among organizational members are difficult to capture with quantitative methods that assume stability. Since many aspects of organizational life, such as leadership, motivation, satisfaction, and commitment, cannot be directly observed and measured but must be inferred, there is a danger of misinterpretation and seeing what the observer wants or expects to see rather than what is really there.

The difficulty of understanding the reality of others objectively, that is without superimposing one's own set of ideas, distinguishes the social from the physical sciences and has led many researchers to adopt a critical stance toward this particular method. Especially in the study of organizations, there is the keen awareness of their complexity and the cognitive demands inherent in describing and analysing organizational behaviour. Systems scientists such as Boulding (1956), for example, argue that individuals are cognitively ill-equipped to comprehend systems at a level of complexity higher than our own. The difficulty of understanding ourselves as individuals is only magnified when it comes to groups of people and social entities such as organizations. This conundrum is well expressed in the simple but profound Sufi fable of the three blind men who happen upon an elephant and each make sense of the encounter based on their cognitive capacity but fail to comprehend reality objectively. Without painting too gloomy a picture of organizational research, there is a lot of evidence to suggest that our cognitive resources are limiting our understanding of organization; a limitation afflicting researchers and managers alike.

A second major limitation to quantitative research is related to the application of knowledge obtained. The primary goal of researchers, and certainly that of quantitative research, is to explain reality and, perhaps, understand how events are related to each other. It is not the primary objective of researchers to solve problems or decide what action to take. The goals and tasks of researchers and managers, thus, differ, with one attempting to make sense of what has already happened, the other to influence what is about to happen. Much of organizational and HRD research, thus, does not translate directly into practice, although it might explain what has happened and suggest action that might be fruitful and promising. While research findings often inform practice and contribute to decisions, they are not the only factor. Organizational action requires attention to many more situational contingencies than a research study can typically account for. Despite many years of research, social scientists have not developed general theories that might apply in many or most circumstances. On the contrary, much theorizing in the last 20 years has resulted in an appreciation of how situationally bounded organizational action is. It is commonly acknowledged that scientific theories cannot be general (applying in a wide variety of situations), simple (using a small number of variables), and accurate at the same time (Langley 1999). Accurate theories typically include many contextual variables and thus lack simplicity. Theories that are general and use a manageable number of variables typically lack accuracy.

The role of research thus cannot be to solve problems or make decisions – this is much better done by experienced practitioners – but to provide frameworks for understanding and guiding action, thus influencing practice indirectly. Therefore, HRD practitioners should take care to understand the descriptive nature of research findings and not confuse them with prescriptions or recipes for practice.

Conclusions and key learning points

This chapter has addressed several conceptual and practical aspects related to quantitative research and hopefully provided some insight into the strengths and limitations of this method. Organizations are complex social institutions where HRD professionals are faced with a myriad of practical problems and where quantitative research might provide information and insight into some major issues and problems. The chapter began with a very brief overview of the history and philosophy of this method and then illustrated the research process and the components of a research report by using a published article. Finally, several limitations were discussed that relate to the nature of organizations and the cognitive limitations of individuals to understand and, thus, control organizations. The role of researchers and their contributions to the practical work of HRD professionals and managers were also discussed.

References

Avolio, B., Bass, B. and Jung, D. (1995) *MLQ: Multifactor Leadership Questionnaire: Technical Report*, Palo Alto, CA: Mind Garden Press.

Babbie, E. (1986) *The Practice of Social Science Research*, Belmont, CA: Wadsworth.

Boulding, K.E. (1956) 'General systems theory – the skeleton of science', *Management Science*, 2(3): 197–208.

Chronbach, L.J. and Suppes, P. (eds) (1969) *Research for Tomorrow's Schools: Disciplined Inquiry for Education*, New York: Macmillan.

Creswell, J.W. (1994) *Research Design: Qualitative and Quantitative Approaches*, Thousand Oaks, CA: Sage.

Flew, A. (1984) *A Dictionary of Philosophy*, New York: St. Martin's Press.

Holton, E.F. and Burnett, M.F. (1997) 'Quantitative research methods', in R.A. Swanson and E.F. Holton (eds) *Human Research Development Handbook*, San Francisco: Berrett-Koehler 65–87.

Howell, D.C. (1992) *Statistical Methods for Psychology*, Boston, MA: PWS-Kent.

Hunt, S.D. (1994) 'On the rhetoric of qualitative methods: towards historically informed argumentation in management inquiry', *Journal of Management Inquiry*, 3(3): 221–34.

Kuchinke, K.P. (1998) 'The influence of leadership styles on subordinates' attitudes towards their leaders and towards performance: a comparison of US and German manufacturing employees', *Human Resource Development International*, 1(3): 291–308.

—— (1999) 'Leadership and culture: work-related values and leadership styles among one company's US and German telecommunication employees', *Human Resource Development Quarterly*, 10(2): 135–55.

Langley, A. (1999) 'Strategies for theorising form process data', *Academy of Management Review*, 24(4): 691–710.

McMillan, J.H. (1992) *Educational Research: Fundamentals for the Consumer*, New York: HarperCollins.

Morris, M.W., Leung, K., Ames, D. and Lickel, B. (1999) Views from inside and outside: integrating emic and etic insights about culture and justice judgement, *Academy of Management Journal*, 24(4): 781–96.

Pedhazur, E.J. and Schmelkin, L.P. (1991) *Measurement, Design, and Analysis: an Integrated Approach*, Hillsdale, NJ: Lawrence Erlbaum.

Shulman, L.S. (1981) 'Disciplines of inquiry in education: an overview', *Educational Researcher* June/July: 5–23.

Swanson, R.A. and Holton, E.F. (1997) *HRD Research Handbook: Linking Research and Practice*, San Francisco, CA: Berrett-Koehler.

University of Illinois (1999) *Human Subject Participation in Survey Research*, Champaign, IL: Institutional Review Board.

11

WRITING THE RESEARCH STORY

Sally Sambrook

Aims and contributions

This chapter addresses one of the key processes of any research activity. The aim of this chapter is to explain how, as a doctoral student, I approached the task of writing the research story, given that the PhD was conducted from an interpretative perspective. This is an important point to make because it suggests a different and alternative way of writing 'up' the research findings, one that does not consider the writing to be a separate activity, detached from conducting the research, and one that does not consider the researcher to be detached from what she is creating and writing about. This chapter suggests that writing the research story can be conceptualized as struggling to craft an artistic and honest product, rather than the neutral reporting of empirical findings.

The chapter is structured to address the following questions.

- *What* is the research story about – fact or fiction?
- *Why* write the story – to try to make personal sense, to inform others, to get a qualification?
- *When* do you start – and stop – writing?
- *Who* are you writing for – yourself, your examiners, your participants, your public?
- *How* do you construct and present the story – as an objective reporter or reflexive writer?

We could add the small – but important – issue of *where* to write – both as in where to disseminate or publish your findings, and where to locate yourself to achieve the most effective writing environment.

After reading this chapter the researcher should be able to:

- describe different perspectives on conducting and writing about research;
- analyse the merits and limitations of different perspectives;
- reflect upon and critically evaluate her own perspective;

226

- answer the above questions as they apply to her own current/proposed research project; and
- explain the needs of various stakeholders when writing about the research.

As Koch (1998) asks, 'Story telling: is it really research?' Borrowing her thoughts, in this chapter I argue that a story can be considered as a legitimate research product. It could also be considered as a particularly appropriate research product for interpretive research, where meanings are constructed and explored. Rather than then attempt to 'write these up' in a clinical report, why not just 'tell the story'? As Koch (1998: 1182) states, 'Story telling has been used for centuries as a powerful vehicle for communication.' We use stories to help make sense of the social phenomena we have created. Stories (myths and legends) are a significant part of our cultures and provide a means of helping us understand our lives. Stories give theoretical explanations believable or 'real life' meanings and therefore help us to learn. In this chapter, I tell the story of my doctoral research project. The doctoral thesis told not only the story of the emergence of HRD in the health service (the scene), but also narrated the tale of a novice researcher and her co-researchers (the characters) coming together to create new meanings and understandings (the plot).

Theoretical and empirical context

This section reviews both the theoretical and empirical context of the research from which this chapter is drawn. Here, I address the *content* of the research – that is, what was being studied – and the *process*, that is, how HRD was investigated. The context of this chapter is a three-year doctoral programme, entitled 'Models and Concepts of Human Resource Development: Academic and Practitioner Perspectives'. Thus, in terms of content, the thesis explored how academics and practitioners made sense of the emerging concept of HRD from a British perspective. In terms of my research methods, the academic perspective was investigated through a review of existing literature, conceptualized as the means by which academics theorize and practise HRD in the public domain (through products such as course programmes, textbooks and conference papers). This element is explored in more detail in a later chapter. The practitioner perspective focused on HRD strategies and practices within a specific context – the British National Health Service (NHS). The study was conducted from an interpretative perspective, with the storyteller engaged in ethnographic research. This involved gathering accounts of HRD from practitioners, by observing, questioning and examining both their spoken and written words. It is from these accounts that I crafted my research story, and this is explained below. However, there is one key point I wish to make, and this is made by many other researchers (Saunders, Lewis and

Thornhill 1997). It is this: *thinking* about the research project is very closely related to *writing* about the project.

When thinking about the research project, and as a means of clarifying the research question and methods to be used, it is useful to use the framework of examining and answering the 'what', 'why' and 'how' questions (Watson 1994b). What are you researching, and so, what are you going to be writing about? The 'what' defines the area in which the research is located, articulating the associated concepts and their relationships. Why are you researching, and writing about, this? The 'why' is concerned with the reasons for conducting the research; perhaps resulting from a gap in the literature which leaves social experiences without theoretical explanations; or an organizational problem in a novel context (see Chapter 18). These two dimensions form the basis of the conceptual model. The 'how' raises two further questions – how philosophically, and how practically? For example, philosophically, which position do you take on the conception of science and the creation of knowledge, and, practically, which technical methods will you use? Answering these 'how' questions help identify and answer the 'what' and 'why'. It also helps to identify what contribution the research might make to expanding public knowledge. To explain the context of the doctoral research upon which this chapter is based, the next section answers the what and why questions. The question of 'how' is explored in the following section – methodological issues.

The 'what'

Managing and developing people is a key area of organization theory and practice. There is an extensive literature on the broader topic of employment management – or human resourcing as it is now more commonly referred to – which encompasses the specialist occupational roles associated with recruiting, rewarding, developing and relating with employees. I focused on managing the development of employees. Traditional approaches to training and development are well-documented (Reid and Barrington 1994; Buckley and Caple 1995). There is now an increasing amount written about HRD (Megginson, Joy-Matthews and Banfield 1993; Stewart 1991; Stewart and McGoldrick 1996; Lee 1997a, 1998a,b). The term HRD seems to depict a subtle shift in the role, status and practice of the 'training and development' function. In my thesis, I suggest that HRD has been talked into being and accomplished through talk. From an academic perspective, analysed through a review of relevant literature, HRD is purported to be (or is talked about as being) the more strategic approach to managing and developing people. To investigate the practitioner perspective, I decided upon a specific organizational environment – the British NHS.

There are many changes occurring within the NHS. Some of these have some bearing on human resourcing, and particularly HRD. Some of these changes include increasing consumerism and technological advancements, but perhaps recent government policy (The NHS and Community Care Act 1991) resulting in the creation of the internal market and Trust status have impacted most significantly upon the management and funding of healthcare providers. Other changes, or potential sources of 'external' influence, include the activities of professional bodies, such as the General Medical Council (GMC), British Medical Association (BMA), United Kingdom Central Council for Nursing, Midwifery and Health Visiting (UKCC) and Royal College of Nursing (RCN), and European initiatives specific to the health service. How these are interpreted and then acted upon influence the way work is organized and managed within, in this case, two Trust hospitals. As Burchill and Casey state:

> British medical training and practice have excellent world-wide standing and the same is true of its research . . . [however]. The professions contain elements of inflexibility; financial management could be improved; and the same is true of general management. General reforms of training are in place. Some of these are related to the needs of the internal market. A key point is that we do not confuse the needs of this market with the overall issues of training and development.
>
> (1996: 121)

These changes can be seen to create new training and development needs and influence the activities of specialist practitioners.

At a national level, the NHS Training Agency (NHSTA) was created in 1983, ahead of the establishment of general management in the NHS, following the Griffiths report. It was replaced in 1991 by the NHS Training Directorate (NHSTD), created to meet increasing demands for customer responsiveness (Mabey and Salaman 1995), and under the control of the human resources director. In 1996, the NHS training division was disbanded, and its functions were split into two. In part, it was replaced by the self-financing Institute of Health and Care Development (IHCD) based at Frenchay Healthcare Trust. This is a NHS trading agency working both as a consultancy specializing in human resources development and an awarding body. The other part is a development unit based at Quarry House, Leeds, retained by the NHS Executive and with responsibility for overall policy and strategy. The split of the NHSTD itself is interesting. One part is concerned with development (HRD) strategy, the other with operational HRD. This split mirrors the distinction emerging in academic literature between strategic HRD and HRD strategies (Walton 1999). To find out more about HRD in the health service I contacted the IHCD 'help desk' and was told that trusts 'do their own thing now'. Very little was known about local activities. When planning the practitioner element, I had considered how to investigate HRD in the health service – a nation-wide survey or case-study approach. With this information, I decided to focus on activities in two local Trust hospitals, looking at development issues – and how the development function relates with HR and corporate strategies.

The 'why'

The purpose of the research was to investigate the academic development of this new concept of HRD and then examine how this related to changing practices in the development arena within the NHS, investigating the reasons practitioners use to explain these changes. As Lee states, 'if SHRD is to be legitimised as an academic discipline or as an important aspect of practice, then further attention needs to be paid to the conceptual base from which we work' (1997a: 98). I tried to respond to Lee's plea for further study of HRD, in that I examined how academic resources and structural changes in the role, status and activities of development practitioners impacted upon their individual work orientations, shared meanings, senses of identity and career development. I also explored the meanings attached to the terms training and development and human resource development (HRD) by both academics and specialist practitioners in the context of British work organizations, as much of the literature related to American experiences. In addition, this project focused specifically on organizations within the health service sector, where 'significant change has taken place in education and organizational and professional development . . . [but] development of HRM capacity and best practice in human resources has become patchy. The available research, albeit limited, supports this analysis' (Heron 1997). There was little research into the changing role of the development function.

There were two key reasons why I felt this topic was worthy of investigation in this particular sector. The first was the context of change within the health service, particularly in the sphere of training and development. The second was the identification of a gap in contemporary literature relating to training and development within hospitals. Whilst there is an increasing amount written about HRM in the national health service (see for example Leopold, Glover and Hughes 1996), there is little theoretical or empirical material concerning the complex processes of training and development in Trust hospitals. Managing development in the health service is a complex process (Burchill and Casey 1996: 124). A review of the literature revealed how each specific professional area was managing training, education and development, for example management development for clinicians (Dopson 1996; Ashburner 1996), and continuing professional development for doctors, nurses and PAMs, together with organization development (Stewart 1993) and management development (Thompson 1994). The responsibility for co-ordinating this rests with specialist human resourcing (HR) practitioners. There was, however, very little literature that examined this complex role. In their very informative text, Leopold, Glover and Hughes (1996) explored the relationship and tensions between management and professionalism in the health service, and examined the role of human resource managers. However, there was no mention of the role of human resource *development* specialists – whose role is to manage and co-ordinate the development of professionals and managers, amongst others – nor the training and development function. Burchill and Casey propose 'to examine issues associated with overall staff development within the context of a NHS trust' (1996: 120) in their chapter entitled 'Human Resource Development', but then proceed to describe what is generally labelled 'training and development', and make no reference to HRD. In addition, they state that, 'Training and development are, of course, a part of human resource planning' (ibid.: 124). Therefore, the identification of a 'gap' in the literature was the second reason for conducting this research.

There was also a third reason why I chose this sector – my personal experience of, and interest in, how training and development is managed in hospitals. From my experience, there did not seem to be much co-ordination between the different health professionals and the training specialists, nor between identifying and meeting individual and organizational development needs. As a former nurse, I had been interested in and exposed to training and development, both as a trainee and as a clinical nurse with training duties. To investigate practitioner perspectives in some depth, I chose to focus on one area of British work organizations. To generate and sustain my own interest in the project, I chose the health service, a sector with which I was already familiar. More specifically, I chose to study the hospital organization, where I had had previous experience of training and development, and had posed myself questions about how it was managed and co-ordinated, albeit only from the nursing perspective.

My story is now beginning to unfold – I have set the scene and explained (or perhaps rationalized) why this is an important story to tell.

Methodological issues

The 'how'

Having discussed the 'what' and 'why' of the project, I now briefly explain the emergent research design. To explore academic perspectives, I conducted a review of the (academic) literature to trace the creation/adoption and development of HRD as a discursive construction. It seems standard practice (Easterby-Smith, Thorpe and Lowe 1991: 46) to begin a research project with the literature review stage, gathering background information to frame the empirical stage. For this project, the literature review has not been 'merely' background material but one of the two resources from which to analyse models and concepts of HRD. This is discussed in more detail in Chapter 19. Adopting a processual approach (Watson 1994a; Lee 1997a) attention has centred on not trying to discover *what* HRD 'is', but studying *how* 'development' is managed, practised and theorized by occupational specialists, and to some extent by line managers.

As the project moved forward, and became an investigation of models and concepts of HRD specifically within the NHS, I had to choose how to undertake the empirical research element. Managing development within NHS Trust hospitals is, I suggest, a complex series of inter-related contractual, social, psychological, political and cultural processes between development specialists and 'others', whether other HR specialists, business/ line managers responsible for their own and the development of their employees, external providers and learners themselves. The second aim of the project was to develop an understanding of the concepts and models used by specialists to inform their practices and make sense of their occupational activity. To achieve this, I felt I had to get close to practitioners, and observe them in their natural settings. I chose to use an ethnographic case-study approach. Ethnography can be defined as a distinct research style where 'the researcher tries to immerse himself or herself in a setting and to become part of the group under study in order to understand the meanings and significances that people put upon their own behaviour and that of others' (Easterby-Smith, Thorpe and Lowe 1991: 38). The main reason for adopting this ethnographic case-study approach was the breadth and depth of analysis (from the broader organizational context to more focused attention to 'everyday' detail) that I felt was necessary to understand how, for example, the social, political and contractual processes occur. Yin (1994) argues that,

> the distinctive need for case studies arise out of the desire to understand complex social phenomena. In brief, the case study allows an investigation to retain the holistic and meaningful characteristics of real life events – such as individual life cycles, organisational and managerial processes, neighbourhood change, international relations and the maturation of industries.
>
> (1994: 3)

Within a case-study approach, I chose to investigate internal documents referring to organizational and HRD strategies and objectives – the 'intended'; and then interview and observe twenty practitioners and some of their clients, for example, line managers (notwithstanding that line managers can also have a training role) – the actual or 'real'. When examining the development functions, activities and specialists in each organization, I did not treat HRD as if it objectively existed (adopting an external realist position), and then attempt to present a black and white snapshot picture of 'it', the function. My aim was to gather material relevant to actual, and possibly, changing practices in real contexts, noting Storey's concern that too many case studies 'tend to exaggerate the degree of change. They bestow upon it a coherence and neatness which distorts reality. Moreover, they rarely give details of the real difficulties encountered' (1992: 17, in Harrison 1997: 15). This suggests an idealist position. Adopting a reflexive approach – for example revealing my reasons for including certain research materials and not others, and including material that seemingly did not fit with my emerging theorizing – I hoped to overcome this possible weakness. I also hoped to demonstrate how the relationships and practices associated with HRD are always in a state of emergence, are continually being *negotiated* and are therefore difficult to research. To do so requires exploring the deeper, more colourful processes, which are difficult to capture. This requires the researcher to be almost part of the activities, trying to experience the changing relationships and appreciate the social, political and contractual processes in order to begin to understand and *jointly* construct a version of the organizational and occupational reality. Watson (1994b) describes this approach as achieving a *mediated* reality, which can help overcome problems associated with taking either an external realist or idealist position. This notion of both the researcher and the participants constructing this reality is discussed in more detail later in this chapter. The researcher, and reader, need to get close to practitioners to understand how social, political and contractual processes and relationships may 'cause' HRD to exist *as if* it were an object outside the minds of the people who 'create' it.

For my doctoral research, and from a philosophical perspective, HRD was conceptualized as a discursive construction and discursive action (Sambrook 1997). I wanted to explore how HRD has been talked into being, how it is talked about, and how it is accomplished through talk. Thinking of HRD as a social and discursive construction helped me investigate how the concept has been talked into being, and created through words. Conceptualizing HRD as discursive action enabled me to explore how it is accomplished through words. Once I had established these initial research questions my research design needed to focus on methods which would enable me to gather evidence of how HRD was talked about. The research investigated how HRD has been talked into being, is talked about and is accomplished through talk. My focus was on words, phrases and discursive resources used to create, describe, analyse and achieve 'HRD'. Therefore, practically, the emphasis was on analysing internal documents describing HRD, gathering individual's own 'accounts' of HRD, and observing HRD practices. This required the use of discourse analysis – analysing how HRD was thought and talked about. However, writing 'up' social science research – or, more accurately, writing the research 'story' is problematic, given that the researcher has only subjective 'accounts', rather than 'facts' from which to craft the story, and the researcher herself has a hand to play in 'constructing' and shaping the final tale. This research story can then become part of the extant literature. However, rather than focus on the content, here I examine the process of writing the research story. A key feature is the role I played in crafting this. My story relates particularly to the postgraduate task of writing, but some issues could be relevant to all social scientific research activity.

The research

So, what is my story?

The essence of my thesis was the construction of a typology of three 'ideal types' or approaches to developing employees. These three ideal types – or discourses – were identified as I analysed the literature and empirical material. The three types refer to changes detected in the ways in which academics and practitioners talked about HRD. Of course, these ideal types do not 'represent' any true 'reality'. However, they serve as a theoretical tool to enable academics and practitioners to analyse, and perhaps consider changing, their own discursive practices. My typology was constructed out of their words (see, for example, Sambrook 2000).

What I presented in my thesis was more than the outcome of three years of work as a Researcher in the Department of Human Resource Management at Nottingham Business School (NBS). My background as a qualified nurse and as a mature Business Studies undergraduate shaped my thoughts (personal theories), feelings and values, and aspirations. This was my own account of how years of interest in the topic culminated in a three-year project to investigate changes in training and development from both academic and practitioner perspectives. This account takes the reader through the processes, and reports just as much about my personal learning experiences as it does issues related to learning, training and development as the subject of study. As Easterby-Smith and colleagues state, 'researchers are not keen on self-disclosure, and they rarely explain precisely where their ideas and questions have come from' (Easterby-Smith et al. 1991: 46). Yet, it is important to give an inside and first person view (Bryman 1988) of the research process. Conducting postgraduate research, I felt a need to account for my actions and explain how I acted 'within a view of the world and one's own existence in which both are situated and complex' (Lee 1998b: 3), what Lee (1996) describes as Holistic Agency. I also wished to reveal the quirkiness and 'messiness' of the process and illustrate how this differs from the textbook approach – supposedly linear, rational and goal-oriented (Bryman 1988). I tried not to give my account in the form of the reconstructed logic of the textbook process, but follow my logic-in-use (Kaplan 1964). The process was not as orderly as one might expect, and I did not wish to give the reader the illusion of a tidy process by writing in a way which applied reconstructed logic (Silverman 1985: 4).

Whether personal, postgraduate research, or commercial, externally funded research, it is important to understand the process as well as the product of research. However, particularly in postgraduate research, there is a personal attachment to the subject and product. Using my doctoral research as an example, the process I experienced and the outcomes I reported were inextricably intertwined. I felt very much a part of the project, unlike the detached scientist. I tried to overcome the criticism that 'scientific practitioners have traditionally ignored the role they play in shaping the outcomes of their research' (Gergen and Gergen 1991: 76). The project involved an element of social interaction, and like Barnes (1994), I questioned the methodological possibilities and ethical justifications of objective social science research. What I reported in my thesis could not be completely objective. As Gergen and Gergen argue, there is no means of achieving an 'observer-free' picture of nature (ibid.). Before I began, and during the project, my own subconscious and value-laden assumptions influenced my orientation to, and theorizing about, the topic. I was aware that 'value suppositions guide the framing of theory and fact' (ibid.: 77). Yet, I tried to be as detached as possible, especially when I was writing. My way of achieving this was by declaring, and at times it felt like even admitting, all I could about my involvement in the project. This was not an easy task. I made mistakes. I found some parts of the process very difficult, and yet I tried to reveal all of this so that the reader could make their own judgement as to the honesty of my reporting.

In considering how I might 'report' the research, I searched for a term that could describe and explain my approach. I considered action research, although this seemed to require more active involvement in organizational change processes (Easterby-Smith *et al.* 1991). I explored feminist research, where subjectivity and process issues have been acknowledged (see, for example, Oakley (1981) on the role of interviews, and Holloway (1989), who states she uses her 'own method' and reveals her involvement). A review of the literature describing the 'reflective practitioner' (Schon 1983; Eraut 1995) led me to the notion of myself as a 'reflective researcher' – showing myself to myself. A further stage is showing myself to the reader. The term 'reflexive' describes the interchange between research and human behaviour (Giddens 1989: 687), and in this case, between this research project and my feelings and actions. So in the thesis, I took a reflexive approach (Steier 1991), writing reflexively to reveal to the reader something of myself, the nature of my involvement in the research settings and the value positions lying behind my thoughts and words. I tried to adopt a self-questioning approach to my beliefs, assumptions and practices (Lee 1998b: 3).

Who am I writing with, and for?

It is useful to think of knowledge as a social and cultural construction. Knowledge is constructed by people with their own interests, goals, and interpretations, for example. In my thesis, I did not construct knowledge purely by myself. Instead, I argue that the thesis was *co-produced* – in the sense of my creating the account *with* the participants' co-operation and contribution – rather than by me standing apart and attempting to *discover* the 'world' of that research. My assumptions and activities therefore had to become part of the investigation (Steier 1991). For me, that meant writing in the first person, which did not mean putting me at the centre of the research, but acknowledging the role I, amongst others, played. I agree with Lee who recognizes the 'power of the personal' and argues that 'there is something developmental about coming close to another person's situated complex view of the world that is hard to discount, and that cannot easily be replicated by more impersonal articles of theory or practice' (Lee 1998b: 4).

As well as recognizing the contribution of others, that is, by using their words, it is also useful to consider for whom you are writing. I wanted to construct something readable, like the work of Watson (1994a). What I attempted to do was write in a way that was accessible to those with whom I had co-produced this knowledge, as well as in a way that was reassuring for those who may be embarking on research projects and may be bewildered – as I was – by the idealized process presented in the standard textbook. My justification for this personal and inside perspective is that I believe it will provide a more human and arguably more realistic account (Bryman 1988) than that offered in most theoretical, academic texts. My justification is neatly captured in the claim of Nichols and Beynon that

> so much of what passes for 'theory' . . . fails to connect with the lives that people lead, whereas most descriptive social surveys too often fail to grasp the structure of social relations and the sense which people make of them. It is almost as if another way of writing has to be developed; something which 'tells it like it is' even though in any simple sense this is not possible; something which is theoretically informed yet free from theoretical pretentiousness, and which destroys the gap between the abstract and the concrete.
>
> (1977: viii)

I wanted to move away from

> conventional social research that dulls the imagination; locks the observed inside rigid category systems having little or nothing to do with the culture of the researched, but everything to do with our research culture; promotes an insidious institutionalisation

of social boundaries that separate 'us' (the observers) from 'them' (the observed), and perhaps most telling has become rather tedious, if not boring, thus losing its power to convince.

(Maanen, Manning and Miller in Rose 1990: 5)

I could not report like that because I did not experience the research like that. I practised what can be called the ethnography of 'intimacy rather than distance . . . and of contingent understanding rather than detachable conclusions' (Rose 1990: 6). Rather than standing on the outside looking in, this reversal from conventional methodological practices took me over to the 'other side,' to take part, return and then textualize the others' points of view (ibid. 10) and synthesize with my own. This was a reciprocal process and not a self-centred product. I tried to enhance, rather than de-privilege, the voices of those with whom I interacted (Steier 1991). The reference to the 'power to convince' reminds us of Koch's comment that story-telling is a powerful means of communication, a means of convincing others to believe your portrayal of the research scene, the characters and the plot.

There is, though, the danger with this approach that what is created could be accused of being highly anecdotal (Dingwall 1980) and lacking theoretical generalization. For example, how far would you go to reconstruct the world of the research faithfully, warts and all, or would you reconstruct and co-produce – in the sense that what you produce is partly achieved through the participants' subjective contributions – only selective bits? My thesis presents only a partial view of HRD in the UK. It is a partial account recited by one person (Lee 1998a: 528). If this is a theoretical description, it is *my* description. How scientific is this, given that it is the product of my own involvement (Hammersley 1992)? Yet, it is also the product of those who talked to me. The text is polyphonic (Rose op. cit.: 56–7) – drawing on my own voice and emotional reactions; the critical and theoretical voices of academics through their existing literature; and the conversations, gestures and reactions from the daily lives of people whose experiences I am trying to understand. I do not go as far as Rose and live the ethnographic life as part of them, but I do 'cross over' and try to create, from this experience, knowledge which is realistic, accessible and relevant to academics and practitioners alike.

Why write the research story?

There could be several reasons for conducting, and writing about, your research. There may be an academic requirement – where you are required to submit a written assignment in the form of a report or dissertation. As a researcher, you may wish to develop your academic career – where you are expected to write/publish your research as a requirement of the research assessment exercise (RAE). There may be an organizational requirement – where your manager requests a written analysis of a current problem and recommendations for action, which you are asked to submit as a management report. Or, you may have altruistic reasons – believing that you have something important to share, in whichever community (academic or practitioner).

Having identified these different reasons, it is apparent that there are different audiences for the product of your research activity. Who you are writing for may influence how you write – that is, the style and structure of your final research output.

Style and structure

It would be reasonable to suggest that there is no 'one best way' to write about your research. It depends on whom you are writing for and why. However, any piece of work should have a clear structure, and as the word implies, a story should have a beginning, a middle and an end. It also helps to set an imaginable scene (by describing the context in detail), build an intriguing plot and have some interesting characters. But, this sounds like science fiction, not science fact. Watson (1999) would agree, and even suggests the notion of *science faction*. For example, as researchers, if we agree to assure confidentiality, then we must obscure the identity of our characters. To do this, we give the characters 'false' names and mix up the 'data' to protect the participants, to ensure nothing can be attributed to them. So, in fact, we do not completely accurately report the 'facts'. But, to the extent that everything we report is true and has happened, the story is not complete fiction.

If the audience requires a traditional report, then useful guidelines are given in other texts (see, for example, Saunders, Lewis and Thornhill 1997; Easterby-Smith, Thorpe and Lowe 1991). However, this chapter focuses on writing the research story. If you decide to write a research story, there are still some key requirements. For example, writing for academic assignments, the story should include an abstract, rigorous analysis, a well-constructed argument, and meaningful conclusions. This should be articulated in a discursive style with a logical structure and clear, coherent sentences. Also, it is important to check institutional guidelines, for example, word count, and technical requirements. When considering your style, there are tensions between objectivity and subjectivity. To what extent do you describe your personal involvement, bearing in mind that the product should not be too self-centred as this is generally considered to be non-academic and hardly generalizable. I thought the writing should be complex and clever, so initially I used long, complex sentences. However, as I soon learned, as a researcher you should aim to get your message across in a clear and simple style. If you are writing for academic journals, it is important to recognize their particular (and differing) house styles. For instance, the *International Journal of Training and Development* (*IJTD*) seems to prefer more empirical and quantitative research, reported in a 'scientific'

Table 11.1 Summary of general differences in the structure and style of writing

	Management report	Research story
Overview	Executive summary	Abstract, prologue
Structure	Sections, sub-sections, numbered	Chapters, headings
Writing style	Concise, brevity, objectivity	Discursive, subjectivity
Evidence	Facts, data	Accounts, material

manner. Conversely, *Human Resource Development International* (*HRDI*) acknowledges the possibility and utility of diverse approaches to, and ways of writing about, HRD research. In addition, specifically practitioner journals seem to prefer articles that focus more on practical solutions and lessons to learn, generalizability, and a good story. The organizational audience may be different again. A management report should include an executive summary, be succinct, perhaps using bullet points for brevity, and clearly structured. These general differences can be summarized in Table 11.1.

A key factor in developing your writing style is the content of your research – what are you researching, and writing about?

What am I writing about?

In my doctoral research, historically, my topic of study was 'training and development'. However, I focused on the recent developments, and particularly on the emergence of HRD. I wanted to explore how HRD had emerged in the British NHS context, how HRD had been talked into being and how HRD was accomplished through talk. To achieve this, I needed to access this 'talk' and gather 'evidence'. This raises the question of what type of evidence? Academic accounts were accessed and gathered from the literature review. This is relatively straightforward, based on analysing texts and articles to trace how the concept has emerged, and what discursive resources are employed. From this analysis, I identified changes in the way HRD was talked and written about. Practitioner accounts were gathered from internal documents, interviews and observations. In considering how to write the research story, there is also the issue of how to write 'up' observation notes, and in particular, interviews.

The interview process provides two areas of study: the process of making sense and the sense that is made (content). What (content) was I going to use in my story, given the process of making sense by participants can be messy? The interview method is not without problems. First, there are issues associated with this interpretative research style, for example the degree of structure, interviewing skills, obtaining trust, as identified in Easterby-Smith, Thorpe and Lowe (1991). There are also the issues of 'truth', how perceptions are constructed and articulated, confidentiality, ethics and negotiation, for example. Mishler (1986) explains that the interview is a joint product of what the interviewer and the interviewee talk about, and how they achieve this. The interview is a speech event; it takes the form of a jointly constructed discourse, creating mutually shared understanding and meaning; the meanings of questions and answers are contextually grounded (Mishler 1986). Others note how it can take speakers several 'turns' or attempts to convey their meaning, and words have no meaning in isolation (ED 1994). This mutual sense-making and subjective interpretation leads some to question the objectivity of the interview process. In this research, interviews were conducted to explore practitioners' experiences, in an attempt to reveal the rich and complex interpretations of professionals trying to make sense of their 'enacted' (Weick 1979) environment, and to achieve a better understanding of how they construct their own versions of the reality (Berger and Luckmann 1967) of the development function. What I tried to do through the interview process is what one practitioner tried to do with a client, and she reported similar difficulties. 'I don't have a view of their reality. I try to understand it, but I'm not part of it.' This raises issues of how to write about this reality.

Also, in an Employment Department funded project examining the use of the word 'training' (ED 1994), researchers note the many variables that can influence an interview. These can be categorized as dialectal (class, gender, age) and diatypic (mode, whether written or spoken, and tenor, the relationship between speakers, for example, the potential power imbalance). In addition to class, gender and age, how the researcher presents herself can influence both the process of sense making and the sense that is made. My dress, for example, had an influence on the interview. One of the participants explained that her impression of me influenced which language she spoke: 'I could have used big words if you'd had big shoulder pads, thick make-up and hair up. I'd have used long words. But I felt as if I was using my natural language.'

The interview is something with which we are all familiar, but can easily create difficulties – philosophical and political. Oakley (1981: 36–7) is critical of interviewing when it is interpreted as a method from the dominant (positivist) social science paradigm. Alternatively, she argues for a model of questioning which is based on grasping the subjectivity of the interview experience. Oakley argues that personal involvement 'is more than dangerous bias – it is the condition under which people come to know each other and to admit others into their lives' (op. cit.: 58). I argue that my personal involvement was necessary to get to know practitioners, for them to feel I could understand their meaning(s) and appreciate their situations. Although I presented the research design as 'scientific' to demonstrate this was a rigorous piece of research, I tried hard not to present the interview as a scientific piece of enquiry, seeking objective facts. Instead, I attempted to follow the model of a semi-structured conversation, where I got to know something about the person. Most of the time this worked well, as the following quotations might suggest.

Has it been an interview – it was more like a friendly chat, we must do this again.

How did you manage to make this feel so relaxed, not like an interview?

How did you manage to follow what I said, and still pick up the threads?

Sometimes, the semi-structured model failed. Some participants seemed unclear as to what I was actually asking them to talk about. There were a few comments, such as,

Oh Gosh that is a *very* broad question, I don't know where you're coming from, what do you mean?

Does that answer your question?

Sorry, I've gone off the point . . . sorry, I'm not being very clear there . . . is this OK?

This leads to another problematic aspect of the interviews. Semi-structured interviews are an appropriate method for exploring complex issues, allowing un-thought-of themes to emerge, but are difficult to manage, direct, and then analyse. As a Senior Nurse asked me, 'Do you always do this as a conversation, like today? How do you analyse all these open questions? Give me a tick box questionnaire any day.' Other interviewees' comments included:

I didn't realize I was being interviewed. I thought we were chatting. We must do this again.

I bared my soul, now burn the tape.

This sounds silly. I hope you won't write all this down.

However, other extracts reveal some participants' difficulties with the semi-structured interview process.

I'm going off all over the place here.

I am getting back to the point of what training and development is . . . this is a very complex way of telling you what training and development is about. I'm sorry, I'm rambling because it's extremely complicated, and difficult to say what it is because it is a bit of this, you know. I know I'm digressing, but I'll get back to the question in a minute.

I was a bit worried I'd get something wrong, or it would be rubbish.

Is this OK?

However, the key question is – how are you going to use this material? As we can see from the extracts cited above, the account is often confused as interviewees try to make sense, thinking out loud. Therefore, when writing your story, do you 'tidy up' these accounts to make textual sense? Which 'bits' do you use?

An interview is a pattern of interaction where the outcome of research is influenced by the interpretation of individuals involved (their own experiences, background) and the research topic itself (Mishler 1986). My own involvement will have influenced the interview and research outcomes, and I tried to acknowledge this. Rather than treat these various influences as problems that distort the interviewees' responses, they can be investigated to provide a richer understanding of individuals' experiences. Rather than think of interviews as a 'scientific' way of 'discovering facts', my interview technique sought to engage participants in natural (but prompted) conversation. Thought of as such, interviews yield 'accounts'. Accounts are not fixed, but are statements revealing how people account for their thoughts and actions at a particular time. Accounts give an account of behaviour, behaviour that people can be held accountable for (Feldman 1995). They can be requested, as during my interviews, or spontaneous, when people fear their behaviour may not be interpreted as they would like. During my observations, people offered accounts to place their behaviour in the context they thought would be appropriate for such behaviour.

I do not treat people's accounts as providing definitive facts about their experiences. As one participant said, 'I can only give you perceptions, not facts.' Perceptions of strategies and practices will vary, not only between different practitioners, but also between the same individuals at different times. People have built their own picture of what the development function is, as an object, and what it is like to work there, but this picture can change, depending on mood, work pressures, their perceptions of me, what they believe I want to hear. In this sense, perspectives will be subjective. As Potter and Wetherell (1987) point out 'discourse analysts have noted how the same person can produce quite different stereotypical categorisations depending on the demands of the situation'. This refers back to the notion that people construct (think about, put ideas together) their accounts of reality, and when asked to do so during an interview, these accounts will be influenced by my presence, and the prevailing conditions (mood, workload, family events, etc). I could have re-interviewed these people on a different occasion and found they could have constructed different accounts. Therefore, the accounts I draw upon now cannot be judged as either right or wrong. The accounts provide a snap-shot picture of how participants interpreted the reality of there and then. Future events will shape future constructions.

This raises questions about the reliability, validity and generalizability of such research. Yet, these are criteria applied in quantitative research. What might be more appropriate (parallel) criteria for qualitative research are dependability, credibility and transferability (Lincoln and Guba 1985). Credibility is assured if the researcher provides faithful descriptions or reproductions of, say, her observations and interviews, and offers all possible interpretations and potential misfits. On the issue of reliability/dependability, I have said that if I repeated the interviews people could (and almost definitely would) give different accounts. Their 'realities' would have changed, due to environmental factors, organizational developments, personal circumstances and changes in me. The frame of reference, or of reality construction, is dynamic, and can never be 'recovered' from the past or repeated. However, I have provided accurate reproductions of observations and accounts. The reliability of my own interpretation could be questioned, and I do not deny that other researchers could have influenced the process in different ways, and reached different interpretations. But that somewhat misses the point of ethnographic case-study research, which seeks to generate an understanding of complex phenomena in a specific setting. There can be no universal or replicable answers. Credibility refers to the ability of other researchers being able to audit your research. This can be achieved by adopting a reflexive approach, explaining your reasons for including particular material, the choices you made and providing a clear audit trail. On this second point, to what extent can the interpretation be valid, again I would question whether asking if this is the right interpretation is the wrong question. 'Is this an honest interpretation' may be a better question. From the evidence I present, and through my reflexive approach, I let the reader judge whether my interpretation is credible. On the final issue, conclusions from your research might be transferable depending on the extent to which you give enough detail of the context. This will enable other readers to judge whether your theorizing can explain similar phenomena in other situations, and offer a better understanding of that context. In terms of generalizability, I have said that the research has been exploratory, and thus, difficult to reach broad-sweeping generalizations. However, this research can contribute towards a better understanding of HRD, not only in the two Trust hospitals, but also within the wider context of the NHS, and in the context of the changing nature of HRD generally. Thus, I would argue that my findings and theorizing are transferable.

Still on the issue of reliability and validity, Mehan (1979: 15) focuses on three weaknesses of field-studies – their anecdotal quality, resting on a few exemplary instances culled from field notes; the lack of selection criteria; and the inability to view the original data to enable alternative interpretations (Silverman 1985: 12). I tried to give reasons for the inclusion of certain quotations, and attempted to explain the circumstances, or the context, of the quotations. This helps the readers judge for themselves my own interpretation of the material. I also tried, where possible and relevant, to include examples of 'deviant cases' (ibid.: 21), where participants' comments have contradicted my theorizing. I tried, throughout the project, and particularly during the writing, to give a 'true' picture of the HRD practitioners and practices in the two Trust hospitals. I tried to construct an accurate account, to craft a plausible story. I would argue that, from an ethnographic stance, the findings are reliable and valid – or true – to the extent that a person reading this story would be better placed to conduct themselves successfully in the setting where the research was carried out – that is the HRD function of an NHS Trust hospital (Watson 1996).

So far, I have considered some of the problems and issues associated with gathering material from which to craft the research story. Next, I consider the problem of actually writing the story.

How do I construct and write the research story?

The purpose of writing the research story is not simply to describe or report empirical activities. The story is more than just 'what's going on'. The aim is to identify and solve a puzzle, or to construct an answer to a theoretical question, or try to create a theoretical and generalizable explanation for certain organizational phenomena. Psychology and sociology, for example, are theoretical pursuits. They are also possible legs of the HRD theoretical stool (McLean 1999; Swanson 1999). The purpose of theorizing is to develop further understanding of the world as human beings (individually and collectively) experience it. I am neither psychologist, nor sociologist, but have an interest in the way the world works, how I and others 'fit in', the role of work, and the role of training and development. Academics develop theories, but as Watson (1977) clearly states, academics must respect and retain a closeness to the problems experienced by those living and working outside the insulated world of academic institutions. In my PhD, I needed to say that I had experience of both the academic and practitioner perspectives. As a clinical nurse, I had been involved in training activities, both (practically) in our outpatients' department and (theoretically) in the School of Nursing. As a Research Officer, I was (practically) involved in teaching activities and had been on the 'receiving' end of postgraduate courses. So in answer to Watson's (1977) concerns, I do feel that in writing my research stories and in constructing my theories, I have not only respected, but also remained close to those I studied.

Developing relationships then becoming detached

Undertaking ethnographic research requires you to become part of the setting you are studying, to develop relationships. The researcher can become an 'honorary member' (Feldman 1995: 62), even a friend. I became quite attached to some of my collaborators. Yet this closeness can hamper the final stages of the research process, when the researcher has to interpret events and accounts, adopt a critical approach and comment about the organization and individual members. Having become an insider, the researcher must now be able to be critical, yet it is emotionally difficult when people have been so generous with their time and effort. There is a great fear of offending these co-producers. Having seen the situation from their perspective, as the researcher, I must now create my own interpretation, which includes their understanding, but also encompasses wider implications and broader generalizations. The key step to detachment, for me, was to change the names of the hospitals and participants. I had promised to do this for reasons of confidentiality, but I wonder what would I have done if participants had wished to be revealed? It is easier to be critical of an impersonal 'training manager', rather than 'Sally Sambrook' in person.

Some analysis

In terms of analysing the material, this was not a separate and distinct stage following collection, but ongoing, on a preliminary basis, throughout the fieldwork phase. The material I had at my disposal was more than twenty transcripts of interviews (each between six to ten pages in length), umpteen pages of hand-written notes recorded during the numerous meetings I attended, additional notes recorded on whatever was available and internal documents. As Feldman (1995: 1) reveals,

> the task can be overwhelming. One sometimes feels that review ing the data only reinforces the complexity and ambiguity of the setting. While it is well to remember this complexity and ambiguity, the task at hand is to create an interpretation of the setting or some feature of it to allow people who have not directly observed the phenomena to have a deeper understanding of them.

The ongoing analysis was probably implicit, and iterative, influencing how I asked questions, refined some and followed areas of emerging significance. There can be a tendency to postpone the detailed analysis, as I did, particularly if there is a large amount of material to analyse and in a untidy format, for example scribbles hurriedly written on scraps of paper in between meetings, and even on bus tickets when ideas have come to mind, sat in the pub, with no notebook to hand! Having completed the fieldwork, there was a period of 'intense' analysis, realizing the rather enjoyable stage was over, and I now had to make sense of it all.

Each of the interviews was recorded and transcribed to provide a text of the accounts. This was time consuming, but as Bryman (1988) points out, you have to transcribe yourself as others may not understand the jargon and content. In addition, I felt the process helped me to 'get to know' the material. My attention was also drawn to 'good quotes', but this could lead to dangerous limited selection. In response, does the researcher present all the transcripts for the reader to examine and interpret? This seems impractical and pointless. There is no unique solution in this research project. No matter how objective and scientific I may try to be, your interpretation could be equally 'right' (or 'wrong').

During my observations, I made notes, describing what *I* observed, that is whatever caught my attention. Obviously, this was not everything that could have been observed, and others could 'see' these in different ways. My notes captured what I thought was important. As a method, observing is physically demanding – listening to maintain involvement and provide appropriate responses, for example, body language, nodding, as well as trying to make notes as discretely as possible. Afterwards, I often had to make additional notes, and then make connections between the observations. Those being observed sometimes looked unsettled as I scribbled as they spoke. I often reiterated that nothing said could be attributed to them. One even commented, 'we're going to rugby tackle Sally when she leaves to find out exactly what she has written about us'.

From an analysis of practitioners' accounts and these observation notes, I tried to create my own interpretation, and theoretical explanation, of HRD within the case studies. This was based on existing academic models and concepts of HRD and how they may be applied in the hospital setting. However,

> the tricky part of this interpretation creation, of course, is to create an interpretation that is neither simply the application of some pre-existing theory to your data nor only a description of how the members of a culture understand particular phenomena ... The goal is to develop one's own interpretation of how parts ... fit together or influence or relate to one another that is intrinsic to the setting one has studied, and at the same time, sheds light on how similar processes may be occurring in other settings.
>
> (Feldman 1995: 2)

The difficulty is to avoid presenting exclusively the interpretations made by the people I studied, and those made by other theorists about phenomena similar to the ones under study. The process of interpretation should lead to new understandings, and new knowledge. Referring to my model of the literature review, in Chapter 18, the aim of research is to penetrate, extend and/or develop theoretical explanations – in my case, existing models and concepts of HRD within the NHS context – if not create new ones. As with the notion of paradigmatic diversity, there are many analytical methods available to the qualitative researcher. What I was investigating was HRD as a discursive construction and as discursive action. What I was analysing, therefore, were the varying discourses academics and practitioners used in their theories and accounts of training and development practices. This can be referred to as discourse analysis. Discourse analysis recognizes that the language people use does not merely describe how they view the world, but can demonstrate how they actually construct this world. We use language to construct HRD. HRD could be judged as 'good' or 'bad', depending on whether it improved a practitioner's position of influence, or secured more revenue for an academic department, or 'caused' a line manager 'extra' work, for example. Language creates, sustains and changes what we mean by HRD, organizations, whatever. As Gergen (1992) suggests, language is part of the process whereby people through individual and social action make sense of the world, therefore language does not merely describe action but is action in itself.

In attempting to find out about HRD, that is the sense people make of the development function, and their activities within it, I have had to understand the processes involved in how this sense is made. Discourse analysis not only examines the content of accounts, but also the purpose and consequence of that content (Potter and Wetherell 1987: 168). Individual's accounts serve many functions; how they choose to frame their explanations and how they actually construct these explanations. In terms of the process, we make sense of things by giving them some sort of order. We have an innate human need to sort and organize our thoughts (Watson 1994a). However, we do not always think before speaking, but during and after. Weick suggests the process of sense making follows the recipe (although incomplete) of 'how can I know what I think until I see what I say' (1995: 135). We can say something 'daft' and then think about what has come out and start to develop these thoughts. Interviews are often characterized by their contradictions (Potter and Wetherell 1987). When it comes to reporting these conversations, as I have already noted, there is the issue of how to translate verbal communication into written prose, whether the researcher includes the 'daft' utterances or 'tidies up' the language to make (textual) sense.

In summary, the subjectivity and messiness of social science research potentially causes concern of how to achieve academic rigour when writing the research story. This is where I have found the notion of reflexivity – adopting a critical approach – particularly useful. By this I mean being careful not to discard elements which did not appear to fit the initial patterns developing in the researcher's mind, and trying to challenge the emerging conclusions as 'outsiders' might. I tried to ensure the process was as rigorous and systematic as possible, given the nature of my research questions and my role, far removed from the remote, detached scientist, but close to, part of and very much involved in that research. The fact that I am reporting on my experiences during a doctoral programme, where the research was of great personal interest, may be a significant reason for this 'non-detached' involvement. However, many issues still concern me as I engage in commercial, externally funded research, where I am more personally distanced from (or not so emotionally attached to) the research questions and the participants.

Having explored some of the key issues regarding what material you use to construct your story, and how to overcome some of the problems of validity, reliability and generalizability (or credibility, dependability and transferability), the final question is 'when' to write.

When should you write the research story?

During the research project, there are several different stages, where the processes and purposes of thinking and writing vary slightly. For example, the initial stage involves writing the research proposal. At this stage, your thinking and writing could be creative and flexible. It is useful to get something down on paper and accept you will probably have to revisit it several times. The final outcome could vary from your original idea, but this is just a feature of the emergent nature of the research process. If you read my doctoral research proposal, you might smile when you compare it to my final thesis. At the next stage, when you begin the literature review, it is useful to write up your notes in a draft chapter. This helps to set the scene in your mind. Borrowing Eco's words, this process provided me with a ladder (cited in Fisher 1996). Early on, I included much detail and description in my chapters. Later, I gained the confidence to more critically analyse the literature and synthesize it with my own thinking. But, that early work enabled me to climb up the ladder from general description to specific critical analysis. This early writing gave me something to build on; to go back and prune or refine as my understanding developed. Being required to write a progress report gave me the opportunity to try to pull together the results of my critical literature review and initial interpretations of the empirical material. At this stage, I was able to see the whole product, to question my original aims, and to prepare for the crafting of the final story. It might be tempting to leave any writing until you feel you have something well thought out to put down on paper (a final draft). However, my overall recommendation is to start as soon as possible. As Weick (1995) asks, how can I know what I think until I see what I say – or write? Getting your thoughts onto paper forces you to think, make links and critically evaluate. Writing exposes your theorizing. Some can write a first, almost final, draft. However, I needed many attempts. I needed to see what I thought, before I could think some more.

Throughout the fieldwork I referred back to my conceptual framework, revising the links between the concepts, and between academic and practitioner accounts. It is worth noting how the project evolved since my earliest thoughts and aspirations in April 1995. Then, the research design was somewhat more 'ambitious', attempting to investigate and map out 'models' of HRD, using case studies from various economic and industry sectors. It was not until almost two years later that I felt the design was robust and I had a clearer view of the objectives and potential outcomes. It was a worrying process getting that far, as I seemed not to follow a 'rational' and logical approach, but be swayed as 'new' information and informants came my way. In a sense, I muddled through (Lindblom 1959). It was only through reviewing the literature and actually undertaking the fieldwork that I was able to make sense of what I wanted to achieve and refine the shape of the project and the thread of the story.

Until I began the formal process of writing the thesis, interpretations of the literature review and empirical material seemed unconnected and overwhelming in quantity and complexity. For brief periods I felt unable to make sense of the research, and felt like giving up. I would then consider the time and effort people had contributed to help me achieve my personal goal, and one not necessarily of much benefit to themselves or anyone else. It was more this sense of loyalty to the participants that kept me going, rather than the sense that I had something important to contribute. The discipline of writing focused my attention on bringing together practitioners' accounts in a conceptual/theoretical framework, challenging the links, looking for exceptions or alternative conclusions and justifying my arguments. Writing a thesis was a bit like studying for exams. For so much of the student's time is spent trying to cram in lots of knowledge and theories and examples. There then comes a point when the student has to start trying to piece together all of this and pull out of it some personal understanding.

Once that time comes, it is important to identify *where* you write best. As with studying for exams, the researcher needs the time and space to start emptying the mind. Some of my clearest thoughts emerged when I was away from my desk, seemingly thinking of nothing. However, where I did some of my best thinking was not always where I could write, for instance walking in the countryside. From experience, and advice from other researchers, it is useful to carry a small notebook with you to capture these crucial thoughts. There are various places where you might write. This could be at home, at work, in the library, on the train. A factor, which might influence your choice, is the medium in which you compose your story. For example, do you write straight into a word-processor, or do you make hand-written notes first? Again, from my own experience and from other researchers I have talked to, it is useful to set aside blocks of time – and physical space. It is not easy to pick up and put down your manuscript in short bursts, as you lose the thread of your story, which means you might have to trace back to your earlier thought patterns before continuing to write. This makes the process unnecessarily time-consuming, which does little to help you finish crafting your story. So, how should I finish this story?

Critical analysis

Before finishing this story, it is worth considering first the issues this chapter raises for the conceptual development of HRD, and for developing methods of researching HRD. It has been suggested that there is a direct connection between thinking and writing about HRD. Your philosophical perspective shapes your flow of words. For example, if, as a researcher, you think of HRD as a social construction, and engage in research exploring meanings associated with this conceptualization of HRD, then it is probable that you will wish to present your findings in a manner that reveals your hand in constructing the research story. From my experience in submitting papers to a range of journals, this approach to writing the research story is far from being commonly acceptable. I have received reviewers' comments asking for removal of all references to 'I' and, instead, reporting the analysis of 'data' in the third person. This requirement to rationalize and depersonalize the research and writing process I find difficult to achieve. So, do I avoid submitting my 'stories' to such 'scientific' journals, or do I play the game and (re)construct an objective and neutral report? Is there not a danger in developing two opposing approaches to researching and understanding HRD? Philosophically, there is talk of both paradigmatic incommensurability and multi-paradigmatic perspectives, and methodologically of 'mixed methods' and pragmatic pluralism. When it comes to presenting research findings, should we perpetuate paper incommensurability or strive for penned pluralism?

Conclusions and key learning points

To conclude, I have suggested that the research story is like any other story – it sets the scene, has characters, and gradually reveals a plot. This may sound rather artistic, rather than scientific. However, in this chapter, it has been suggested that the investigation of HRD takes the form of social, rather than natural, science. Choices have to be made about the approach to the research, the researcher's conception of science and her position on knowledge generation. In the natural sciences, there is a tradition of 'writing up' experiments, where the author is the detached, objective scientist, in the hygienic, controlled, laboratory setting, merely recording observations and making logical deductions and theoretical generalizations. In the social sciences, the researcher cannot be detached from the human setting in which she conducted her investigation – she has contaminated the scene by her own presence, and, as author, can manipulate the story, intentionally or otherwise. Writers need to be aware of, and highlight, the limitations of their research, and consider the epistemological, political and ethical problems in reporting their findings. Social science research aims to be scientific in that material is gathered in a systematic manner, analysed with rigour and reported as honestly as possible. The author needs to explain her role in writing the story to enable others to make their own judgements as to the honesty (or objectivity) of the tale.

In attempting to construct the tale, I suggest there are five questions that, when answered, can help to clarify the process and product of writing the research story. Answers to these questions provide the key learning points of this chapter.

First, the researcher needs to consider whom she is writing for. This influences what will be written and how. For example, there will be differences between the requirements of academic (MPhil, PhD) versus professional (MBA, MSc HRD) qualifications, seen as the difference between a discursive thesis versus a concise management report. By identifying your audience, you might decide that a story is not appropriate, in which case you will need to consider a more 'orthodox' report.

Writing a research story is a different way of reporting research associated with an alternative conception of science, of knowledge and of knowledge creation. This alternative approach has emerged to address problems encountered when applying 'scientific' methods to social science research. This way of writing is not presented as the 'best' approach, but a different one. Whether you choose to adopt this approach, and whether you are comfortable with this 'un-scientific' style, will depend upon your approach to research and your research questions.

Other issues include what material you use to construct your story, when you start and stop, and where you write best.

There is no one best way – it all depends, upon the different purposes, time-scales, and audiences of the research. It is important to identify your own most effective way. However, it is also important to remember the issues of credibility, dependability and transferability of your story.

Discussion questions

1 Consider your current/planned research activity and identify the target audience(s) for your written outputs.
2 Which would be the most appropriate 'form' of writing in those cases, and why?
3 What problems might you encounter when writing the research story?
4 How might you overcome these?

References

Ashburner, L. (1996) 'The role of clinicians in the management of the NHS', in J. Leopold, I. Glover and M. Hughes (eds) *Beyond Reason: the National Health Service and the Limits of Management*, Stirling Management Series, Aldershot: Avebury, 3–14.

Barnes, M. (1994) 'Objective science or social interaction? Researching users' views of services', *Research Policy and Planning*, 12(2): 1–29.

Berger, P.L. and Luckmann, T. (1967) *The Social Construction of Reality*, Harmondsworth: Penguin.

Bryman, A. (ed.) (1988) *Doing Research in Organisations*, London: Routledge.

Buckley, R. and Caple, J. (1995) *The Theory and Practice of Training* (third edn), London: Kogan Page.

Burchill, F. and Casey, A. (1996) *Human Resource Management: the NHS, a Case Study*, Macmillan Press.

Dingwall, R. (1980) 'Ethics and ethnography', *Sociological Review*, 28: 871–91.

Department of Health (1991) *NHS and Community Care Act*, London: HMSO.

Dopson, S. (1996) 'Doctors in management: a challenge to established debates', in Leopold *et al.* (eds) *Beyond Reason: The National Health Service and the Limits of Management*, Stirling Management Series, Aldershot: Avebury, 173–88.

Easterby-Smith, M., Thorpe, R. and Lowe, A. (1991) *Management Research: an Introduction*, London: Sage.

ED (1994) *Training: an exploration of the word and the concept with an analysis of the implications for survey design*, Research Series No. 30, Sheffield Employment Department.

Eraut, M. (1995) 'Schon Shock: a case for reframing reflection-in-action', *Teachers and Teaching: Theory and Practice*, 1(1): 9–22.

Feldman, M.S. (1995) *Strategies for Interpreting Qualitative Data*, Qualitative Research Methods Series No. 33, California: Sage.

Fisher, C. (1996) 'Managerial stances: perspectives on manager development', in J. Stewart and J. McGoldrick (eds) *Human Resource Development: Perspectives, Strategies and Practice*, London: Pitman, 28–46.

Gergen, K. (1992) 'Organization theory in the post-modern era', in M. Reed and M. Hughes (eds) *Rethinking Organisation*, London: Sage, 207–26.

Gergen, K. and Gergen, M. (1991) 'Towards reflexive methodologies', in F. Steier (ed.) *Research and Reflexivity*, London: Sage, 76–95.

Giddens, A. (1989) *Sociology*, Cambridge: Polity Press.

Hammersley, M. (1992) *What's Wrong with Ethnography?* London: Routledge.

Harrison, R. (1997) *Employee Development*, London: Institute of Personnel Management.

Heron, R. (1997) *Managing Human Resources in the NHS – a Service Wide Approach*, keynote speech delivered at the Annual HRM Conference, Nottingham Business School, the Nottingham Trent University, December.

Holloway, W. (1989) *Subjectivity and Methodology in Psychology*, London: Sage.

Kaplan, A. (1964) 'Power in perspective', in R.L. Kahn and E. Boulding (eds) *Power and Conflict in Organisations*, London: Tavistock, 11–32.

Koch, T. (1998) 'Story telling: is it really research?' *Journal of Advanced Nursing*, 28(6): 1182–90.

Lee, M.M. (1996) 'Holistic learning in new Central Europe', in M.M. Lee, H. Letiche, R. Crawshaw and M. Thomas (eds) *Management Education in the New Europe*, London: Internal Thompson, 249–66.

—— (1997a) 'Strategic Human Resource Development: a Conceptual Exploration', *Proceedings of the AHRD Conference*, 92–9.

—— (1997b) 'The developmental approach: a critical reconsideration', in J. Burgoyne and M. Reynolds (eds) *Management Learning: Integrating Perspectives in Theory and Practice*, London: Sage, 199–214.

—— (1998a) 'Human Resource Development in the United Kingdom: a Partial Exposition', *Proceedings of the AHRD Conference*, 528–35.

—— (1998b) 'HRDI: a journal to define', *Human Resource Development International*, 1(1): 1–6.

Leopold, J., Glover, I. and Hughes, M. (eds) (1996) *Beyond Reason: the National Health Service and the Limits of Management*, Stirling Management Series, Aldershot: Avebury.

Lincoln, Y.S. and Guba, G. (1985) *Naturalistic Enquiry*, London: Sage.

Lindblom, C.E. (1959) 'The science of muddling through', *Public Administration Review*, Spring: 79–88.

Mabey, C. and Salaman, G. (1995) *Strategic Human Resource Management*, Oxford: Blackwell.

McLean, G. (1998) 'HRD: a three-legged stool, an octopus or a centipede', *Human Resource Development International*, 1(4): 375–7.

—— (1999) 'Get out the drill, glue and more legs', *Human Resource Development International*, 2(1): 6–7.

Megginson, D., Joy-Matthews, J. and Banfield, P. (1993) *Human Resource Development*, the Fast Track MBA Series, London: Kogan Page.

Mehan, H. (1979) *Learning Lessons: Social Organisation in the Classroom*, Cambridge, MA: Harvard University Press.

Mishler, E. (1986) *Research Interviewing: Context and Narrative*, London: Harvard University Press.

Nichols, T. and Beynon, H. (1977) *Living with Capitalism: Class Relations and the Modern Factory*, London: Routledge and Kegan Paul.

Oakley, A. (1981) 'Interviewing Women: a contradiction in terms', in H. Roberts (ed.) *Doing Feminist Research*, London: Routledge and Kegan Paul, 30–61.

Potter, J. and Wetherell, M. (1987) *Discourse and Social Psychology: Beyond Attitudes and Behaviour*, London: Sage.

Reid, M. and Barrington, H. (1994) *Training Interventions: Managing Employee Development* (fourth edn), London: IPD.

Rose, D. (1990) *Living the Ethnographic Life*, Qualitative Research Methods Series No. 23, Thousand Oaks, CA: Sage.

Sambrook, S. (1997) 'HRD as a discursive construction', proceedings of the Strategic Direction of HRM Conference, The Nottingham Trent University, December.

—— (2000) 'Talking of HRD', *Human Resource Development International*, 3(2): 159–78.

Saunders, M., Lewis, P. and Thornhill, A. (1997) *Research Methods for Business Students*, London: Pitman.

Schon, D.A. (1983) *The Reflective Practitioner: How Professionals Think in Action*, London: Temple Smith.

Silverman, D. (1985) *Qualitative Methodology and Sociology*, Aldershot: Gower.

Steier, F. (ed.) (1991) *Research and Reflexivity*, London: Sage.

Stewart, J. (1991) *Managing Change through Training and Development*, London: Kogan Page.

Stewart, J. (1992) 'Towards a model of HRD', *Training and Development*, October: 26–9.

—— (1993) *Organisation Development: History, Perspectives and Relevance to NHS Organisations*, Bristol: NHSTD.

Stewart, J. and McGoldrick, J. (eds) (1996) *Human Resource Development: Perspectives, Strategies and Practice*, London: Pitman.

Swanson, R. (1999) 'HRD theory, real or imagined?' *Human Resource Development International*, 2(1): 2–5.

Thompson, D. (1994) *Developing Managers for the New NHS*, Harlow: Longman.

Walton, J. (1999) *Strategic Human Resource Development*, London: Financial Times/ Prentice Hall.

Watson, T.J. (1977) *The Personnel Managers*, London: Routledge and Kegan Paul.

—— (1994a) *In Search of Management: Culture, Chaos and Control in Managerial Work*, London: Routledge.

—— (1994b) 'Managing, Crafting and Researching: Words, Skill and Imagination in Shaping Management Research', *British Journal of Management* 5, special issue, S77–S87, June.

—— (1995) 'Rhetoric, discourse and argument in organisational sense making: a reflexive tale', *Organisational Studies*, 16(5): 805–21.

—— (1996) Proceedings of the Hospitality Management Research Conference, The Nottingham Trent University, 10–11 April.

—— (2000) 'Ethnographic fiction science: making sense of managerial work and organisational research processes with Caroline and Terry', *Organisation*, 7(3): 489–510, IS 1350–5084, Sage.

Weick, K.E. (1979) *The Social Psychology of Organising* (second edn), Reading, MA: Addison-Wesley.

—— (1995) *Sensemaking in Organisations*, California: Sage.

Yin, R.K. (1994) *Case Study Research: Design and Methods* (revised edn), California: Sage.

12

ETHICAL ISSUES
IN HRD RESEARCH

Rona S. Beattie and Marilyn McDougall[1]

Aims and contribution

Ethical issues are floating constantly beneath the surface of what
we do, and they typically receive too little public attention within
and beyond the research community.

(Miles and Huberman 1994: 289)

The overall aim of this chapter is to explore a range of ethical issues and
dilemmas in empirical HRD research through the vehicle of an action
research project in a major public sector organization. The focus of the
research was the implementation and evaluation of a pilot mentoring and
peer-mentoring programme for middle managers.

The research team's interest in ethics in HRD has been growing over the
last few years. This mentoring programme was a particularly appropriate
vehicle for exploring ethical issues and dilemmas because of the sensitivities
that can arise from processes which are integral to mentoring relationships
and programmes. A key issue for such relationships is the trust between
participants. There is therefore an important need for researchers to be
cautious that their interventions – particularly in Action Research – do not
breach such trust and thus damage this approach to learning.

This chapter argues that due to the potentially intrusive nature of
research into HRD issues at both individual and organizational levels there
is a need to consider the possible ethical dilemmas that can emerge. It
encourages researchers and practitioners to recognize and develop strategies
to resolve such dilemmas appropriately, and presents a useful framework
to support this process.

Theoretical context

The concept of mentoring is one which has played an important role in learning and development both within and outwith the world of work. As it relates
to work organizations it has been defined as 'a process in which one person

255

(mentor) is responsible for overseeing the career and development of another person (protégé) outside the normal manager subordinate relationship' (European Mentoring Conference 1994). In traditional mentoring, the mentor is usually at a different level in the organizational hierarchy – usually more senior (Clutterbuck 1991). Mentoring relationships have been described in terms of career and psychosocial functions (Kram 1983). The former includes sponsorship, visibility in the organization, coaching, protection by the mentor, and access to challenging assignments. The latter involves role modelling, acceptance and confirmation, counselling and friendship. From the individual's perspective, a mentoring relationship can aid awareness of the growth of specific knowledge and skills; and can help them cope with current demands (Cunningham and Eberle 1993). For organizations, benefits have included improved succession planning and management development, better communication, increased productivity especially during induction, and improved staff morale (Clutterbuck 1991).

There is a further concept which builds on the strengths of traditional mentoring and which takes into account that peers can play an important role in facilitating effective learning in their colleagues (Smith 1990); in improving motivation (Evenden and Anderson 1992); and in managing careers in flatter structures (Holbeche 1995). This is peer mentoring, defined as 'a process where there is mutual involvement in encouraging and enhancing learning and development between two peers, where peers are people of similar hierarchical status or who perceive themselves as equals' (Beattie and McDougall 1995: 3). To date it seems that there are significant benefits to be achieved for both individuals and organizations from this process (McDougall and Beattie 1997).

Particularly in times of organizational change, benefits to individuals have been identified as mutual support, increased confidence, mutual learning, gaining a different perspective on issues; organizational benefits have included the opportunity for synergy and cross-fertilization of ideas and experiences (McDougall and Beattie 1995).

In both traditional and peer mentoring relationships, a crucial component in ensuring effective learning and development is the existence of trust between participants (Cunningham and Eberle 1993; Beattie and McDougall 1998). This learning intervention therefore particularly highlights the challenge for organizations in meeting the ethical demands which such an intervention presents where it is important to respect the trust built up by participants and ensure no breaches of confidence.

Empirical context

The organization

City Housing Services (CHS) is the department within Glasgow City Council, which is charged with exercising its extensive statutory powers and duties in relation to housing in the City, in accordance with Council policy. CHS is responsible for setting the long-term strategy for the City and directing investment and partnership with other agencies to meet the housing needs and attain the City's objectives. It provides a comprehensive housing service across all tenures and on the basis of equal opportunities for all. CHS' main activities are as follows:

- managing, maintaining and investing in the Council's own stock of 105,000 houses and factoring 20,000 former council houses;
- paying or arranging Housing Benefit and Council Tax benefit for around 90,000 council tenants, 21,500 housing association tenants, 13,000 private tenants, 6,500 Scottish Homes and 30,000 owner occupiers each year;
- together with the Social Work department and Housing Benefits, providing appropriate packages of accommodation and support for people with special needs, including an alarm service to approximately 13,500 households;
- providing advice, assistance and accommodation as appropriate for about 13,000 households who present as homeless each year;
- assisting in the retention and upgrading of the private traditional sandstone stock via the provision of grants;
- managing the improvement, redevelopment and/or disposal of unsatisfactory council property and of the area in which they are situated;
- provide services to people requiring community care including housing adaptations, sheltered homes and housing resettlement.

Vision and strategy

The main strategic objectives of CHS cover housing and estate management, best value, staff and management and investment. As has been stated in the service plan for 1999/2000 it is a key aim 'to have the best staff, providing the best service, achieving the best value'. Key issues facing the Housing service, as defined in CHS' service plan 1999/2000 are as follows:

- changing tenant profile
- addressing poverty and disadvantage
- managing estates better
- improving access
- increasing housing choice, developing mixed neighbourhoods
- social rented supply/demand
- lack of money for the service
- Community Housing Trust, Glasgow Energy and Signposts
- role of the Council in the future.

The Department is preparing at present for the proposed transfer in 2001 to a Community Housing Trust, and this will involve transferring the entire Council housing stock (100,000 houses and flats) to a newly formed Community Housing Trust independent of local authority control. CHS is therefore preparing for this major transitional event and has recently initiated a staffing reorganization and to begin a large-scale consultation with City residents affected by the change. Managers and their staff require to adapt to a cultural change with many staff having worked in local government for over twenty years.

Staffing

There is a staffing establishment of 2,144 staff, comprising 1,264 administrative, professional, technical and clerical staff and 880 manual staff. Management of the central stock is decentralized to some thirty neighbourhood offices, grouped in five divisions. Other key sites are the Wheatley House headquarters, George Street Housing Benefit office, the Hamish Allan Centre, eight hostels and thirty-one concierge sites.

Learning and development strategy

In 1999 the CHS management board introduced a Learning and Development Strategy which would complement the new Human Resource Strategy for the Department. The Learning and Development Strategy is aimed at supporting all staff in coping with the changes, which present such an important current challenge to individuals and to the organization. The strategy indicates the organization's commitment to the promotion of continuous learning and self-managed learning in addition to a comprehensive training programme for all managers and staff.

Part of this strategy has been the introduction of a pilot mentoring programme for middle managers. This included two approaches to mentoring, with an equal number of traditional and peer-mentoring pairs. The board agreed to this pilot with the anticipation of possible expansion throughout the department, to be considered after comprehensive evaluation of the programme. Possible expansion of a mentoring programme inter-departmentally would perhaps be considered in the longer term. This could take the form of senior members of staff, potentially up to Directorate level, being encouraged to develop a mentoring relationship with a member of staff at the same level in another Council department. In the long term also, there is the possibility of establishing mentoring relationships between the CHS and the private and voluntary sectors.

Methodological issues

Research objectives

There were two strands of research objectives in this project. Applied objectives of particular interest to the host organization were to implement and evaluate a pilot mentoring and peer-mentoring programme for middle managers. Theoretical objectives were to explore similarities and differences in process and outcome between the two approaches to mentoring.

Choosing a research design

It has been argued that ethical issues in management research are very complex (Snell 1986). Key factors that will influence research design, questions and ethics have been identified as the subject of study, the researchers, stakeholders, the context and the model of research being used (Easterby-Smith, Thorpe and Lowe 1991).

The subject of study

The subject of this study was the development of middle managers through a pilot mentoring and peer-mentoring programme. As discussed above, the need to develop middle managers had been recognized by the organization as this group was particularly affected by organizational change and was also expected to be key drivers of future change.

Researchers

Six researchers were involved in the project – two were academic HRD researchers, who also acted as consultants to the host organization for the implementation of the mentoring programme. One of them had a long-standing involvement in other aspects of the organization's HRD strategy and had a local government background, which it was felt contributed to enhancing understanding of strategic and HRD issues in local government. The other had extensive experience of consultancy and research with a wide range of organizations. The four other researchers were the organization's HRD manager, and three HRD practitioners, all of whom are IPD qualified. The in-house team was responsible for implementing and managing the pilot programme and also adopted a role as facilitators to support individual mentoring relationships.

Stakeholders and context

Within the host organization there were various stakeholders. These were as follows:

- The in-house HRD researchers. In the three years before this project, this group had developed and delivered a range of innovative and valued HRD interventions. These established their credibility, and it was important that this initiative would continue this trend and further enhance their professional standing. For this stakeholder group therefore this project was important, as failure could undermine what had recently been achieved and was planned for the future.

- The senior management of CHS, in particular the Director of Housing. He viewed this initiative as playing a critical role in enabling middle managers to adapt to the new roles they were to be required to undertake as the organization prepared itself for the possibility of moving towards new status in terms of a Community Housing Trust. Approval from the Departmental Board was therefore readily forthcoming, and emphasis was placed on the importance of evaluation as a means of assessing effectiveness of this initiative for the Housing Department in the first instance, and possibly longer term, for the Council as a whole.
- The mentors participating in the mentoring programme who were prepared to share their knowledge with less experienced colleagues at a time of considerable organizational pressure.
- The protégés participating in the mentoring programme who had expressed a desire to learn from more experienced managers.
- The peer mentors who were keen to participate in mutual learning with another colleague at the same level.
- The participants' line managers who were generally positive about having their staff developed through this process.

From an academic perspective there were also various stakeholders. These were as follows:

- The academic researchers for whom this collaboration with a major local employer was important in terms of enhancing their personal and professional development.
- The academics' university. This would gain from academic and professional outputs from the project, as well as contributing to the university's mission of enhancing education–industry links.
- The wider academic community. It was hoped that results from this research would contribute to expanding knowledge in this increasingly important field of HRD.

The HRD practitioner community was a stakeholder to this project in that results could inform policy and practice in this field. Preliminary findings have already been utilized as teaching material for HRM professionals studying for IPD qualification.

Model of research

Action Research has been defined as aiming 'to contribute to both the practical concerns of people in an immediate problematic situation and to the goals of social science by joint collaboration within a mutually acceptable ethical framework' (Rapoport 1970: 499 in Gill and Johnson 1997: 62).

This discussion focuses primarily on the process of action research – for a fuller discussion of the roots of Action Research and the debate over its definitions, see Dickens and Watkins (1999). Action Research assumes that any social phenomena are subject to continual change, with the researcher perceived to be part of the change process itself (Easterby-Smith, Thorpe and Lowe 1991). Two features which are generally present in action research studies are as follows:

1   A belief that the best way of learning about an organization or social system is by trying to change it. This study involved managing change through the introduction of mentoring for middle managers.
2   The belief that those individuals most affected by, or involved in implementing changes should, as much as feasible, be involved in the research process. In this project the implementation team were directly involved in the research design, data collection, analysis and evaluation (Easterby-Smith, Thorpe and Lowe 1991).

A potential challenge arising out of research collaboration between academics and managers is whether the focus of the research will be on solving the particular organizational problem or theory building (Gill and Johnson 1997). Despite this challenge, it has been noted that Lewin – the originator of Action Research – recognized the need to improve collaboration between researchers and argued that academics should engage in theory building by becoming involved with research on practical problems (Cunningham 1993 in Dickens and Watkins 1999). Such involvement, unlike many other forms of management research, requires collaboration. This according to Peters and Robinson 'must take place within a mutually acceptable ethics framework governing the collection, use and release of data' (1984 in Dickens and Watkins 1999: 18). Such an ethical framework is the subject of this chapter.

According to Dickens and Watkins (1999) action research involves various stages:

•   The action research team identifies a problem in their particular context. In this instance this was the need to develop middle managers to help drive a major change programme.
•   On occasion an external facilitator is required to unfreeze the group dynamics so that the participants can proceed with change. Here the academic researchers were utilized to facilitate the thinking processes of the in-house team and to present an initial workshop for participants to introduce them to the concept of mentoring.
•   After identifying the problem, data is collected from a range of sources within the organizational context. Such sources may include interviews

and surveys. These were used in this project and supplemented by focus groups.

- Given the nature of involvement in action research all members of the team should participate in the data collection phase. This was the case in this study.
- Analysis of data and possible solutions. Here: 'the team must make meaning of the data and introduce that meaning to the organization. The feedback to the community may act as an intervention itself, or the action researchers may implement more structured actions that create change within the system. The interventions can be considered experimental, as the action team members next test the effects of the changes they have implemented by collecting more data, evaluating the results, and reformulating thoughts or redefining the problem in the system' (Dickens and Watkins 1999: 133).
- Finally the action research team continue moving through the above cycle until they have solved the problem they identified initially.

It has been suggested (Dickens and Watkins 1999) that approaches to Action Research that adhere closely to Lewin's principles can add value to organizations. In particular that democratic participation and social action, and moving between analysing a problem and re-conceptualizing that problem, have great potential to facilitate organizational learning. This requires group decisions and group commitment to improvement.

Within this Action Research framework quantitative methods were rejected in this study, because of the difficulties of identifying and isolating the impact of variables contributing to a complex learning process. In addition, given the holistic nature of mentoring and peer mentoring, it was considered that quantitative approaches would not capture effectively the learning processes involved and would not contribute appropriately to inform the future development of the mentoring programme.

The research

Stages were identified for the development and implementation of the mentoring programme, and each stage was reviewed and informed the implementation of the following stage. The stages were as follows:

Initial research

This involved a literature review and consultations with other organizations which had implemented mentoring.

Preparation of the project proposal and setting up the programme

The first stage of the project was ensuring that there was commitment and support from the Board. This was successfully achieved. It was agreed from the outset, that the programme was to be managed and supported by four internal facilitators, all of whom were members of the training team. All had participated recently in educational programmes such as MSc/Diploma in HRM or Certificate in Training Practice, and were thus aware of the issues and features of effective mentoring programmes. Each facilitator was dedicated to particular mentoring pairs, and their role is to provide advice, support and counselling. In-house training was provided for the facilitators about this role, and further clarification emerged during seminars as participants' expectations and needs became clearer.

The training team considered options as to how to recruit appropriate participants, and decided to be proactive in this process, approaching colleagues known for their positive approach towards self-development. Of the twenty finally included, almost half (nine) had completed or were studying for CTP and several others had attained further education and postgraduate qualifications. Programme application forms and explanatory programme and mentoring notes were issued to those to be involved.

It was decided from the outset, that it would be appropriate to include an equal number of both hierarchical and peer-mentoring relationships in this pilot, with a view to assessing their progress and any issues arising. Participants were allowed to choose the type of developmental role they would play.

As to the pairing process, facilitators were aware of insights from mentoring literature on mentor 'pairing' selection, and the importance of individual choice in this matter. However, they felt that many of the participants were unlikely to know others well enough to be able to make an informed decision about potential partners, and so the option of individual selection was considered inappropriate. Learning styles of potential participants were identified. Thereafter facilitators proceeded with selection and suggested pairings based on their own subjective views about participants, anecdotal information known about the individual colleagues, and this was complemented by information about learning styles. It was recognized that there was an element of risk in this approach, and it was felt that its prudence or otherwise would become apparent in the course of the pilot programme.

Support for participants was considered by facilitators to be a key feature of the pilot. Training and learning events were to be planned and delivered by academic staff from Glasgow Caledonian University (GCU). In addition there were also separate briefings by CHS for participants and their line managers, and these are outlined below. The four facilitators agreed their own principles of behaviour and form of contact with participants. This included the importance of coaching rather than leading, developing rather than instructing; and covered frequency of contact and importance of regular reviews. It was decided that throughout the project there would be a 'drip-feed' of relevant articles to participants to aid their learning and awareness on mentoring issues, though care is taken to ensure the participants are not overloaded with material.

Pre-programme evaluation

This explored a range of issues including mentoring experience, expectations and concerns through semi-structured interviews with mentoring pairs, their line managers, and the facilitators.

Programme launch

The programme was launched by a senior member of the Board.

Seminars

Participants

These sessions were structured similarly for each group and were complementary to the introductory session for all participants by GCU. They involved opportunities to gain insights and reflection on: learning styles, the mentoring role, skills and characteristics, the range of anticipated learning outcomes, managing and developing the relationships, exercises and case-study role-playing, the use of learning logs and learning contracts, and the support role of training team facilitators. The suggestion was made by mentors that they should meet together to provide each other with support. It was agreed that this should be driven by the mentors themselves in the first instance.

The main issues arising from these sessions were concerns about potential lack of support and commitment from some line managers; and about the difficulty of developing the partnerships effectively while coping with the pressure of heavy workloads. Participants were asked to share notes of meetings and conversations with the academic researchers only, in particular highlighting any critical incidents in their relationships. There was some reluctance to share this information and thus this element was abandoned.

Line managers

The seminar for line managers was well attended by the managers of participants with seventeen out of twenty taking part. The purpose of the session was to introduce them to the concept of mentoring and this was carried out through presentations, a training video on mentoring which had been developed by David Clutterbuck, discussions about the practical value of mentoring to their colleagues. Outputs from participants' workshops, including their concerns about potential lack of line manager support, were also shared with managers.

Managers were concerned about how their busy staff would manage their time spent on mentoring. One senior manager asked what level of input and support was required from him as he neither wanted to interfere nor appear disinterested. After a discussion the term 'tacit support' was deemed to be appropriate to describe line managers' roles in supporting their subordinate. By this the group meant support without interference. The managers were assured that the partnerships should not undermine their authority and that there should be a flexible and mutually support-ive 'triangular' relationship between the manager and the mentor pairs. The CHS annual appraisal for staff known as EDR (Employee Develop-ment Review) is seen by managers as critical to the personal development of their staff. It was suggested that mentoring was a parallel device which could enhance the personal development aspect of the EDR when parti-cipants were being appraised by their line manager.

Establishment of mentoring relationships

The pace of initial meetings was tempered by the summer holiday period. However, several pairs managed to hold first and second meetings during the summer during which times ground rules and an initial agenda were developed. One pair requested the facilitator to assist with their initial meet-ing to help establish their ground rules. The communication link between participants and facilitators has been through occasional telephone con-versations and electronic mail to confirm general progress. A joint progress meeting was arranged. In addition to discussing progress and scope for further assistance from facilitators, this session will included a training session on self-development and holistic personal development planning.

Initial evaluation

This was designed to explore progress and initial impact, and involved semi-structured interviews with the mentoring pairs, questionnaire to parti-cipants' line managers and a focus group discussion with facilitators. At the time of writing this is ongoing.

An end of pilot evaluation

This is planned to involve semi-structured interviews with all internal stakeholders.

Decision about the future

Following the final evaluation a decision about future mentoring develop-ments will be made.

Critical analysis

Having considered the characteristics of this project particularly the number and range of stakeholders concerned, the Action Research methodology and qualitative methods adopted, and the very nature of the subject of the study – mentoring – it was clear that this work had the potential to raise important ethical dilemmas and issues.

It has been identified (Miles and Huberman 1994), that there are particular ethical dilemmas and issues that typically require attention in qualitative research. These are used below as a framework for discussion of this project.

Worthiness of the project

Both in-house and academic researchers were in no doubt that this work was worth undertaking as there were potential benefits to all of the stakeholders. In particular, the research had the potential to facilitate the management of change within the organization, and the empirical approach could enhance understanding of different types of mentoring in facilitating management learning.

Competence boundaries

Miles and Huberman challenge researchers to consider whether they have the expertise to conduct research of good quality. Also they are asked to consider the extent to which they are prepared to learn from others, given that both novice and experienced researchers are 'always exploring things they do not quite know what to do' (ibid.: 291).

Within this team of researchers there was an appropriate mix of competences and experiences and importantly, a willingness to learn from each other. The two academics involved had different backgrounds and strengths which complemented each other. They valued the exposure to pragmatic transformational change issues and current organizational life, which was gained through working with practitioner colleagues. The in-house researchers had already gained applied research experience through professional studies and welcomed the opportunity to work with academic colleagues.

Informed consent, privacy, confidentiality and anonymity

Respondents were told at the beginning of the project that there was to be an ongoing research evaluation of its progress. In addition, this plan was repeated at the outset of each individual interview and willingness to participate was ascertained. Consent was therefore given on an informed basis. In general respondents supported the research, in some cases seeing it as an indicator of the organization's commitment to and valuing of this initiative.

The research team was highly sensitive to the need to protect the privacy, confidentiality and anonymity of those involved. While this is a core value of the researchers involved, its importance was particularly heightened given that the research focused on one organization, and there was a multiplicity of stakeholders involved. In addition the literature on mentoring, the subject under study, stresses the central importance of confidentiality to develop the trust required for effective learning.

As part of the original research design, the academic researchers had proposed that participants keep a diary of their learning experiences as means of encouraging their reflection and providing rich data on their learning processes. It was proposed, for reasons of privacy, that such diaries would only be seen and analysed by the academic researchers. However, respondents indicated that they felt this was potentially intrusive and this was immediately respected. Participants were subsequently encouraged to keep learning logs for purposes of personal reflection only.

As part of the overall research protocol there was agreement between researchers that confidentiality of responses would be protected. For example, the transcription of interview tapes was delayed at one point in the project to ensure the involvement of a secretary experienced in undertaking confidential personnel work.

The majority of respondents were assured that their anonymity would be preserved, and care was taken in presenting findings both internally and externally, that individuals would not be identifiable. Several key stakeholders were recognizable because of their unique position in the organizational hierarchy, and their permission was sought prior to any dissemination.

Benefits, costs and reciprocity

This relates to the extent to which there is a balance between participating parties. In this particular project there was no monetary advantage to either practitioner or academic researchers, but rather a mutual exchange of benefits and costs. Academic researchers gained entry to the organization and project. This was particularly valued as it built on a particular research interest and was also important in terms of material for academic publications in due course. For organizational experts, there was a gain in terms of the involvement of the academics and this helped to convince senior management of the importance and appropriateness of the project. The research design also offered a benefit to participants in the mentoring project, as the interviewing process aided their understanding of mentoring, and facilitated their reflection on their learning. There was also an important mutual benefit in that the involvement of six researchers meant that the workload and costs of the project were spread.

Reciprocity was an important characteristic of this research and was part of a wider collaborative arrangement with this organization involving the delivery of in-house programmes; academic supervision of Diploma and Master's degree dissertations of practitioner researchers; and the provision of placements by the host organization for full-time HRM students.

Harm and risk

There was the potential for this research to be threatening to some stakeholders – particularly the HRD team. There was a potential threat to their credibility and that of the mentoring process, as the action research methodology encouraged a frank consideration by participants of problems and issues at various stages. This was however accepted as a reasonable risk by the in-house researchers, and indeed they recognized that introducing mentoring into the organization would not be problem-free. Another potential risk – this time for participants – was the failure of a mentoring relationship which could have an impact on their profile and standing in the organization. The in-house team made it clear to participants that the breakdown of any mentoring relationship would not be viewed critically.

Honesty and trust

This project was built on an already high-trust relationship between academic and in-house researchers that had resulted from prior collaborations. In addition, ground rules were established at the outset regarding how the project should be conducted, what would be roles and responsibilities, etc. Honesty and trust were also integral to the relationship between researchers and respondents. As discussed above, research participants gave informed consent based on promises made by researchers about the purpose and process of the research, and dissemination of the findings. Such promises were always kept. There was an interesting parallel with this issue, in that honesty and trust have been found to be central to successful mentoring and peer mentoring relationships as was mentioned earlier.

Intervention and advocacy

Miles and Huberman challenge researchers to consider their most appropriate course of action, in circumstances where there is 'harmful, illegal, or wrongful behaviours on the part of others during a study' (1994: 293). No such circumstances arose. However, researchers discussed this hypothetically and all were clear that they 'couldn't stand by, or condone' behaviour which was illegal. In a situation where harmful or wrongful behaviours were apparent, practitioner researchers were clear that their organizational role would supersede their researcher role. Academic colleagues felt that their decision making on this would be constrained by their lack of professional expertise where matters related to technical aspects of the housing sector.

Research integrity and quality

It could be suggested that the circumstances of this project were conducive to subjectivity in analysis due to the HRD team's stake in the mentoring project. The practitioners were very aware of this and had sought the involvement of academic colleagues partly to offset this possibility. They in turn were aware of the team's desire to have them involved for this reason and were confident of ensuring a rigorous approach. The development and observation of a strict research protocol enhanced data collection and the reliability and validity of findings.

Within the research team there was the somewhat unusual situation of academic researchers interviewing the practitioner researchers on their role as facilitators. During a project review session this issue was discussed, particularly whether this might contaminate research results. The practitioner researchers were quite clear however that whilst being interviewed they were in facilitator rather than researcher role.

Ownership of data and conclusions: use and misuse of results

The research team discussed throughout the project, issues about ownership of data and use of results. It was therefore clear to all parties that data was owned equally. There were also discussions and agreement on where and how to disseminate outcomes. The latter included a range of approaches such as joint conference papers and joint practitioner articles with both practitioner and academic researchers involved and named; academic outputs from academic researchers with acknowledgement of practitioners' contributions; and internal and local government reports from the practitioner team. A project brief was developed at the outset outlining aims and objectives, and roles and responsibilities. However, there was no written contract which set out formally the relationship and the team was comfortable that this was not necessary – largely because of the long-standing and successful nature of the association.

Conflicts, dilemmas and trade-offs

The research team discussed the potential for conflict for practitioner researchers, from their dual role of facilitators of the mentoring process and researchers of the project's progress. It was felt that as evaluation of their activities was an integral element of the ethos of this particular HRD team, and something they rated highly, they were accustomed to engaging in self-criticism and that this therefore was not problematic. In addition they had a vested interest in the project's objective evaluation, as this was to provide the basis for future mentoring strategies, which they wanted to be successful. While this was not perceived as a problem by any of the stakeholders to the research, the point was made that the involvement of academics was a means of neutralizing any 'risk of contamination' of such internal conflict of interest.

With regard to the relationship between researchers and respondents there was a potential for a dilemma to arise for the in-house researchers.

To enhance objectivity in both their facilitator and researcher roles individual members of the team worked with those participants of whom they had little prior knowledge or involvement. The in-house researchers did however perceive there to be the potential risk of some participants continuing with the pilot because they did not want to let themselves down and also not to disappoint members of the HRD team for whom they felt some loyalty. To minimize this it was stressed at various stages of the project that individuals should not feel an obligation to continue if the process was not appropriate for them.

Conclusions and key learning points

As the field of HRD grows it is important to recognize that the subject of research often includes issues which are sensitive for individuals and organizations. This has already been recognized in the Code of Professional Conduct and Disciplinary Procedures published by the IPD (1998). It is worth highlighting that all researchers in this field who are members of the Institute – whether academics, practitioners or consultants – are subject to this code. While the focus of this specific study was mentoring, this is only one of a range of HRD interventions where researchers should be aware of potential ethical dilemmas so as to minimize inappropriate intrusion and to ensure avoidance of harm to individuals and organizations.

Action Research has an important role to play in dealing with live HRD problems, and through this, in contributing to the testing of key HRD concepts and the development of theory and good practice. It is recognized, however, that there are limitations in this approach because of the potential conflict of roles of 'researcher' and 'consultant'. There may also be some tension between organizational and academic objectives in research. HRD researchers therefore will want to be clear and explicit about the balance between pragmatic and theoretical aims when using this approach. As has been mentioned in the literature on Action Research there is the possibility of conflict between organizational goals and the development of theory. In this project all of the researchers believed that these were not mutually exclusive and indeed were complementary. It was also intended that all stakeholders would benefit from the research, including respondents who had the opportunity to reflect on their own learning processes.

Ethical dilemmas and conflicts did arise from this action research project – as they may with other – research methodologies. Researchers should be aware of this and as part of the data collection and evaluation processes involved, should review and resolve ethical issues. The framework adapted here from the work of Miles and Huberman (op. cit.) has been found to be particularly helpful in facilitating such a discussion. In this project it was decided that in parallel with the data collection and review process, there would be regular reflection by the team on ethical matters arising and resolution of such when appropriate.

From this collaborative project there were a number of features which helped in the resolution of ethical dilemmas. One of these was shared values between researchers on core issues such as the importance of learning, the protection of anonymity, privacy and confidentiality, and the willingness to adopt a flexible approach in the interests of learners and the organization. An example of these values being practised was the team's willingness to comply with respondents' wishes about not keeping a diary for the academic researchers to analyse as they felt it would be intrusive, despite the fact that this would have given a rich insight into the mentoring relationships. This flexibility is also consistent with an Action Research approach. The second feature was open communication between the researchers involved. There were various examples where this was important in addressing potential ethical dilemmas. These included the explicit discussion from the outset about the existence of mutual benefits, and the establishment and review of ground rules as they related to issues such as ownership of data and dissemination of results. A third was a good rapport among all of the researchers involved which made it easy to raise or resolve any issues or concerns. This was facilitated by the high degree of trust between all members of the research team.

In conclusion, an explicit commitment by all researchers to taking an objective stance is critical to ensuring validity and reliability in HRD research. In addition, it is in the interests of all involved in this area of work, to recognize that ethical dilemmas are likely to be implicit in undertaking such research. It is important therefore that researchers in this field undertake to integrate into their project design opportunities to debate and resolve ethical issues in HRD research.

Note

1 The authors would like to acknowledge the contributions of Carol Naismith, Dorothy Christie, Gerry O'Keefe and Michelle Skivington of City Housing Services, Glasgow.

References

Beattie, R.S. and McDougall, M.F. (1995) 'Peer mentoring: the issues and outcomes of non-hierarchical developmental relationships', working paper presented to the British Academy of Management Annual Conference, Sheffield.
—— (1997) 'Inside or outside HRM? Locating lateral learning: two case studies from the voluntary sector', in C. Mabey, T. Clark and D. Skinner (eds) *HRM – the Inside Story*, London: Sage, Open University.
Clutterbuck, D. (1991) 'Everyone needs a mentor', London: IPD.
Cunningham, J.B. (1993) *Action Research and Organisational Development*, Westport, CT: Praeger.
Cunningham, J.B. and Eberle, T. (1993) 'Characteristics of the mentoring experience: a qualitative study', *Personnel Review*, 22(4): 54–66.

Dickens, L. and Watkins, K. (1999) '"Action Research": Rethinking Lewin', *Management Learning*, 30(2): 127–40.

Easterby-Smith, M., Thorpe, R. and Lowe, A. (1991) *Research Methods: an Introduction for Managers*, London: Sage.

European Mentoring Conference (1994), Sheffield Hallam University, September.

Evenden, R. and Anderson, G.C. (1992) *Management Skills – Making the Most of People*, Wokingham: Addison-Wesley.

Gill and Johnson (1997) *Research Methods for Managers* (2nd edn), London: Paul Chapman.

Holbeche, L. (1995) 'Peering into the future of careers', *People Management* 31 May: 26–8.

Institute of Personnel and Development (1998) *Code of Professional Conduct and Disciplinary Procedures*, London: IPD.

Kemmis, S. and McTaggart, R. (1988) *The Action Research Planner*, Victoria, Australia: Deakin University.

Kram, K. (1983) 'Phases of the mentor relationship', *Academy of Management Journal*, 26(4): 608–25.

McDougall, M. and Beattie, R.S. (1995) 'Peer mentoring to support transformational change', paper to the Scottish Conference on Organisational Transformations, Glasgow, November.

—— (1997) 'Peer mentoring at work', *Management Learning*, 28(4): 423–37.

Miles, M.B. and Huberman, A.M. (1994) *Qualitative Data Analysis* (2nd edn), Thousand Oaks, CA: Sage.

Peters, M. and Robinson, V. (1984) 'The origins and status of action research', *Journal of Applied Behavioural Science* 20(2): 113–24.

Rapoport, R.N. (1970) 'Three dilemmas in action research', *Human Relations*, 23(6): 449–513.

Smith, B. (1990) 'Mutual mentoring on projects', *Journal of Management Development*, 9(1).

Snell, R. (1986) 'Questioning the ethics of management development: a critical review', *Management Education and Development*, 17(1): 43–64.

13

IMPLEMENTING NETWORKED LEARNING WITH HRD PROFESSIONALS INTERNATIONALLY

Catherine Edwards

Aims and contribution

In this chapter I present a reflective and analytic account of an aspect of curriculum development of a postgraduate course for human resource development professionals which was undertaken as a process of longitudinal action research. My role whilst undertaking this research was as course director. Earlier published work (Edwards and Hammond 1998) discusses the introduction of e-mail discussion into this distance learning programme to enhance dialogic learning and critical thinking. The reason for introducing e-mail discussion forums and then the intranet was to complement text-based and face-to-face teaching and learning aspects of the course with collaborative networked learning using these information and communication technologies (McConnell 1994; McConnell *et al.* 2000). In particular the intention was to exploit the potentially collaborative and dialogic attributes of electronic communicative technologies through what Hodgson names as a constructionist orientation (Hodgson 2000).

Theoretical context

Previous action research

The earlier research phases in which e-mail discussions were introduced produced results that led to two main conclusions for this particular programme. The first was that all students participating and sharing their perspectives with us on the experience of trying to make this technology work for critical dialogue felt that they wanted to see more sustained use of ICT in programme design and delivery, despite difficulties with access, the technology itself and tentativeness for some in sharing ideas through

273

this medium. The second was that as a course team we realized we had to continue to model the emphasis on collaborative learning and critical thinking throughout all aspects of course delivery and design, and keep learning ourselves how to make best use of this medium to fulfil these aims. We realized that networked technologies alone, without preparatory debate and evaluation, would not necessarily be used collaboratively or to promote the development of critical perspectives amongst course participants.

The analytical evaluation of this first phase of the action learning project led to the design of a dedicated intranet by a member of the course team; staff development and training in use of this intranet and the Web for learning and research; and a collaborative exercise amongst the course team in developing critical discussion themes using a simple e-mail discussion list. This latter took place over several months. Different members of the team took responsibility for learning how to lead and moderate discussions.

An intranet for cross-cultural communications and learning

The next phase of the action research was to discover how postgraduate HRD students might assist us in our development as a learning community in using the intranet for collaborative critical learning and research.

The purpose of the intranet and associated technologies was to offer a forum for students on this programme, world-wide, to share perspectives relating to their learning and professional practice. Together we wanted to explore our different interpretations of learning networks and networked learning. We wanted to begin to comprehend and consciously work with our diverse culture-bound understandings. We felt this should better prepare us for using online discussion software to communicate and learn across the trans-cultural boundaries created by different languages of origin, different regionalities and nationalities, educational formations, occupational and professional orientations, genders. We knew that the critical perspectives we hoped to share would be informed by those differences, implicitly and explicitly. We wanted to begin to tease out some nuances of interpretation within those differences in relation to these particular concepts and processes.

Chapter structure

The next section of the chapter gives further descriptive background about the course and its locations, the course team and the postgraduate students who participate. This is followed by a section that explores the strengths and limitations of action research. It discusses how the story of the account might be variously read and dilemmas for the writer in establishing an authoritative voice from within the tentativeness of non-replicable research. A summary of the research 'evidence' is presented in the next three sections focusing on the process of gathering definitions and meanings; how these HRD professionals encountered networked learning and how they positioned themselves as prospective trans-cultural communicators in relation to their national location and identity in particular.

Learning outcomes

Readers will thus gain insight through this account into research purpose, focus, context, circumstance, process and findings, and into my retrospective perception of its contribution and its flaws. Those particularly interested in methodology should find this situated within the debate about construing reflection and evaluation (here in relation to the process of a curriculum development) as research. Those particularly interested in designing and developing networked learning in course curricula will find relevant the ways in which students and tutors talked about and prepared themselves for new ways of communicating.

Empirical context

The programme in the study was a postgraduate degree in training and development. It was designed for post-experience human resource development professionals whose current job involved them in the management of learning with adults in the workplace, in preparation for paid employment, or in urban or rural community development initiatives.

Course structure

The course originally comprised an induction into postgraduate distance learning, four modules and a dissertation. The modules covered the core curriculum under the following headings: Training and Development policies, theories and practices; Training and Organisation; Managing Diversity; and Auditing and Researching training and development. The modules were taught through interactive text, small group face-to-face discussion, individual tutor support and residential schools. One residential weekend per module comprised a range of group-work exercises, lectures, peer teaching and presentations. All assessed work required that students learn to focus on theoretical debates, reflections on practice and the relationship between these. The final dissertation had to include an element of empirical research, normally related to the students own workplace or work-related preoccupations.

Curriculum design and student support teams

The text-based modules were authored and updated by ten members of the full-time academic staff and a further ten or so commissioned authors. This course team of around twenty-four full- and part-time academic and professional practitioner staff was actively researching and practising in the following areas: evaluation and assessment; gender in training and development; strategic human resource development and its relationship to national economies; critiquing competencies within an international context; training and the environment; reflective practice in professional development and networked learning and new technologies in a cross-cultural context.

All materials' authors also played active roles in other aspects of course delivery, design and student academic and pastoral support. Students were organized into tutor-led groups of around eight to ten per group. They were strongly encouraged to construe the groups as learning sets and to 'bond' with one another as a means of combatting the isolation of long-distance studentship and to promote the kind of perspective sharing essential for the development of critical thinking. The social bonding could often be so successful a process that tutor group members had to be almost prised out of their small groups at residential weekends in order to collaborate and network more broadly within their year group. However, many students struggled to engage as deeply as they said they would have liked, with critical intellectual debate, immersed as they were in daily working and family lives and coming regularly but only occasionally to their 'study' lives. The wrench of constantly being interrupted from pursuing threads of debate became more consciously acute during the dissertation process. Online discussion offered a new possibility for enhancing the integration of academic learning with daily life.

Tutor and student profiles

All tutors on the programme were active contributors to the course curriculum from their research. Two were professors and the rest were qualified to at least Master's level with over half the team possessing or working towards doctorates. The disciplinary background of staff reflected the interdisciplinary nature of the course curriculum and ranged from education and management through to continuing education, philosophy, psychology, sociology, politics, economics, environmental science, linguistics, organizational behaviour and organizational development. All tutors also had extensive practitioner experience as adult educators, trainers, or human resource developers.

Students ranged in age from mid-twenties to early sixties with a modal age of around 35 at the inception of the course which became gradually lower over a period of ten years to around late twenties by the time this study took place. Males numerically dominated recruitment by around two thirds to a third in the early years of the programme. This shifted in later cohorts to around 50 per cent in all three locations. In Ireland and the UK one or two of the more recent cohorts had a majority of women of over 50 per cent and one year group in Ireland a majority of 75 per cent. These changes were not the result of a proactive recruitment campaign to attract more women participants and reasons for the changes have yet to be researched.

Students' job roles included training manager, trainer, training and development consultant, company directors, special needs co-ordinator, community and rural development educator and co-ordinator, equal opportunity officer, personnel manager or line manager with special interest in learning and development, director of community school. Workplaces encompassed the whole range of industrial, service, public and private sectors. Students came from their own consultancy businesses, large multinational manufacturing industries, national banks, building societies and insurance companies, local service and tourism industries, health and social services, local government, armed forces, education and vocational training organizations, religious and community based networks for local and regional development.

There was a preference for social science based degrees as entry qualifications, but students were also accepted with degrees in engineering and sciences as well as a number with no first degree but with a relevant professional qualification and appropriate experience. Final grades awarded to students consistently showed low correlation between entry qualification and postgraduate achievement.

Programme locations

The programme had three administrative bases, one in the UK, one in Eire and a third in Singapore. Each location had a local co-ordinator who offered student and tutor support. Between 95 and 100 per cent of students recruited to the programme in Eire were Irish nationals, with a very small number from the North of Ireland. Students choosing the Singapore location were normally local and from one of Singapore's three main cultural communities: Chinese, Malaysian, or Indian, though there were occasionally students from Europe (UK and Ireland mainly) working full time in Singapore. Around two thirds of students at the UK location were of UK origin and around a quarter to a third were from Europe or overseas living and studying temporarily in the UK.

Country-specific additions to the curriculum materials were specially commissioned for Singapore and for Ireland particularly in the areas of the history of training and development, the role of the trade unions and professional bodies and the local socio-economic context and conditions.

Course aims

The aims of the course were to re-engage human resource development practitioners, who may have been away from formal academic study from anything between two and twenty years, in a stimulating process of learning and research into theoretical foundations and frameworks which could inform their own professional practice and contexts. Students were particularly encouraged to increase their capacity for critical reflection and analysis of the relevance of published literature to their professional domains as educators and trainers of adults. There was a strong emphasis on sharing and evaluating the wide range of conceptual, theoretical and experiential perspectives that could be brought to bear on work-related issues. Apart from debates they encountered in the literature, as distance learners these students were dependent upon regular but infrequent face-to-face contact moments in the course and occasional telephone contact with tutor and peers as spaces in which they could discuss, debate and share the development of their ideas. A common self and course critique was the frustration felt at only getting so far into the intellectual development of a particular theme when it was time to pack up and move back to individual and somewhat isolated study. The aspiration behind first the e-mail and then the intranet initiatives was to increase and enhance opportunities for continuing this sharing and development of thinking, learning and critique beyond face-to-face contact, to any place and time the students had access to a networked computer.

Forces for change

The curriculum was shaped and co-ordinated by module co-ordinators and the course director. In the period during which this developmental study took place a regular more collaborative curriculum review process was established. The process involved full- and part-time academic staff, student representatives and focus groups with students, which were conducted at residential weekends. The content and design of the curriculum had hitherto been informed by staff research and practice interests, student feedback about professional relevance, contemporary developments in the field and technology-led approaches to distance teaching and learning.

McConnell (1994 and 1998) introduced collaborative networked learning for postgraduate professional students in the same department and the Just in Time Open Learning (JITOL) project under his direction had funded the first phase of this action research. The particular pedagogic challenge from this quarter was a rejection of 'traditional' text-based materials in favour of a course constructed around students' own individually and collectively chosen curricula, which they created from Web-based and published sources and their own electronically mediated discussions.

In this study, however, networked learning was being introduced into an existing course. Pragmatism would suggest that an accommodation with existing teaching and learning strategies and media would have to be accomplished. But from a pedagogic perspective also, it was deemed by students and the course team alike that the so-called 'didactic' text-based materials were of continuing value as a 'secondary source' alongside 'primary source' material to be found in other published literature.

Students were no more or less likely to perceive this 'body of knowledge' uncritically, once introduced to its proper pedagogic purpose, than they would a piece of information downloaded from an Internet site or a text authored by an established academic authority. In effect this meant combining both what Hodgson calls the 'dissemination and developmental orientations' of our pedagogic practices with this 'so called constructionist approach to education' (Hodgson 2000: 139), although I read her as suggesting they must be sequential rather than co-existent. Hodgson optimistically, in my view, suggests that such a constructionist or constructivist approach may help us to overcome 'boundaries created due to such aspects as cultural and language differences'. The perspective being put forward in this chapter builds on Hodgson's ideas. But it suggests that for networked learning to achieve this ambitious and worthy aim, explicit awareness raising processes in relation to participants' self-concept and formative experiences as culturally situated networked learners needs to take place. This research looks at how that process was initiated in this one instance.

Methodological issues

Curriculum development 'through' and 'as' action research

Rationale for change

Curriculum development can be stimulated by various internal and external desires or requirements for change. It may be planned without debate with the student body in advance of delivery, or entail some peremptory co-opted student representation. It can be imposed following internal institutional or external govenmental policy requirements, or those of a professional body in cases of joint accreditation (this programme did not have professional accreditation status). In the case of a curriculum so strongly linked to a particular profession there can be perennial difficulties accommodating university requirements of 'research-ledness', with the 'market-led' demands surfacing in some aspects of student feedback. One can also, as in this case, attempt to undertake curriculum development experimentally and collaboratively with the (sometimes conflicting) interests of different stakeholders variously taken in to consideration (Fullen 1999). Charlier, Bonamy and Saunders (2000: 1) cite Fullen's ideas about complexity theory as a helpful way of naming the 'need to accept complexity or diversity as a given in the design of change process'. Here we were not just accepting it as a given but addressing aspects of the diversity amongst us as part of the change process in order that our diverse identities as communicators be acknowledged in their contributing agency to our construing of the curriculum. This might create further insight into our own differently (dis)empowered discourses essential for a deeper understanding of our purposes and capacities for engaging in the sharing of perspectives for critical thinking. It was for this reason that it made sense to plan and construe these curriculum developments towards greater access to and use of networked learning, as action research. We could thus invite ourselves as course team members and student participants to critically explore and debate the shaping of new developments and devise processes in which we would be encouraged to begin to confront our own learning agendas and our identities within learning networks in preparation for using them cross-culturally within an international student cohort. But it is important to clarify that the collaborativeness of the research was not particularly democratic. It should be construed as learning centred (rather than learner centred) as it could not presuppose equality of responsibility towards the eventual shape and nature of the 'outcomes'. There was always a sense in which any student voice was a co-opted voice because the decision to incorporate or ignore any new suggestion remained with the course team and course director.

The research

Researching 'action'

Deciding to give the name 'action research' to a process of curriculum development is problematic. First, there are issues of focus, as I have found myself saying to students over the years, in distinguishing what makes it 'research' rather than a 'project'. In this instance I propose that collaboration with participants around the very definitions and concepts of networked learning in which 'snapshots' (Levin 1993) of their past and current experiences were systematically sought, recorded and then presented to them for further reflection and subsequent action, supports a claim for this process as action research (Wellington 1996).

Critical analysis

Aiding and abetting our research claims we have on the one hand a contemporary body of writings that maps research orientations attempting to give gravitas and authority to what is inevitably a non-replicable process. These writings could be typified in the seminal quote by Kabir, 'If you have not lived through something it is not true', at the front of Reason's *Human Inquiry in Action* (Reason 1988). But they also encompass a rich feminist research legacy and recent writings of African centred researchers (Asante 1998). On the other hand many current introductory research texts still construe qualitative approaches to research as attempting to reclaim concepts of reliability and validity originally framed within a positivist tradition (as discussed in Bell 1997; Blaxter, Hughes and Tight 1996; Miles and Huberman 1994; Gill and Johnson 1997).

Reflexivity in research

Claiming reflexivity through the portrayal of any research process or procedure under a particular self-revealing light is equally problematic due to the variety of interpretations and critiques of Schon's original premise (1983 and 1987) that we should seek to name and therefore 'know' how and why we perform our professional roles in order that we can change what we do according to changes in circumstance or new (moral) enlightenment. Critics of Schon have acknowledged the need to situate an individual's engagement with change (through the naming of personal moral values, action and intent) within a broader organizational and political context in order to arrive at a more complex but 'realistic' account of how the locus of control in change and the shape and texture of change agency can be understood. Fullen's (1999) essay on complexity theory attempts to illuminate a crucible of theoretical frameworks which ultimately undermines any scholarly attempt to derive explanatory or predictive stances from the study of 'variables'.

My intent was to continue with action research which would stimulate an awareness of change (towards using online learning media) at at least two further levels the second of which was reflexive and the third evaluative (Wellington 1996: 16). The second phase of the research then was to increase our self-awareness and our awareness of others, as potential networked communicators and learners in preparation for group formation and discussion with others we might never meet face to face. The third phase was to systematically record how we were using the technology and how useful we found it for enhancing dialogic learning and critical thinking. Data from this second phase remains only partially gathered and accessible to me due to my moving to another job role in a different institution, perhaps a not altogether uncommon occurrence during an action research process.

Gathering data about ourselves as networkers

At the first residential weekend in the first year cycle of the programme and in each of the three locations, UK, Eire and Singapore, students and tutors met as focus groups. These involved twenty-five students and three tutors and myself (in the role of course director) in the UK; twenty-eight students and three tutors and myself in Eire and eight students and one tutor colleague who led the inquiry in Singapore. On each occasion the entire group of tutors and students present met together and we conducted a questionnaire using oral prompts following which participants wrote or drew their response and the different meanings, definitions, experiences and understandings were then discussed. Participants were asked to define the terms 'network', 'networking' and 'networked learning and learning network'. They were then asked to sketch or describe existing networks they belonged to which contributed to their professional learning; to suggest ways in which learning networks might enhance their learning on this academic programme, and to note whether or not they thought their national location and/or cultural identity had any significant influence on the way they might engage as networked learners.

Gathering data to evaluate how we used the technology

There had already been some recording of frequency and nature of use of e-mail discussion lists during phase one (Edwards and Hammond 1998). This was extended with full cognisance and permission of all participants, to use of the internationally accessible intranet, though as stated above, my researcher role came to an end fairly soon after the second phase of the research was launched.

Eliciting definitions and meanings

It is essential to note that the questions devised to elicit participants' definitions and meanings-in-use were being asked within a context of inquiry which had already been identified by some of them and their tutors. They had expressed concern to pursue intellectual and professional debates and argument further than always appeared to be possible within the 'time' constraints of face-to-face learning phases of the course. Some participants had found that the asynchronicity and privacy offered by e-mail discussion lowered barriers to critical debate because they could take much more time to make a considered response to another's point of argument or perspective. Others felt much more self-conscious that their partially developed ideas, in text, formed a permanent record of their intellectual insecurity, 'incompetence', or tentativeness. However, it was remarkable that all expressed serious interest in integrating aspects of networked learning into the programme. The 'bottom line' was that they felt they ought to be up to date with new technological developments and be able to use it themselves in their professional lives, for teaching and learning.

So it was in pursuit of acceptable and more emotionally comfortable ways of taking these aspirations forward that we thought to make links between our anticipated experiences as electronically 'networked learners' and our current and past experiences of networks, networking and how we used networks for (professional) learning. The idea was that we acknowledged we would bring these expectations with us to our intranet networking and that it would serve us well to become more aware of the different and divergent interpretations and practices amongst us, especially as we were set to network with other participants from diverse cultures.

There was also an underlying theme about collaboration in learning. Networked learning is generally associated in the literature with collaboration (McConnell 1994; Hodgson 2000). As networks require, by definition, informal and voluntary associations between people, rather than formal institutionalized or structured relationships, they are necessarily collaborative. One could even say that it is only at moments of collaboration that a network actually comes into being, as participants' definitions suggested, by means of its fluid and flexible attributes.

But the conceptual 'mapping' of this almost structural configuration of collaboration onto 'collaborative learning', and the counterposing of it with individuated and/or competitive learning began to seem oversimplistic. At best it became understood as an attempt to address social affiliation needs rather than critical learning needs, when we explored different understandings of collaborativeness afforded by networking in participants' experiences.

Analytical framing

Initially we 'borrowed' an analytical framework so that we could more easily compare and contrast participants network, networking and networked learning definitions. We used Philip Seed's (1990) framework of network features, network types and relational qualities. It seemed apt as Seed, originally working with computer networks, transferred these networked communications concepts to the field of social work as a way of helping social workers and clients negotiate around different perceptions of assessed need, professional and informal carer roles and service provision. Here we were almost doing the reverse by taking social and professional network mapping across to our practice as putative computer mediated networkers.

Network types and meanings in Ireland

Networks and networking were mainly described in pragmatic terms: 'connecting as a means to an end'; 'a system of information exchange'; 'organizational linkages'. Networks could be typified as supportive, developmental, career oriented, problem-solving, entertaining and 'humanizing' routine aspects of work. Network relationships included work colleagues, professional associations, family, friends and local community, international colleagues (for some in multinational organizations). Key features included a superficial 'absence of hierarchy', a 'willingness to share, help, facilitate, openness, a reaching out, a reciprocal process', 'giving and getting a "hand up" in professional life occasionally in relation to what was perceived as "insider" information'.

Network types and meanings in the UK

Networks and networking were described as 'ways of sharing information to mutual benefit' of 'accessing the experiences of others', of 'tapping into other peoples' brains, knowledge, experience, ideas'. In response to this particular definition we discussed why we might also feel reticence or resistance to networking as a way of preserving a notion of 'self' with respect to such intrusion. By contrast with the spirit of informal definitions from Ireland, they were defined by some as 'organized, regular, professional contracts with others to exchange and co-operate'.

Networks were typified as local workplace centred, regional, European, global. But network relationships included family, community and friendship groups as well as particular named colleagues and fellow students on the course.

Network types and meanings in Singapore

Networks and networking were described or typified either in pragmatic terms as 'a framework for connecting items together', 'organizational linkages including personnel', 'a process in which connections are made amongst people of various organizations to fulfil a task/work project or to make referrals'. Or they were seen as ways of sustaining personal and professional identity and cohesion: 'a group of people with similar interest, related knowledge and frequently in the same or related professions'; and 'a community of people who have a common interest, purpose or identity'.

Network relationships included the construction, for several in the group, of professional relationships as friendships.

HRD practitioners using networks for professional learning

Using networks for (professional) learning in Ireland

Students suggested they could optimize the use of networks for learning by: preparing information in advance to share with others and being organized (in person, by phone and/or with computerized filing systems) to categorize received information; being able to assimilate useful tips and 'tip-offs' relating to the whereabouts of further information (most favourable if in the form of personal contacts and URLs, but not so useful if relating to library locations, titles of texts or addresses of organizations – library access was a serious issue) and ways of managing data. The similarity in use of personal contact and Internet-based networking was a sense of speed and short-cutting. Those fearing that electronic networking encourages a disposition towards easy access antipathetic to the kind of slow and steady scholarship which leads towards academic critical thinking would not gain any reassurance in these findings. Students felt networking helped them 'solve problems fast' but were also quick to point out that spending hours tracking down a particular source simply wasted time and did not necessarily lead to a more scholarly approach to the text once found. They did occasionally use networks for debate and discussion of professional issues in general over and above the brief sharing of information, but not to the extent of critical debate we were working towards on the course.

Using networks for learning in the UK

- Diverse perspectives: (1) 'Gives me new ideas and insights.' (2) 'Linking a wide variety of knowledge and experience hence putting things in different perspective, offering options. Bringing new and exciting dimensions into situations which have looked dull and lifeless. Life bringing.' (3) 'Getting a broader view.'
- Developing critique: (1) 'Challenges what I think and do, usually in a constructive way.' (2) 'Being able to compare my learning with the views and opinions of others. Being able to debate topics.' (3) 'Clarify own thoughts, verify own thoughts, gain momentum to turn reflection into generalization. Comparing.' (4) 'Others' ideas broaden my understanding-introduction of different approaches, theories.'
- Motivational support structure: (1) 'Provides me with continuous access to learning and support.' (2) 'Increases confidence and lessens sense of isolation which can impair motivation to learn.'
- Enhanced capacity: (1) 'Enables me to do work which I otherwise could not do or would have great difficulty doing.' (2) 'Getting knowledge, understanding from many sources pooling resources.' (3) 'Left to my own devices I could quite often deviate from the given topic for an assignment. My networks enable me to solicit feedback from others and externalize my reflection process. Once an idea is externalized you can witness your view changing as you speak/write.' (4) 'Vastly increases my available pool of skills, knowledge, resources, short cuts, tricks and tips.'
- Time (and thought) saving: (1) 'Reduces reinventing the wheel'. (2) 'Rapid contact, rapid exchange, rapid assistance.'
- Reflexive potential: (1) 'An outlet for feelings and thoughts worthy of evaluation and feedback in a supportive environment.' (2) 'Sharing of ideas and approaches often makes me reflect on my own practice in a way which doesn't normally occur on a day to day basis.'

Using networks for learning in Singapore

I have devised the following categorizations:

- Access to information: (1) 'The process of gathering information from people who have established links with the learner.' (2) 'Where an exchange of information takes place.'
- Mutuality: (1) 'A learning network is when people of a network actively learn from one another.' (2) 'To gather together to learn from one another, may or may not come from similar background or knowledge.'

(3) 'A system of interactors communicating with one another with the objective of learning.'

- Commonality of purpose: 'a group or community of people who have a common purpose of wanting to share resources and learning in a common field or area of interest'.

Exploring cultured interpretations of networking

Anecdotal experience by members of the course team including myself, working with students from and in different cultures on the same programme of study led to the desire to explore the extent to which students felt national cultural identity should also be taken into account in preparing for networked learning internationally. Each group was asked to note and then discuss whether they were aware national identity had any influence on their experiences and interpretations of networking and networked learning. We discussed both the dangers of internalized and externally attributed stereotypes and also the dangers of being 'blind' to significant difference if we were to attune our communications to and thus our learning from each other. This was done within the context in which theories of equal opportunities, anti-oppressive practice (Donald and Rattansi 1992) and trans-cultural (D'Ardenne and Mahtani 1989) communications already formed part of the taught curriculum.

In Ireland

Students in Ireland seemed aware that they were perceived as being a nation of social networkers and that this stereoptype did have useful resonance in much of their experience. But individually they took quite different stances in response to the prompt that network experiences and expectations might be culture-bound, as one might hope they would given the discourses around diversity and difference they were already studying on the programme. My own classification of responses is as follows:

- Total rejection of stereotype: 'it depends totally on the individual, there are differences in the way people relate to each other and they may not be consistent. What is Irish culture? Who defines it?'
- Fond embrace of stereotype (specifically in relation to peers on the course): (1) 'people have been supportive and open, quick to network. In January (first meeting) we were strangers, 8 March (second meeting) we are friends'. (2) 'I believe Irish people are naturals when it comes to networking.'
- Ironic caricature: (1) Networking in the pub with drink as the ice-breaker. 'We like to talk but we are not always honest up front.'
- Honest self-exposure: (1) Very social beings but reticent for quite a while before trusting people – pub oriented social life. (2) Instrinsically

the Irish are competitive with networking taking place on the golf course and in the pub in an informal way. (3) 'There is still a certain amount of "knowledge is power" attitude but it is improving.' (4) 'Our competitive nature can be a problem. We will share knowledge if it does not give the other person a big advantage.'
- Relation to time and place: 'May be a big difference between rural and town. Or it's not where you live but how long you have lived there. Have you had the time to build a network?'

In the UK

Students in and from the UK talked about the limiting effects of a culture of individual self-reliance in pursuing more collaborative learning strategies. They also discussed wanting the need for permission to share in such a way that they would not be deemed to be 'cheating', an issue which led us to revisit definitions of plagiarism within this context. There was also a positive recognition that a culture of freedom of opinion lent itself well to engagement with critical academic debate. Individual perspectives demonstrated a fair breadth of interpretation in the range of stances elicited in response to this prompt.

- Internalized 'reserved' stereotype: (1) 'Initially I might be less open and more reserved in my interaction with others when networking, but after a time would be more comfortable and enjoy it.' (2) 'As a nation we tend to be reserved. Starting small networks can accommodate the reservedness.' (3) 'Not sure my answers [to question areas above] reflect my feelings which I think are "British" of unease in the social network situation. I believe I see network in reference to learning as a different kind of elephant.' (4) 'perhaps one of the reasons people choose distance learning is that they are happy to work in isolation "doing their own thing". However, is this particular to UK culture? I don't know.' (5) 'English culture of "stiff upper lip" its common for us to have a "be strong" driver – I feel there's an inherent reluctance to admit to our own weaknesses and ask for help. This is compounded by adulthood and professionalism superimposed on top.' (6) 'Traditional reserved British are sometimes slow to open up to unfamiliar new contacts. Overcoming the shyness is the biggest barrier.' (7) 'Possibly the formality given to the concept and process of networking.'
- Oblique reference to social class structure: 'Your face fitting with perception, trying to meet expectations, realistic or otherwise.'
- Reference to democratic rights: (1) 'must respect people's option to participate. Be careful about the IT phobic amongst us'. (2) 'Perhaps freedom to voice opinions?'

As noted in the introduction some students based in the UK were from other cultures:

- Issue of organizational confidentiality: 'Active sharing of ideas can be done in both cultures as long as organization for which you work is fine with it.'
- Internalized stereotype of Asian reticence: 'Not afraid to show "mistakes". Can be difficult in Asian cultures.'
- Contrast between 'individual' and 'collective' cultures: 'Working in Africa for 12 years I have learned that there is much more networking in African societies (even traditionally) than in Western countries. Africans in general are very network-oriented (family, tribe, clan, caste).'
- Lack of cultural bias a cultural characteristic?: 'I don't feel able to comment – my networks consist of multinational sources. However, as a Scot it may be my culture means I don't recognise any cultural bias due to national characteristics!'

In Singapore

The most remarkable result in this section from the students in Singapore was the lack of response. Out of nine respondents five left this section blank or simply said 'no'. As this was the only site in which I was not present when the research questions were explored I have very limited insight. It could simply be that the purpose of the question was not explained in the same detail as it was in Ireland and the UK. Or it could be from a sense of uncertainty or lack of identity with Singaporean nationality, as opposed to Chinese, Malaysian, Indian or ex-patriot European. Being 'Singaporean' is a historically much more recent phenomenon than is the case with either of the other two major national groups. In discussions the group talked about collaboration being very much a way of life in their communities and that indeed they had difficulty in not collaborating over some aspects of academic study. Explored further this was held to mean that they did not feel comfortable challenging and arguing in public and thus appeared to be at a disadvantage in critical debate. They needed explicit permission and coaching to challenge tutors in particular. The four who did answer the question individually said:

- Singaporean stereotype: 'I am not sure but perhaps there is discomfort in confrontation and questioning of authority which may curtail creativity.'
- Singaporean central political policy on community involvement: 'Getting involved with the Community Club, providing my services to the public.'
- Polarized views on networking as 'support' in Singapore: (1) 'I understand the Singapore Alumni [of this programme] is uniquely active

and supportive of the programme and current students.' (2) 'People may not be so forthcoming in sharing ideas (unless they know you well enough) but will certainly be happy to receive information and ideas – this could be due to our social and political backgrounds.'

Other cultural configurations

There were also participants from all three groups who felt that (national) cultural difference had very little bearing on how they used networks for learning. They felt either that their professional identities were already trans-national and more influencial than the culture of their country of origin or workplace. Or they perceived their organizational culture was the predominant influence upon collaborative learning behaviours and approaches.

- Organizational resourcing and attitide: 'I do believe [my responses] are intrinsically related to organizational culture. Resources available to me as an employee of large organization might not be available to an independent consultant. Or the cost of those resources might prohibit an individual from benefitting. I am able to spend time on the Internet via my office PC – with the consent of my employers.'
- Main cultural issue is new technology itself: 'Irrespective of culture, most people need to socialize. New technology is changing how we do this. Online learning whether it be written, audio or even video link-age cannot replace the complexities of a face-to-face discussion.'

Tutors' perceptions

Tutors were either from and based in the UK or from and based in Ireland. Tutors for students in Singapore travelled across from the UK (on one occasion from Ireland) and maintained e-mail, fax, or postal links with students in between visits. Their own experience of the value of networks for learning might differ from the advice they would give to students:

- Networks offer minimal support but worth sustaining: 'Networking is not a major developmental aid for me, but I'd advise students to get into the habit of communicating with other members of the network. Initially this can mean sharing information about anything. Keep talking. Feeling someone is out there sharing your pain, but knowing contact is legitimate and welcomed help when you need to seek help with learning issues.' Did not note anything culture-specific about their perceptions – students in UK and Singapore used e-mail to keep in contact (UK based tutor also working in Singapore).
- Networks keep learning fresh and reflective: this tutor felt networking offered opportunities 'to reflect and discuss situations, see ways in which things might be improved or recognize more clearly why they

went well'. Would recommend to students that networking 'encourages discussion and debate – seeing the experience as dynamic, stimulating, exciting'. Culture-specific observations included: 'Who you know and who knows who is a powerful undercurrent in Ireland. People use networks to get access to information and jobs but seem far more wary of learning from others where it does not have a perceived "payoff". Women are less likely to have a powerful network or to see their contacts and colleagues as being powerful enough to offer help and assistance in terms of learning and development. Learning from those not labelled "expert" and accredited as such is a difficult concept for some people in Ireland to feel comfortable with. There is a hierarchy of educational/intellectual status which places credibility on "book learning" and far less on learning through experience or learning by listening and discourse with one's peers. People come around to it when it is introduced positively. I have just found there to be an initial resistance which can be quite startling.' (Ireland-based tutor).

- Getting the idea across: picking up on this last point a third tutor claimed they learned a great deal from their several academic networks 'expecially in new areas'. He recommended that the most important thing was to persuade students to 'use fellow students as a resource. Once they get the idea and start doing it they will learn for themselves'.

- Networking for peer comparison: this tutor felt networks 'help me benchmark myself against others. You don't always know what you don't know. Linking with others helps address this'. He also wondered if, although we often don't recognize what is inherent in our own cultures, British stiffness discourages face-to-face networking. (UK-based tutor)

- Envy as a learning motivator: another tutor recommended that students 'stay envious' if it would inspire them to push their understanding forward. (UK-based tutor)

Conclusions and key learning points

In order to draw on our findings and make good use of them for the purposes of curriculum development we felt we had made a serious attempt to sketch some of the boundaries and operant limitations arising out of the cultural habits, mores and shared meanings of this international and variously dispersed group of students. Our cultural habits and mores were deemed to influence our interpretation of and engagement with any group learning processes designed, especially online networking, to promote discourse and dialogue.

Within the relatively short life-span of a student's engagement with a course, we might only expect that they partially adapt to our co-operative modes of learning especially if their professional 'norms' are located in highly competitive business environments. Thus our data and our data gathering gave us a point of departure from which we could then discuss the extent to which we wanted and were able to develop a course culture of negotiated collaboration. In doing this we became aware of the need to respectfully value a corresponding need for competitive, non-collaborative learning behaviours and approaches.

Overall the research indicates many similarities in definitions and meanings related to networking and networked learning. There are also a number of differences in experience of and expressed interest in collaborative learning using networks in general and our new online network in particular which we felt it had been well worth investigating in advance of launching this new medium.

It is worth re-emphasizing that the findings, being part of an action research process, are to be construed as contributions to our own learning-in-progress. They are to be seen in the light of an 'internal' debate and not as accurate factual representations of people's perceptions, feelings, or experiences. They gave us a means for and an experience of sharing ideas and language which we could then build on. Their purpose was to prepare the course team and students to take account of each others' varied interpretations when we planned to use our intranet with its online discussion capability.

In particular I must reiterate that the 'findings' on cultural identities and difference as networkers emerged in the context of a critical debate about the nature, value and limitations of stereotypes and were not left as literal and unexplored areas of discourse.

Future plans

Preparations for the next phase

Early analysis of intranet usage following these preparatory investigations and discussions revealed that students depended quite considerably upon leadership by tutors in pursuing discussion beyond the sharing of information and social support towards more critical debate. This was not altogether surprising and mirrored role-influenced discursive behaviours typical of face-to-face seminars and discussion groups. Tutors appeared much more comfortable in taking the lead following dedicated staff development days on use of the intranet and Web-based research, and also following informal and structured and minuted discussions about the developments and their academic role within them. It was recognized early on that this was an area of learning in which none of us would ever be able to claim 'expertise'. Taking an action research approach to developing our curriculum in this way we would be confident we had created spaces to solicit perspectives which should enhance leadership of this learning community and its purposes.

References

Asante, M.K. (1998) *The Afrocentric Idea*, Philadelphia, PA: Temple University Press.

Bell, J. (1997) *Doing Your Research Project*, Milton Keynes: Open University Press.

Blaxter, L., Hughes, C. and Tight, M. (1996) *How to Research*, Buckingham: Open University Press.

Charlier, B., Bonamy, J. and Saunders, M. (2000) 'Provisional stabilities for change in Learnet: bridging tools for transforming learning cultures', unpublished paper presented at Networked Learning 2000 Conference, Lancaster: Universities of Lancaster and Sheffield.

D'Ardenne, P. and Mahtani, A. (1989) *Transcultural Counselling in Action*, London: Sage.

Donald, J. and Rattansi, A. (1992) *'Race', Culture and Difference*, London: Sage/Open University Press.

Edwards, C. (2000) 'Introducing networked learning with human resource development professionals internationally', *Networked Learning 2000 Conference*, Lancaster: Universities of Lancaster and Sheffield, 94–7.

Edwards, C. and Hammond, M. (1998) 'Introducing email into a distance learning course', *Innovations in Education and Training International*, 35: 4.

Fullen, M. (1999) *Change Forces, the Sequel*, London: Falmer Press.

Gill, J. and Johnson, P. (1997) *Research Methods for Managers*, London: Paul Chapman.

Hodgson, V. (2000) 'Changing concepts of the boundaries within ODL', in M. Ascencio, M. Foster, V. Hodgson and D. McConnell (eds) *Networked Learning 2000: Innovative Approaches to Lifelong Learning and Higher Education through the Internet*, Proceedings of the 2nd International Conference, Lancaster: Universities of Lancaster and Sheffield, 139–44.

Levin, J. (1993) *Sociological Snapshots: Seeing Social Structure and Change in Everyday Life*, Newbury Park, CA: Pine Forge Press.

McConnell, D. (1994) *Implementing Computor-Supported Co-Operative Learning*, London: Kogan Page.

—— (1998) 'Developing networked learning professionals: a critical perspective', in Banks, S., Graebner, C. and McConnell, D. (eds) *Networked Lifelong Learning: Innovative Approaches to Education and Training through the Internet*, Proceedings of the 1998 International Conference, Sheffield: Sheffield University, v.i–v.xi.

McConnell, D., Noakes, N., Rowe, P. and Stewart, W. (2000) 'The practice of networked learning: experiences of design and participation', in M. Ascencio, M. Foster, J. Hodgson and D. McConnell (eds) *Networked Learning 2000: Innovative Approaches to Lifelong Learning and Higher Education through the Internet*, Proceedings of the 2nd International Conference, Lancaster: Universities of Lancaster and Sheffield, 220–8.

Miles, M. and Huberman, M. (1994) *Qualitative Data Analysis*, Beverley Hills, CA: Sage.

Reason, J. (ed.) (1988) *Human Inquiry in Action: Developments in New Paradigm Research*, London: Sage.

Schon, D.A. (1983) *The Reflective Practitioner: How Professionals Think in Action*, New York: Basic Books.

Schon, D.A. (1987) *Educating the Reflective Practitioner: Toward a New Design for Teaching and Learning in the Professions*, San Francisco, CA: Jossey-Bass.

Seed, C. (1990) *Introducing Network Analysis in Social Work*, London: Jessica Kingsley.

Wellington, J.J. (1996) *Methods and Issues in Educational Research*, Sheffield: USDE.

14

IMPLICATIONS FOR REFLECTIVE HRD PRACTITIONERS OF THE INFLUENCE OF LIFE EXPERIENCE ON MANAGERS' CAREER DECISIONS

Goronwy Davies and Tony Wilson

Aims and contribution

We consider that the range of current HRD research in relation to careers is heavily biased towards either the psychological or sociological approaches with the result that the definitions are closely defined from within the academic environment. In order to illustrate the effects that a different perspective can give, we have chosen to use Grounded Theory methodology to identify the definitions that individuals apply to their own careers and the factors that affect the decisions they make about their careers. Using this methodology it is possible to close the gap between research and the lived experience of people in employment. It offers a means by which practitioners can inform and develop their practice based upon the lived experience of employees rather than upon an academic abstraction. Such research is becoming important for HRD practitioners to enable them to respond sensitively to the impact of the breakdown of many of the tenets upon which HR management practices are based. An example of this is the instability of employment. This is currently the reality for many employees as a result of the changes that have occurred in industrial and commercial organizations in Britain in the 1980s and early 1990s. These changes have been well documented, Benbow (1995) found that 90 per cent of large employers had restructured their organizations over the previous five years, with 66 per cent having shed at least one layer of management. Further, 40 per cent of employers expected to restructure their organizations in 1996 and 60 per cent expected to do so again. Of those restructuring, 75 per cent expected there would be job losses at all management levels. Eastman Kodak reduced its labour force by 12,000 during the period 1988–93 (*Economist* 1995). This continuous process of restructuring means that organizations are becoming less hierarchical and flatter (Herriot and Pemberton 1995; Inkson and Coe 1993; Nicholson and West 1988). In these circumstances Kanter (1989) predicts that in future there will be unstable employment environments where employees will not be able to make decisions and take action that will ensure continuous employment with a single employer. Further, Hutton (1995) argues there is evidence that in such an environment employers are unable to commit themselves to long-term relationships with employees.

This and other trends in the workplace have and will continue to create difficulties for employees wishing to manage their careers and indeed their lives. These trends have consequences for the way individuals define career and make decisions about the management of that career. Such changes in definitions enable the individuals to reframe their values, which in turn has implications for those who employ them. HRD practitioners who are able to recognize these changes and use the insights gained to inform their employment practices will become more effective.

Theoretical context

Definitions of career

Academic career theory has developed a number of different ideas concerning careers, all of which may be at variance with the meaning of the word in use in every day language. Adamson, Doherty and Viney (1998) survey the different academic meanings of the concept and contrast the traditional disciplinary orientations of sociology and psychology as applied in the 1970s and early 1980s. Sociologists view the 'career' as 'the unfolding of social roles, emphasizing individual's contributions to the maintenance of the social order'. They have also discussed the 'career' as 'social mobility, seeing the series of positions held over time as indicators of social position'. Psychologists on the other hand have viewed the 'career' as vocation by matching personality and occupation; as 'a vehicle for self realization and individual growth'; and as 'a component of the individual life structure'. The weaknesses of these orientations is that they emphasize relatively stable personal, social and organizational structures and seek explanations which when examined reflect the methodological structure of the discipline.

Adamson, Doherty and Viney (op. cit.) also discuss the multidisciplinary nature of current academic discourse. They indicate that this discourse has focused on the careers of women, career transitions, the consequences of organizational restructuring upon alienation, and notions concerning career commitment and organizational loyalty. However, what is apparent in this literature is that the concept of career that has been developed, is academically based, is not grounded in the current experience of managers and appears not to have been questioned (Herriot 1992).

As examples, Arnold (1997), Arthur, Hall and Lawrence (1989) and Hirsch, Jackson and Jackson (1995) define 'career' as a sequence of work experiences over time. More specifically, Greenhaus (1987) defines 'career' as a pattern of work-related experiences that span the course of a person's life. These views emphasize the centrality of work and it is implied that work experience is continuous. No reference is made to the direct experience of managers through time where commonly and anecdotally, managers report they have had enforced breaks in their work experiences over the last fifteen years. Currently, it appears that careers for the majority are being appraised as short term, present oriented and non-hierarchical in terms of traditional views concerning work-based career progression. We suggest that in terms of career definitions a reorientation of purpose may have taken place through time because of the way work has been restructured over the past fifteen years. If this is the case, then there are questions that need to be asked concerning whether current academic interpretations of career decision making take these changes into account.

Career decision making

Academic career decision making has been heavily influenced by theories of career motivation. That is, the particular models have been developed in the context of historical definitions as discussed above. For instance, London (1983) develops a trait factor theory that identifies career resilience, career insight and career identity as important factors in career motivation. Career resilience is defined as the ability to adapt to changing circumstances even when the circumstances are disruptive or discouraging, career insight is defined as the ability to be realistic about the self and career and to put these perceptions to use in establishing goals, and career identity is defined as the extent to which one defines oneself by work. London suggests that resilience is a persistence/maintenance component, insight is the energizing/arousal component and identity is the direction of motivation component within the theory. London and Noe (1997) have updated the model to elucidate situational conditions that influence motivation and have a direct bearing on decision making. They specify the organizational conditions for resilience, insight and identity and suggest that person–situation interactions need to be understood in order to explain career decisions and behaviour. Prospective rationality suggests that the situation predicts the resilience, insight and identity of the individual, which in turn affects the individual's decisions and motivation, whereas retrospective rationality processes predict how behaviours influence the individual's feelings of career motivation and perceptions of the situation.

As with many trait factor theories, which attempt to focus on a dynamic process, the model may not be sufficiently robust to provide a useful insight into the changing circumstances within which career decisions are currently being negotiated and disrupted. London (1997), however, does distinguish between problem-focused and symptom-based strategies for coping with career barriers. London suggests that people who are resilient and have external support develop constructive, problem-focused coping strategies. Those who are vulnerable and lack support develop defensive, ineffective and possibly destructive, symptom based, coping responses. Latack, Kinicki and Prussia (1995) considered the process of appraisal involved in coping with and adapting to job loss. They suggest that individuals compare their status on various life facets with a referent goal or standard. These individuals then make a cognitive assessment of the extent to which discrepancies are seen as harmful or threatening before each individual sets a coping goal that becomes the individual's overall desired end.

Further, Howard and Bray (1988) suggest that personality characteristics are associated with career motivation and therefore career decision making. They suggest that as a person ages motivation changes due in part to changing career experiences. They found that managers' work involvement, optimism about their futures, job satisfaction and identification with management declined over time. Noe, Noe and Bachhuber (1990) report that individuals move through different career stages depending on their age. Less than 30 years of age individuals are preoccupied with learning their role and associated behaviours (Trial Stage). Between 31 and 45 years of age individuals develop career goals and have higher levels of career identity, insight and resilience (Stabilization Stage). After 46 years of age individuals have a decreased involvement in work with a decreasing importance placed on career goals (Maintenance Stage). Further they suggest career decisions are affected by situational characteristics as defined by managerial support for employee development and the particular job characteristics experienced by individuals. They report work conducted by Slocum and Cron (1985) which suggests that careers are best conceptualized as consisting of three stages which differ in the importance of work, family and personal issues at different points in time.

Currently, it is evident that individual managers in their careers, however defined, will have experienced several job changes brought about by a variety of circumstances. This has meant that managers will be less able to plan each career move long in advance. In a more dynamic, less certain employment market they will need to develop different decision-making approaches based on the continuous updating of their skills to maximize their ability to respond to each employment opportunity as it arises. Viney, Adamson and Doherty (1995) suggest that some organizations are now offering opportunities for individuals to develop their skills and competencies to increase their marketability or employability. They also suggest that the emphasis is becoming one where the individual will have to continuously consider their strengths, weaknesses, skills and attributes with reference to their perception about the nature of work opportunities that may materialize in the future in order to plan and affect their own personal development. There has been a shift from the deliberate development of people to match the organization's views of its human resource needs to an approach that emphasizes the individual's responsibility for their own career development (Herriot and Pemberton 1995). Individuals, careers, career decisions, situations and organizations are currently in a state of flux.

Implications

It appears there is a need to explore whether career definitions on the ground are changing in response to individual managers' experience of work. Heckscher and Donnelon (1994) suggest we have moved into a post-bureaucratic era in which we will have to accommodate to broader theoretical concepts, more fluid organizational structures and pervasive uncertainty. The literature concerning career motivation and decision making needs to accommodate both the emerging definition of career as well as the changing organizational pattern. The study of decision making as reported above either de-contextualizes the process, or refers to situations in terms that do not account for the transitory nature of the interaction between individuals at work and the organization. This appears to be the person–situation paradox. A more appropriate focus is one which grounds ideas concerning the definitions of careers in the experience of managers over the last fifteen years, and considers how individuals have made decisions, coped with and survived their work environments over that period of time, whilst attempting to maintain an acceptable lifestyle.

Methodological issues

As aspects of employment-related career management are well researched, this research aimed to identify the different aspects of an individual's life experience, which have influenced career and career decisions. The study focused on the experience of managers as a group because they have experienced the greatest turmoil in the last fifteen years and therefore would have had greater reason to develop strategies for self-managed career development. Part of the research was designed to identify whether the trend for self-managed career development was an experienced reality and whether current definitions of career 'fit' this reality.

In order to address these issues in depth, a qualitative grounded theory approach was used (Glaser and Strauss 1968), involving interviews with twenty-five members of a professional institute of management, located in the West Midlands. Twenty-five managers (twenty-two males and three females, aged between 34 and 61) were interviewed out of a possible pool of eighty-two. Those interviewed were members of the pool who could make themselves available for interview at a specific time. All of the collaborators in the research had been available for work since 1980. Each interview was semi-structured and lasted for approximately an hour. The main aims and questions of the researchers structured the first interview. Strauss and Corbin (1990) suggest the analysis of the preceding interview should form the basis of a developing analysis for the subsequent interviews.

After careful consideration this process of analysis was not followed after the first four interviews because the researchers came to the view that such a process encouraged the development of fixed interpretations of the data. Initially, this preliminary data was thought to be similar when comparisons were made, but on reflection further interviews not contextualized in this fashion provided data which was different, richer and more varied in the meanings that could be attributed. This was a direct result of understanding and applying Glaser's (1978) comments concerning the improvement of theoretical sensitivity. The first twenty interviews were transcribed verbatim; the other five were analysed directly from the tape recording. For those interviews transcribed a copy of the transcript was sent to the informant, who was asked to check that it represented an accurate account of the interview. In the event that an informant suggested modifications, the original recording was checked and the transcript modified only if the recording confirmed the informant's point. The transcripts were not analysed until the informant had confirmed that it was an accurate account of what they had said. The preliminary analysis from the taped interviews was also checked by informants to establish that the analysis reflected their views.

For the remainder of the analysis the method set out by Strauss and Corbin (op. cit.) was closely followed to ensure that the richness of the data was retained. This change required that, at the preliminary analysis stage, each interview was coded and analysed separately. As a check upon the analysis, a single transcript was given to a group of six other independent researchers. They were asked to undertake preliminary coding and then justify their coding to the group as a whole. The exercise provided a number of insights into the issues raised by the informant and in doing so considerably increased the richness of the interpretation of the data. The process was most useful and the improved interpretation influenced the subsequent analysis. After the categories were developed for each interview they were then brought together before further analysis developed the axial codes upon which subsequent conclusions were based. The analysis of each transcript was then re-examined against the analysis of the preceding interviews until theoretical saturation was reached. This extended the time taken but it allowed the analysis to be more open and receptive to the nuances of each individual interview.

The researchers decided to stop collecting more data because they had met the criteria for both appropriate depth, appropriate analysis of core axial codes and for the development of appropriately sensitive theoretical concepts (Strauss and Corbin op. cit.).

The research

By applying the grounded theory methodology the researchers established a large body of data which would be impossible to report in great detail.

As there is a limitation of space the researchers will present the main propositions of the theory which is grounded in the experience of the managers. The key five theoretical constructs are career, career decisions, balance, employment action and life events.

Career

All the managers, in our study, had experience of more than one form of employment relationship with an organization, including temporary, part time, permanent, or full-time. In addition many managers had experienced redundancy in the last fifteen years. From the interviews a consensus emerged about the elements that defined the idea of the nature and purpose of their career. They were asked to describe their own idea of the nature of a career. We report that their descriptions of career had three elements: the first concerned skills, education and experience; the second concerned the relationship individual had with an employer; and the third concerned the need to maintain and develop individual lifestyles. As a result the grounded definition of career that informed this research was as follows: 'A career is the long-term accumulation of education, skills and experience that an individual sells to an employer or employers, to try to provide the lifestyle that he or she wants for himself or herself and dependants.'

Clearly, this definition does not stress employment-based achievement as the outcome of career choices and employment. Rather it concentrates on that individual's attempt to achieve a balance between work and life-style. That is, the managers in the research were stating that the purpose of a career was to provide an appropriate lifestyle. (The definition of lifestyle included reference to the person's current and future aspirations in relation to the standard of their personal and domestic way of life.) They made decisions that attempted to maintain a balance in the relationship between demands and their aspirations at work and those of the other aspects of their life. We found our managers made decisions within a personal framework of values, beliefs, aspirations and expectations concerning appropriate levels of personal satisfaction, either domestically or at work. It was interesting that some of the respondents emphasized the satisfaction in community related activity was part of their definition of personal aspiration:

> I want to see myself as a recognized figure in the local community . . . that is a sort of career goal. To develop the scope of my role in the community, in the local community and within my profession.
>
> (34-year-old male respondent)

Many of those with a family emphasized the importance of their family in making decisions about their own job:

> My family is the most important thing [in my life], work comes second. [If my wife was offered a better job which meant that we had to move] I would certainly consider moving [and giving up my job].
>
> (38-year-old male respondent)

It was noticeable that those respondents who had invested considerable time and effort in achieving a high level of academic qualification saw it as an investment that they would want to be realized in terms of increased future earnings. Without exception they translated the need for greater earnings in terms that related to their own and their family's lifestyle:

> I've put a lot of effort into getting qualified, I want a job that recognises that and in turn gives me the money to let me and my family enjoy life.
>
> (53-year-old respondent)

> I financed my own MBA so I don't owe my present employer anything. My next job is to sell myself, with my qualifications, for as much as I can get. I want financial security and to keep a roof over [my family's] heads.
>
> (34-year-old respondent)

It should be noted, however, that one of the older managers reported that: 'A career is a journey through working life which is influenced more by others than by yourself' (61-year-old respondent).

Career decisions

In analysing data what became apparent was the differences in the extent to which individuals believed, at the beginning of their working lives, they could or should be in control of their working lives. Through the research there was clear evidence suggesting that many managers, who started work in subordinate posts expected little support for career development from the organizations in which they worked. However, after a short period of years in work they recognized that they needed to take greater control of their career for themselves. Within this broad context it also became clear that there were different influences, in relation to work, lifestyle, and their careers that individuals acknowledged that had an effect on their career decisions and beliefs about their effectiveness. These were as follows:

1   Individual influences: personal attributes such as personal/professional skills, education, perceptions, beliefs concerning effectiveness of their control and balance.

2   Domestic influences: relationships with others of greater or lesser personal significance and the responsibilities that those relationships impose upon the individual.

3   Employment influences: a negotiated contract that provides intrinsic satisfaction but also the means of enabling the individual to satisfy the demands and responsibilities in the other areas of his/her life.

In some cases the individual believed that these influences were apparent within the one area but the majority identified that the most common situation was one in which there was an interaction between them.

Within each of these areas which influenced decision making we found differences that suggested an individual's family background, formal education and experience, that is his/her personality, framed their perceptions. These individual personal styles set individual evaluations of personal aspirations and satisfaction experienced in the context of decisions made personally, domestically and in employment. Additionally, there was evidence that the environment in which these factors interacted had an effect upon the way and extent to which each individual would respond. Whilst there are events in society that overwhelm the ability of the individual to make choices, the majority of decisions made by the managers took into account the environment as it existed at the time of choice.

We also found that personal aspirations and the satisfaction experienced provided a framework that individuals applied when evaluating the effects of change in the different areas of their career. For instance, some reported that they responded to changes in satisfaction levels experienced at work by acknowledging that this was having an effect on their beliefs concerning their effectiveness and the quality of relationships they were experiencing domestically. Several collaborators reported changes in levels of satisfaction, some indicated that there were implications for other aspects of their lives, and some did not. We believe that this was because of the way individuals framed their perceptions of these events in a way that was specific to them and, therefore, different from others.

Balance

The definition of career applied by managers implies an attempt by individuals to create and maintain a balance between work-related demands and those of their own self-esteem, their family and its lifestyle. The relationship between the individual and work is perceived as satisfying, if it provides for the maintenance and development, by that individual of an appropriate lifestyle. If these elements are in balance, the individual will experience a form of psychological equilibrium leading to satisfaction, and maintenance of the status quo: 'There are more things in life than aspiring to bigger and better things . . . what you need is a balance between work and your private life' (9-year-old respondent).

This status quo may be dynamic in that it can include the situation in which the individual seeks regular advancement in terms of skills, status, reward, or lifestyle. However, if they are not in balance, for example if the individual is made redundant, then he or she will experience an imbalance as the possibilities for lifestyle maintenance become threatened. Commonly, this imbalance led to the high levels of anxiety and the experience reduced some managers' capacity to respond rationally to the situation.

> You don't know quite what to do (following a notification of redundancy). I hadn't prepared a CV, I should have but I didn't. I was so shocked it took ages to get one sorted out.
>
> (48-year-old male respondent)

However, managers also reported that changes in the circumstances in one area of their lives could create imbalances in other areas, and it was difficult to predict how a specific event would influence their decisions. They had to choose between various actions that they could take to adjust to one or more of their individual, domestic, or employment circumstances.

A manager having decided that he or she was deficient in some skill area might commit time usually devoted to the family for personal development. If this action successfully addressed the issue, the short-term imbalance in the domestic situation was seen to have been worth it. They felt that after the initial turmoil and anxiety experienced when imbalance was identified, they became more satisfied as a result of taking the appropriate action. This response occurred with managers who were consistent in managing their careers. With those who had an *ad hoc* response to career management, efforts to restore balance were also unpredictable and *ad hoc*. It was reported by some who had experienced difficulties in domestic arrangements that these difficulties had led to a reduction in the level of commitment to organizational career. Also, these difficulties affected decisions and/or actions taken which could have led to the adoption of a different form of employment and of lifestyle.

> Well, I got sacked . . . My wife had decided to walk out on me, so all kind of things were happening at the time . . . I'm sure that I contributed to it by . . . arguing with the FD (Financial Director).
>
> (43-year-old respondent)

> . . . my daughters are in their teens and I don't really fancy [the life of a consultant] so I decided to join them [a new employer].
>
> (52-year-old respondent)

What was reported shows that if one aspect of an individual's life is affected and creates a perceived imbalance relative to other aspects, then the anxiety experienced acts to motivate action. The action taken attempts to restore a balance between the personal, the domestic and the employment relationship to maintain lifestyle commitments.

Employment action

We found that individuals took action that attempted to effect a change in relation to their employment (employment action) either to maintain the current balance in their careers or to reduce the anxiety caused by perceptions of the possibility for imbalance sometime in the future. In this way individuals attempted to exert control over the circumstances created by a change that could occur in relation to them personally, domestically, or in their employment. However, individual beliefs about their own ability to control the outcome of any action taken and its beneficial effects varied within the group of managers interviewed. We found that managers were proactive or reactive dependent not only on their beliefs as mentioned but also on the individual's perceptions of their personal, domestic and employment circumstances. Much depended upon the individual's belief about how amenable these circumstances were to moderation; the repertoire of skills and actions available to him or her and the extent to which a particular action was thought to be prejudicial to the maintenance of balance in other areas of their life.

This is a simplification of a complex issue, for, in reality, managers had the view that there were areas in their life in which they could be proactive in making decisions concerning action whilst in others they reported they could only react to the situation as it emerged. Managers identified that there were unexpected life events that had minor or major effects on the career decisions they made.

Life events

All the collaborators in the research gave accounts of events in their lives over which the individual had little or no control, the consequences of which had a significant impact upon that person's life and career. The range of such events was considerable and varied from a near fatal road accident to divorce.

> I had a wonderful driving accident . . . I think it was God with a yellow card saying 'watch what you are doing', so I started to look for another job.
>
> (53-year-old respondent)

> After I got over the shock of the divorce, I realised that I was happier being on my own . . . My career really started to take off. I am very content.
>
> (46-year-old female respondent)

We found that the impact of such events on career decisions may be direct or indirect. A direct impact was, for example, where managers decided to end current employment and find an alternative, perhaps by 'down shifting' which is a deliberate decision to work at a lower level of responsibility than in the past, accepting what is seen as a less affluent lifestyle. An indirect impact, reported by managers, was where the event led to a re-appraisal of some or all of the different aspects of a career as defined by the individual, where the non-work circumstances dictated the nature of the employment commitment.

An important issue established with managers was the extent to which individuals believed that they could exercise control over events. To a large extent respondents who had experience of resolving or recovering from conflicts believed they had achieved greater balance and control over more areas of their life. They perceived that there were courses of action that could be taken that would be effective. In addition they appeared to have a greater repertoire of actions they could deploy.

> I have been in this job for 18 years and I have never had to think of moving . . . now I will be 50 in three weeks time and my job will end next month, there's not a lot I can do, I wish I knew what would be best.
>
> (50-year-old respondent)

However, the success or otherwise of an employment action taken was also a function of the extent to which an individual had support from others. The quality of support was important for the career decision made, for taking risks in career decisions and for employment actions taken. For single people with few domestic responsibilities the opportunity for the creation and development of a broad support network of other people depended largely upon an individual's personality.

> I have a guy who I used to work for years ago we are really good friends and we always talk over problems with one another. He was a great support when I was made redundant and I helped him with some personal problems.
>
> (57-year-old respondent)

In contrast those managers with permanent relationships and with dependants reported that the level of support they received depended on both their partner's and their own attitude to taking risks within their set of domestic relationships.

> I would certainly discuss it [a job-related problem] with my wife and perhaps family and a couple of close friends.
>
> (33-year-old respondent)

Oh there were problems [involved in taking a new job], I talked it through with my wife, who has been incredibly supportive.

(58-year-old respondent)

Critical analysis

The research indicates that definitions of career in current usage are at variance with academically oriented definitions as reported earlier. The definitions used by our managers confirm the shift in emphasis identified by Adamson, Doherty and Viney (1998). We found that it was more important to study the 'everyday usage' of the term 'career' as this reflected the way in which the individual manager approached the problem of making meaningful career decisions. We have found that the definitions used by our managers emphasize a utilitarian psychological contract with employers. This showed that individuals made career-related decisions because of their current experience of work and their dissatisfaction with their own definition of themselves, their social status and lifestyle. We show that managers use a broader canvas with which to make career decisions. The underlying purpose of their work careers was short term and utilitarian but designed to support themselves and their families in a desirable long-term lifestyle. This concurs with the views of Bailyn and Schein (1976) and the findings of Schein (1978) that people's concern for the family significantly affects their view of their careers. Watkins and Drury (1994) report that studies show that many employees would willingly reduce their working hours to spend more time on family or community responsibilities.

We established a clear link between career definitions in use and the effects that these definitions have on career decisions. Each individual has to make decisions that affect the continuity of employment and the progress of his or her career. More employees want more control over their careers according to Giles and West (1995). Gunz (1989) writes of career transitions that represent choices between opportunities presented to individuals by organizations. However, Guest and Mackenzie (1996) found that whilst managers recognized the need to manage their own careers, far too many could not find the time and did not accord it sufficient priority to make it happen. Indeed Griffiths (1980) reported that in 75 per cent of 500 major American companies less than 25 per cent of the workforce participated in career development activity. The management of an individual's career requires them to respond to a variety of situations. Goffee and Scase (1992) identified that managers responses to career disappointment varied according to a number of factors including, for example, their age, gender, marketable skills, family commitments, and so on. We found some managers were consistent in the way they approached the management of their careers, others were less consistent and responded in a more random way to issues. As we report earlier London (1997) distinguishes between problem-focused and symptom-based strategies for overcoming career barriers. However, his explanation refers to work barriers and does not explain the possible effects of utilizing these strategies in relation to the effects of life events and the consequences of both for a manager's lifestyle.

Equally the work of Derr (1986), Holland (1985) and Schein (1978), which focuses on the decision making at the beginning of a career, and Noe, Noe and Bachhuber (1990), discussing career stages throughout a working life, was not particularly helpful. This literature fails to provide an insight into how managers have made career decisions regularly throughout a working life characterized by turbulence in the work environment and sometimes turbulence in their personal lives.

In a study of 532 male middle managers Bartholome and Evans (1979) found that half were dissatisfied with the way in which they were investing time and energy in their professional rather than their private lives. Bhagat and Ford (1990: 99–112) describe how

> In a modern society, work and non-work roles are becoming increasingly interdependent. However, while considerable knowledge exists concerning the effects of variables specific to each of theses roles on the psychological well-being of individuals, relatively little research attention has been directed to the nature of the interactions that exist between them.

This research has identified that there is an interaction between work and lifestyle that impacts on the career decisions an individual manager would make in order to maintain a form of psychological balance.

The causes of work and family conflict have been identified by Greenhaus and Beutell (1984), whilst Cooke and Rousseau (1984) have examined the prevalence of conflicts between work and family life, particularly for women. They found that a substantial minority of workers experienced such conflict. Their work did not show whether this was more prevalent amongst managers although they identified the principal causes as long working hours. We found that the first response our managers made to such a situation was to resolve the problem at work if possible. If this was unsuccessful we found the likelihood of the individual changing employment was increased, as was the likelihood of some change in the individual's domestic situation. Bell and Staw (1989: 232–51) suggest that

> to the extent that the person has made previous attempts at personal control he or she should understand what is involved in making these attempts. To the extent that these attempts have been rewarded in the past, the person will have learned which sort of attempts have high probabilities of success.

Clearly what we found was a complex of experiences reported by managers which represented their experiences of life, not only work. We believe that London's (1983) concept of career identity needs to be modified. Through the data we found that managers adopted a multiple identity in relation to lifestyle contexts. We found that lifestyle needs motivated managers as much as career identity needs. However, we also found, as Bell and Staw (1989) suggest, that 'because most people want to feel efficacious, they are likely to attempt some measure of control over their environments'. We found that this extends outside the environment of work and covers both domestic and private environments. Our findings lead us to believe that if individuals needs for control are frustrated in one of these environments they will attempt to exercise greater control over the others. We found that frustration in an attempt to control their work-based career caused the majority of managers, in this study, to seek greater control in other areas of their lives. This confirms the findings of Goffee and Scase (1992) who suggest that for male managers there appears to have been a distinct shift in personal priorities over recent decades. In our view, unfulfilled career expectations, together with the increasing dissatisfaction and uncertainty associated with programmes of organizational restructuring, have encouraged them to withdraw psychologically from work and to seek greater personal rewards in their private lives. This is a view that is repeated by Tyson (1995) in his comment that 'If anything lifestyles are changing to give greater emphasis to home life and to more personal values.'

This view can be refined by reference to Bell and Staw's (op. cit.) model of personal control in organizations. They argue that an individual's ability to self-monitor reflects a tendency to rely on features of the situation when making organization-based choices. They distinguish between high self-monitors who are situation dependent, and low self-monitors, who rely on their own inner state in making choices. We found that when individuals failed to achieve an acceptable level of control in a preferred environment (work, home and leisure), they would attempt a higher level of control in one of their other environments. We found that managers applied control strategies like this in environments that were amenable to the level of control that was acceptable to them as individuals. Therefore, we believe that control strategies do not apply to organizational choices only; they are also applied to establish the priorities given to different aspects of the interaction between career and lifestyle as we discuss it here. This is congruent with Super's (1986) findings.

Clearly the focus of the research was on career definitions and career decisions. However, issues concerning balance, control and coping with changes in career were also found to be important in terms of their possible effects on decisions made. We found that the personal characteristics of individuals and the ability they developed 'to sculpt' (Bell and Staw op. cit.) an appropriate career pathway as individuals was important. We also found that distinctions could be drawn between proactive and reactive managers in relation to how they responded to critical events like redundancy. This relates to Bell and Staw's (ibid.) classification of 'situational receivers' and 'active interpreters' where the coping strategies we identified resonated with London's (1997) categorization of symptom-based and problem-focused strategies. We found that the personal attributes and beliefs of an individual manager would tend to enable distinctions to be drawn between those managers who would be able to cope with the exigencies of situations as they developed, and those who would have greater difficulty.

For instance, we found that the proactive managers in the group believed that they could exert some positive control over situations and events as they evolved. Whereas those who were reactive to events tended to believe they could not exert control and consequently were poorly prepared to deal with the events as they occurred. The proactive group of managers tended to respond better to these events such as redundancy in that they were prepared to seek out support networks and use them. They reported that they believed that they suffered considerably less stress than others they knew in a similar situation. This supports the finding of Granovetter (1973) and Perri 6 (1997). These proactive managers also believed that taking responsibility for managing their own careers was important in learning to cope with such events.

Conclusions and key learning points

In this research we show that there has been a clear shift in the way that managers address issues concerning the management of their careers in the light of the experience they have gained through work over the past fifteen years. We provide evidence to show that:

1 Personal, domestic and employment critical events create situations that lead to re-appraisals of decisions made with regard to career and career development.
2 There are individual differences in terms of responses made to unpredictable critical events that can occur during the course of a career.
3 Career decisions made by this group of managers strive to maintain a form of balance between the personal, the domestic and the employment aspects of an individual's life.
4 Responsibility for career development is beginning to be recognized as the responsibility of the individual manager and not of organizations, but this shift is dependent on how individuals define career and on whether or not they have experienced critical employment events.

Theoretically, the evidence we present supports the view that individual managers are slowly realizing that organizations may be paying 'lip service' to the rhetoric of HR professionals when advocating organizational change strategies. Those of our managers that had experienced a significant employment event, such as redundancy believed that they were responsible for the development of their own career and that organizations were unreliable in terms of providing appropriate means for development. Many believed that employers were over demanding in their requirements of managers who believed that their relationship with work organizations was likely to be impermanent. This lends some support to views of Hutton (1995) and Kanter (1989) and develops the idea of the individual being responsible for their own career development (Herriot and Pemberton 1995).

Relationships that are important to a person can be described in terms of individual psychological contract. The evidence of this study suggest that for some managers the dominant psychological contract is with their significant others outside their current employment. As a result, we found career decisions do not always take into consideration or depend upon issues related to either the employer or the individual's employment.

In our research there was some evidence that managers as a group, had redefined the psychological contract with organizations for which they worked. The uncertainties in employment that many of these managers have experience over the last fifteen years, have led them to adopt strategies for maximizing their relationship with organizations, but not at the same level of commitment as in the past. The creation and maintenance of a domestic and personal lifestyle now balances that commitment. As managers felt and perceived that organizations had a different form of commitment to them, they expressed a different, more cynical and instrumental commitment to their employing organization. Managers' expected organizations to provide opportunities for the development of their marketability and employability (Viney, Adamson and Doherty 1995), as well as providing adequately for the maintenance of the preferred lifestyle. Managers also sensed that organizations implicitly and sometimes explicitly communicated a relative lack of opportunities for development that they were able or prepared to offer their employer. Many spoke about the relative impermanence of the employment relationship. Herriot (1992) suggests that relationships between individuals and organizations are permeated by a psychological contract of mutual expectation. He suggests that if there is clear communication of these expectations then the understanding of the organizational and the individual will match and a balance will be achieved and maintained. We provide evidence to show how individual managers are adjusting to the changes by adopting career strategies that have as their purpose the maintenance of lifestyle, rather than the survival of a work-defined career.

Implications for HRD practice

This research demonstrates that there are substantial disparities between the perspectives of involved individuals which results in a different definition of 'career' as compared with that posited by academic career theory. We believe that this is caused by the academic stance being heavily focused upon two approaches. The first, the psychological approach, is focused upon the relationship between the individual employee's personality and his or her career, in which 'career' is defined in terms that relate to the personal demands of the individual. The second, the sociological approach, is focused upon the relationship between the employer and the employee, in which 'career' is defined in terms that balance the demands of the employer with those of the employee as they occur in the working environment. Both offer a model for explaining the relationships that affect the individual but neither fully recognizes the importance of the broader basis upon which the individual seeks to define his or her career in terms of the achievement of a lifestyle for the individual and his or her family. Nor do the current academic approaches take account of the impact of domestic and personal changes upon the decisions the individual makes in relation to the management of his or her career. It is these later aspects that emerge as important issues to the individual, from a methodology that is grounded in the lived experience.

It is clear that a gap exists between theories that HRD practitioners use and upon which they base their practice and the lived experience of the individuals affected by that practice. By exploring this gap there is an opportunity for practitioners to discover different realities and to use the insights gained to better inform their practice. In order to understand the differences and to attempt to close the gap, practitioners will need to be aware of the alternative perspectives that may be obtained by viewing a problem using different research methodologies. The reported study demonstrates that research grounded in the lived experience of the participants can challenge the accepted academic definitions and the understanding of a subject. In addition, it can illuminate an issue in ways that are not readily seen from other perspectives. Vigorous qualitative research is difficult and challenging; it breaks away from the more usual quantitative methodologies and requires the practitioner to develop new analytical skills and perspectives. We suggest that the investment in time and effort to develop and secure these new skills are worthwhile in that they enable the practitioners to gain fresh insights.

At the most basic level our research implies that HRD practitioners need to recognize that for an individual, the opportunity for involvement in career development may be seen as having a deleterious impact upon their lifestyle. In the face of such a possibility it is for the practitioner to set out the implications of the development for a participant's lifestyle so that the individual may make assessments based upon information rather than on speculation. It may be helpful here to point out that no assumptions can be made about the ambitions of an individual; the only way in which they can be identified is by approaching the person directly. Too often individuals have to be coerced into participating in HRD activities because they are unsure about the implications for their careers, as they define them. Such situations occur when those who initiate an individual's involvement have made assumptions about what that individual seeks to achieve. HRD practice needs to recognize that whilst few individuals may openly reject opportunities that may lead to promotion, they will be consciously assessing the impact that such a promotion will have on their lifestyle.

As we have outlined individuals report that they need to achieve balance between the different influences on their lives. The activities of the HRD can have profound impact upon this balance. The reactions from an individual will depend upon his or her assessment of the extent to which the imbalance will distort his or her current lifestyle or that to which he or she aspires. It may be difficult for a given individual to articulate his or her concerns over the achievement of a particular balance, particularly if the ethos within the workplace seeks to ignore the domestic and personal influence upon the individual's life.

Employees who fail to respond to the opportunities offered by HRD may be seen by less perceptive employers as lacking motivation or ambition. Whilst this may be true, it is important to recognize that some employees may have their ambitions focused outside their current employment. There is much speculation on the causes for the growing number of employees who are reported as lacking an employment-focused ambition. One explanation, which has resonance with our work, is that the lack of security and reduced confidence in the continuity of their employment leads employees, to focus their ambitions on themselves or their family situation, in which they are better able to create a sense of control, security and continuity. Such changes would explain the following responses by an individual who perceives that there is a significant imbalance in his or her life:

Downshifting, the deliberate search for and acceptance of a lower paid less demanding post.

Plateauing, where the individual no longer actively seeks promotion or career development in order to derive greater satisfaction from his or her personal or domestic life.

Major Career Change, faced with the prospect of not being able to achieve an acceptable level of satisfaction or lifestyle, the individual seeks to find employment that does offer greater balance within his or her life.

Whilst the first of these actions becomes self-evident such a deliberate rejection of the ethos of the majority can raise concerns for the employer and the individual's colleagues. In the second case, it can sometimes take the HRD practitioner a little time to realize that an individual has decided not to actively pursue further career development. Indeed, it is possible that the individual has not come to a conscious decision but rather simply allowed the active of the management of his or her career to lapse. In the third situation, the wish expressed by an employee to change career direction can present the HRD practitioner with a considerable challenge. Support for such person would imply that the employer is willing to invest time and effort in someone who is actively trying to leave their employ. It may also challenge both the employer's and the HRD practitioners' perceptions on acceptable or realistic career choices.

HRD practitioners should recognize that their approach to issues depends upon their perceptual framework that, in turn, depends upon a particular epistemological foundation. As we have demonstrated, approaching issues using different methodologies can challenge preconceptions and offer fresh and cogent insights that can confront and inform their practice.

References

Adamson, Doherty and Viney (1998) 'The Meaning of Career Revisited', *British Journal of Management*, 9(4): 251–9.

Arnold, J. (1997) *Managing Careers into the 21st Century*, London: Paul Chapman Publishing.

Arthur, M.B., Hall, D.T. and Lawrence, B.S. (1989) *Handbook of Career Theory*, Cambridge: Cambridge University Press.

Bailyn, L. and Schein, E.H. (1976) *Life/Career Considerations as Indicators of Quality of Employment*, in A.D. Biderman and F. Drury (eds) *Measuring work quality for social reporting*, New York: Wiley.

Barham, K., Fraser, J. and Heath, L. (1988) *Management for the Future*, Project Report, Ashridge College.

Bartholome, F. and Evans, P. (1979) 'Professional lives vs. private lives: shifting patterns of managerial commitment', *Organisational Dynamics*, Spring: 2–29.

Bell, N.E. and Staw, B.M. (1989) 'People as sculptors versus sculpture: the roles of personality and personal control in organisations', in M.B. Arthur, D.T. Hall and B.S. Lawrence (eds) *Handbook of Career Theory*, Cambridge: Cambridge University Press.

Benbow, N. (1995) *Survival of the Fittest: Institute of Management, Research Report*, London: Institute of Management.

Bhagat, S. and Ford, D.L. (1990) 'Work and non-work issues in the management of occupational careers in the 1990s', in J.C. Quick, R.E. Hess, J. Hermalin and J.D. Quick (eds) *Career Stress in Changing Times*, Binghampton, NY.

Cooke, R.A. and Rousseau, D.M. (1984) 'Stress and strain form family roles and work-role expectations', *Journal of Applied Psychology*, 69(2): 252–60.

Derr, C.B. (1986) *Managing the New Careerist*, San Francisco: Jossey-Bass.

Economist (1995) 'The Salaryman Rides Again, management focus', *Economist* 334, 2 February.

Giles, M. and West, M. (1995) 'People as sculptors versus sculptures: what shape career development programmes?', *Journal of Management Development*, 14(10): 48–64.

Glaser, B. (1978) *Theoretical Sensitivity*, Mill Valley, CA: Sociology Press.

Glaser, B. and Strauss, A. (1968) *The Discovery of Grounded Theory*, London: Weidenfeld and Nicolson.

Goffee, R. and Scase, R. (1992) 'Organisational change and the corporate career: the re-structuring of managers' job aspirations', *Human Relations*, 45: 363–85.

Granovetter, M.S. (1973) 'The strength of weak ties', *American Journal of Sociology*, 78: 1360–80.

Greenhaus, D.K. and Beutell, N.T. (1984) 'Sources of conflict between work and family roles', *Academy of Management Review*, 10: 76–88.

Greenhaus, J.H. (1987) *Career Management*, New York: Dryden Press.

Griffiths, A.R. (1980) 'Career development: what organisations are doing about it', *Personnel*, 57(2): 63–9.

Guest, D. and Mackenzie, D.K. (1996) 'Don't write off the traditional career', *People Management*, February: 22–5.

Gunz, H. (1989) 'The dual meaning of managerial careers: organisational and individual levels of analysis', *Journal of Management Studies*, 26(3): 225–50.

Handy, C. (1989) *The Age of Unreason*, London: Random – Century.

Heckscher, C. and Donnelon, A. (1994) *The Post-Bureaucratic Organisation: New Perspectives on Organisational Change*, Thousand Oaks, CA: Sage.

Herriot, P. (1992) *The Career Management Challenge: Balancing Individual and Organisational Needs*, London: Sage.

Herriot, P. and Pemberton, C. (1995) *New Deals: the Revolution in Managerial Careers*, Chichester: Wiley.

Hirsch, W., Jackson, C. and Jackson, C. (1995) *Careers in Organisations: Issues for the Future*, IES Report 287, Brighton: Institute of Employment Studies.

Holland, J.L. (1985) *Making Vocational Choices: a Theory of Personality and Work Environments*, Englewood Cliffs, NJ: Prentice-Hall.

Howard, A. and Bray, D.W. (1988) *Managerial Lives in Transition: Advancing Age and Changing Times*, New York: Guilford Press.

Hutton, W. (1995) *The State We're In*, London: Cape.

Inkson, K. and Coe, T. (1993) *Are Career Ladders Disappearing?*, London: Institute of Management.

Kanter, R.M. (1989) *When Giants Learn to Dance*, New York: Simon and Schuster.

Latack, J.C., Kinicki, A.J. and Prussia, G.E. (1995) 'An integrative process model for coping with job loss', *Academy of Management Review*, 20: 311–42.

London, M. (1983) 'Towards a theory of career motivation', *Academy of Management Review*, 8: 620–30.

—— (1997) 'Overcoming career barriers: a model of cognitive and emotional processes for realistic appraisal and constructive coping', *Journal of Career Development*, 24(1).

London, M. and Noe, R.A. (1997) 'London's career motivation theory: an update on measurement and research', *Journal of Career Assessment*, 5(1): 61–80.

London, M. and Stumpf, S. (1982) *Managing Careers*, Reading, MA: Addison-Wesley.

Nicholson, N. and West, M. (1988) *Managerial Job Change: Men and Women in Transition*, Cambridge: Cambridge University Press.

Noe, R.A., Noe, A.W. and Bachhuber, J.A. (1990) 'An investigation of the correlates of career motivation', *Journal of Vocational Behaviour*, 37: 340–56.

Perri 6 (1997) *Escaping Poverty: From safety nets to networks of opportunity*, London: Demos.

Pleck, J.H., Staines, G.L. and Lang, L.L. (1980) 'Conflicts between work and family life', *Monthly Labour Review*, 103(3): 29–32.

Scase, R. and Goffee, R. (1989) *Reluctant Managers: Their Work and Life Styles*, London: Unwin Hyman.

Schein, E.H. (1978) *Career Dynamics: Matching Individual and Organisational Need*, Reading, MA: Addison-Wesley.

Slocum, J.W. and Cron, W.L. (1985) 'Job attitudes and performance during three career stages', *Journal of Vocational Behaviour*, 26: 126–45.

Strauss, A. and Corbin, J. (1990) *Basics of qualitative research: Grounded Theory Procedures and Techniques*, Newbury Park, CA: Sage.

Super, D.E. (1986) 'Life career roles: self-realisation in work and leisure', in D.T. Hall (ed.) *Career Development in Organisations*, Englewood Cliffs, NJ: Prentice-Hall.

Tyson, S. (1995) *Strategic Prospects for Human Resource Management*, London: Institute of Personnel and Development.

Viney, C., Adamson, S.J. and Doherty, N. (1995) 'Organisations' expectations and career management of fast track recruits', paper to The New Deal in Employment Conference, City University Business School, December.

Vrakking, W. (1991) 'The Innovating Organisation', *Long Range Planning*, 23(2): 94–102.

Watkins, J. and Drury, L. (1994) *Positioning for the Unknown: Career Development for Professionals in the 1990s*, Bristol: University of Bristol.

15

GOING NATIVE!

Ethnographic research in HRD

Rona S. Beattie

Aims and contribution

This chapter aims to enhance understanding of the processes, benefits and challenges involved in ethnographic research by exploring the operational and ethical issues involved in undertaking such research. This will be achieved through discussing and evaluating the experiences of a part-time doctoral researcher who undertook research in a voluntary organization of which she is a member. It is hoped that this chapter will contribute to greater understanding of the reality and challenges involved in conducting research in an organization to which the researcher belongs.

The rationale for using participant observation as a research process will be explored, in particular highlighting its role in preparing the researcher for more substantive empirical research, including in-depth interviews, through the opportunity to immerse oneself in the organization. The chapter will discuss the advantages of participant observation, e.g. flexibility and the ability to develop more intimacy with respondents thus providing greater access to information and the motives of respondents. The disadvantages of such an approach are also explored including the potential for the researcher to have an influence on those being researched, particularly given her 'management' role in the organization.

The chapter will:

- explore taxonomies of field roles and provide a rationale for the role selected;
- describe how access was negotiated;
- describe how the research was conducted to minimize researcher impact;
- discuss the practicalities of participant observation including such issues as maintaining objectivity, personal style, keeping field notes and the requirement for stamina;
- outline how ethical issues were dealt with given the dual role of researcher and manager.

The chapter will conclude with the author's personal reflection on this research experience, which she feels gave her a powerful insight into the culture, life and history of the organization. She does, however, acknowledge the risk of going 'native'.

Theoretical context

Introduction

The theoretical area being investigated is the role of the line manager as a developer of people and their part in linking individual and organizational learning. A role that has been defined as 'The Developmental Manager actively develops self, staff and peers' (Beattie 1996: 1).

This role is seen as increasingly important (AMED 1991; Mumford 1993; Heraty and Morley 1995; IPD 1995) but Mumford argues that it has been neglected in the management development literature compared to other topics. Mumford notes that 'The increased attention to development on and through the job inevitably throws greater weight on managers themselves as developers of others. Surprisingly little (literature) is available on this' (1993: 227).

This increasing involvement was confirmed by an IES study investigating the skills required for managers in the twenty-first century, which confirmed that key skills needed included development, coaching and counselling (Bevan, Toye and Frost 1995).

Whilst there is an extensive literature on specific developmental roles, such as mentoring and coaching, much of it is prescriptive, and there are relatively few examples of empirical research exploring the day-to-day interactions between managers and their staff which facilitate or inhibit learning. Indeed Mumford argues that looking at processes and coaching are an inappropriate place to start. He suggests that

> instead of leaping into the use of these terms it is more sensible to start from where managers are, to look at ways in which they are experienced in helping others, and only then to look at whether words and processes such as coaching and mentoring are useful.
>
> (Op. cit.: 94)

This would suggest that research strategies that adopt a phenomenological approach incorporating an ethnographic element would help us understand what managers actually *do* to help others learn. The use of participant observation to gain an insight into managerial life was used successfully by Watson (1994). He argues that the key is to get 'closely involved . . . with managers to learn more about the day-to-day activities of managing and especially, to find out how managers cope with (manage!) the challenges that their work roles entail' (Watson and Harris 1999: 16).

This research is therefore attempting to explore the developmental inter-actions between line managers and their staff to identify the behaviours of effective developmental managers, thus addressing this gap in HRD knowledge. It is argued that an analysis of significant episodes or critical incidents from individual's careers where managers have had a positive (or negative) impact on the development of their staff could provide a deeper insight into the behaviour of developmental managers.

Presented below is an overview of current knowledge on this topic.

Devolving HRD to the line

It has been argued that the growing interest in human resource manage-ment *per se* has heightened interest in management and the development of management skills, given that in all models of human resource manage-ment 'the job of the manager is fundamentally reconstructed and is seen as pivotal' (Salaman 1995: 12). In the 1990s it was recognized that there was a growing trend towards line management involvement in HRM in the UK and Europe, which was expected to continue (IPD: 1995).

In particular there was a growing recognition that responsibility for a range of HRD activities had been devolved increasingly to line managers (AMED 1991; Mumford 1993; Cabinet Office 1993; Bevan and Hayday 1994; Heraty and Morley 1995; Bevan, Toye and Frost 1995; Ellinger, Watkins and Barnas 1999). The rationale being that devolving of staff development responsibilities can be highly effective as the assessment and delivery of training is delivered to employees in the workplace. Indeed Salaman argues that the central role of the manager and the essence of management are to improve subordinates' work, and indeed that 'key managerial competences . . . are those which support the management of performance or the management of learning, for this is seen as the key activity of managers *qua* managers' (1995: 5).

However, the effectiveness of such an approach depends significantly on the individuals who are carrying it out (Heraty and Morley 1995). There is therefore a pressing need to identify the development needs of line managers with regards to their developmental roles (AMED 1991). However, before addressing managers' development needs it has to be recognized that there are potential barriers to effective devolution of HRD.

Barriers to effective devolution

Various Cabinet Office reports (1991, 1993) have identified barriers to greater delegation of human resource development responsibilities. These included: the perception of managers that they will gain little from taking on such responsibilities; lack of time; lack of strategic direction from the organization; inadequate support from personnel and top management; lack of role clarity; and lack of accountability and performance monitoring.

317

A number of Bevan and Hayday's respondents identified a conflict between developmental and operational objectives, in particular they highlighted that they experienced role ambiguity between 'the need to be both a task-orientated business manager and a more socially-orientated manager of people' (1994: 16). This was exacerbated by the devolution of other business activities.

Bevan and Hayday (op. cit.) identified three key problems. First, in the area of assessing individuals managers were uncomfortable about using appraisals to determine pay and to identify development needs. Some managers were also reluctant to make medium- or long-term predictions about individuals' potential, and felt they had insufficient knowledge to make such judgements, 'and that they need more guidance on how to perform this role' (ibid.: 8). Second, regarding corporate matters HRM managers felt there was a conflict between having a devolved approach to personnel accountability whilst trying to maintain a corporate view. For line managers the challenge here could be letting their staff move to other jobs within the organization. Third, for line managers a consequence of having responsibility for staff development requires them having to be aware of, and discuss the needs of individual members of staff. Yet, 'for many the annual appraisal interview often represents too much dialogue, so conducting an ongoing dialogue with individuals about their work preferences, development and career potential can be a low priority' (ibid.: 8–9). Many managers expressed concern abut how they could cope with pressure from staff demanding some sort of career development and progression, particularly in those organizations which had become flatter. Concern was also expressed by a significant minority 'that actively developing some staff would amount to training subordinates to be better than them. This was for some a threatening notion, and one which HR managers had not seemed to recognise' (ibid.: 9).

One of the key concerns emerging from the IPD's (1995) study was the competence of line managers to carry out HRM roles. Both line managers and personnel managers felt that there was a lack of support for line managers, particularly in the area of training for line manager. This lack of training not only covered personnel management issues, but also more general management training issues particularly those relating to motivation, a key skill and knowledge area for effective staff development. Lack of resources, a heavy workload, lack of time and a resistance from line managers were all reasons given for ineffective training of line managers.

Relationship between line managers and the HRD/M function

A key factor identified in the literature as influencing the effectiveness of line managers in delivering HRD effectively is the relationship between line managers and the HRM/D function (Bevan and Hayday 1994; IPD 1995; Heraty and Morley 1995).

Bevan and Hayday (op. cit.) identified evidence of tension between the HR function and line managers, which sometimes limited the extent to which real devolution can be achieved. Three reasons for such tension were suggested. First, that some line managers are unwilling to accept that devolved staff management is part of their job. Second, that even amongst those line managers accepting that managing staff is part of their role, most have a limited view of the things they should be doing and of those which they expect to be conducted by or led from the corporate personnel function. Third, that there was reluctance from personnel professionals to release their responsibilities to line managers contrary to public statements.

The IPD study (1995) found that responsibility for training and development tended to be shared, but with a greater involvement of personnel in consultation with line managers. This study tended to take a very traditional perspective of training by focusing on systematic training and on training courses in particular, with no consideration of the role of managers in providing 'direct' developmental support. The study identified that personnel were more heavily involved in the administration and delivery of courses, whereas line managers had more responsibility for determining who attends training. Some organizations had progressed further and made managers responsible for the design, delivery and timing of training. In these situations personnel adopted the role of providing guidance, support, 'trainer training' and the provision of resources. Conversely, in some organizations managers felt that

> of all the personnel issues delegated to the line, line managers were probably weakest in ensuring that staff was adequately trained and in monitoring their development. This is mainly because it is an area that does not demand immediate attention. As one line manager explained: Managers only think about training if a problem occurs.
>
> (Ibid.: 21)

Bevan and Hayday (op. cit.) suggest that to maximize the potential of the partnership between personnel and line management the following need to be implemented.

- Be clear about what HR role line managers want and what skills they need to perform them.
- Define what 'ownership' really means – distinguish it from 'dumping'.
- Clarify the training and support available to the line and how it can be accessed.
- Move from rule books and procedures to standards and values.
- Review the state of HR development in the organization: how well equipped are the line managers to cope with increased pressure from staff?
- Keep two-way communication channels open.

Supporting line managers in their developmental role

The Cabinet Office (1993) proposed a model for effective HRD devolution, which included: the need for a coherent HR strategy derived from organizational goals; top management commitment to change by its behaviours and actions; effective communication of strategy to managers; clearly defined roles for line managers; line management involvement in establishing the agenda; the HRM function must provide support to help line manager's perform their new roles; line managers must be made accountable to ensure they take their responsibilities seriously; and HRD should be evaluated to make sure that the new approaches are helping the organization meet its objectives.

Bevan and Hayday (op. cit.) suggest that two models of HR support to line managers emerged from their case-study organizations. The first involves the HRM function providing training to line managers in those areas they found difficulty, notably staff development. Organizations adopting this approach spent time persuading managers that by investing time on staffing matters they could have a tangible impact on their business goals. Line managers that the researchers spoke to, however, reiterated the paradox they faced – delivering short-term goals at the expense of progressing medium- or long-term goals. In some organizations there was an attempt to clarify the criteria against which line managers' performance was to be assessed, thus suggesting to managers that their staff management accountabilities were of similar standing to their other business targets.

The second involves aligning the HRM function more closely to operational management, and involves a more explicit client–customer approach, in effect adopting an internal consultancy approach.

The line manager as developer: the conduit between individual and organizational learning?

It has been suggested that there has been significant research into the psychology of individual learning and much theoretical debate about organizational learning. However, there has been little empirical investigation into how individual learning contributes to organizational learning (McDougall and Beattie 1998). Yet there has been recognition that 'individuals are the primary learning entity in firms, and it is individuals which create organizational forms that enable learning in ways which facilitate organizational transformation' (Dodgson 1993: 377–8). A proposition of this research is that line managers could act as a key channel between individual and organizational learning by participating in 'learning partnerships' with their staff and others given that

> Learning processes within organisations usually involve interaction between individuals. It is important, therefore, to consider

members of the organisation and their relationships, and to analyse the contribution which these relationships make to organisational learning.

(Probst and Buchell 1997: 148)

Ellinger, Watkins and Barnas also argue that 'organisations that aspire to become learning organisations must encourage managers to adopt new roles as coaches, trainers and educators if learning is to become distributed and continuous at multiple levels within the organisation' (1999: 387). Now, therefore, seems timeous to explore the nature and outcomes of developmental interactions within organizations.

Central research questions

The central questions of this research are as follows. First, to explore the interaction between managers and learners within developmental relationships. Second, to identify the distinctive behaviours of developmental managers within the voluntary sector. Third, to identify what motivates voluntary sector managers to develop staff. Finally, to examine the role of the developmental manager as a conduit between individual and organizational learning. This chapter focuses on the process of initial empirical research into one of the selected case-study organizations, Quarriers, which utilizes participant observation to explore organizational variables.

Empirical context

Quarriers is a voluntary organization providing social care services for children, families and people with a disability throughout the West of Scotland. It is both a registered charity and a company limited by guarantee. The charity was originally established in the late nineteenth century as a children's village in the countryside sixteen miles from Glasgow. Whilst the village still exists physically, the majority of its services are now delivered in projects within the communities that service users live in.

Following changes in social care policy in the 1970s the organization struggled to adapt, particularly in the field of childcare, and indeed was in a state of near collapse. However, the 1990s saw considerable change with the shift in services from an institutional to a community basis. In 1993 the organization had 200 employees and a turnover of £4 million; by 2000 the organization had expanded to over 900 employees and had a turnover of £16.5 million. Quarriers is now one of the leading and fastest growing social care charities in Scotland. Much of this success can be attributed to the new senior management team appointed to turn the organization round and their effective collaboration with the Council of Management.[1] This transformation can be seen in recent strategic management of the organization, which had seen it adopt the desire to become a learning organization (Beattie and Ross 1997). This has also been recognized externally by two recent national awards for the quality of its services and the achievement of IiP.

Methodological issues

Epistemological debate

The epistemological debate in the social sciences, and management research, is dominated by two research paradigms – positivism and phenomenology (Easterby-Smith, Thorpe and Lowe 1991). The central tenet of positivism is that the social world exists externally and that its properties should be measured by objective methods, rather than being inferred subjectively through sensation, reflection, or intuition. Whereas the phenomenological view is that the world and reality are not objective and exterior, but that they are socially constructed and given meaning by people (ibid.). In this study it is argued that developmental relationships are constructed by managers and their staff, whilst being interpreted both by respondents and the researcher.

Easterby-Smith, Thorpe and Lowe, describing the task of the social scientist, suggest it,

> should not be to gather facts and measure how often certain patterns occur, but to appreciate the different constructions and meanings that people place upon their experience. One should therefore try to understand and explain why people have different experiences, rather than search for external causes and fundamental laws to explain their behaviour. Human action arises from the sense that people make of different situations, rather than as a direct response from external stimuli.

> (Ibid.: 24)

Andersen, Borum and Kristensen also distance themselves from the rational approach of positivism advocating that the researcher see the world as it is as needs to empathize with the field as

> The field is a field that, through symbolic interaction, ascribes meaning to things and phenomena in a community of reflexive discourse. A micro-cosmos in its own right, in which individuals relate practically to phenomena in which the researcher is interested. Consequently the researcher can learn much more from empathising with the field's creation of meaning than from viewing the field as a sub-contractor of data.

> (1995: 144)

The central theme of this study is to understand and explain why people have different constructions and meanings regarding their developmental experiences at work and it was therefore felt that a phenomenological approach, utilizing qualitative methods as they are 'interpretative techniques which seek to describe, decode, translate and otherwise come to terms with the meaning, not the frequency, of certain more or less naturally occurring phenomena in the social world' (Van Maanen 1983: 9) was the most appropriate research strategy.

Research methodology

An explanatory case-study methodology has been adopted to gain a holistic perspective of developmental relationships in the organization. The first phase of fieldwork involved participant observation to gather data on a range of organizational variables and to prepare the researcher for the second phase of fieldwork. The second phase of fieldwork involved two stages of in-depth interviews. The first to gather data on behaviours of developmental managers utilizing critical incident techniques, the second based on a behavioural event interviewing process to test the validity of behaviours identified. This chapter reports on the writer's experiences of the first phase of this empirical work.

Participant observation

Participant observation has its roots in ethnography, where researchers focus on the manner in which people interact in observable and regular ways (Gill and Johnson 1997) and participate in 'people's daily lives over an extended period of time, watching what happens, listening to what is said and asking questions' (Hammersley and Atkinson 1983: 2).

Watson describes graphically the process of undertaking ethnographic research with managers which involves:

> feeling one's way in confusing circumstances, struggling to make sense of ambiguous messages, reading signals, looking around, listening all the time, coping with conflicts and struggling to achieve tasks through establishing and maintaining a network of relationships. But this is what we do all the time as human beings. This is how we cope with our lives. And it is what managers do in their more formalised 'managing roles'.
>
> (1994: 8)

He goes on to suggest that both the work of researcher and managers are similar crafts.

> Both crafts involve close attention to language, formal and informal, speaking and writing as well as observing. And it is through

323

language, formal and informal, official and unofficial, that the bulk of the business of management is conducted. It is through speaking to each other that all of us make sense of the worlds we move in, whether we are trying to make sense of things as managers, as researchers or as part of our ordinary daily lives.

(Ibid.)

Given this potential insight into management and organizational life offered by ethnography it seems appropriate that a study seeking to understand developmental interactions utilizes such an approach.

Ethnographic studies satisfy three simultaneous preconditions for the study of human activities:

1   the need for an empirical approach;
2   the need to remain open to elements that cannot be coded at the time of the study;
3   a concern for grounding the phenomena observed in the field (Baszanger and Dodier 1997).

The advantages of participant observation include flexibility and the ability to develop more intimacy with respondents thus providing greater access to information and the motives of respondents. The disadvantages include: the closeness to unique events may limit their classification and generalizability; intimates may be an atypical sample; presence of researcher may influence behaviour; and, unusual events may be viewed as normal by the researcher (Gill and Johnson 1997). However, in this study these limitations will have been minimized by the use of other methods such as interviewing and archives.

Taxonomies of field roles

Easterby-Smith *et al.* (1991) identify four types of participant observation roles. First, the 'researcher as employee' adopts the role of employee, which may or not be explicit. This is appropriate where the researcher needs to be fully immersed and experience the work or situation directly. Second, they identify the 'researcher as explicit role'. Here the researcher has negotiated their entry and can move around, observe, interview and participate in the work as appropriate. The third role is 'interrupted involvement'. In this role the researcher moves in and out of the organization to deal with other work or to carry out other forms of complementary data collection, such as interviewing. There is little actual participation in the work of the organization. The final role is that of 'complete observer'. This is a much more detached role where the researcher engages in no interaction with the research population but merely observes, similar to the approach used in work-study. This last role has little to offer the phenomenological researcher seeking to understand the world of those being studied.

The choice of field role is influenced by a number of factors including: the purpose of the research; costs; level of access; the extent to which the researcher participates in the field setting; the researcher's comfort with a particular role; the extent to which the researcher's identity and role are communicated; and the amount of time the researcher has available (Easterby-Smith, Watkins and Barnas 1991; Gill and Johnson 1997).

Operational issues

Operational issues that need to be considered by the participant observer include the negotiation of access; consideration of the researcher's impact on and relationships with those being observed; the maintenance of object-ivity in interpretation of observations; the personal style to be adopted in observation; and the approach taken to field notes (Lofland 1971).

Ethical issues

Ethical issues in ethnographic approaches arise from the relationship be-tween researcher and host organization; and between the researcher and subjects studied (Gill and Johnson 1997). Miles and Huberman have also identified a number of ethical issues that were appropriate for consideration in this ethnographic research phase: the worth of the project; consent; benefits, costs and reciprocity; honesty and trust; privacy; confidentiality and anonymity; and intervention and advocacy. They suggest that researchers are often faced with dilemmas between ethics and research rigour and that 'you often face a choice between two goods, where choosing one means, to some degree, forgoing the other' (1994: 295). An example of such a choice is the potential conflict between the demands of validity and avoiding harm. Further ethical dilemmas include: the implications of using overt or covert observation (Lofland 1971; Easterby-Smith, Watkins and Barnas 1991; Gill and Johnson 1997); the concern that individuals may feel *obliged* to co-operate; and the potential for pressure on the researcher to disclose specific observations.

The implications of the choice of roles and the resolution of operational and ethical issues for this study with particular reference to Quarriers are discussed below.

The research

A personal account of participant observation

Roles

As a full-time academic, undertaking a part-time PhD, the most appropriate role for me was a combination of 'interrupted involvement' and 'explicit role' (Easterby-Smith, Thorpe and Lowe 1991). This approach through explicit negotiation allowed me to move around the organization, observe, interview and participate as appropriate, whilst still maintaining contact with normal employment duties. This hybrid role facilitated the operational and ethical requirements of both the organization and myself.

The role of 'researcher as employee' (ibid.) was inappropriate, as the main work of this organization is social care and I do not have the appropriate skills to carry out this sort of work. There was, however, a small element of this latter role as I am a member of the organization and was able to utilize this role in management committee activities, such as meetings. Thus the research role could also be described as a 'participant-as-observer' (Gill and Johnson 1997), given my membership of the organization. The 'complete observer' role (Easterby-Smith, Thorpe and Lowe op. cit.; Gill and Johnson op. cit.) was not only regarded as an anathema but was also viewed as being inappropriate in social care settings, where service users would have found the lack of interaction both intrusive and potentially threatening in what is after all their homes. The only time that this role was used was during a meeting of the organization's Directorate, the senior management team, where it would have been inappropriate for a member of the Council of Management to interact – despite the temptation to do so on one particular agenda item close to my heart!

Operational issues

Negotiating access

Access was initially discussed with the 'main gatekeeper' to the organization – the Director of Human Resources. It was stressed that this was principally an exercise in getting to know the organization, as preparation for more substantial research in the future. It was also stressed that visits to projects would be handled sensitively, with minimal disruption and no intrusion into 'private' activities, for example staff supervision sessions or observation of personal care of service users. In particular I did not want projects putting on anything special for visits, rather to see them as they are.

It was also stressed that everything heard and seen would be treated in the strictest confidence. There would be no report back on individuals and individual projects to senior management. A composite report would be provided after the research was completed, but it would not be possible to identify any individuals from it. Finally, it was stressed that it should be made clear to all potential participants that they were free to refuse involvement, as I did not want to abuse my position as a volunteer 'manager' of the charity.

The next stage was discussion with the Chief Executive. He was very supportive and was keen that a range of projects would be involved. The proposed research was then discussed at a Directorate meeting involving the Service Directors and in principle they agreed to facilitate the research. They did however, quite rightly, ask that a short written summary of what the research involved should be provided so that staff in projects could be informed and asked if they wished to participate, that is *informed consent*, and this was complied with.

Participant observation in practice

The main phase of participant observation was during a three-week period, although given my role in the organization it continued on a more low-key basis during my normal duties for the organization, for example attendance at committee meetings and attendance at training courses relevant to the research study. The programme for the three-week period was organized by the Human Resources Department based on my instructions. In effect they organized an 'induction programme'.

A range of activities was included in this participant observation process. Visits to a cross-section of projects, representing different services and older and newer parts of the organization, were undertaken and included: respite care units for children and adults with learning disabilities; projects for the young homeless; short-term residential projects to support children from families with a range of problems; a residential school for children with emotional and behavioural problems; and residential units for adults with learning disabilities. It was felt that it was more appropriate to see a range of projects to provide breadth and to get a 'feel' for the organization, rather than spend a long time in one particular project which may have provided more depth but may have been atypical of the organization as a whole. This proved so during the research, as I quickly became aware of the diversity created by different types of work activities and between old and new projects.

These visits involved: an informal interview with the project leader which included such topics as the project's history, purpose, staffing and a description of a 'typical day' in order to see 'their' world; a tour of the project; and participation in project activities where appropriate, for example lunch with service users and staff. These visits also provided an opportunity to observe interaction between managers and staff, and between staff and service users. Overall these visits provided a valuable insight into the front-line work of the organization and indeed provided a number of examples of developmental incidents. Examples of a couple of visits are described below.

At a service for adults with learning disabilities insights into a 'typical' day demonstrated the types of activities that staff were involved in for example: person-centred planning; shopping with service users; supervising cooking; supporting service users on outings, for example meals, holidays, medication (although some service users self-medicate); and interaction with other agencies, for example social work, Adult Training Centres, day centres, community service (e.g. getting offenders in to do the garden). The team leader described how she saw the philosophy of the organization, which she felt 'values and focuses on the needs of the individuals, their dreams, aspirations. It gets staff to think about the dreams and aspirations of service users and try to help them achieve as much as possible'. There was physical evidence of this approach in the project with person-centred plans and their realization being presented graphically on the kitchen wall. Interestingly she also said that this philosophy had been beneficial to her by making her more self-aware, opening her mind to new ideas and that it had been translated to her personal life. Whilst at the project I was able to observe two staff interacting with a service user. Both interacted in a compassionate and interested way. They discussed her supermarket shopping, her shopping for a forthcoming holiday with one of the staff and her plans for more shopping. They also took the opportunity to reinforce messages about eating food in the right date rotation and budgeting her money. She became the centre of attention when she came into the kitchen. She was introduced to me and she subsequently showed me round the project, which is in a modern, attractively furnished and decorated house.

A typical day at a childrens' project was described as:

6.45 a.m.	Children starting to get up, dressing, breakfasting, etc.
8.30 a.m.	School buses start to arrive
9.00 a.m.	Children at school
9.00 a.m.–3.00 p.m.	Team leader will do administrative work; key workers will do activities like shopping, decorating and reports
3.00 p.m.	Shifts overlap by one hour
	Children return, clothes, etc. changed
	Range of activities, e.g. walks, playing, watching TV/video
4.30–5.30 p.m.	Tea
6.00–7.30 p.m.	Bus run, TV, painting activities
7.30 p.m. on	Getting children ready for bed, time depends on level of dependency

8.45–9.00 p.m.	Bedtime
9.45 p.m.	Day staff go off
Night	Night staff do laundry, tidy up and are available to help any children during the night

The project leader at this Children's Respite project reported that staff take great pride in doing laundry at the week for the child's parents and packing their case. This was seen as a symbol of their care for the child. If their clothes and belongings are being well looked after, there is a chance their child is too. Also, at a practical level they felt the last thing a parent wanted after a break was to be faced with a massive pile of washing! Throughout my visit to this project I could hear chatter and laughter, both from children and staff; it felt a happy place to be and was well equipped to support the diverse needs of the children using the service.

There was observation and participation in a number of meetings. I have also been able to participate in a range of training courses covering issues such as the organization's values built round the mission statement and staff development. I have acted very much as a participant in these programmes working alongside managers and staff. Discussions with key informants also provided valuable insights into the learning climate of the organization. An additional benefit of such discussions is that one key informant has expertise not only in adult learning but also pre-school learning, and the insights given by her into early learning provided alternative models of developmental relationships.

Other activities included a visit to the craft centre, staffed by volunteers, which provides additional income to the charity and participation as a judge in a caption tie-break contest run by the fund-raising department where the prize was a day out to a concert by one of the UK's leading bands.

The researcher's impact

The human resource staff reported a range of reactions to proposed visits – happy, bemused and 'what's in it for us?' In previous interactions with staff at various events, I had been invited to visit a number of projects by staff keen to 'show off' their projects.

In practice, without exception staff, some of whom had been met before, were both welcoming and open. Most knew who I was and what my organizational role was – although one relatively new project manager asked for an explanation of the role of a Council of Management member. Most staff appeared comfortable and confident to speak about the work of their project. Although a few appeared initially nervous they soon relaxed. Few used these visits as an opportunity to gripe, although a number of concerns were expressed about certain organizational policies. One of the unexpected hazards of this type of research was the numerous cups of tea and biscuits, which had to be consumed!

One of my initial concerns was that projects might put on special events or present their project in an artificially positive light. Whilst staff devoted time and effort to the visits themselves, there was little impression of the projects being 'sanitized' for these visits. Indeed it is difficult to do this given the unpredictable nature of some service users and it was a common experience for discussions with staff to be interrupted by service users. A tour of one project revealed a kitchen, used by service users not staff, full of dirty pots and plates, reflecting the reality of working with this particular client group – if the project wanted to create a false impression the kitchen would have been cleaned by staff. I was also pleased that staff and managers were comfortable to deal with service user or staffing issues prior to spending time with me.

Not only were staff welcoming, but so also were service users, for whom my arrival created great interest and to whom I was described as the 'boss's boss'. In many projects it was service users rather than staff who gave the tour of their home, which provided yet another invaluable insight into the work of the organization and its staff.

One activity where I was particularly concerned that I may have had a constraining impact on behaviour was at a meeting where everyone appeared to behave in a very restrained manner despite a number of difficult issues being discussed. Following the meeting a number of key informants were asked independently if the meeting had reflected a typical meeting of this group and I was told that it did. It was reported that there was an unwritten rule that when people got heated with each other over specific issues during the meeting they always publicly demonstrated by the end of the meeting that their relationship with each other was unaffected.

Maintenance of objectivity in observations

Prior to commencing this research into Quarriers I felt it was necessary to make a conscious effort to put to one side existing preconceptions – about the organization as a whole, projects and individuals – which had largely been formed through involvement in strategic activities. Overall the maintenance of objectivity was achieved, although it was inevitably fascinating to hear about particular events from a front-line perspective which had previously only been viewed from a senior management perspective.

What I was not prepared for were the various emotional feelings that were experienced. After some visits I felt elated at seeing the amount of positive work being done to help the vulnerable members of our community. A particular 'high' was having lunch with the children in one of the small residential units and seeing how secure they were in this environment, watching their preparations for a Spice Girls dance routine and playing 'keepie uppie' with one of the boys. Other visits, particularly those for the young homeless, caused feelings of distress that such projects were still required in the late 1990s, just as they had been 125 years ago when our charity was founded. On one visit I felt some discomfort at being shown round an establishment by service users with behavioural problems. Although staff were in the vicinity I was concerned about how I would react if the service users presented challenging behaviour. I was also greatly impressed by the amount of fund-raising that staff engaged in to purchase 'extras' for their projects.

Personal style in observation

Lofland (1971) suggests that researchers engaging in participant observation need to pay due attention to their behaviour and dress. Great care was taken to remind individuals about the purpose of the research and to stress the confidentiality of anything seen or heard. When interviewing a relaxed style and loose structure were adopted. At all times interest in what was being said or shown was maintained. This approach seemed to work. Generally, I merely gave a few prompts as most respondents talked willingly and volunteered much of the information required. In terms of dress code generally 'smart but casual' attire was worn, particularly in settings where children were present. More 'business-like' clothing was worn at formal meetings.

Approach to field notes

Good practice suggests that field notes should be written up as soon as possible after observation to minimize loss of data. The nature of some observations allowed, with the permission of respondents, brief notes to be taken during observations. Immediately following observations where possible I recorded fuller notes either in writing or by Dictaphone. I also recorded how I felt during the observation. On return home full field notes were then written up on a PC. It was felt important to do this to minimize the risk of confusion between different experiences. On occasion this proved problematic where two observations followed closely one after the other. Full writing of field notes was also sometimes disrupted by the demands of my job. I also found, although advised in advance by a colleague, that I was not fully prepared for how tiring it was to return from a day in the field and then have to start writing up field notes in the evening. Ethnographers need stamina and discipline!

Ethical issues

Relationship between researcher and host organization; and between researcher and subjects studied

Perhaps unusually for an academic researcher the research was being carried out in an organization of which the researcher is a member, indeed

I, along with my fellow council members, carry significant responsibility for the governance of this organization. Whilst this position potentially removed many of the barriers to access experienced by many researchers I was concerned that there was a risk of abusing my position, after all I was asking those who report to me for access and there may have been a danger that they would feel obliged to co-operate when it was not appropriate. As far as possible I am confident that this position was not abused, as negotiation was carried out carefully with senior managers with whom I work closely, more as a partner than a superior. Furthermore, the individuals concerned themselves are strong personalities and do not shy away from putting across their opinions. This was demonstrated by their view that one part of the organization should not be included in this initial study and this was complied with happily.

It could be argued that the nature of many social care and voluntary organizations tends to perhaps be more informal and less conscious of status than parts of the public and private sectors. As a consequence staff may be less likely to be intimidated by a visit from an 'authority figure' and I was never aware of putting people on the spot. Indeed a significant number of staff volunteered to participate in future phases of the research and appeared genuinely interested in the research topic, and this has proved to be so in subsequent phases of the research. In addition many staff are used to being involved in research studies either from outside agencies or by social work students who have placements in the organization.

Worth of the project

I believe that the project is of worth in that the results will hopefully illuminate an area of adult learning where there is currently limited insight – the interaction between managers and their staff within developmental relationships. It is also hoped that this research will provide a better understanding of what developmental managers do and thus help management educators and developers provide appropriate support to managers. Denzin (1997) after all argues that ethnographers should not only interpret the world, but also help change it. Individual employees, managers, developers and fellow academics have indicated that they feel this research is worthwhile.

Informed consent

As discussed above in *Negotiating Access* attempts were made to ensure that all participants were fully informed about the nature of the research and their role in it. Whilst subjects were informed prior to the commencement of the research, it was still necessary on some occasions where individuals appeared unclear about its purpose to remind them and advise them that it was not necessary to participate.

Benefits, costs and reciprocity

Clearly I as a researcher benefited from this period of participant observation as it made a significant contribution to my research. It is however equally important that participants gain too and are not subjected to 'ethnographic vampirism' (McLaren 1991). Therefore the organization will be given a report providing valuable data on the learning climate of the organization and on the role that managers play in supporting learning, this is particularly significant given the organization's ambition to be a learning organization (Beattie and Ross 1997). It is hoped that for individual subjects they in the short-term gained from reflecting on their own learning, indeed this has been confirmed in later interviews, and in the longer-term gain from managers being better equipped as developers.

Honesty and trust

Whilst it is hoped that few qualitative researchers are dishonest or abuse trust, it has been suggested that some have been 'economical with the truth' about the true purpose of their research (Miles and Huberman 1994). It is this writer's view that the greatest abuse of trust is committed by those who conduct covert research – in effect an invasion of other people's civil liberties. Within Quarriers it is critical that trusting relationships are not breached. Within Quarriers I have a long-term role and a breach of trust would make this position untenable.

Privacy, confidentiality and anonymity

Key issues to consider here are the level of intrusion into people's lives, the use of information gained and the maintenance of anonymity. In this study intrusion has been minimized by limiting participant observation to manifestations of work which are generally publicly observed. Therefore staff supervision sessions have been excluded, despite the fact they would provide valuable data for this research, as these are normally conducted in private and individuals may raise personal issues.

Confidentiality has been preserved by not informing senior managers of what junior staff have said, and vice versa. On occasions senior managers asked how the 'visit' was going. These questions seemed to arise more out of courtesy rather than to find out what was being said about them or the organization as a whole. The reply was always 'fine' without any details being provided. Also the organization was assured that no commercially sensitive material would be published or shared with those outside the organization. As a trustee of Quarriers this is a responsibility that had to be followed in any case.

Anonymity will be preserved for front-line staff and managers. This has already been tested this by giving a trusted informant an anonymous

19

POSTSCRIPT

The future of HRD research

Jim McGoldrick, Jim Stewart and Sandra Watson

Introduction

In writing the concluding chapter to their 1996 edited book (Stewart and McGoldrick 1996) two of the editors of this volume made the following statement.

> We do not, completely at least, discount the possibility of a definitive analysis of the nature and meaning of HRD. Such an analysis is though not yet available and is unlikely to be so for the foreseeable future.
>
> (p. 303)

It is encouraging to note that the predictive element of that statement has, so far, turned out to be true. The work and debates examined in our introductory chapter are evidence enough that meanings attached to the term HRD remains diverse. Any reading of the chapters in between that chapter and this one would add weight to that argument. So, a first conclusion to be drawn is that HRD continues to provide a rich and diverse field for academic research and theorizing. A related conclusion is that the work presented in this volume provides evidence of a growing maturity within and for that research and theorizing. The work also suggests a growing connection with and relevance for the problems, challenges and concerns of professional practice. That too is encouraging and suggests a healthy future for HRD research.

Common themes

Having made those opening and optimistic remarks, the task remains to attempt to identify some common themes arising from the book, and to use these to speculate on the future for HRD research. Given the diversity already referred to, this is by no means an easy task, though it is made description of a positive developmental critical incident and she was unable to identify the project or individuals concerned. It will be more difficult to preserve the anonymity of those in key roles such as the Chief Executive, Director of Human Resources and Training specialists and they have been offered the opportunity to read drafts before publication.

Intervention and advocacy

Miles and Huberman pose the great moral question for the 'fly on the wall' researcher – '*What do I do when I see harmful, illegal, or wrongful behaviour . . . ?*' (op. cit.: 293). In the case of Quarriers my position as a Director and Trustee had to take precedence over my role as researcher and any such incident dealt with under those legal obligations. Fortunately, this dilemma was not faced. I did, however, have to restrain myself from advocating on behalf of the Director of Human Resources on an issue we both believe in passionately. However, as this arose at a meeting which a Council member would not normally attend I would have been abusing my position.

Critical analysis

Participant observation was used in this doctoral research to gain insight into the influence of organizational variables on developmental relationships, such as: the organizations' history, culture and work; learning climate and HRD strategy; and managerial roles. These insights provided valuable information prior to interviews being conducted with respondents. To gain worthwhile data through interviewing it is essential that the researcher establishes rapport with respondents, rather than impose the academic world on them. To facilitate this an understanding of the language and culture of the respondents is helpful (Fontana and Frey 1994). It is therefore argued that an element of practical immersion in the organization where respondents are based allowed the development of this empathetic understanding prior to interviewing. Although care had to be taken not to lose objectivity.

Roles

Overall the adoption of the participant observation role described above worked well, giving the required 'feel' for the culture and work of the organization to inform the next phase of research – in-depth qualitative interviews. A major disadvantage was the interruptions created by the demands of 'paid' employment, which created distractions and at times undermined the immersion effects of participant observation.

Operational issues

The investment of time to *negotiate access* with key stakeholders proved invaluable as it facilitated a highly effective research process by ensuring that visits could be made across the organization and that staff were confident to participate.

The value of observing a *breadth* of activities in the organization provided more holistic insight into the organization, than would have been possible if I had only spent time in a few projects. An unexpected benefit was the insight into learning provided by a specialist employee.

From my perspective I believe that I had minimal *impact* on the research population. Two factors contributed to this. First, I already had a relationship with the organization and was thus not viewed as a 'stranger'. Second, staff are well used to being participants in research studies.

Maintaining *objectivity*, as far as possible, was achieved by reminding myself that I was observing the organization from a researcher's rather than a manager's perspective. This only slipped when observing projects dealing with particularly vulnerable groups which led to understandable, but unexpected, emotional responses.

The consideration of appropriate *personal style* for different groups in the research population proved useful as all appeared to be comfortable with my presence and were willing to engage with me.

The experience of recording and writing-up *field notes* very much reflected the good advice contained in the ethnographic literature. To maximize accuracy and richness it was vital to write up notes as soon as possible. Wherever possible it was helpful to write up one observation before embarking on another to minimize data loss and confusion. Such practice however requires great discipline and the avoidance of distractions – which I did not always achieve.

Ethical issues

The consideration of ethical issues at the design phase and during the initial ethnographic phase were viewed as critical by a social care charity given its own ethical values in particular the respect for the dignity of the individual. By giving due attention and priority to such issues helped further develop trust with the organization and its employees, thus facilitating the later phases of the research.

Conclusions and key learning points

The conclusions and key lessons from this experience of participant observation are outlined below, some are specific to this case but others have wider application. It was critical for the outcomes of my research that I was explicit about my role to all participants, not just senior management.

This openness was respected by many individuals and resulted in high levels of co-operation. This experience may be helpful for those grappling with the overt: covert dilemma.

I had to accept my own limitations and that there were aspects of the work of Quarriers for which I did not have the requisite abilities, and therefore my role tended more towards the observer end of the participant–observation continuum, although I still interacted with the research population. I also had to take care not to express my opinion about specific events, policies, or individuals where I would be abusing my position or would breach confidentiality. Ethnographic researchers need to take care not to meddle in the affairs of the organizations they are researching.

Clear benefits were gained from investing time in carefully negotiating access, gaining the support of key informants and by being clear about what was required from the organization. Therefore planning, whilst retaining flexibility, can enable the ethnographic researcher to maximize their time.

The researcher's impact on the population studied is always an issue with participant observation, particularly where the research is conducted on an overt basis. Throughout this period in Quarriers I tried to ensure that gatekeepers and individual workers did not feel pressurized to participate in the research. I also tried throughout to adopt a friendly, low-key approach and was always genuinely interested in what people had to show and tell me. Ethnographers need to consider if they can adopt the appropriate personal style for the environment in which they are operating.

The limitations of 'interrupted involvement' were experienced resulting in a loss of some of the feeling of immersion in an organization's culture that can be gained from ethnographic approaches. However, many part-time researchers have to accept this particular role for pragmatic reasons.

Utilization of this research approach has resulted in the acquisition of powerful insights into the culture, life and history of this organization which in the long run I hope made me a more competent and credible researcher when I revisited this research population. I would encourage other qualitative researchers to adopt such a strategy prior to engaging in interviews to facilitate their insight into organizational life.

An additional benefit of the flexibility of adopting an ethnographic strategy was the scope to learn from respondents not only about practical aspects of social care and learning but also about theoretical and philosophical aspects of both these subjects. Ethnography can be a powerful learning experience for academics.

One of the most unexpected results during the participant observation research was the range of feelings experienced and this may suggest a danger of (being and) getting close to a research population. This was perhaps the closest I came to 'going native'. At times these feelings could be quite draining, at other times there was a desire to take action.

Ethnographers need to be sensitive to their own emotions and acknowledge when these may impact on their judgement.

Although as far as possible field notes were written up as soon as possible after observation periods, this was not always possible and there was little doubt the greater the time between observation and writing the less reliable the data recorded. Ethnographers need to exercise great discipline to ensure they maintain the necessary discipline to record their observations in a timely and accurate way.

A key lesson from this is that it is critical to consider and discuss ethical issues at all phases of research – preparation, conduct, analysis and publication – and that these debates whenever possible should be conducted with respondents. Otherwise the potential to do harm and/or bring research into disrepute becomes a very real possibility.

Finally, it is hoped that this very personal account of a novice ethnographer's experiences of preparing for and entering the 'field' provides some useful insights for those considering adopting a similar research strategy in the future. I am grateful to all those who participated in this research for letting me into their world.

Note

1 The researcher, a full-time academic, is a member of the organization's Council of Management and chair of its Human Resources subcommittee, in effect a charity trustee and a company director.

References

AMED (1991) *Developing the Developers: Improving the Quality of the Professionals Who Develop People and Organisations,* London: Association for Management Education and Development.

Andersen, I.B., Borum, F. and Kristensen, P.H. (1995) *On the Art of Doing Field Studies: an Experience-based Research Methodology.* Copenhagen: Handelshojskolens Forlag.

Baszanger, I. and Dodier, N. (1997) 'Ethnography: relating the part to the whole', in D. Silverman (ed.) *Qualitative Research: Theory, Method and Practice,* London: Sage.

Beattie, R.S. (1996) 'Developing a conceptual framework and methodology for the developmental manager in the voluntary sector', a paper presented to the British Academy of Management Annual Conference, Aston University, September.

Beattie, R. and Ross, Z. (1997) 'The learning organisation – an empirical test in the voluntary and non-profit sector', a paper presented at The Second International Research Symposium on Public Services Management, Aston Business School, Aston University, September.

Bevan, S. and Hayday, S. (1994) *Towing the Line: Helping Managers to Manage People,* Brighton: Institute of Manpower Studies.

Bevan, S., Toye, J. and Frost, D. (1995) *Managers for the Millennium,* Brighton: Institute of Employment Studies.

Cabinet Office (1991) *Developing People for Results through the Line,* London: HMSO.

—— (1993) *Encouraging and Supporting the Delegation of Human Resource Development Responsibilities to the Line*, London: HMSO.

Denzin, N.K. (1997) *Interpretative Ethnography: Ethnographic Practices for the 21st Century*, Thousand Oaks, CA: Sage.

Dodgson, M. (1993) 'Organisational learning: a review of some literatures', *Organisation Studies*, 14(3).

Easterby-Smith, M., Thorpe, R. and Lowe, A. (1991) *Management Research: an Introduction*, London: Sage.

Ellinger, A.D., Watkins, K.E. and Barnas, C.M. (1999) 'Responding to new roles: a qualitative study of managers as instructors', *Management Learning*, 30(4): 387–412.

Fontana, A. and Frey, J.H. (1994) 'Interviewing: the art of science', in N.K. Denzin and Y.S. Lincoln (eds) *Handbook of Qualitative Research*, Thousand Oaks, CA: Sage.

Gill, J. and Johnson, P. (1997) *Research Methods for Managers* (second edn), London: Paul Chapman.

Hammersley, M. and Atkinson, P. (1983) *Ethnography: Principles in Practice*, London: Routledge.

Heraty, N. and Morley, M. (1995) 'Line managers and human resource development', *Journal of European Industrial Training*, 19(10): 31–7.

Institute of Personnel and Development (1995) *Personnel and the Line: Developing the New Relationship*, London: IPD.

Lofland, J. (1971) *Analysing Social Settings*, Belmont, CA: Wadsworth Publishing Company Inc.

McDougall, M. and Beattie, R. (1998) 'The missing link? Understanding the relationship between individual and organisational learning', *International Journal of Training and Development*, 2(4): 288–97.

McLaren, P. (1991) 'Field relations and the discourse of the other', in W.B. Shaffir and R.A. Stebbins (eds) *Experiencing Fieldwork*, Newbury Park, CA: Sage, 149–63 (cited by Miles and Huberman 1994).

Miles, M.B. and Huberman, A.M. (1994) *Qualitative Data Analysis* (second edn), Thousand Oaks, CA: Sage.

Mumford, A. (1993) *How Managers Can Develop Managers* (second edn), Aldershot: Gower.

Prost, G. and Buchell, B. (1997) *Organisational Learning: the Competitive Advantage of the Future*, Hemel Hempstead: Prentice Hall.

Salaman, G. (1995) *Managing*, Buckingham: Open University.

Storey, J. (1992) *Developments in Human Resource Management*, Oxford: Blackwell.

Van Maanen, J. (1983) *Qualitative Methodology*, London: Sage.

Watson, T. (1994) *In Search of Management*, London: Routledge.

Watson, T. and Harris, P. (1999) *The Emergent Manager*, London: Sage.

16

CONVERGENCE AND DIVERGENCE IN HRD

Research and practice across Europe

Jean Woodall, Alison Alker, Christina MacNeil and
Sue Shaw

Aims and contribution

The US origin of the field of HRD has had a powerful effect upon its emerging evidence base and has been very influential in shaping the research agenda. However, the recent emergence of European scholarship in this field would suggest that diversity in HRD practice involves more than differences of degree along the dimensions originating in the US debate. This chapter reviews the nature of research and practice in HRD across Europe, and provides some reflection upon the extent of divergence and convergence in HRD practice both within Europe as well as between Europe and the USA. It does so by reference to a number of scholarly papers presented at a conference on HRD in Europe held at Kingston University in January 2000, and by scrutiny of earlier debate on comparative European HRM and employee relations.

Theoretical context

Human resource development as a field of academic study is of relatively recent and primarily US origin. The main milestones were probably MacLagan's HR 'wheel' (1989) differentiating HRD from other HR functions and the formation of the US Academy of Human Resource Development. As Walton (1999) notes, the field of HRD has expanded beyond training and development to include:

- a strong connection to corporate strategy
- clarifying who benefits from learning
- individual responsibility for learning
- inclusion of non-employees
- extension into team learning

- incorporation of organization development (OD)
- incorporation of career development
- emphasis upon internal consultancy
- focus upon organizational learning
- link to knowledge management and intellectual capital of an enterprise.

However, such a laundry list can convey a misleading impression of consensus, as evidenced in the debate between two leading US academics in this field (Swanson 1992; Swanson 1999; McLean 1998, 1999), and also in the introductory reflections from an earlier text edited by two of the editors of the current volume (Stewart and McGoldrick 1996), and some attempt has been made to provide an outline of current definitions of HRD to identify common themes (Weinberger 1998). Swanson argued that the main processes of HRD were 'organization development and personal training and development for the purpose of improving performance at the organizational, process, and individual/group levels' (Swanson op. cit: 3). Stewart and McGoldrick (op. cit.) emphasized the importance of culture, leadership, and commitment in making the connection between the strategic direction of the organization, and individual behaviour and practice.

In addition to the debate around the definition and scope of HRD, academic research in the field of HRD remained strongly influenced by US scholars (Weinberger 1998), until the foundation of the University Forum for HRD in 1995, a UK-based network of over 30 universities offering Master's level programmes in HRD and providing an opportunity for scholarly dialogue, and the current volume is a typical outcome of this. Some of the member universities also collaborated with a number of European partners in 'EURESFORM', an EU-sponsored programme for the mutual recognition of common learning outcomes in HRD programmes. Eventually, a growing awareness of the similarities and differences between European approaches and practice in HRD led to the proposal for a scholarly conference – the First Conference on HRD Research and Practice Across Europe: Convergence and Divergence in the European HRD Agenda – which was jointly sponsored by the UK University Forum for HRD and EURESFORM and held in the UK at Kingston University in January 2000. The second half of this paper endeavours to provide an overview of the main themes that surfaced at the conference. However, before doing so, it is important to reflect upon some key features of the European context within which HRD is practised.

In reflecting upon the contextual factors that potentially influence HRD, we are fortunate to be able to draw upon the findings of earlier research on HRM in Europe (Sparrow and Hiltrop, 1994; Hegewisch and Brewster 1993; Pieper 1990), and European employee relations (Hyman and Ferner 1994; Ferner and Hyman 1998; Ferner and Quintanilla 1998, Marginson 2000). The main findings on HRM in mainland Europe are summarized in Table 16.1.

Table 16.1 Contextual factors influencing HRD in mainland Europe

1	More restricted employer autonomy
2	Less stress on market processes
3	Less emphasis upon the individual, more emphasis upon the group
4	More emphasis upon workers than managers
5	Increased role of 'social partners' in the employment relationship
6	Higher level of government intervention or support in many areas of HRM

Source: After P. Sparrow and J.-M. Hiltrop *European Human Resource Management in Transition*, London: Prentice-Hall, 1994, p. 30

While acknowledging that HRD is a distinct field of scholarly research and practice in relation to HRM, it has to be acknowledged that the contextual factors in mainland Europe are an important influence upon HRD outcomes. If anything, the UK context is somewhat closer to the US experience, and it is a mistake to assume that the rest of Europe is mirrored in UK practice. So, for example, the historical role and development of HR professionals varies considerably across Europe, as do their career paths (Tyson and Wikander 1994). So, for example, in the UK a strong professional body representing both HRM and HRD practitioners regulates initial training. Elsewhere in Europe this does not happen, and HR professionals can undergo very different training. So, in Germany the extensive legal responsibility of HRM professionals for collective employee relations necessitates a strong legal training, while their counterparts in HRD are more likely to have a background in adult education or psychology. There are also differences in the extent to which HR activities are contracted out (very high in the Netherlands and Belgium) and also in the extent to which HR responsibilities are devolved to line managers (particularly high in the UK and Denmark, but much less so in France). The involvement of HR professionals in corporate governance is also highly variable with no direct relationship between this and representation on corporate boards. In addition, there are widely different emphases upon empowerment, the role of communication, the importance of training and career management, and the role of pay in performance management.

The conclusion of these earlier studies in HR was that Anglo-Saxon models of HR did not fit comfortably with the reality of HR in mainland Europe. At best mainland European countries could be grouped into three: 'Latin', 'Central' and 'Nordic'. So, HRM and employee relations in the 'Latin' countries of France, Portugal, Italy and Spain are characterized by ideological divisions between the trade union confederations, a persistently strong state presence in business ownership, and the key role of trade unions in regulating many aspects of employee relations and welfare. Conversely the 'Central' countries of Germany, the Netherlands, Switzerland and Austria would feature a strong corporatist macro-economic

341

management, a strongly legalistic 'dual system' of interest representation in employee relations, to exert co-determination over wide areas of corporate business practice, including training and development, and trade union movements (with the exception of the Netherlands) that are non-political and all-encompassing. Finally, the 'Nordic' countries of Denmark, Finland, Norway and Sweden would feature a highly centralized and institutionalized manner of handling collective bargaining based on a long-standing compromise between business and labour, endorsed by predominantly social democratic (with some occasional exceptions) hegemony in political life.

However, a recent publication (Brewster and Holt Larsen 2000) would argue that the Netherlands, UK and Ireland share much in common with the 'Nordic' Group. The key features identified are a democratic approach to HR, a low power-distance culture, an acceptance of legal regulation, a history of strong state ownership, and high levels of trade union membership. In particular, they signal out a strong commitment to competence (especially in the Scandinavian countries, UK, the Netherlands and Ireland), embracing various forms of flexibility (mainly functional in Germany and Finland, but very high part-time employment in the Netherlands) that contrasts strongly with southern European countries. These countries also share an acceptance of the decline of the traditional career and greater line manager involvement in HR. However, it would be a mistake to argue that these countries are all very close to North American practice within HR. So, in most 'Northern' European countries except UK and Ireland working hours in excess of 48 per week are not worked by more than 5 per cent employees, short-term contracts are not extensively used, and variable pay systems do differ, with PRP and bonuses being commonly used in the Netherlands and Denmark, but profit sharing very common in France and Germany, and employee share ownership plans (ESOPs) in UK and Ireland (Brewster and Holt Larsen 2000). Yet, there is a risk that the distinctions between the different national business and employee relations systems become overdrawn. There are two additional international dimensions that complicate the European context for HRD. The first is globalization, and the second is the specific impact of the European Union.

While it is easy to list the key features of globalization (the expansion of international markets; the increasing vulnerability of domestic business 'champions' to international competition; the accelerating velocity of business transactions aided by information communications technology, and the internationalization of production by means of multinational corporations (MNCs)), it is less easy to ascertain what this might mean for HR at the firm level. Even within MNCs there is considerable debate as to whether there is a general trend towards either 'homogenization' of HR practice across different companies and sectors, or a move from 'polycentrism' towards distinctive company-based employment systems (Marginson and

Sisson 1994), or towards greater heterogeneity between MNCs with a simultaneous corporate 'isomorphism' (Ferner 1997). Recent research (Ferner and Quintanilla 1998) would suggest that there is a 'nationality' effect on MNC HR practice strongly influenced by the country of origin, but mediated through the context of policy and practice in the host country. The resulting tensions force MNCs into various adaptation strategies, the most important of which is 'Anglo-Saxonization': a convergence in MNC structure and behaviour around a model of international operation typical of highly internationalized British or US MNCs. Home business systems can differ substantially in terms of the inter-relationship between market structure, the financial system and the nature of corporate governance and control systems. So, for example, long-term relationships with banks and a relatively low degree of reliance on the stock market as a source of finance in Germany can be contrasted with the 'short-termist' focus upon share price typical of UK and US firms, with their consequent heavy reliance upon financial control and performance management systems and the predominance of the finance function over the commercial and production functions.

The interrelation between this and labour market institutions such as the nature of collective bargaining, the system of vocational education and skills acquisition, plus the division of labour within the enterprise, has significant implications for approaches to human resources in general, and to HRD in particular. So, for example, in Germany this involves a view of human resources as an investment in the firm, encouraging employment stability for core workers, accompanied by flexible work organization and the acquisition of skills through heavy investments in training (Marginson and Sisson 1994). Yet, at the same time the influence of traditional German approaches to management development and managerial career development will often persist in German MNCs which emphasize the long-term acquisition of specialist expertise within a specific management function, as opposed to the more Anglo-Saxon career 'tournament' or 'carousel' of frequent moves across different functions, and even companies spurred on by performance-related pay systems that link executive remuneration to personal and corporate performance, all underpinned by general executive development programmes.

Thus, the growth of global business adds considerable complexity to the context of HRD practice within Europe. In addition, at the supranational level, 'the structures and institutions of the EU and the EEA are creating an economic, political, and regulatory space whose character and dynamic are distinctive when set against wider global developments' (Marginson 2000: 11). Unlike any other region in the world, the EU and the European Economic Association (EEA) have political institutions that have considerable capacity to control the process of international economic integration. This is evident in the implementation of the programme to create a single European market which has involved considerable rationalization and restructuring of European industry, and a competition policy that has opened up national markets to European-wide competition, such as in airlines and telecommunications, and financial markets. This has had the effect of encouraging European companies to organize on a pan-European basis, and for international companies based outside Europe to inwardly invest in order to consolidate their presence. It is therefore not surprising that cross-border mergers and acquisitions involving both European and US-based companies have increased, and the single market has also led to the creation of new European scale companies through joint ventures and strategic alliances (ibid.: 11–13). These developments illustrate why the pattern of HRD policy and practice has become so complicated, and why distinct European regional management structures have been created within international businesses – Eurocompanies emerging in certain industries and sectors, as distinct from the global corporation.

Finally, it is important to acknowledge the strength of small and medium-sized enterprises (SMEs) throughout the European economy, and also that the state sector until very recently was very prominent in Austria, France, Italy, and Spain (Ferner 1994). Across the EU, over 99 per cent of businesses employ less than twenty-five people, and SMEs (those employing less than 250) account for two thirds of total EU employment, and 55 per cent of total business turnover. However, there is considerable variation between EU countries, both in terms of the relative sizes of SMEs (micro-businesses employing less than ten people predominate in the southern European countries of Greece, Italy, Spain and Portugal, while SMEs tend to be on average much larger in the 'Nordic' and North European countries). Measure of government support for SMEs also vary with substantial investment in human capital for management and workforce training in Denmark, Finland, Norway, Portugal, and the UK, and a close integration of SMEs within active labour market policies in Belgium, France and Germany (European Network for SME Research 1995). However, in contrast with the USA, where since 1993 70 per cent of the 18 million new jobs created have been in SMEs, the infrastructure of public–private partnership is not so well developed in respect of guaranteed loans and venture capital, and the transfer of R & D from universities to SMEs (House of Lords 1999).

So, in conclusion, the contextual basis for convergence and divergence in HRD practice is complex: the different origins and scope of the field of HRD, different national business systems, the differential impact of globalization upon business located within the EU and EEA; the persistence of distinct national business systems, and the strong position of SMEs. All these shape the European agenda for HRD. There are both similarities and differences between European countries, and also with the USA. It is therefore to be expected that this will influence the European HRD agenda. To date there have been few comparative studies of HRD practice between Europe and the US, and few between different European countries. Such a project requires a community of European scholars of HRD sufficiently familiar with the prevailing US models of HRD, to be able to devise a common research design. The First Conference on HRD Research and Practice Across Europe, held at Kingston University in January 2000, can be seen as a step in this direction, providing an opportunity for exchange of ideas for around seventy delegates from the UK, France, Italy, Spain, Germany, the Netherlands and Finland.

Research issues

Documentary data have traditionally played a key role in social science research, but methods of analysis vary, as does the perceived centrality of documents. The debate over the use of documents in research concerns validity, reliability, representativeness and generalizability. Textual analysis is less concerned with notions of validity and more concerned with the context and meaning of emergent concepts or themes. In this sense themes are not treated as fixed entities, but as fluid and emergent phenomena. In an attempt to produce an interpretative lens to assess the divergent and convergent research and practices, each paper was systematically reviewed to identify the focus of the content. As a result key themes were seen to emerge, which were then used to order the papers and form the basis for the proceeding discussion. Although this could be seen to be utilizing the underlying principles of textual analysis, it does not conform with the positivist view of content analysis, with its emphasis on quantitative measurements of derived data. In contrast the informal analysis for this chapter was rather loosely formulated, almost intuitive in nature, using terms defined by the researchers.

The call for papers was issued in May 1999 and abstracts were invited which subsequently passed through a refereeing process. In all, twenty-eight papers were presented and grouped into eight streams:

- research methodologies for HRD
- knowledge management
- organizational and individual learning
- HRD policy
- HRD business strategy and performance
- managers and careers
- learning technology and evaluation.

What follows is a summary of the highlights of the conference, and full copies are published in the conference proceedings (Woodall 2000). However, the table of contents from the proceedings is reproduced in Appendix I, and several of the papers have subsequently been published in *Human Resource Development International* and other journals.

345

Methodological issues

The adoption of diverse methodologies and epistemological standpoints was a striking feature of conference contributions. While the requirements of evidence-based practice have forged a close link between scholarly research and HRD practice, the resilience of constructivist and reflective research designs is remarkable. So, on the one hand, there were papers like Shipton *et al.*, Wognum *et al.* and Straka and Schaefer, which adopt a positivist research design drawing on questionnaire survey data to test established theoretical frameworks and constructs. Shipton *et al.* provided a quantitative study using longitudinal data to establish the existence and significance of variables which might predict how organizations become learning organizations, and Wognum *et al.*'s paper was a similarly framed survey of the extent to which HRD was vertically integrated within organizations. Straka and Schaefer were examining the conditions that promote self-directed learning in the workplace, arguing that there is a relationship between experienced workplace conditions, and interest in self-learning and learning strategies. While all three papers could be held to have policy implications they are very different in approach from others which were either more firmly grounded in practice such as the papers by MacNeil, Shelton and Short. Other research designs included Action Research (Shelton; Trehan *et al.*), and also much more constructivist research designs drawing upon metaphor (Baste), and even philosophical reflection (Bonet *et al.*). The overwhelming impression left is that HRD research in Europe welcomes a wide range of research designs and methodologies, and that in particular, a traditional critically reflective European discourse that seeks to explore and challenge concepts and frameworks is strongly present (see papers by Bassett-Jones; Gourlay; Woodall).

Knowledge management and organizational and individual learning

The link between HRD and the emerging field of knowledge management was a dominant theme at the conference. There was also much overlap between the papers in this stream, and those in the stream on organizational and individual learning, so all seven papers are considered together. Despite a variety of research designs varying from theoretical reflection (Gourlay; Bonet *et al.*; Tomassini; MacNeill), case studies (Poell and van der Krogt), action research (Shelton) and questionnaire surveys (Capetta *et al.*); there was a remarkable similarity in the points made, including:

- a challenge to the epistemological basis of theories of knowledge management (including the empiricist, rationalist and situated cognition theories of knowledge) and the relative implications of these for the role of HRD in promoting and maintaining knowledge management in organizations;

346

- questioning whether organizations can really 'manage' knowledge, unless they accept the different learning strategies of individual employees, and accept the socially constructed nature of the learning process;
- following from this, the importance of recognizing and including all the different stakeholders in the learning process;
- the importance of proactive facilitation that recognizes both the dynamic nature of organizational learning, and power relations;
- and the essential importance of equal attention to 'people processes' (especially culture change, training, education and facilitation) as well as technology for successful knowledge management.

A key feature of several papers was a criticism of Nonaka and Takeuchi's (1995) model for the creation and dissemination of both explicit and tacit knowledge, as both a simplistic and inaccurate representation of what happens. All papers argued very strongly in favour of adopting a model that recognized the socially constructed nature of knowledge and learning, and hence argued strongly for the role of HRD in reinforcing existing learning cultures and processes, rather than modelling mechanistic technology-driven alternatives, and through creating climates of sharing and trust backed up with wider human resource policies for employment security, recognition and reward. In general the papers in these two streams took the debate around knowledge management and organizational learning to a new level, and away from simple, prescriptive systems frameworks.

HRD policy

This stream combined two working papers that explored the implementation of public policy initiatives in HRD (Alker, Shaw and Holman) with an investigation of learning processes that could contribute to greater competitiveness for SMEs (Trullen et al.). All three papers illustrated the manner in which HRD is present in the public policy agenda in Europe. Government labour market policy embraces public post-compulsory vocational education and training, and in many European countries this has been used to spearhead innovative thinking in HRD (especially in the UK with the use of the VET system to pioneer developments in work-based learning and competence development). Two of the papers in this stream covered the implementation of vocational education and training initiatives to improve the labour market prospects of employed adults in the UK (Alker); and the competing and conflicting stakeholder agendas in lifelong learning, and the challenge that this presented to the paradigm of UK higher education (Shaw and Holman). Successful implementation was held to depend upon responsiveness to different stakeholder needs. While the first two papers drew principally upon UK fieldwork, that by Trullen et al. is drawn from a collaborative research project carried out by four

European universities, and reported on preliminary findings. These indicated the key importance of two major factors to effective learning in SMEs: organizational culture in creating the necessary climate of trust and encouragement of risk-taking for learning, and the importance of group learning and informal networking.

HRD, business strategy and performance

While a public policy focus is a distinctive feature of much HRD research in Europe, so is a clear focus upon business strategy and performance, as illustrated by the papers of Shipton *et al.*, and Wognum. Both of these used survey research designs drawing upon data from a number of organizations. The former drew upon longitudinal questionnaire survey data from eleven companies to identify and assess the significance of a number of variables (competitive success, environmental uncertainty, organizational structure, approach to HRM, and quality orientation) in correlating with the propensity to support organizational learning. Significant correlation was found with HRM strategy where a developmental rather than a radical transformative perspective was important, and a correlation with quality orientation where the decentralization of decision making and the use of projects teams encouraged a learning orientation. Wognum's paper was also based upon a large questionnaire survey focusing upon the extent to which HRD is vertically integrated within organizations at three organizational levels: strategic, tactical and operational. The paper focused upon the process of alignment rather than the outcome, and this was operationalized in terms of four main variables: participation, information, formalization and decision making. The findings indicated that whilst individuals were interested in achieving alignment, this did not in practice happen, with a consequent lack of vertical integration within HRD policy-making and implementation processes. So both these papers illustrate the complexity surrounding strategic HRD. Organizational learning may only be possible in certain strategic HR contexts where there is little pressure for radical change, and where it is integrated with quality management. On the other hand, despite the prescriptions of many HRD texts, the actual achievement of strategically aligned HRD may be an elusive goal.

HRD practitioner roles and skills

All three papers in this stream attempted to go beyond the largely prescriptive literature in this field. Chivers *et al.* reported on a longitudinal study of alumni of the first UK university Master's degree programme in Training and Development at Sheffield University, to ascertain whether respondents felt prepared to meet greater organizational demands in learning and development, and particularly learning outside the traditional vocational education and training environment. Data were collected by means of semi-structured interviews with a large sample of alumni. The findings reflected that these HRD professionals were working in turbulent and uncertain environments that had led many to move into self-employment. Other aspects of their role included changes in organizational structures and work structures, loss of responsibility for training delivery and a growing emphasis upon self-directed, work-related and informal learning, mainly focused upon individuals (with some increasing focus upon group learning and organization development). The main obstacle was carrying out their responsibility in the absence of a learning culture within their organizations, and frequently facing line manager hostility. The implications were that many had developed negotiation and political skills and were more assertive in self-development and marketing themselves. A separate study of practising HR developers in Finland (Valkeavaara) also noticed how the changing and ill-defined context within which HRD is practised, has been very influential in extending the basis of expertise beyond the knowledge and skill base acquired in initial training. The main findings stressed the centrality of change agency to the work role, and that high levels of analytical managerial, developmental and coaching competences were essential if the HRD professionals were to be able to engage flexibly with their work. While the changing role of HRD professionals has been acknowledged to include more time devoted to the facilitation of informal learning and change management, these papers illustrate the growing importance of political skills, ability to function in conditions of considerable uncertainty, and acquiring a wider repertoire of general management skills. Such evidence has considerable bearing on the future for professional training in HRD.

Managers and careers

A large number of papers were focused upon management learning and careers. Several of the papers here challenged conventional approaches to management development. Walton's interim findings of an exploratory comparison of mentoring in Europe reported considerable differences in both definitions of the practice and its cultural acceptability. Although well established in Scandinavia and well suited to countries with low power distance and a high tolerance for uncertainty, it was likely that MNCs would act as a trigger for the spread of mentoring across Europe. Woodall provided a methodological critique of the way in which UK survey research on management development has investigated the growing significance of work-based management learning, and especially informal and incidental learning, followed by suggestions for future research designs. Klink *et al.*'s exploration of the competencies required by graduates in the Netherlands also provided a critique of different approaches to the definition and measurement of competencies, suggesting the influence of organizational context is more important than knowledge of the professional domain, and that a more holistic approach to competency is required. Finally, Lankhuijzen's working paper was concerned with the research question of the relations between managers' psychological career contracts, personal HRD activities, and their orientation towards job mobility. All these papers indicated the potential impact of organizational context, and changing labour market situations upon the ability of individual managers to take responsibility for their own development and employability. The message was that prescriptions for management development and HRD must be placed within context.

Learning technology and evaluation

This stream contained two papers outlining two online tools to assist learning and two evaluation studies. Stoyanov *et al.* outlined a Web-based performance support system to assist managers in solving ill-structured problems by means of concept mapping, and de Vries illustrated how online expertise centres can be used as a key element in study support for students while they are in work placements, and he went on to indicate the potential of this as a key tool in lifelong learning. The other papers included Short's case study to illustrate the application of a model to learn from training 'breakdown' in order to improve course quality, and Zolingen's evaluation of a new instruction model for on the job training in post offices in the Netherlands focusing upon training outputs, processes, inputs and organizational context. The latter illustrated again the problems encountered when there is a high reliance upon human facilitation by mentors, but little involvement of them in the process of programme design, and insufficient flexibility in the instructional model.

Conclusion and key learning points

The HRD agenda in Europe

It is clear that this conference attracted a very diverse range of contributions, which in themselves indicate the breadth of the HRD agenda in Europe. In as much as it is possible to identify common themes, they are as follows:

- HRD in Europe is a much more 'fuzzy' concept than is understood within the USA. There are no recognizable boundaries, and the disciplinary base is not confined to areas such as systems theory, labour economics, organization development, adult education, etc.
- HRD research in Europe welcomes a wide range of research designs and methodologies.
- The European tradition of critically reflective discourse that seeks to explore and challenge concepts and frameworks is also present in European HRD research.

- There is an acute awareness that many of the established prescriptions of professional practice (e.g. competencies, mentoring, strategic integration of HRD, HRD practitioner skills and roles) are not wholly adequate and require adaptation to cultural circumstances.
- 'Managing' learning in organizations is less about adhering to formal procedures for design, delivery, etc. of instruction, and increasingly about creating the environmental conditions (including building trust, fostering networks, and working with a range of stakeholders) within which learning can take place.

Maybe there is much more scope for cross-European comparative evidence-based research? While there are indications that some is already underway, it is to be hoped that this conference has provided the impetus for more sharing of ideas, and there are intentions to convene an annual conference on HRD research and practice across Europe on a regular basis.

Acknowledgement

The authors would like to thank Dr Chris Rees and Dr Tony Edwards of Kingston Business School for their critical comments and advice on developments within European HRM, and Professor Robert Blackburn and colleagues at the Small Business Research Centre at Kingston Business school for information on comparative developments in the small business sector in Europe.

References

Brewster, C. and Holt Larsen, H. (eds) (2000) *Human Resource Management in Northern Europe*, Oxford: Blackwell.

European Network for SME Research (1995) *The European Observatory for SMEs.* Third Annual Report, Zoetermeer, Netherlands.

Ferner, A. (1994) 'The state as employer', in R. Hyman and A. Ferner (eds) *New Frontiers in European Industrial Relations*, Oxford: Blackwell, 52–79.

Ferner, A. (1997) 'Country of origin effects and HRM in multinational companies', *Human Resource Management Journal*, 7(2): 19–37.

Ferner, A. and Hyman, R. (eds) (1998) *Changing Industrial Relations in Europe*, Oxford: Blackwell.

Ferner, A. and Quintanilla, J. (1998) 'Multinationals, national business systems and HRM: the enduring influence of national identity or a process of Anglo-Saxonisation', *The International Journal of Human Resource Management*, 9(4): 710–31.

Hegewisch, A. and Brewster, C. (1993) *European Developments in Human Resource Management*, London: Kogan Page.

House of Lords (1999) *Promoting Small and Medium Enterprises in the EU*, Select Committee on the European Communities, Session 1998–9, 20th Report. House of Lords Paper 115.

Hyman, R. and Ferner, A. (eds) (1994) *New Frontiers in European Industrial Relations*, Oxford: Blackwell.

Marginson, P. (2000) 'The Eurocompany and Euro Industrial Relations', *European Journal of Industrial Relations*, 6(1): 9–34.

Marginson, P. and Sisson, K. (1994) 'The structure of transnational capital in Europe: the emerging Euro-company and its implications for industrial relations', in R. Hyman and A. Ferner (eds) *New Frontiers in European Industrial Relations*, Oxford: Blackwell, 15–51.

McLean, G. (1998) 'HRD: a three-legged stool, an octopus or a centipede', *Human Resource Development International*, 1(4): 375–7.

—— (1999) 'Get out the drill, glue and more legs', *Human Resource Development International*, 2(1): 6–7.

McLagan, P. (1989) *Models of HRD Practice*, Arlington, VA: ASTD Press.

Nonaka, I. and Takeuchi, H. (1995) *The Knowledge Creating Company*, Oxford: Oxford University Press.

Pieper, R. (ed.) (1990) *Human Resource Management: an International Comparison*, Berlin: de Gruyter.

Sparrow, P. and Hiltrop, J.-M. (1994) *European Human Resource Management in Transition*, London: Prentice Hall.

Stewart, J. and McGoldrick, J. (eds) (1996) *Human Resource Development – Perspectives, Strategies and Practice*, London: Pitman.

Swanson, R. (1992) 'Human resource development: performance is the key', *Human Resource Development Quarterly*, 6(2): 205–13.

Swanson, R.A. (1999) 'HRD theory, real or imagined?' *Human Resource Development International*, 2(1): 2–5.

Tyson, S. and Wikander, L. (1994) 'The education and training of human resource managers in Europe', in C. Brewster and A. Hegewisch (eds) *Policy and Practice in European Human Resource Management: the Price Waterhouse Cranfield Survey*, London: Routledge.

Walton, J. (1999) *Strategic Human Resource Development*, London: Financial Times/ Prentice Hall.

Weinberger, L. (1998) Commonly held theories of human resource development, *Human Resource Development International*, 1(1): 75–93.

Woodall, J. (ed.) (2000) *First Conference on HRD Research and Practice Across Europe: Conference Papers*, Kingston upon Thames: Kingston Business School.

Appendix I

Table of contents from conference proceedings of *The First Conference on HRD Research and Practice Across Europe*, Kingston, January 2000 (ISBN 1–872058–67–1)

Contents   Page

17

USING ACTION RESEARCH TO EXPLORE THE DEVELOPMENT NEEDS OF SECOND GENERATION ASIAN SMALL BUSINESSES

Clare Rigg, Kiran Trehan and Monder Ram

Aims and contribution

Research into small firms' HRD practice and needs in general has overwhelmingly been quantitative, focused on training, and concentrated on investigating larger enterprises, tending to exclude businesses with fewer than fifty employees. There is very limited information on HRD within minority ethnic firms and no more than speculation on the development needs of 'second generation' South Asians[1] in self-employment.

This chapter will relate the experience of a consultancy project that deployed action research to investigate the development needs of second-generation South Asian small business owners and aspiring entrepreneurs. The intention is to use this account to introduce the reader to the following:

- the origins, aspirations and characteristics of action research;
- diversity of traditions and approaches to action research;
- the potential application of action research to researching HRD;
- pitfalls of implementing the ideals of action research, particularly in research conducted as funded consultancy.

The chapter argues that action research in this context can address concerns over rigour and reliability. However, the process requires a constant struggle to maintain credibility with entrepreneurs who are acutely aware of costs of participation, funders who are part of a pervasive contract culture, and the small business research community which is still in the process of establishing its disciplinary credentials.

Theoretical context

Action research, an approach first associated with the work of Kurt Lewin in the 1940s (Lewin 1946, 1947), has been a valuable, if somewhat neglected, approach to management research. Doubts about its methodological precision, rigour and generalizability have contributed to its comparatively marginal location in the field of management research (Eden and Huxham 1996). However, the approach, with its characteristics of practitioner-orientation, continuous reflection and collaborative methodology, has had particular appeal for work with marginal groups (e.g. Brown and Tandon 1983; Whyte 1991). Intuitively, there are important reasons why the small business community should be a fertile ground for such an approach. First, the small business field has a pronounced policy and practitioner orientation (Stanworth and Gray 1991). Second, small businesses have been the target of a plethora of training, enterprise support initiatives (Bennett and Robson 1999). Finally, governments of all political complexions have vied with each other to champion entrepreneurship, although it is doubtful if their policies have been entirely efficacious (see Storey 1994, for a review). For these reasons, the 'user' perspective has been a defining feature of the rhetoric, if not the reality, of the small business sector. Somewhat paradoxically, the similarly practitioner inclined paradigm of action research is extremely rare within published accounts of small enterprises.

The importance of the small business sector to the UK is well documented (Storey 1994); moreover, over the past two decades, small firms have been seen as the source of economic growth and renewal across the European Union (ENSR 1997). The promotion of training has been an important means of supporting small enterprises. Encouraging training in small firms has been an explicit feature of the policy-agenda for at least a decade. The Competitiveness White papers of 1994, 1995 and 1996 attached considerable importance to the training needs of small firms. Much of the remit of Training and Enterprise Councils (TECs) was to promote skills and training in small businesses; and programmes like the nurturing of 'training champions' in small firms continue to flourish (Curran et al. 1997). Despite this level of interest, there remains a deficiency of understanding of human resource development (HRD) needs of small business owners, managers and employees (Matlay 1999). Research into small firms HRD practice and needs has overwhelmingly been quantitative (Matlay 1999), has taken a narrow definition of training, detached from wider human resource strategies (Pettigrew, Arthur and Hendry 1990), and has concentrated on investigating larger enterprises, tending to exclude micro-businesses (1–10 people) or very small firms (11–49 employees). The call has been for research that is more specialized (Pettigrew, Arthur and Hendry 1990), longitudinal and qualitative (Westhead and Storey 1997), as well as research that is relevant to practitioners (Gibb 1999).

The debates on training in small firms have effectively by-passed ethnic minority businesses (Westhead and Storey 1997), despite mounting evidence of distinctive needs of such firms (see Ram and Jones 1998, for a review). Published evidence suggests that previous attempts by enterprise support providers to engage with Asian businesses have been hampered by a 'top-down' approach (Ram and Sparrow 1992), or insufficiently close ties with appropriate businesses (Marlow 1992). Against this background of limited information, there has been considerable speculation on the progress, problems and prospects of 'second-generation' South Asians in self-employment. Some commentators argue that the second generation is more likely to pursue 'professional' careers rather than maintain the tradition of entrepreneurship noted in the South Asian community (Metcalf, Modood and Wirdee 1996). In contrast, others maintain the second generation might be utilizing their comparatively favourable education credentials to develop businesses in non-traditional 'knowledge-intensive' sectors, such as computer software, music production and financial services (Ram and Jones 1998).

Action research defies simple definition, despite its increasing acceptance and application in social and organizational research. Eden and Huxham offer what they call a 'starting point for an exploration of the nature and boundaries of action research . . . [which] involves the researcher in working with members of an organization over a matter which is of genuine concern to them and in which there is an intent by the organization members to take action based on the intervention' (1996: 1).

There are three broad traditions within action research, which can be divided into a focus on organizational development, on social change and on personal development.

Early action research was concerned with social understanding and change. Action research became academically formalized as an approach to social research in the 1940s with Kurt Lewin's work on food habits (Lewin 1943) and tackling race relations issues (Lewin 1946) and Collier's research with native Americans' (Collier 1945). Lewin's approach was to design hypotheses and test them in workshops, collecting data on the changes achieved through the process of the workshops. The approach of action research for social change became popular within some community development projects (e.g. Nottingham Youth Action, Chesterfield, and Birmingham Settlement, within the UK). The defining principles of this approach being collaboration between researchers and research participants, concern for empowerment and emancipation of marginalized groups through the process of constructing and using their knowledge, and intent to take action. This tradition displays a keen awareness of issues of power and attention to the researchers' values. This approach encompasses participatory action research, for example: Whyte 1991; Fals-Borda and Rahman, who talk of 'the enlightenment and awakening of common peoples' (1991: iv); human inquiry (Heron 1981); co-operative inquiry (Reason 1988); and new paradigm research (Reason and Rowan 1981).

Many of these approaches, of participatory action research and co-operative inquiry, have been deployed within organizations, as well as for social issues. However, for many years in the UK, managerial action research was most influenced by a socio-technical systems approach to organizations, particularly at the Tavistock Institute (e.g. Clark 1975). Elsewhere in the world organizational development applications of action research have been employed in organizational activity concerned with democratization of work, for example in Sweden (Elden 1979; Elden and Levin 1991).

From the 1980s a third tradition in the use of action research has developed, where the concern is for personal development. In education and health this is well developed in the context of improving professional practice (e.g. Hart and Bond 1995) and has more recently gained popularity in management research (e.g. Whitehead 1994). Eden and Huxham link this development to Argyris and Schon's ideas of the reflective practitioner (1978) and double loop learning (1974). Argyris and Schon argue that people develop by identifying their 'theories in use' through reflection on action – what they term 'action science' (Argyris, Putnam and Schon 1985). Torbert (1981, 1991) also contributes to the focus on personal development, through concern with individuals' implicit cognitive models, although he also advocates collaborative inquiry as a method of working.

With such a variety of approaches and priorities for action research, can we go beyond Eden and Huxham's starting point above? They themselves have developed an extensive set of fifteen key characteristics (1999 – see Box 17.1), which they argue constitutes valid action research. We have found it valuable to consider how these principles can inform a research process, to provoke thought and to aspire to. However, in practice we find they are too complex to apply in their entirety, which Eden and Huxham acknowledge, describing the fifteen principles as standards which are 'probably not an achievable challenge' (1999: 284).

Elden and Chisholm (1993: 126–9) suggest a more distilled characterization of five features of action research:

1   value choice – action research is purposeful, frequently informed by the researcher's objectives for change, and interpretive;
2   contextual – action research is grounded in the participants' definitions of their context;
3   scientific method – action research is conducted within the basic social science rules of 'scientific inquiry', for instance concerned with validity;
4   participation – action research is conducted collaboratively or interactively with people involved in the research problem;
5   knowledge diffusion – action researchers contribute to knowledge through writing, dissemination and generating theory.

Box 17.1 Eden and Huxham's fifteen characteristics of action research

1 Action research demands an integral involvement by the researcher in an intent to change the organisation. This intent may not succeed – no change may take place as a result of the intervention – and the change may not be as intended.

2 Action research must have some *implications beyond those required for action or generation of knowledge in the domain of the project.* It must be possible to envisage talking about the theories developed in relation to other situations. Thus it must be clear that the results *could* inform other contexts, at least in the sense of suggesting areas for consideration.

3 As well as being usable in everyday life, action research demands *valuing theory*, with theory elaboration and development as an explicit concern of the research process.

4 If the generality drawn out of the action research is to be expressed through the design of tools, techniques, models and method then this, alone, is not enough. The basis for their design must be explicit and shown to be related to the theories which inform the design and which, in turn, are supposed or developed through action research.

5 Action research will be concerned with a system of *emergent theory*, in which the theory develops from a synthesis of that which emerges from the data and that which emerges from the use in practice of the body of theory which informed the intervention and research intent.

6 Theory building, as a result of action research, will be incremental, moving through a cycle of developing theory to action to reflection to developing theory, from the particular to the general in small steps.

7 What is important for action research is not a (false) dichotomy between prescription and description, but a recognition that description will be prescription, even if implicitly so. Thus presenters of action research should be clear about what they expect the consumer to take from it and present it with a form and style appropriate to this aim.

8 For high quality action research a high degree of systematic method and orderliness is required in reflecting about, and holding on to, the research data and the emergent theoretical outcomes of each episode or cycle of involvement in the organisation.

9 For action research, the processes of exploration of the data – rather than collection of the data – in the detecting of emergent theories and development of existing theories, must either be replicable or, at least, capable of being explained to others.

10 The full process of action research involves a series of interconnected cycles, where writing about research outcomes at the latter stages of an action research the processes of explicating pre-understanding and methodical reflection to explore and develop theory formally.

11 Adhering to characteristics 1–10 above is a necessary *but not sufficient* condition for the validity of action research.

12 It is difficult to justify the use of action research when the same aims can be satisfied using approaches (such as controlled experimentation or surveys) that can demonstrate the link between data and outcomes more

transparently. This in action research, the reflection and data collection process – and hence the emergent theories – are most valuably focused on the aspects that cannot be captured by other approaches.

13 In action research, the opportunities for triangulation that do not offer themselves with other methods should be exploited fully and reported. They should be used as a dialectical device which powerfully facilitates the incremental development of theory.

14 The history and context for the intervention must be taken as critical to the interpretation of the likely range of validity and applicability of the results of action research.

15 Action research requires that the theory development which is of general value is disseminated in such a way as to be of interest to an audience wider than those integrally involved with the action and/or with the research.

(Reprinted by permission of Sage Publications Ltd from Eden, C. and Huxham, C. 1999: 285 @ C. Eden and C. Huxham, 1995)

The idea of cycles is fundamental to action research. One of Eden and Huxham's fifteen principles is the notion of incremental theory building through a cycle of theory-to-action-to-theory (1999). Reason talks of 'cycling and recycling between action and reflection so that issues are examined several times in different ways' as a contribution to validity in co-operative inquiry (1994b: 327).

Visually, action research can usefully be conceived of as a cyclical process of actions and reflection, which we illustrate in Figure 17.1.

New knowledge of a 'social system' (Lewin 1946) derives from the attempt to change it, from the stages of problem diagnosis, intervention and evaluation, leading to new problem diagnosis, and so on – a cycling of action and reflection.

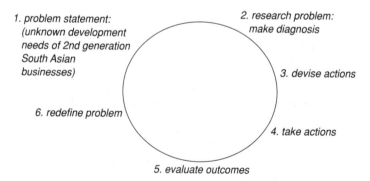

Figure 17.1 Action research cycle
Source: Derived from Lewin (1946)

Empirical context

In an effort to move beyond the speculation into second-generation needs outlined above, we are mindful of the criticism of 'imposing' initiatives without consultation. Birmingham Business Link Enterprise (BBLE) commissioned the University of Central England's Enterprise Research Centre to undertake an initiative to ascertain the business development needs of second-generation South Asians.

The brief we drew up with the funding client, was to:

- facilitate a collaborative process with second-generation South Asian small business owners (existing and aspiring);
- through this process, to reveal the particular business development needs of the target group;
- involve them in the design of appropriate interventions.

Presenting the brief in this manner enables us to reinforce the difference between action research and consultancy. Rather than tacking on research to what could have been a pure consultancy exercise, the basic principles of action research were explicated during interactions with the funder. Hence, following Ormerod (1995: 5): 'A reasonable objective might be to conduct consultancy as action research making sure that prior assumptions and research questions are stated, prolonged analysis is included and reliance on judgement and expertise is minimised.'

It was significant that the BBLE officers were prepared to sponsor an action research project since, as a qualitative approach, with unpredictable outcomes, this runs counter to their organization's 'instant measurable output' culture, and was therefore an unknown risk. However, the discomfort of risky territory rumbled throughout the project, influencing our later methods and affecting the client relationship, as will emerge.

The Second Generation Asian Entrepreneurs project straddled the organization and social development rationales of action research. At one level Asian entrepreneurs are part of a marginalized group, a minority within both the business community and wider UK society. Although there is an above average level of higher education amongst second-generation Asian entrepreneurs (Curran and Blackburn 1993), they are not usually *au fait* with academic research terminology and practice, which consequently disempowers them within a research context. However, at another level, some individual entrepreneurs are hugely successful and amongst the most wealthy, and hence economically powerful people within the country.

The setting as we began our case study was one with a number of interested parties: there were clearly ourselves as researchers and participants, the yet-to-be-found entrepreneurs; three Asian business support agencies, through whom we hoped to recruit participants, and BBLE, the paying client. This was action research as a consultancy project with a complex client-system (Cockman *et al.* 1992), encompassing all the other parties.

Methodological issues

Why action research?

It seemed clear to us that so many development interventions for small firms in general, and minority ethnic firms in particular, have been ill-advised because their conception has been divorced from the prospective clients (see also Curran *et al.* 1997). We saw action research as an approach that might be more fruitful. We were also sensitive to the fact that much consultancy in the 'expert' tradition, whilst it might enlighten a particular problem, often leaves clients as ignorant and powerless in the face of ongoing problems (Cockman *et al.* 1992; Schein 1999). We believed that the only way second-generation South Asian entrepreneurial development needs would be addressed on an ongoing basis is if the entrepreneurs had an ongoing, collective voice within both the Asian business networks and the wider business support industry. Again, a participative approach to research seemed to offer the possibility for us as researchers to leave some kind of second-generation South Asian entrepreneurial infrastructure behind when the research project ended. An additional interest in deploying action research was the potential for development of individual participants in the course of their involvement in the project. Action research as an approach can encompass a range of research methods. However, because of our concerns with what participants might gain in the process of the research, we rejected a perspective which set the entrepreneurs as passive objects of research, for instance using methods such as questionnaires or interviews, alone, without participation.

In terms of potential cycles within action research, our objectives for this project addressed just part of the cycle, as indicated by italics in Figure 17.2. This partial action research cycle was a direct consequence of the research being commercially funded. As consultants we had no control over whether or how stages 4–6 might be implemented. We could but advise the paying client.

Despite our concerns that being impotent to deliver might impede our credibility with entrepreneurs, we wanted the project to be participative and for them to identify and design interventions they thought were needed. We saw our role as facilitating this identification and design.

Which action research tradition?

In considering which action research tradition to work with, we elected to follow Peter Reason's model of co-operative inquiry (Reason 1988). It would be good to be able to claim it was a process of systematic and

1. Establishment of authentic collaboration
- *initiation*
- *finding a group*
- *contracting*
- *devising an overall research plan*
- *roles*
- *group facilitation*

2. Progress of the inquiry
- *formulating a model for research*
- *putting the model into practice*
- *reflecting on experiences and making sense*

3. Writing

4. Validity procedures

5. Endings

Figure 17.2 Stages in co-operative inquiry
Source: Adapted from Reason (1988) with permission of Sage Publications Ltd

reasoned choice, but that was not so. It was simply that we liked the principles within it because they seemed to speak to our concerns for participation and 'user voice'; the literature offered an outline programme we could adapt to our purposes, so we adopted it.

> Co-operative inquiry is a way of working with other people who have similar concerns and interests to yourself, in order to under-stand your world, make sense of your life and develop new and creative ways of looking at things, learn how to act to change things you may want to change and find out how to do things better
>
> (Reason and Heron 1998)

Co-operative inquiry aspires to genuine collaboration between the initiators of research and the participants; to equal status between all parties. Research is done *with* people not *on* them, working collaboratively in an inquiry group. Reason explains a co-operative inquiry group as being one 'in which the intent is that all members work together fully as co-researchers' (Reason 1994a: 18). Reason articulates four phases of action and reflection:

- Phase One: people come together who have a common interest to agree their focus and research questions; they agree to take some actions.
- Phase Two: group members (the co-researchers) apply their agreed actions and record outcomes. These are reflected on.
- Phase Three: Co-researchers engage in more activity.

- Phase Four: The group reassembles to share their experiences and reflections and agree a new cycle of actions and reflection.

Reason proposes six stages to setting up a co-operative inquiry, which are adapted in Figure 17.2. (He has a sixth stage, seeking supervision from other experienced action researchers, which he recommends for long projects, which we omitted because ours was so short.) In the following section, The Research, we relate how we tried to implement each stage in researching development needs with second-generation Asian entrepreneurs.

The research

Establishment of authentic collaboration

Initiation – 'selling action research'

From the outset, aspirations of genuine collaboration face the contradiction that someone has to initiate the project and in doing so starts the process with greater ownership and knowledge than any subsequent participants. As the initiators, we were committed to the project and had more knowledge of action research processes; hence we were concerned from the outset to try to encourage the participants to share ownership. The project could also only begin if sufficient numbers of business owners were convinced there was a point in dedicating several evenings of their time over several weeks to the project. To this end, our publicity material tried to sound appealing:

> This is your opportunity to become part of an exciting initiative aimed at responding to the particular needs of existing businesses and the next generation of Asian entrepreneurs . . . You will have a chance to contribute to the design of enterprise support for new and existing Asian businesses. There will also be an opportunity to meet with other business owners and be introduced to the wide range of packages of services available to you.

Finding a group

Our intention was to form three or four groups of about ten people in each, including women, aspiring entrepreneurs, fast-track businesses and other existing businesses, so as to be able to explore differential needs as well as commonalities. We started by circulating the membership networks of the main three Asian business support groups in Birmingham, because one of us had good connections with these. We also used the media, through a radio chat show, and a press release. Interested individuals were invited to a high-profile launch involving the business groups as well as the funder. Our intentions here were partially to explain the project and try to 'sell' action research to prospective participants. But we were also aware of a subtext: to sustain credibility with the funder by demonstrating the numbers of people interested. Our ambivalence epitomizes the tensions that ran throughout the project, between the quantitative output orientation of the funders and the necessary imprecision of early stages of action research.

From our promotional efforts we signed up around thirty people, who were invited to one of several initial group meetings. However, one problem this method produced arose from the in-built dominance of business groups by men. We recruited very few women. To rectify this we turned to other, more female networks – putting the word out through families and Asian women community workers. This route produced a group of women prospective entrepreneurs.

Contracting

Reason (1988) argues that a co-operative inquiry group cannot simply be set up, rather that co-operative inquiry emerges as co-operative processes are negotiated and learned. Contracting is the stage of beginning to evolve from a collection of individuals into a group; it is the early one or two meetings where expectations are shared, the method of co-operative inquiry is explained and participants are guided to discuss commitment to, and roles within, the project. The process of these contracting meetings is important in contributing to building the co-operative spirit. In our project, there was a tension between the power held by us as initiators, and our desire for co-operation. If we were too clear and fixed about how the project would proceed, there were risks of dependency, resistance, or stagnation within the groups. However, we were also alert to the possibility that if we were too flexible, and apparently directionless, the groups could flounder in confusion and ambiguity. There was a risk the groups or some members within them could take over. We also had to deal with a sense that our credibility was damaged by appearing uncertain in the context of a fast-moving, action-orientated small business culture.

Our intention had been to facilitate the formation of three or four consistent groups. We began a contracting process through initial meetings with participants, but it was also at this stage that some of our problems began. Although attendance at each meeting averaged fifteen, the individuals varied, as work commitments, conflicting priorities and interest intervened. Over the two months in which group meetings took place around forty people were involved in total, very few (six) actually withdrew from the project, and twenty-four attended the final meeting. All made a contribution, but the core which could be most closely described as a co-operative inquiry group was a group of eight men, and the separate group of eight women.

We found an underlying tension between the drawn out, discursive style of co-operative inquiry and the entrepreneurs' culture of quick action, and 'talk for action'. Reason (1988) suggests initial meetings use small group discussions as icebreakers – we found we could never persuade the business owners to break into small groups. He also suggests the contracting meetings end with a closing round in which each person is asked to state their resentments and appreciations as a result of the meeting. In our notes we wrote: 'Could we really get small business people to do this?'

Devising an overall research plan

This is the stage of agreeing an outline of working arrangements, actions and meeting times. Although there was enthusiasm for the method, and commitment from many individuals to seeing some positive outcomes from the project, there were many instances where meeting times were selected to fit individuals' schedules, only to find they did not turn up; or people offering venues that did not then materialize. At this stage we felt we were limping through uncertainly, from a meeting of four one week, to a turnout of twenty-two the next. Whilst we tried to facilitate establishment of ground rules, the idea itself was not well received. We proposed a research structure for discussion, but the response was very much 'OK let's get on with it'.

Roles

A goal of co-operative inquiry is to identify and use group members' skills and resources, as another way of building participation. For us this became particularly pertinent as some individuals' networks helped expand and sustain the group's membership, as we discuss below.

Group facilitation

Reason (1988) suggests inquiry groups usually need facilitation to help them through three stages of group development:

- coming together, feeling included, overcoming anxieties;
- working on the inquiry task, handling differences, power struggles;
- a full co-operative relationship in which individuals each have a place, differences are respected, struggles are productive.

He suggests co-operative inquiry can also be upsetting, because it can challenge some of peoples' norms and habits, warranting 'distress facilitation'. We know, from facilitating groups in another context which work over a two-year period, that this is frequently true. However, within this short project we found difficult process issues did not surface, probably because the time and frequency of meeting did not build sufficient intensity. Although at the end of meetings we would ask questions like 'how do you feel?' or 'what do you think is working well, not so well?', these can be hard to answer for people whose working culture does not allow for questions about feelings (Hofstede 1994). Again the short time of the project was a barrier to building familiarity with this mode.

Progress of the inquiry

Formulating a model for research

We proposed a framework of questions, derived from Peter Senge (1993), as a structure for the participants to share their experiences and views. These are shown below.

Where	Where do you want to be in one year? Where do you want to be in three years? What will assist you? What is constraining you?
Why	What is constraining you? Why?
How	How can you make the most of assisting factors? How can you move through the constraints?
What	What do you need to help you overcome the constraints? How can supporting interventions be made?

We also offered to organize meetings on any themes which participants would find useful.

Putting the model into practice

The early stages of the project could be characterized as 'initiators left eating the biscuits'. We seriously wondered if the project would take off, and cursed the action research literature's apparent optimism. We kept a positive spin on progress with the funding client, and maintained pressure on the business groups to deliver more of their promised contacts. Because we found the uncertainty difficult to handle and were concerned to retain credibility with the funder, we resorted to a short, traditional, quantitative telephone questionnaire, so that we would at least have something to write up for this client, despite our scepticism of this method.

Then without warning, about half way through, the hoped-for 'shared ownership' took off. A few individuals seemed to decide they were intensely interested. Recruitment was boosted through family networks, and numbers rose to around twenty each meeting. Participants were diverse, including several young aspirant entrepreneurs, some well-established business owners, with just a couple of millionaires. We also followed up new contacts and the group of women was assembled. Both these incidences showed our reliance on our initial contacts was misplaced, and that often there is a need to tap into different networks. It was an important reminder of the need for any network to ask who is not involved and how else they could be contacted, for example, through community groups, sports or music venues, not simply through established business networks.

In structuring the group discussion we followed Senge's framework of questions, above, which proved productive as a way of generating information for the funder's brief, but also was a mechanism for participants to exchange experiences. Meetings were often characterized by individuals offering each other advice. We no longer had to take the initiative in organizing the meeting times, or in communicating to absent group members. Participants also took up the offer of information inputs, for which we organized an input by BBLE on sources of support. For us, this meeting served two additional purposes, first, to demonstrate to BBLE (the project sponsor) that there were bodies engaged in the project, and second, to make an intervention which might enhance the development of some of the businesses.

Throughout the project one person, from the academic team, but not an active project participant, recorded discussions through note taking.

Reflecting on experiences, making sense and writing up

The spirit of co-operative inquiry implies that all participants should engage in, and share ownership of the sense making and the writing up. Reason says: 'Presumably co-operative inquiry leads to co-operative reporting, and so the writing of any report should be a shared business' (1998: 38).

We could have chosen to do this collaboratively with a sub-group; we could have handed it over entirely to a sub-group; but instead we suggested a mechanism that still maintained engagement of participants, but could not honestly be claimed as collaborative. We proposed that we would pull together what we thought the process had revealed and write up a draft report for presentation to all participants for discussion and written comment. The other participants readily accepted this, but two said they would also prepare their own presentation.

So, what was going on here? For us, as the project contractors, we felt responsible for delivering something to the funder that we could feel was credible. Quite consciously we suggested a mechanism for writing up that involved a degree of sharing, but kept us in control. In referring back our draft to other participants we were seeking validation, but the power of the pen cannot be denied, and we held on to the power to determine the language and select the particular stories to relay, in short to construct the reality of development needs presented to the funder.

For the two participants preparing their own report, they made explicit that they had their own individual agendas to convey to the funder, beyond the collective interests of the project group. We were happy that they had the space to do this, but we deliberately manœuvred to dissociate ourselves. Funded research is a political game, and the other participants seemed to accept that we were trying to balance a desire for them to have a voice, with our desire to maintain credibility with the funder. They knew we knew they had other agendas. Perhaps trading is such a lifestyle that it passes without question when applied to these relationships.

Validation

'Co-operative inquiry claims to be a valid approach to research with persons because it "rests on a collaborative encounter with experience"' (Reason 1994b: 327, citing Reason and Rowan 1981). As such, Reason argues it relies on a 'critical subjectivity' of researchers – being self-aware, discriminating, self-reflexive and critical. He recommends processes to promote validity, that include 'cycling and recycling between action and reflection so that issues are examined several times in different ways, exploring authenticity of participation within the group . . . and establishing norms whereby group members can challenge unwanted assumptions' (Reason 1994b: 327).

At each meeting we referred back what had come out of the previous ones; the draft report was circulated and commented on, and the final presentation to the funder was shared. As we elaborate below there was genuine participation, with differences of opinion, although there were also silencing factors as well.

Ending

After the penultimate meeting, at which the two draft reports were debated, it was agreed that the project would be ended by a formal presentation meeting to which the funder, the three Asian business groups and all participants would be invited. The spirit of collaboration was maintained, in that the platform would be shared. However, it would not be jointly owned, in the sense that we would introduce the project process and key findings; three participants would speak to convey the three key groupings that had emerged as needing differential attention – a young aspiring businessperson, a woman and an established entrepreneur; and the separate report would also be presented. The funder and the business group representatives would be asked to respond.

This final meeting was well attended and the atmosphere amongst participants was upbeat. The feedback they gave us was that they had found the project worthwhile and interesting. Useful contacts had been made; new ideas had been sparked; advice had been exchanged; new business proposals had been spawned. Several business owners welcomed the direct connections they had established with BBLE and the Asian business groups who offered further discussion to take up the challenges that had been thrown to them. Although we were withdrawing there was considerable energy amongst other participants to carry on trying to implement some of the ideas and it felt as if the project had a momentum that was now independent of us, the initiators.

Critical analysis

Reflecting on this experience of using action research to investigate development needs, was it successful? What would success look like? If we refer back to the aspirations of action research outlined above, and of co-operative inquiry in particular, we would have to ask the following questions:

1 Did the project create valid knowledge?
2 Were participants empowered by their involvement?
3 Were participants developed *en route*?
4 Did the project produce actions to solve the problems?
5 From the perspective of the sponsoring client we would also have to ask whether their brief had been satisfactorily met.
6 Was it a genuine collaboration?
7 Did the project work as a piece of action research?

In terms of the content we are confident the project yielded new insights into the development needs of second-generation South Asian entrepreneurs in Birmingham. Whilst focusing on this new core group, we were able to differentiate between the needs of different types of existing and aspiring business owners within this group. The findings echoed research into generic small businesses in some senses yet was sufficiently sensitive to identify some specific needs. So as a research method for generating knowledge about HRD we were pleased.

The project was short term, with participants really only involved for two months, which contrasts with much action research work which can spread over years (Elden and Chisholm 1993). This does not provide much scope for participants to work through anxieties or to become reflexive. Nevertheless, in that some participants took the initiative to promote their own agendas with the funders, and that many of the participants wanted to continue to meet and translate the project's aims into interventions, there is evidence of a degree of development and empowerment. We use the term empowerment in the sense of moving from 'passivity to action' (Belenky *et al.* 1986: 54), where people gain new insights and understandings into their situations, which heightens their capacity to make changes. This is particularly so collectively.

However, the concept of empowerment is problematic, even within the realms of co-operative inquiry. There is an assumption of community, of equity within an inquiry group, and of individualism within the collectivity.

It is implied that if some participants take on a task they are acting for the group rather than themselves. Yet the complexities of power relationships are ever present. For example, this project was permeated by gender and family relationships. Structurally, many women were excluded by the initial networks we used to promote the project and recruit participants, because they were not part of them. The evening timings of meetings, and the university location further excluded them. To make the project accessible, we had to communicate through other, more female networks, and to meet in the day, at women's houses. The fact that two of the team were women, and in particular that one was an Asian woman, helped to make contact with women.

Family networks proved more fruitful for recruiting participants than the Asian business groups we initially relied on, producing cousins, aunts and nephews for the inquiry. Yet family relations also structured the power dynamics of the inquiry group, so a young nephew may not openly challenge a middle aged, high status uncle, whether from respect or fear of consequences.

When does ownership become highjacking? Co-operative inquiry promotes joint ownership by initiators and other participants. Yet there seems a fine line between encouraging participants to take control, to fully participate, and watching the agenda be taken over by a minority's self-interest, no matter how you try to facilitate the group to recognize it. It seems to us more realistic to conceive of facilitation as a political process, not just a psycho-dynamic one, in which you may aim to give participants as much voice as possible, but in which you also have to be honest about the extent to which you want to keep control. And perhaps we surprised ourselves by how much control we wanted to retain.

The importance of relationships

The intensive involvement of participants inherent to action research is heavily dependent on a process of exchange, as described in other research (Ram 1998). For example, on the first meeting with the group of women, before they agreed to participate, it took two hours of general conversation with them questioning the researcher about a range of issues outside the project, before the first mention was made of the research. The fact that the researcher was also a South Asian woman paved the way, both in terms of language and in terms of building trust.

Overall the project was only possible because of who we were – particularly that two of us are second-generation South Asian, which opened the doors to networks.

Client expectations

As funded research this client relationship needed managing throughout. Whilst this is true of all consultancy, we would argue the need was enhanced by the messiness and uncertainty of action research. The process is necessarily slow to begin, and even we felt uncomfortable with that. The strengths of the approach lie in its depth and the outcomes are predominantly qualitative, which runs counter to the quantitative performance measurement culture of the TECs and to the 'common sense positivism' we would argue permeates this society. Despite our convictions we made a sop to these expectations by adding the quantitative survey to the inquiry group work, in order to bolster numbers. However, Bryman (1988) has argued 'the practice of social research is also governed by constraints other than those of theory. The decision to combine (or not to combine) qualitative and quantitative methods is subject to a variety of considerations concerning the funding context and the available financial resources [etc.]' (cited in Brannen 1992: 17).

We made a point of keeping the client updated throughout, albeit minimizing the uncertainty we were feeling at times. We emphasized to the client that the outcomes of action research lie as much in the process for the participants, and the continued activity beyond the project, as in the final written document. Even some of the client's quantitative targets had been met, with the generation of new inquiries to them. However, ultimately we do not think we were successful in managing the funding client's expectations since his main comment after the final, collaborative presentation was 'the report's a bit thin'.

Was it a genuine collaboration? Heron himself recognizes that 'even if all group members contribute fully, influence hierarchies may become established' (1998: 56). We found a tension between our academic discourse and the entrepreneurial discourse of the other participants. We felt a constant battle, particularly early on, to establish our credibility with them. We would talk the talk of co-operative inquiry: of participation, valuing their experience, joint ownership, dialogue. They were dismissive of what they termed 'academic twaddle', and wanted to see useful outcomes, quick action.

In the sense of action research as a process characterized by action, participation, cycles and theory generation (Elden and Chisholm 1993), we are happy that action research was appropriate for the project in that it was addressing a genuine problem, with the intention to inform interventions, even if not to make them within the time-frame; that it successfully engaged participation from a range of people; and that we are attempting to theorize from the experience. However, our thoughts are that the genuine collaboration advocated by collaborative inquiry was not possible to achieve in this project, for two key reasons. First, because it was too short to work through issues of power, diversity and the academic/business cultural differences. Building groups from diverse members is always challenging and time-consuming, even though frequently productive (Reynolds and Trehan 1999). The second reason arises from using the method of collaborative inquiry for consultancy, where the funder is also not part of the inquiry group, yet retains a strong interest in the outcomes. The messiness and uncertainty of action research will always cause tension in an output-orientated contract culture, but collaborative inquiry requires the initiators, as consultants, to give up control for the project direction and outcome, whilst still retaining sole responsibility to the client.

In retrospect we would have created less dilemma for ourselves, and arguably retained more integrity, if we had chosen a less ambitious form of action research participation. In our attempts to achieve egalitarian co-researching relationships with the business owners, consistent with co-operative inquiry, we felt we acted more as facilitators in the minimal interventionist process consultation style (Schein 1992). It may have been more appropriate to have deployed a more confrontational approach, to move things more quickly in the time-scale; to challenge some of the power dynamics within the group more forcefully; to expose the hidden agendas we knew were present.

Conclusions and key learning points

In conclusion, we would argue that action research is a valid method of research for gaining greater depth of understanding into the development needs of second-generation South Asian entrepreneurs. However, the process requires a constant struggle to maintain credibility with entrepreneurs who are acutely aware of costs of participation, funders who are part of a pervasive contract culture, and the small business research community which is still in the process of establishing its disciplinary credentials.

The principles inherent to a social change tradition of action research, such as co-operative inquiry, were arguably unattainable within the short-term, entrepreneurial culture, and consultancy context where the client was not a participant. It would perhaps have been easier to work with a model of participation which puts less emphasis on the idea of equitable co-researching, with less aspiration of openness, honesty and equality.

Questions

1   How appropriate is action research for HRD consultancy?
2   What are the potentials and pitfalls of taking an action research approach to HRD research?
3   What are the differing approaches that can be taken to action research, and what are their comparative advantages and disadvantages?

Note

1 In talking of South Asians we are referring to those with ethnic origin from India, Pakistan or Bangladesh. By 'second generation' we refer to those who were born, or have grown up from childhood, in Britain.

References

Argyris, C., Putnam, R. and Schon, D. (1985) *Action Science*, San Francisco: Jossey Bass.

Argyris, C. and Schon, D. (1974) *Theories in Practice*, San Francisco: Jossey Bass.

—— (1978) *Organizational Learning: a Theory of Action Perspective*, Reading, MA: Addison-Wesley.

Bennett, R.J. and Robson, P.J. (1999) 'The use of external business advice by SMEs in Britain', *Entrepreneurship and Regional Development*, 11: 155–80.

Belenky, M.F., Clinchy, B.M., Golderger, N.R. and Tarube, J.M. (1986) *Women's Ways of Knowing: the Development of Self, Voice and Mind*, New York: Basic Books.

Brannen, J. (1992) *Mixing Methods: Qualitative and Quantitative Research*, Aldershot: Avebury.

Brown, D. and Tandon, R. (1983) 'Ideology and political economy in inquiry', *Journal of Applied Behavioural Science*, 19: 277–94.

Bryman, A. (1988) *Quality and Quantity in Social Research*, London: Routledge.

Clark, A.W. (ed.) (1975) *Experimenting with Organisational Life*, New York: Plenum.

Cockman, P., Evans, B. and Reynolds, P. (1992) *Client-Centred Consulting*, London: McGraw-Hill.

Collier, J. (1945) 'United States Indian Administration as a laboratory of ethnic relations', *Social Research*, 12: 275–6.

Curran, J. and Blackurn, R.A. (1993) 'Ethnic enterprise and the high street bank', ESRC Centre for Research on Small Service Sector Enterprises, Kingston Business School.

Curran, J., Blackburn, R., Kirtching, J. and North, J. (1997) 'Small firms and work-force training: some results, analysis and policy implications from a national survey', in M. Ram, D. Deakins and D. Smallbone (eds) *Small Firms: Enterprising Futures*, London: Paul Chapman Press.

Eden, C. and Huxham, C. (1996) 'Action Research for the Study of Organizations', in S. Clegg, C. Hardy and W. Nord (eds) *Handbook of Organization Studies*, London: Sage.

Elden, M. (1979) 'Three generations of work democracy experiments in Norway', in C. Cooper and E. Mumford (eds) *The Quality of Work in Eastern and Western Europe*, London: Associated Business Press.

Elden, M. and Chisholm, R.F. (1993) 'Emergent varieties of action research: introduction to the special issue', *Human Relations*, 46: 121–42.

Elden, M. and Levin, M. (1991) 'Cogenerative learning: bringing participation into action research', in W.F. Whyte (ed.) *Participatory Action Research*, London: Sage.

ENSR (1997) *The European Observatory for SMEs – Fifth Annual Report*, European Network for SME Research, Zoetermeer: EIM Small Business Research and Consultancy.

Fals-Borda, O. and Rahman, M.A. (1991) *Action and Knowledge*, New York: Apex Press.

Gibb, A. (1999) 'Entrepreneurship and small business management: can we afford to neglect them in the twenty-first century business school?', *British Journal of Management*, 7(4): 309–22.

Hart, E. and Bond, M. (1995) *Action Research for Health and Social Care: a Guide to Practice*, Buckingham: Open University Press.

Heron, J. (1981) In P. Reason and P. Rowan (eds) *Human Inquiry in Action: a sourcebook of new paradigm research*, Chichester: Wiley.

—— (1998) 'Validity in co-operative inquiry', in *Human Inquiry in Action*, London: Sage.

Hofstede, G. (1994) *Culture and Organizations*, London: HarperCollins.

Lewin, K. (1943) 'Forces behind food habits and methods of change', *Bulletin of the National Research Council* CVIII: 35–65.

—— (1946) 'Action research and minority problems', *Journal of Social Issues, 2*: 34–46.

—— (1947) 'Frontiers in group dynamics: channel of group life: social planning and action research', *Human Relations*, 1: 143–53.

Marlow, S. (1992) 'Take-up of business growth training schemes by ethnic minority owned small firms', *International Small Business Journal*, 10(4): 34–46.

Matlay, H. (1999) 'Evaluating training initiatives and support: lessons from Britain', ISBA Conference, Leeds, November.

Metcalfe, H., Modood, T. and Wirdee, S. (1996) *Asian Self-Employment: the Interaction of Culture and Economics in England*, London: Policy Studies Institute.

Ormerod, R.J. (1995) 'Combining management consultancy and research', *Omega* 24(1): 1–12.

Pettigrew, A., Arthur, M. and Hendry, C. (1990) *Training and Human Resource Management in Small and Medium Sized Enterprises: a Critical Review of the Literature and a Model for Future Research*, Sheffield: Training Agency.

Ram, M. (1998) 'Trading places: the ethnographic process in small firms research', *Entrepreneurship and Regional Development*, 11: 95–108.

Ram, M. and Jones, T. (1998) *Ethnic Minorities in Business*, MK: Open University Press.

Ram, M. and Sparrow, J. (1992) *Research on the Needs of the Asian Business Community in Wolverhampton*, Wolverhampton TEC Ltd. and Wolverhampton Chamber of Commerce.

Reason, P. (1988) *Human Inquiry in Action*, London: Sage.

Reason, P. (1994a) *Participation in Human Inquiry*, London: Sage.

—— (1994b) 'Three approaches to participative inquiry', in N.K. Denzin and Y.S. Lincoln (eds) *Handbook of Qualitative Research*, Thousand Oaks, CA: Sage.

Reason, P. and Heron, J. (1998) *A Layperson's Guide to Co-operative Inquiry*, www.bath.aac.uk/carpp/LAYGUIDE.html.

Reason, P. and Rowan, P. (eds) (1981) *Human Inquiry in Action: a Sourcebook of New Paradigm Research*, Chichester: Wiley.

Revans, R.W. (ed.) (1982) *The Origins and Growth of Action Learning*, Bromley: Chartwell-Bratt.

Reynolds, M. and Trehan, K. (1999) 'Propositions for incorporating a pedagogy of difference in management education', paper presented to Critical Management Studies Conference, Manchester.

Schein, E. (1999) *Process Consultation Revisited*, London: Addison Wesley.

Schon, D. (1983) *The Reflective Practitioner*, New York: Basic Books.

Senge, P. (1993) *The Fifth Discipline*, London: Century Business.

Stanworth, J. and Gray, C. (eds) (1991) *Bolton Twenty Years On*, London: Paul Chapman Press.

Storey, D. (1994) *Understanding the Small Business Sector*, London: Routledge.

Torbert, W.R. (1981) 'Why educational research has been so uneducational: the case for a new model of social science based on collaborative inquiry', in P. Reason and P. Rowan (eds) *Human Inquiry in Action: a Sourcebook of New Paradigm Research*, Chichester: Wiley.

Torbert, W.R. (1991) *The Power of Balance: Transforming Self, Society and Scientific Inquiry*, Newbury Park, CA: Sage.

Westhead, P. and Storey, D. (1997) *Training Provision and Development of Small and Medium Sized Enterprises*, Research Report 26, London: HMSO.

Whitehead, J. (1994) 'How do I improve the quality of my management?' *Management Learning*, 25: 137–53.

Whyte, W.F. (1991) *Participatory Action Research*, London: Sage.

18

A NEW APPROACH TO THE LITERATURE REVIEW

Sally Sambrook

Aims and contribution

This chapter explores the practice of conducting a literature review, necessary in any research project. The aim of this chapter is to explain how, as a doctoral student, I approached the task of reviewing the literature in the field of HRD, and to explore the role of the literature review. I share a model I developed during my doctoral research that enabled me to identify both relevant material and potential gaps in the existing literature. The model could help researchers identify a number of factors. First, existing theoretical explanations of HRD, second, new areas where such explanations can be developed and expanded and third, even new theoretical explanations – that is, develop new knowledge and understandings of HRD.

It is anticipated that after reading this chapter the researcher will be able to:

- understand the role of the literature review and knowledge generation;
- organize a search of relevant literature;
- identify gaps which current/future research could attempt to fill (even if only partially); and
- synthesize existing literature with one's own theoretical explanations.

Theoretical and empirical context

In my earlier contribution to this volume (Chapter 11) I described my approach to researching HRD in the NHS and gave an account of how a researcher might write the research story. This story might then become part of the extant literature, available to others in the public domain, whether through conference presentations and papers, or journal articles, or – although less accessible – as internal organizational documents. In the earlier chapter, I suggested that writing the research 'story' was a newer approach to presenting research findings, diverging from the more positivist approach where the researcher is the 'detached' scientist reporting 'facts'. A similar argument can be applied to the literature review. I would argue that the role of the literature review is not necessarily a detached and 'background' element of the research process, but an integral part and an additional potential source of enquiry.

The context of this chapter is a three-year doctoral programme, entitled 'Models and Concepts of Human Resource Development: Academic and Practitioner Perspectives'. The academic perspective was investigated through a review of existing literature, conceptualized as the means by which academics theorize and practise HRD in the public domain. The practitioner perspective focused on HRD strategies and practices within a specific context – the British National Health Service (NHS). I wanted to explore how HRD has been talked into being, how it is talked about, and how it is accomplished through talk. I conceptualized HRD as a social and discursive construction (talked into being, created through words) and as discursive action (accomplished through words) (Sambrook 1998, 2000). Once I had established these research questions my research design needed to focus on methods which would enable me to gather evidence of how HRD was talked about. My focus was on words, phrases and discursive resources used to create, describe, analyse and achieve 'HRD'. This meant that, in this research, the literature review was not 'merely' background material but one of the two resources from which I was able to analyse models and concepts of HRD. The literature review was a key source of academic words. Hence, my approach to the literature review was not one where the review was merely 'background', but a source of material in itself. This forced me to think carefully about how I would manage a review of HRD literature. During my early search, I identified that much of the HRD literature emanates from America. However, I wished to investigate the emergence of HRD within the British context – this focused my later search. I then reviewed existing British literature and identified a gap in terms of the NHS context. This provided a space for my own research to attempt to fill – to provide an explanation of HRD within the British health service.

Methodological issues

This section explores the role of the literature review in the research process, explains some of the techniques involved and considers some of the problems associated with this activity.

What is a literature review?

It is useful to begin with some explanations and definitions of the literature review. As Easterby-Smith, Thorpe and Lowe (1991: 145) state: 'Researchers undertaking projects, whether theses, dissertations, or funded by outside agencies, need to display a knowledge of the literature in their chosen field.' Jankowicz explains that, 'Knowledge doesn't exist in a vacuum, and your work only has value in relation to other people's. Your work and your findings will be significant only to the extent that they're the same as, or different from, other people's work and findings' (1995: 128–9). To conduct useful research, you therefore need to identify what research has already been conducted in your chosen subject area. This *initial* review can help you to generate and refine potential research topics. Once you have identified this literature, a *critical* review is undertaken to enable you to develop your understanding of the topic and then clarify your specific research question(s) in light of existing studies. There are numerous books on research in the field of business and management that provide practical information about the practice of conducting a literature review. For example, Saunders, Lewis and Thornhill (1997: 36–69) provide a helpful chapter entitled 'Critically reviewing the literature', and Easterby-Smith *et al.* (1991: 145–57) include a useful appendix in their text, and readers are advised to consult these for practical advice.

However, as well as the initial and then critical review of literature (Saunders *et al.* 1997: 36), Easterby-Smith and colleagues (ibid.) identify two different perspectives to the literature review. 'Firstly, when you need to gain a comprehensive overview of the literature in a particular field and second, when you know exactly what items of the literature you require and just need to collect them' (ibid.). The authors 'have borrowed terminology from Selvin and Stuart (1966) and called the former "trawling" and the second "fishing"' (ibid.). *Trawling* involves identifying potentially relevant sources of literature, whereas *fishing* involves the practical aspects of actually retrieving each object in the catch. It is the practice of trawling – or setting the net – that is the focus of this chapter. The first requires (cognitive and creative) skills in setting the net, whereas the second requires (organizational and interpersonal) skills in tracking down the object. To trawl a subject area, it is useful to write a list of the different ways the subject could be described. These terms can then be entered in a library catalogue search tool, or an Internet search engine. For example, when I first attempted to review the literature on 'HRD in the NHS', my search yielded very little. To broaden my scope and trawl a bigger field, I then included concepts such as 'human resourcing', 'training', 'training and development', 'employee development', 'management development' and 'organisation development'. Another way of thinking about this is to consider what might be the 'key words' in your field of study. Of course, the bigger the net, the larger the potential catch, and the bigger the task of fishing. It may be that you wish to restrict your trawl, perhaps to a specific continent, country or industry sector. I focused on the emergence of HRD within the British NHS context. Or, you may wish to trawl deeper waters, and search back in history. I also wanted to explore the origins of HRD.

There are several ways of trawling the literature, including a manual sift through readily available material, or searching an electronic catalogue. The first approach involves sitting in the library and going through various journals to get a feel for the subject area. In the case of researching HRD, journals such as *Human Resource Development International* (*HRDI*), *International Journal of Training and Development* (*IJTD*), *Human Resource Development Quarterly* (*HRDQ*) and *Journal of European Industrial Training* (*JEIT*) may be useful. Or, you might browse through more practitioner-oriented journals such as People Management, published by the Chartered Institute of Personnel and Development (CIPD). The second, and more efficient approach, involves using technology. Most libraries have an electronic, online library catalogue, which allows you to search 'key words', authors, titles and/or organizations. Most libraries will also have search facilities such as BIDS and Internet search engines such as Yahoo or Netscape. It is advisable to contact your local librarian for assistance in using these technologies and retrieving your catch (hence the need for interpersonal skills!).

Sources and types of literature

A trawl can yield several sources and types of literature. There are three sources of literature – primary, secondary, and tertiary (Saunders *et al.* 1997: 43). Literature in the primary category refers to the first publication of the material, for example, the first time that research findings are reported, whether in a book or journal article. It also includes unpublished material, such as internal documents in the form of policy statements or memos. Secondary literature is the subsequent reporting of primary literature. This includes reference to original material in books or articles, where the author summarizes and/or critiques the original material. When a reference seems to be of particular relevance to your research, it is advisable to return to the original primary source. This is because, in compiling the secondary source, the second author has interpreted the original work, and may omit some crucial material that could weaken your arguments or nullify your research findings. Tertiary sources – or search tools – include indexes, abstracts, encyclopaedias and bibliographies.

There are five broad types of literature – books (texts), periodicals (journal articles), theses and research in progress, government publications and official statistics, and reference works, general guides to the literature and guides of literature in specific subject areas (Easterby-Smith *et al.* 1991: 147). In addition, you might wish to explore conference proceedings and organizational documents (internal and external, e.g. HR strategy and job advertisements). For example, at an early stage of my doctorate, I surveyed all NHS HR job advertisements in the IPD's *People Management* journal for one year and conducted content analysis to identify key words in person specifications and job descriptions. This helped me to first identify the phenomenon of a changing role for trainers in the health service, and then consider how I might explore this in more detail.

It is also useful to think of the different audiences for which the literature is written. This can help you when you come to review each 'fish'.

Literature written for an academic audience, such as the periodical *Human Resource Development Quarterly*, is generally peer reviewed, which means the work has been subjected to blind review by peers. This suggests an initial critical review has been conducted by other academic experts in this field, and any major weaknesses in the research/writing will have been addressed. For example, reviewers might have considered the validity and reliability of the research/theorizing. However, this does not mean that the reader need not take a critical approach when reviewing the work.

Literature for a practitioner audience, for example, an article in *People Management*, is not subject to the same rigorous critique. The reader must then consider, for example, to what extent are any methodological issues reported, how rigorous was the research that is being reported, and what is not being reported? If material fished out of your literature trawl is being used to either support or contradict your findings and arguments, you should carefully consider the reliability and validity of what is being reported. These issues have been considered earlier, in Chapter 11.

Why conduct a literature review?

Before examining the innovative approach I wish to introduce in this chapter, it is useful to consider the purpose of conducting a literature review. The literature review, although given limited attention in the methodology text (Cooper 1989: 11), is the usual starting point for a research project. It enables the researcher to begin to identify some of the key themes, and identify gaps, within the field of HRD. Yet, in the key American 'Researching HRD' text (Swanson and Holton 1997) there is no reference to the literature review.

Therefore, the initial purpose is to identify – and map out – the theories and concepts associated with a particular area of study. This can be either an area of personal interest, which you wish to explore, or an area associated with a specific problem you wish to better understand and possibly resolve. Additionally, a researcher might wish to identify existing theories and concepts with a view to challenging their status. The initial literature review helps the researcher plot the existing terrain, to enable them to get a feel for the landscape. This ensures the researcher is aware of previous empirical studies and theorizing, which can inform the planned research project. This initial review also serves (later) to locate the research findings in an existing body of knowledge, and to contribute to the development of a field of study, such as HRD.

Developing a critical approach

HRD academics and practitioners report their empirical findings and/or conceptual theorizing in various media. However, during a review of literature, it is the researcher's role to question what is reported – that is, the researcher should try to adopt a critical approach and consider what was the original research question, how was the research conducted, how have the findings been reported? From this, the researcher might identify weaknesses in the research design, inconsistencies in the reported findings, or an area that could be explored in more detail. This activity can help researchers clarify their own research interests and articulate their own research question more clearly. Also, by developing a critical approach to reviewing how others write the research story, this can help the researcher stand back and take a more critical (objective) approach to their own theorizing and writing. This can help enhance the rigour of the piece of research when it is exposed to public scrutiny – whether in a conference presentation, journal article, or organizational report.

When do I conduct the literature review?

As stated earlier, literature needs to be reviewed early on in a research project. The initial review serves as generating background knowledge, which helps to inform the setting of the research question. Knowing how other studies have been conducted, and their findings, also helps to inform the research design – that is, clarifying what you are researching and how. This includes identifying what type of questions you will be asking (for example, are you interested in finding out *what* is happening, or *why* it is happening, *how* things are happening, or *how many* things are happening), and what types of methods are appropriate to answering these questions.

Once the initial review has been conducted, and you have established your topic of research and specific research question(s), the literature review does not stop there. Indeed, the literature review tends to be ongoing – whilst you are preparing the research proposal, then conducting the empirical research, and writing the research story. In my experience, I have found that there tends to be much activity during the initial stage – as you try to sort out what you hope to achieve from the research project. Then, there is a small amount of literature reviewing activity whilst engaged in gathering the empirical research material (data). Finally, there is much activity again when writing the story, when you are attempting to link empirical findings with other existing knowledge and theorizing. For me, there was also the issue of when to *stop* reviewing the literature. Reading new literature can sometimes spark a new interest and send you off in another direction. This only serves to unnecessarily confuse or delay your research. Having conducted the initial review, this should not be seen as sufficient. The researcher needs to continue – or re-commence – the literature review after the empirical stage to ensure she is referring to the most up-to-date knowledge, and therefore ensuring her own theorizing is as complete as possible. In the case of a PhD, a researcher could conduct the initial literature review in the first year of the programme, and if she does not update this, the theorizing, or linking new empirical findings with existing knowledge, could be two years out of date before it even enters the public domain.

The research

A new approach

Having reviewed some of the practicalities associated with conducting a literature search (the processes of trawling and fishing), the next issue is knowing what to do with the 'catch'. This section presents a means of organizing the output, or the product of your literature review. A new approach is offered to help the researcher organize and manage the literature review. However, as well as providing a means of analysing the literature, this new approach proposes that the 'literature' can have the same status and purpose as data generated through empirical methods and techniques.

The literature review as a source of data

My three-year study sought to explore models and concepts of HRD from academic and practitioner perspectives. This study focused on how HRD has been talked into being, how 'it' is talked about, and how HRD is accomplished through talk. A key feature, therefore, was on the discourses used by two sets of HRD specialists – those practitioners accomplishing HRD in hospitals and those researching, teaching and practising HRD in universities. The practitioner perspective was explored through ethnographic case-study research conducted in two NHS Trust hospitals (see Chapter 11). The academic perspective was explored through the body of literature written by academics. Thus the product of the literature review was treated as a source of data.

The first notion – how HRD has been talked into being – emerged as I explored the origins of HRD, particularly in the UK. I traced the use of the term in academic journals and texts, noting its earliest employment during the late 1980s. From an academic perspective, I noted the development of the 'discipline', with new courses being offered, and then new texts being published and then new 'chairs' in HRD being appointed (Sambrook and Stewart 1998). It could be suggested that HRD was talked into being to create and develop academic careers. HRD can be thought of as a social construction. Once talked into being, and marketed in journals and university prospectuses as a more strategic approach to training and development, it could be argued that practitioners in industry would need to 'buy into' this new academic product. Offered an opportunity to share in this new phenomenon with the potential of transforming training and development into a strategic function, practitioners could then introduce this new concept into their organizations. This could possibly create new job titles and departments, and thus further practitioner careers, too. HRD has now taken on the status of a 'social fact' – academics and practitioners talk of HRD 'as if' it exists as some external reality. New job titles and departments are social facts – their creation has 'real' consequences for individual's identities, activities and careers, and for the organization of work.

Once talked into being, and disseminated through the literature, it is then possible to explore how HRD is talked about. HRD can be thought of as a discursive construction, drawing upon existing discourses to frame activities associated with training and development in a new way. For example, HRD is framed as being strategic, proactive and business-oriented. There is talk of the difference between 'old' training and development and 'new' HRD – extending the earlier debate in the field of personnel and HRM – although some would argue that there is no substantive difference between these concepts, other than merely new labels. However, it is possible to analyse *how* HRD is written and talked about, and the literature provides one source of such data.

Whether called training and development or HRD, much of the activity associated with this specialist occupation is accomplished through talking – for example, direct delivery of training, or talking with managers to identify training needs, presenting lectures, or writing texts. HRD can be thought of as discursive action, where the action is achieved through words. Of course, this presents a potential problem in that HRD could be perceived as 'all talk', particularly in arenas where it is considered that action speaks louder than words.

It has now been suggested that the (written) words of academics, published in the public domain and accessed during a literature review, can be thought of as a source of data. This literature can be analysed for evidence of how the concept of HRD has been constructed, promoted, theorized and challenged. From the literature, we can trace how HRD emerged in North America, and was taken up by British academics. From the literature, we can explore how theories of HRD have been developed from disciplines such as economics and psychology (McLean and Swanson 1999). One purpose of writing journal articles and texts is to explain and perhaps expand HRD beyond its earlier theoretical roots, to help practitioners make sense of their occupational activity. Therefore, in this study, the literature was not considered as background material, but primary evidence of the social construction and accomplishment of HRD through discursive resources. The literature review was not used merely to help frame the research question, it was a source of empirical material which could be measured, categorized and counted. The literature provides a very tangible output of 'doing' HRD. This output can be analysed historically for theoretical perspective, content, purpose, and intended audience. Having already explained how the researcher might trawl the literature,

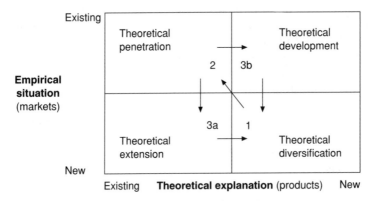

Figure 18.1 The development of theoretical explanations

the remainder of this chapter describes an approach to help analyse this source of data.

The literature review – a new approach

As mentioned earlier, the literature review is the usual starting point for a research project, enabling the researcher to begin to identify some of the key themes, and identify gaps, within the field of HRD. Silverman (1985: 9–10) argues that a review of the literature can provide a 'typology with empty boxes'. These empty boxes identify areas that have been ignored or reveal gaps in existing literature. This raises the issues of how a researcher might go about filling these initial empty boxes. What do you do with the results of your literature review? How do you make sense of your findings? How do you structure this activity? In reviewing the literature relating to HRD and the health service context, and in thinking how I might contribute to future knowledge and literature, I devised my own typology with empty boxes. This typology is based on the marketing matrix developed by Ansoff (1987). It seemed to me that knowledge could be created through four processes, using either existing or new theories (products) in either existing or new situations (markets) (see Figure 18.1 above).

When a researcher commences a particular study, he or she examines the existing literature theorizing existing situations (2). This focuses on knowledge already created. During a literature review, existing theory in an existing situation can be revisited and challenged (or tested) to ensure it still 'fits'. This penetration (2) is similar to adopting a 'critical' approach to theoretical explanation. The researcher is seeking to find flaws in the research methods or reporting of the findings. Such a discovery could then become the focus of the researcher's own study; for example, attempting to replicate the original study but with a more robust methodology. The researcher's findings might support the original theory. If not, the theoretical explanation will be developed in one of two ways – extended to fit a new situation/empirical context (3a), or modified to take into account findings which did not quite fit the original explanation (3b).

When a new situation is encountered and the existing theory fits, then the explanation can be extended (3a). When the researcher finds a theoretical explanation that might explain phenomena in a new context, this could become the focus of the research study – testing the theory in this new situation. The theory can be expanded to explain similar phenomena and their relationships in different settings, thus enabling generalization beyond the original context. The ability to generalize suggests the robustness of a theory.

However, if the researcher tests the original theory and finds the explanation does not quite fit, it might be necessary to refine the explanation to take into account the emerging data. Many such repeated studies can serve to improve the original theory so that it can explain more accurately and meaningfully the emerging findings. If the existing theory no longer quite fits the existing situation, then the theory is developed adapted or modified (3b).

Finally, if a new situation emerges and no existing theory can fit – no matter how refined or adapted – then a completely new theoretical explanation is needed (1), possibly a new paradigm (Kuhn 1970). However, this does not necessarily involve a dramatic leap. Theoretical diversification could build on existing explanations, bringing developments together into a new coherent and comprehensive theory. This is how I made sense of the HRD literature.

I found the typology a useful way of conceptualizing what theoretical explanations already exist and how new knowledge might be created. It gave me a manageable way of dealing with (what seemed like) the onerous task of reading 'as much as I could' about HRD. The typology can be used in several ways, although two key features are worth noting – first, providing a framework to structure the activity and second, assisting in the review process.

I have already suggested that this typology provides a structure for conducting the literature review – it provides a net (or series of nets) for the trawl. The typology can be used to structure a brief overview of the field, perhaps identifying a particular interest or specific question. At this stage, the researcher might be filling the boxes with broad concepts or themes as she begins to categorize the literature. Once these boxes have been filled, and/or you have identified a gap in the literature you should now be in a better position to generate specific research questions. You are now ready to begin a more detailed review. As you focus on a particular interest or question, the typology can then be used to structure a more detailed review, perhaps concentrating your research efforts on testing an existing theoretical explanation in a new situation. You might focus on a particular box to research, and this is where you might later make your own

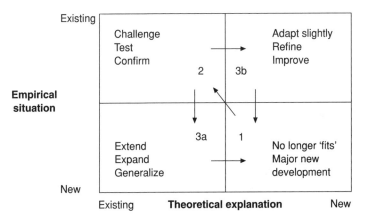

Figure 18.2 Using the typology to review theoretical explanations

contribution to the literature with your findings. For example, you examine all the available literature with a view to adding to it in Stage 3a or 3b.

The typology can also assist in the process of reviewing – that is, helping the researcher critically examine the literature. Her approach to the review might vary according to how the researcher decides to use the literature in her study – for example, as (secondary) background material or as a source of (primary) data. The content of the various objects of literature can be categorized into one of the four boxes. Each of the four boxes has a different focus – whether it is challenging existing theories or developing new ones. The various elements associated with developing theoretical explanations are illustrated in Figure 18.2. This shows the ways in which the typology can be used during the process of reviewing the literature. For example, it could be used to identify the purpose of a particular article or text, whether it challenges an existing theory (2), presents new findings that extend an existing theory (3a), or even introduces a new theoretical explanation (1).

Each object of literature (fish) can be reviewed with this intended focus in mind. For example, if an article claims it is testing out an existing theoretical explanation, does the author clearly state the research objectives and methods? Some research is conducted in the form of a meta-analysis of the existing literature, reviewing numerous studies and looking for consistencies and inconsistencies, and identifying gaps. As well as reviewing current literature and plotting existing theories, this process can also be retrospective.

Hence, a further use of the typology is to provide a framework for exploring the literature retrospectively – where the researcher takes the role of historian. The typology enables the researcher to trace the historical development of a subject, and plot emerging concepts and theories. This

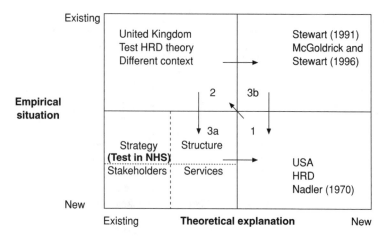

Figure 18.3 Using the typology to review theoretical explanations of HRD within a British context

helped me to categorize the literature (see Figure 18.3) to plot the emergence of HRD (box 1), follow its adaptation and development (box 3b) and find a gap related to how existing theories of HRD might apply to the context of the British NHS (box 3a). However, it could also be suggested that my research has extended a theoretical explanation from the management literature – managing as a discursive activity – to help conceptualize HRD as discursive action. Of course, now that this theoretical explanation has entered the public domain (through conference papers and journal articles), my own work is exposed to critical review, with fellow researchers now seeking to test, expand, adapt, or refute this theoretical explanation.

Practical application

This section illustrates several ways in which the typology can be used, and draws upon my doctoral research. First, I used the typology to structure my initial literature review (Figure 18.3). I found a wealth of literature referring to HRD in America, and was able to trace the origins of HRD back to Nadler around 1970. The earliest theoretical explanations of HRD emerged in the USA, but it was not until the late 1980s that the term entered the UK literature. Then began the debate as to whether HRD represented a new theoretical explanation of training and development, or was merely a new label. This suggests a challenge to HRD's status as a 'new' theoretical explanation and to its explanation of training and development phenomena in the UK context. As British researchers tested out HRD theories in this new national context, the explanations needed to accommodate different variables, such as economic, political and cultural differences. Where explanations valid in the American situation did not fit with new dimensions in the British context, there was a need for the extension and adaptation of the original theories. Several British academics have now filled that gap, either by adapting existing theory or by extending it to a new situation (see, for instance, Hendry 1991; Stead and Lee 1996; Stewart and McGoldrick 1996; Harrison 1997). Although somewhat modified to take account of differences in the organization of work within the United Kingdom (such as the British industrial relations system), a review of UK specific literature reveals HRD as a theoretical explanation of the changing roles and activities experienced by training and development specialists. However, the term is still not widely used by practitioners (Sambrook and Stewart 2000).

Having conducted an initial review and filled the empty boxes, I found a potential gap. When I came to review the literature relating to the health service, applying the matrix to a more specific area of literature, I found very little indeed that examined HRD within the NHS context, and specifically in Trust hospitals (see, for example, Burchill and Casey 1996). This was the biggest gap, and the one I sought to (begin to) fill. Therefore, I had identified a new situation in which to explore HRD – the NHS. I then organized the literature search to take into account my four key research questions, or areas of investigation: HRD and strategy; HRD and structure: HRD stakeholders: and HRD services and products, as illustrated in box 3a of the above figure. This helped me decide where to focus my research activities – in a new setting – and helped me focus on where I could contribute towards a better understanding of HRD – expanding theoretical explanations in a new context. The contents I filled in box 3a then provided a means of refining the literature search and analysis to focus in on four aspects of the HRD literature. Each aspect became the subject of a new typology, reviewing that particular body of literature in more depth. For example, Figure 18.4 illustrates how the typology can help structure the literature associated with HRD and strategy.

This time the boxes in the typology are used to record key themes, discursive resources or even metaphors related to developments in theoretical explanation of strategy and HRD. Alternatively, you could fill in key writers and dates in the relevant boxes. Tracing how strategy has been talked about in the literature, it is possible to note a gradual evolution so although HRD is a new concept (or theory), it is not completely detached from earlier thinking. HRD does not represent a revolution, but an important distinction in how activities associated with developing people are talked about, thought about and practised, sufficient to warrant the 'new theory' label.

The typology can be used to plot how training and development, then HRD has been talked (written) about in the literature. I used literature as a source of primary data – texts and articles were conceptualized as products of practising HRD academics. These products were treated as presenting

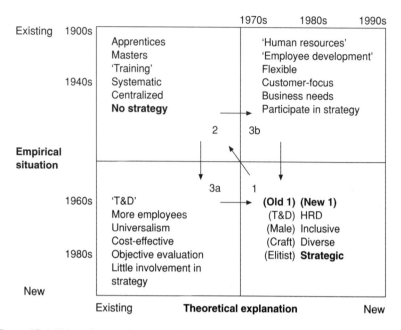

Figure 18.4 Using the typology to review theoretical explanations of HRD and strategy

academic perspectives. They could be analysed in various ways, for example, determining their purpose, content, message and intended audience (for example, students, specialist practitioners or senior managers). Taking a historical stance, the researcher can plot what words and phrases are used during different periods, and how different discourses emerge to frame and make sense of new situations. My own contribution to the literature was in the form of a theoretical explanation of HRD as a model of ideal types (or a typology) of discursive resources, which I labelled *Tell*, *Sell* and *Gel* (Sambrook 1997, 1998, 2000). This typology theorizes and categorizes how academics and practitioners talked about and practised HRD in relation to strategy, structure, stakeholders and services/products – the four key elements of my literature review. The typology comprises three distinct ways of characterizing HRD, in the form of three discourses. The *Tell* discourse can be caricatured as a traditional approach to training and development, where reactive training officers, in a centralized department, tell employees what courses to go on, delivered universally irrespective of learner/business needs. The *Sell* discourse can be described as a more HRD approach where proactive training managers, in a decentralized structure, compete for resources and promote their wares in the internal market, offering a tailored service/product to meet individual/business needs. Finally, the *Gel* discourse involves facilitators and internal consultants operating at a strategic level, advising and supporting learners and managers (also learners) to identify, create and share all forms of learning (formal and informal), pulling together the often disparate elements of individual and organizational learning. It is interesting to note that other researchers reviewing the HRD literature (Garavan, Heraty and Barnicle 1999) have also identified three distinct strands or variations of HRD – a traditional paradigm of classical management, a marketing type philosophy, and a learning organization perspective.

Critical analysis

Although developed for my doctoral research exploring the emergence of HRD within the British NHS, I suggest that the typology has utility beyond this context and purpose. However, whilst I found this typology helpful, its use is not unproblematic. For instance, it is not always easy to fit findings of the literature review into discrete boxes. There could be some degree of overlap, for example, with a piece of literature referring to elements of both theoretical extension and adaptation. Also, developments in theoretical explanations can be slow and evolutionary. It can be difficult to distinguish where, in this gradual shift, theories are extended or adapted. The process of filling the empty boxes becomes a subjective activity. Yet, does this matter? The typology is offered as a means of structuring the literature review to identify key developments and themes in theoretical explanations, and not as a definitive classification.

The typology approach to the literature review is offered as a tool that might aid sense making as researchers trawl through the increasing body of HRD literature – increasing as the topic becomes an academic 'discipline' and as human resourcing becomes an increasingly important organizational function. Indeed, the emergence of the term 'human resourcing' (Leopold, Watson and Harris 1999) further complicates the conduct of the literature review, merging the arguably distinct HRM and HRD into one larger ocean to trawl.

Returning to Silverman's original concept of the typology with empty boxes, he highlights that by even constructing a typology, the researcher is potentially closing off the possibility of analysing peripheral materials. For example, by focusing on fitting theories into boxes the researcher could miss potentially relevant ideas and concepts because they do not fit these preconceived boxes. Also, by labelling something one way, and fitting into one box, this can prevent the researcher from perceiving that in another useful way. However, the literature review, as any part of the research process, is a somewhat complex and messy activity.

Conclusions and key learning points

The key purpose of this chapter has been to introduce a new approach to the literature review. This new approach takes the form of a typology with empty boxes (Silverman 1985), adapted to take account of how theoretical explanations disseminated in the literature might be created, tested, expanded and adapted.

This chapter has offered a new way of thinking about, gathering and organizing material from a literature review. It has been suggested that literature can provide theoretical explanations of, in this case, HRD, and that the purpose of research is to challenge, confirm, develop and expand these explanations, or even generate new explanations. This chapter has provided a model which, used as a structure for the literature review, helps the researcher to identify gaps in existing literature, thereby opening up the possibility of further contributing to knowledge generation and our understanding of HRD.

It has been argued that the literature review is an important and *integral* element of the research process, rather than a distinct stage, somewhat disconnected from 'real' research. Rather than merely providing background material, objects in the literature review can provide a source of 'data'.

Some of the key questions asked in this chapter have been the following:

- *What* is a literature review? What are the different stages?
- *Why* conduct a review of literature, what is its purpose?
- *When* should the researcher begin and stop reviewing the literature?
- *How* might the researcher conduct a literature review? What does this research practice involve?

Answers to these questions provide the key learning points in this chapter.

Key learning points

The literature review comprises two key stages – trawling the subject to identify relevant items, and then fishing to acquire these items. There are many sources and types of literature, with different purposes and target audiences.

The literature review serves several purposes. These include: to identify existing theories and studies in your chosen field; to identify possible research questions based on gaps in the literature or unresolved problems; to inform your research design; and to locate your own theorizing in, and synthesize with, the relevant body of literature.

When synthesizing existing literature into your research project, it does not necessarily have to take the form of 'background' or 'secondary' material. In this chapter, it has been shown that a review of literature can be an integral and empirical element of research, for example, how HRD has been talked into being and is talked about, by HRD specialists – whether academics and/or practitioners.

The literature review can be conducted in several stages – the initial overview, and then the ongoing critical review. However, there is also the issue of when to stop reviewing the literature. This comes down to the researcher's confidence that she has investigated the main and most relevant sources and items of literature.

The new approach introduced in this chapter provides a structure for the literature review. It helps the researcher manage the results of this crucial activity. The typology can be used at different stages of the research project. It can be used to categorize findings from the initial overview, and then to analyse the more focused review of particular bodies of literature.

The typology, although developed for doctoral research, is argued to be of relevance to any research project as a means of structuring the literature review. It provides one solution to the problem of figuring out what to do with the results of all the 'trawling' and 'fishing'. It provides one way of making personal sense of existing theoretical explanations. It also provides a means of identifying potential gaps in the literature that the research can attempt to fill.

Although some answers have been given, with the aim of assisting the researcher get to grips with this often overwhelming activity, there is no 'one best way' of approaching this task. Perhaps much more could be learned by actually engaging in the practice, reflecting on (inevitable) mistakes made and experimenting with different approaches until you find your 'best way'.

Discussion questions

1 What are the reasons for, and advantages of, beginning a review of literature as early as possible during the research project?
2 What help is available at your local library (HEI, college, public, or organization)?
3 How might the typology constrain your literature review?

References

Ansoff, H.I. (1987) *Corporate Strategy*, Harmondsworth: Penguin.

Buckley, R. and Caple, J. (1995) *The Theory and Practice of Training* (third edn), London: Kogan Page.

Burchill, F. and Casey, A. (1996) *Human Resource Management: the NHS: a Case Study*, Basingstoke: Macmillan Press.

Cooper, H. (1989) *Integrating Research: Guide for Literature Reviews* (2nd edn), Beverly Hills, CA: Sage Publications.

Easterby-Smith, M., Thorpe, R. and Lowe, A. (1991) *Management Research: an Introduction*, London: Sage.

Garavan, T., Heraty, N. and Barnicle, B. (1999) 'Human resource development literature: current issues, priorities and dilemmas', *Journal of European Industrial Training*, 23(4/5): 169–79.

Harrison, R. (1997) *Employee Development*, London: Institute of Personnel Management.

Hendry, C. (1991) 'Corporate strategy and training', in J. Stevens and R. MacKay (eds) *Training and Competitiveness*, London: Kogan Page in association with NEDO, 79–110.

Jankowicz, A.D. (1995) *Business Research Projects* (second edn), London: Chapman Hall.

Kuhn, T.S. (1970) *The Structure of Scientific Revolutions* (2nd edn), Chicago: Chicago University Press.

Leopold, J., Harris, L. and Watson, T.J. (eds) (1999) *Strategic Human Resourcing: Principles, Perspectives and Practices in Human Resource Management*, London: Financial Times/Pitman.

Mclean, G. (1998) 'HRD: a three-legged stool, an octopus or a centipede', *Human Resource Development International*, 1(4): 375–7.

Sambrook, S. (1997) *HRD as a Discursive Construction?* Strategic Direction of HRM Annual Conference, the Nottingham Trent University.

—— (1998) 'Models and concepts of human resource development: academic and practitioner perspectives', (unpublished) doctoral thesis, Nottingham Business School, the Nottingham Trent University.

—— (2000) 'Talking of HRD', *Human Resource Development International*, 3(2): 159–78.

Sambrook, S. and Stewart, J. (1998) *HRD as a discursive construction?* Leeds–Lancaster Collaborative Conference on Emergent Fields in Management: Connecting Learning and Critique.

—— (2000) 'Factors influencing learning in European learning oriented organisations: issues for management', *Journal of European Industrial Training*, 24(2/3/4): 209–19.

Saunders, M., Lewis, P. and Thornhill, A. (1997) *Research Methods for Business Students*, London: Pitman.

Selvin, H.C. and Stuart, A. (1966) 'Data-dredging procedures in survey analysis', *American Statistician*, 20, 20–3.

Silverman, D. (1985) *Qualitative Methodology and Sociology*, Aldershot: Gower.

Stead, V. and Lee, M.M. (1996) 'Inter-cultural Perspectives on HRD', in Stewart and McGoldrick (eds) *Human Resource Development: Perspectives, Strategies and Practice*, London: Pitman, 47–70.

Stewart, J. (1991) *Managing Change through Training and Development*, London: Kogan Page.

—— (1992) 'Towards a model of HRD', *Training and Development*, October: 26–9.

Stewart, J. and McGoldrick, J. (eds) (1996) *Human Resource Development: Perspectives, Strategies and Practice*, London: Pitman.

Swanson, R.A. and Holton, E.F. (1997) *Human Resource Development Research Handbook: Linking Research and Practice*, Berrett-Koehler Publishing in association with AHRD and ASTD.

Watson, T.J. (1994a) *In Search of Management: Culture, Chaos and Control in Managerial Work*, London: Routledge.

—— (1994b) 'Managing, crafting and researching: words, skill and imagination in shaping management research', *British Journal of Management* 5, special issue S77–S87, June.

—— (1995) *Sociology, Work and Industry* (third edn), London: Routledge.

—— (1996) Proceedings of the Hospitality Management Research Conference, the Nottingham Trent University, 10–11 April.

easier by use of the word 'speculate'. The book is concerned with both advancing understanding of HRD, and with examining the processes and problems of researching HRD. We referred to this as the distinction between 'content' and 'process' in our Preface. While this represents a questionable distinction, it does provide a useful way of organizing our closing arguments. So, we begin with themes emerging from the book concerning the nature and meaning of HRD.

HRD content

It is evident from the chapters that HRD has a central focus on and concern with learning. While the chapters written by Sambrook and by Lee in particular would question the reifying use of the terms, HRD is clearly concerned with supporting and facilitating the learning of individuals (e.g. Gold et al.), groups or teams (e.g. Rigg et al.) and organizations (e.g. West). Many of the examples in the chapters also emphasize the growing concern with what is becoming known as workplace learning (e.g. Hill, Beattie and McDougall). This focus is supported by and reinforces other work in the field (see for example CIPD 2000, Raelin 2000). Therefore, we can conclude that HRD will be increasingly concerned with facilitating the learning of individuals, teams and organizations through the design, structuring and organization of work itself.

A second theme to emerge is a questioning of the purpose and accountability of HRD practice. This is evident in the chapters by Lee, Hamblett et al. and by Beattie. Thus, HRD is likely in the future to be concerned with a wider constituency and purpose than organizational success. Based on the US literature referenced throughout the book, this is likely to be reflected more directly in the UK and other European countries. Stewart and McGoldrick (1996) also made reference to this trend, drawing in particular on the work of Handy (1994). The work included here seems to confirm that 1996 prediction, and to point to its continuing significance.

A third, though related, theme is HRD as central to power and control processes. The chapter by Hamblett et al. addresses this theme most directly, while others such as Beattie, Sambrook and Gold et al. deal with the issue more implicitly. What is clear from these chapters is that HRD cannot be divorced from organizational and managerial realities, or from wider structural questions affecting the experience of work. Both educators and practitioners need therefore to include such realities and questions in their considerations of what constitutes HRD. We can say at this point that HRD is clearly a political activity.

HRD research

Identifying common themes related to the future of HRD research can best be achieved by borrowing from one of Sambrook's chapters and asking *what, who* and *how*. The previous section begins to answer the first question by suggesting some of the themes or topics which will concern HRD researchers in the future. We can add to that list the focus of SMEs adopted by Hill and that of careers taken by Davies and Wilson. We are confident that these will represent continuing themes for HRD research, as will attempts such as that by Woodall *et al.* to map out a particular European, as distinct from US, understanding of HRD. We also asked our contributors to provide their thoughts on likely themes for future research, and their responses lend support to the topics already discussed. In addition, the following themes were also suggested.

- The whole field of management and leadership development. As well as producing models for predicting future skills needs, a sub-theme in this area will continue to be application of the notion of management competences.
- The links between HRD, HRD strategies and business strategies and performance. The changing context of political, economic and social conditions, including processes of globalization, is a related theme for future research.
- A third theme is the role of HRD in the design and organization of work and work processes at the level of the enterprise. Specific examples in this theme include teamwork and the growth of what is termed emotional work and labour.
- The fourth and final theme has a more individual focus. It is concerned with the relationships between employment, work and careers with the construction of individual identity. Within this broad area, a focus on gender and, for example, exploring differences in learning strategies and methods between men and women, will provide a particular focus for research.

Turning to the question of *who*, it is clear that HRD research is going to become a much more collaborative endeavour in the future. The chapter by Hamlin puts the case for this most strongly and directly. However, the chapters by Gold *et al.*, Rigg *et al.*, McGoldrick *et al.* and by Beattie, for example, all in their separate ways, and through their different examples, make the case for academic–practitioner co-operation in research. Models of academics carrying out research and professionals applying the findings and prescriptions in practice are no longer tenable. It is doubtful that that was in fact ever the case. It will clearly not be the case in the future.

Answering the question of how is also suggestive of a growing trend. The explicit or implicit application of positivist assumptions is clearly going to continue to feature strongly in HRD research. The chapters by, for example, Winterton and Winterton and by Short and Kuchinke are illustrative of this point. They also make a strong case for this to be so by showing the advantages and strengths of those assumptions. Other chapters though equally show the strengths and advantages of more interpretivist assumptions, while some, for example Sambrook on the use of language, point to the potential of (soft) postmodernist analyses. Taken together, the chapters in this book provide an eclectic range of possibilities and potentialities for methodological directions in HRD research. This eclecticism is likely to prove a strength in and for future HRD research. It may also provide HRD research with the opportunity to take a lead in resolving the current debates in the wider field of organization and management theory on the nature and status of knowledge.

Summary

It is clear from the book and from this concluding chapter that HRD as a field of academic enquiry continues to grow in strength. What is also clear is that there are grounds for optimism on the future for HRD research. There are many new questions emerging, and many approaches to adopt in attempts to answer them. While this book does not claim to represent a 'state of the art' or definitive statement on the current position, it does help to signpost future directions. To the extent that it meets the intentions we set, it also provides the basic components of the vehicles needed to make the journey.

Jim McGoldrick
Jim Stewart
Sandra Watson

References

CIPD Consultative document (2000) *Success Through Learning: the Argument for Strengthening Workplace Learning*, London: Chartered Institute of Personnel and Development.

Handy, C. (1994) *The Empty Raincoat: Making sense of the Future*, London: Hutchinson.

Raelin, A. (2000) *Work-Based Learning: The New Frontier of Management Development*, New Jersey: Addison-Wesley.

Stewart, J. and McGoldrick, J. (eds) (1996) *Human Resource Development: Perspectives, Strategies and Practice*, London: Pitman Publishing.

INDEX

Note: Page numbers in **bold** type refer to **figures**. Page numbers in *italic* type refer to *tables*. Page numbers followed by 'n' refer to notes.